The DEPUTY Reader

The
DEPUTY
Reader:
Studies in Moral
Responsibility

Dolores Barracano Schmidt
Earl Robert Schmidt
Slippery Rock State College

Scott, Foresman and Company

The authors gratefully acknowledge the following publishers for permission to reprint
the selections in this book:
The America Press: for excerpts from "Hochhuth in London" by Mary Zavada. Re-
printed from *America*, The National Catholic Weekly Review, by permission of The
America Press.
Appleton-Century-Crofts, Inc.: for excerpt from "Civil Disobedience" by Henry David
Thoreau. Reprinted from *Selected Writings*, edited by Lewis Leary.
The Associated Press: for excerpts from two Associated Press dispatches.
Joan Baez: for letter written to the Internal Revenue Service. Reprinted from *The Catholic
Worker*.
Basilius Presse AG: for "Hochhuths 'Stellvertreter' und die Tradition polemicher
Literatur" by Rolf Chr. Zimmermann; reprinted from *Der Streit um Hochhuths "Stellver-
treter"* by permission of the publisher. For Rolf Hochhuth's reply to a letter written by
Pope Paul VI; reprinted from *Der Streit um Hochhuths "Stellvertreter"* by permission of
Mr. Hochhuth and the publisher. For excerpts from a German television round-table
discussion; reprinted from *Der Streit um Hochhuths "Stellvertreter"* by permission of the
publisher and the participants: Carl Amery, Bischof Dr. Otto Dibelius, Pater Dr. Willehad Eckert, Probst Dr. Heinrich Grüber, and Pater Oskar Simmel, S.J.
The Christian Century Foundation: for "No Letup for 'Der Stellvertreter'" by Ewart E.
Turner; copyright 1963, Christian Century Foundation; reprinted by permission from
The Christian Century, October 16, 1963, pp. 1269–1270. For "The 'Deputy' Controversy"
by Harold E. Fey; copyright 1964, Christian Century Foundation; reprinted by permission from *The Christian Century*, April 22, 1964, pp. 507–508.
The Commonweal: for "The Need for Confession" by Friedrich Heer; reprinted by
permission of *The Commonweal*. For excerpt from "A Question of Judgment: Pius XII
and the Jews" by Joseph L. Lichten; reprinted from *The Commonweal* by permission of
the editor and the National Catholic Welfare Conference.
Encyclopædia Britannica: for excerpts from "Drama" by Adolphus William Ward.
Reprinted by permission of *Encyclopædia Britannica*.
Farrar, Straus and Giroux, Inc.: for "All the World's a Stage" by Susan Sontag. Reprinted
by permission of Farrar, Straus and Giroux, Inc. Copyright 1964 by Susan Sontag.
Jacques Gommy: for "Pie XII devant les massacres de Hitler" by Jacques Gommy. Re-
printed from *L'Homme Nouveau* by permission of the author.
Grove Press, Inc.: for excerpts from *I Cannot Forgive* by Rudolf Vrba and Alan Bestick.
Copyright © 1964 by Rudolf Vrba and Alan Bestick. Published by Grove Press, Inc.
Harcourt, Brace & World, Inc.: for excerpt from *Murder in the Cathedral* by T. S. Eliot.
Copyright, 1935, by Harcourt, Brace & World, Inc.; renewed, 1963, by T. S. Eliot.
Reprinted by permission of the publisher.
La Civilta Cattolica: for excerpt from "La vera storiá e *Il Vicario* di Rolf Hochhuth" by
Father Angelo Martini, S.J. Reprinted from *La Civiltà Cattolica* by permission of the
publisher and the author.

INTRODUCTION

Rolf Hochhuth's play, *The Deputy*, first appeared in West Berlin in early 1963.* Since then, there have been productions in more than twenty cities, radio presentations, and at least ten separate translations of the full text, which is three times as long as the average stage adaptation. The motion picture rights have been sold for $75,000. Nightly riots, the throwing of stink bombs, and actual fist fights between actors bent on giving a performance and demonstrators equally intent on preventing it marked the Parisian run of this work. In London, efforts were made to have the official censor prevent the show's opening; when these measures failed, a printed rebuttal to the author's thesis was included in each program. In New York, pickets carrying banners with the slogan "THIS IS A HATE SHOW" appeared on opening night. The West German government deemed it necessary to apologize for being the country of origin of "this desecration of the sacred memory of Pope Pius XII." Pope Paul VI, while still a cardinal, wrote a letter condemning the play both as history and as literature. Yet no less a person than Dr. Albert Schweitzer strongly supported the author's "solemn warning to our culture admonishing us to forego our acceptance of inhumanity which leaves us unconcerned."

What is there about *The Deputy* that makes it the center of this raging storm? Has the play, as Hochhuth intended, put certain historical facts into proper perspective? Or is it, as its critics contend, a piece of malicious slander from a "sick and twisted mind"? These are matters for you to decide once you have read the play and the articles in this book.

However, the intensely emotional responses to this play are the result of something more than concern for the past; the play's impact is best explained by the challenge it offers to the present. Hypocrisy, complacency, self-delusion, decadent moral traditions, irresponsible authority, unquestioning obedience — these once led to the destruction of millions of European Jews. Do such traits characterize society today? Could another Hitler rise to power? Today? Here? These, too, are questions to be answered.

The selections in Part I of *The DEPUTY Reader*, Conscience and Action: Exploring the Themes, may be taken up while students are in the process of reading the play itself. All deal with the themes of Hochhuth's play, thus pointing out the timeliness and timelessness of the issues with which the work is concerned. Furthermore, they illustrate many forms, styles, and periods of writing — from the Bible to *Life* magazine. The preliminary work of critical reading, analysis, discussion, research, and writing begins here, as does the introduction of the major topic.

The essays in Part II, Play or Polemic: The Literary Perspective, set forth various criteria for judging literature: aesthetic, moral, didactic, historical. The section therefore lends itself to an introductory study of literary criticism, literary terminology, and principles of reviewing — information helpful to the student in evaluating not only *The Deputy* but also the reviews in Part IV. An-

---

*The German title of the play is *Der Stellvertreter;* the British title, *The Representative;* the French title, *Le Vicaire;* and the Italian title, *Il Vicario.*

other topic considered here, that of adapting a play for stage presentation, points out an additional dimension of the problem of communication in drama. *The Deputy* is an historical play, and arguments concerning its historical accuracy have been raised wherever it has appeared. Rolf Hochhuth himself foresaw this and took the unusual precaution of adding an historical appendix to his work. Nonetheless, accusations have been made that the author's documentation is "selective" and that other sources would prove exactly the opposite. Part III, Fact or Fantasy: The Historical Dimension, presents additional facts and opinions with which to answer the questions raised by Hochhuth's play: (1) Was Pius XII more interested in diplomacy than in humanity? More interested in finances than in human lives? (2) Are the Nazi officers depicted by Hochhuth accurately portrayed? Are these the people who are now the good citizens of the German Federation? (3) Are the Auschwitz scenes and statistics factual? Were these facts widely known and generally ignored? (4) How did the "final solution" of the Jewish problem evolve, and who was responsible for it? Another group of essays in this section is concerned with Hochhuth's historical methods and sources. Obviously, some of the questions raised by the play can be answered only speculatively, though numerous attempts to answer them have been made.

Historical information is provided in a variety of forms — statistical tables, documents, personal narratives, newspaper reports — to permit a study of primary and secondary sources. An effort has also been made to include different historical approaches: the heavily psychological explanation offered by Tucker, the intellectual historian's analysis used by Stern, and the legal documentation used by Hilberg are three separate answers to the question of what made Hitler's mass murders possible. Such materials help to show that historical facts do not speak for themselves but need to be arranged and interpreted. Finally, the selections in this section are suitable for a study of logic and/or propaganda analysis.

Part IV, The Critics Speak: Response from Two Continents, is a highly selective survey of world response to *The Deputy,* covering a variety of media — newspapers, magazines, books, radio, television. An attempt was made to include all the major arguments for and against the play and by leading critics, clergymen, and historians. Since the play has been given such extensive coverage, the final decisions about what to include and what to exclude had to be made somewhat ruthlessly. Perhaps the most painful and glaring omission is Dr. Albert Schweitzer's letter in support of the play, an omission dictated by the fact that the letter is used as an introduction to the American edition of the play and is, therefore, generally available.

Original pagination and full bibliographical references are given for each article in this book. Topics for discussion, suggested theme topics, and library assignments appear as materials require. A bibliography, topics for long research papers, and an act-by-act study outline of *The Deputy,* designed to provide information, focus, and topics for writing and discussion, will be found in the appendix.

We wish to express our appreciation for the use of the facilities of the Colorado College Library, Colorado Springs, and the University of Colorado Library at Boulder. We wish also to thank Albert Barracano for his efficient ransacking of "back-issue" book stores; Herman Shumlin, American producer of *The Deputy*, and Bob Maurer, of NBC Monitor, for their information on bringing the play to Broadway; Paul Hallett, of the *National Register*, Denver, for providing us with vital foreign language materials; Dr. Sylvan Berman, of Slippery Rock State College, for his help on the bibliography; and our daughter, Josephine Ann, without whom, to reverse a cliché, this book would have been completed much sooner though life would not have been half as joyful.

Dolores Barracano Schmidt
Earl Robert Schmidt

Slippery Rock State College
Slippery Rock, Pennsylvania

CONTENTS

Part I
CONSCIENCE AND ACTION
Exploring the Themes

Loudon Wainwright

THE DYING GIRL THAT NO ONE HELPED

Those who keep silent are accessories to murder,
and they imperil their immortal souls.

The Deputy, *Act One, Scene Three*

To judge from the recent, bitter example given us by the good folks of a respectable New York residential area, Samaritans are very scarce these days. In fact, if the reactions of the 38 heedless witnesses to the murder of Catherine Genovese provide any true reflection of a national attitude toward our neighbors, we are becoming a callous, chicken-hearted and immoral people. Psychiatrists, poking around in the ruins of character at the scene of the crime, have already come up with some generous, culture-blaming excuses for this grotesque piece of bad fellowship. But the matter calls for something more than sheer indignation. An examination of the pitiful facts of Miss Genovese's terminal experience makes very necessary the ugly personal question each of us must ask: What would *I* have done?

The story is simple and brutal. As she arrived home in the early morning darkness, Kitty Genovese, a decent, pretty young woman of 28, was stalked through the streets close to her Kew Gardens apartment and stabbed again and again by a man who had followed her home and who took almost a half hour to kill her. During the bloody little eternity, according to an extraordinary account published in the New York *Times,* Kitty screamed and cried repeatedly for help. Her entreaties were unequivocal. "Oh, my God!" she cried out at one point. "He stabbed me! Please help me! Someone help me!" Minutes later, before the murderer came back and attacked her for the final time, she screamed, "I'm dying! I'm dying!"

The reason the murderer's actions and his victim's calls are so well documented is that police were able to find 38 of Kitty's neighbors who admitted they witnessed the awful event. They heard the screams and most understood her cry for help. Peeking out their windows, many saw enough of the killer to provide a good description of his appearance and clothing. A few saw him strike Kitty, and more saw her staggering down the sidewalk after she had

"The Dying Girl That No One Helped," *Life,* April 10, 1964, p. 21.

been stabbed twice and was looking for a place to hide. One especially sharp-eyed person was able to report that the murderer was sucking his finger as he left the scene; he had cut himself during the attack. Another witness has the awful distinction of being the only person Kitty Genovese recognized in the audience taking in her final moments. She looked at him and called to him by name. He did not reply.

No one really helped Kitty at all. Only one person shouted at the killer ("Let that girl alone!"), and the one phone call that was finally made to the police was placed after the murderer had got in his car and driven off. For the most part the witnesses, crouching in darkened windows like watchers of a Late Show, looked on until the play had passed beyond their view. Then they went back to bed.

Not all of these people, it must be said, understood they were watching a murder. Some thought they were looking on at a lovers' quarrel; others saw or heard so very little that they could not have reached any conclusion about the disturbance. Even if one of her neighbors had called the police promptly, it cannot be definitely stated that Kitty would have survived. But that is quite beside the point. The fact is that no one, even those who were sure something was terribly wrong, felt moved enough to act. There is, of course, no law against not being helpful.

On the scene a few days after the killer had been caught and had confessed, Police Lieutenant Bernard Jacobs discussed the investigation. "The word we kept hearing from the witnesses later was 'involved,'" Jacobs said. A dark-haired, thoughtful man, he was standing on the sidewalk next to two fist-sized, dark-gray blotches on the cement. These were Kitty's bloodstains and it was there that the killer first stabbed her. "People told us they just didn't want to get involved," Jacobs said to me. "They don't want to be questioned or have to go to court." He pointed to an apartment house directly across the quiet street. "They looked down at this thing," he went on, "from four different floors of that building." Jacobs indicated the long, two-story building immediately next to him. A row of stores took up the ground floor; there were apartments on the upper floor. "Kitty lived in one of them," Jacobs said. "People up there were sitting right on top of the crime." He moved his arm in a gesture that included all the buildings. "It's a nice neighborhood, isn't it?" he went on. "Doesn't look like a jungle. Good, solid people. We don't expect anybody to come out into the street and fight this kind of bum. All we want is a phone call. We don't even need to know who's making it.

"You know what this man told us after we caught him?" Jacobs asked. "He said he figured nobody would do anything to help. He heard the windows go up and saw the lights go on. He just retreated for a while and when things quieted down, he came back to finish the job."

Later, in one of the apartment houses, a witness to part of Kitty Genovese's murder talked. His comments—agonized, contradictory, guilt-ridden, self-excusing—indicate the price in bad conscience he and his neighbors are now paying. "I feel terrible about it," he said. "The thing keeps coming back in my mind. You just don't want to get involved. They might have picked me up as a suspect if I'd bounced right out there. I was getting ready, but my wife stopped me. She didn't want to be a hero's widow. I woke up about the third scream. I pulled the blind so hard it came off the window. The girl was on her knees struggling to get up. I didn't know if she was drunk or what. I never saw the man. She staggered a little when she walked, like she had a few drinks in her. I forgot the screen was there and I almost put my head through it trying to get a better look. I could see people with their heads out and hear windows going up and down all along the street."

The man walked to the window and looked down at the sidewalk. He was plainly depressed and disappointed at his own failure. "Every time I look out here now," he said, "it's like looking out at a nightmare. How could so many of us have had the same idea that we didn't need to do anything? But that's not all that's wrong." Now he sounded betrayed and he told what was really eating him. Those 38 witnesses had, at least, talked to the police after the murder. The man pointed to a nearby building. "There are people over there who saw everything," he said. "And there hasn't been a peep out of them yet. Not one peep." /21/

Topics for Discussion

1. Hochhuth's play, *The Deputy,* is concerned primarily with the sin of omission, with the idea that *not* acting can in itself be evil. In your opinion, did the viewers of Kitty Genovese's death assume guilt by silence?
2. In comparing the apathy of the witnesses of the Austin Street murder of Kitty Genovese to the apathy of the non-Nazi Germans toward the destruction of the Jews, one person commented as follows:

   > . . . Austin Street people ran no risk; they had only to phone the police, and their maximum of inconvenience would have been a few days in court as a witness.
   >
   > The German people, on the other hand, had no police to phone—the police would have arrested them and not helped the victims of the Nazi terror—and any act of assistance (performed, nevertheless, by quite a number of Germans) exposed them to the danger of a concentration camp, if not to a worse fate.
   >
   > . . . [How can one] equate the Austin Street people's failure to phone the police with the German people's failure to revolt unarmed against the S.A. and S.S., or to storm Auschwitz?*

   (a) Do you agree with the statement above, or do you feel that there are some parallels in the two situations? (b) Comment on the statement of another writer that Hitler's rise to power was made possible by just such people as those who witnessed the Austin Street tragedy.
3. A number of theories have been advanced to explain the inaction of the viewers of Miss Genovese's murder. Four are summarized below:

   > The average American TV viewer is fed on such a steady diet of crime and horror that being a passive viewer of violence is natural to him.

   > Deeply imbedded in every man is a fascination for evil and an instinct to destroy. Conscience, social pressure, fear of reprisal may cause a portion of his being to be submerged, but it is never completely removed. Generally, in a situation of this type, people quickly suppress the baser side and act as they have been taught. In this particular instance, apparently, the usual checking devices did not operate. People neither assisted nor withdrew but watched avidly the enactment of their own unconscious urges.

*Hans Neisser, *The New York Times Magazine,* May 24, 1964, p. 62.

Recent activities by civil rights groups and legal commissions have resulted in the enactment of legislation so favorable to criminals and suspects that the average citizen fears to go to the assistance of someone in trouble. This fear is founded on the fact that should the suspect not be convicted, he could seek legal reprisal against all who assisted in his false arrest.

Scientific skepticism is the philosophic basis of modern urban life. Consequently, modern man is conditioned to react cautiously and only after he is in full possession of the facts. Since the Austin Street situation was an ambiguous one, calling for prompt action without knowledge of the participants, conditions, and motives of the event, modern man, having long ago lost his instinctive response to danger, had insufficient stimulus to set him in action.

(a) Discuss each of these theories as it may apply to the witness interviewed in Wainwright's account. (b) Are these theories contradictory? Consider particularly the second and fourth ones.

Theme Topics

What Would I Have Done?
In Defense of Noninvolvement
My Brother's Keeper
On Fighting Apathy

Library Assignments

1. Wainwright refers to "an extraordinary account [of Kitty Genovese's murder] published in the New York *Times*." Using *The New York Times Index*, find the original account of this crime.
2. The peculiar facts surrounding Miss Genovese's murder were the subject of a number of articles. Using the *Readers' Guide to Periodical Literature*, prepare a bibliography of five articles on the subject.

St. Luke

THE GREAT COMMANDMENT: THE GOOD SAMARITAN

Would Christ have turned away?

The Deputy, *Act Two*

And behold, a certain lawyer got up to test him, saying, "Master, what must I do to gain eternal life?" But he said to him, "What is written in the Law? How dost thou read?" He answered and said, "Thou shalt love the Lord thy God with thy whole heart, and with thy whole soul, and with thy whole strength, and with thy whole mind; and thy neighbor as thyself." And he said to him, "Thou has answered rightly; do this and thou shalt live." But he, wishing to justify himself, said to Jesus, "And who is my neighbor?"

Luke 10:25–37.

Jesus answered, "A certain man was going down from Jerusalem to Jericho, and he fell in with robbers, who after both stripping him and beating him went their way, leaving him half-dead. But, as it happened, a certain priest was going down the same way, and when he saw him, he passed by. And likewise a Levite also, when he was near the place and saw him, passed by. But a certain Samaritan as he journeyed came upon him, and seeing him, was moved with compassion. And he went up to him and bound up his wounds, pouring on oil and wine. And setting him on his own beast, he brought him to an inn and took care of him. And the next day he took out two denarii and gave them to the innkeeper and said, 'Take care of him; and whatever more thou spendest, I, on my way back, will repay thee.'

"Which of these three, in thy opinion, proved himself neighbor to him who fell among the robbers?" And he said, "He who took pity on him." And Jesus said to him, "Go and do thou also in like manner."

Topics for Discussion

1. The thirty-eight people who watched the young lady who lived across the street from them being stabbed to death were literally "neighbors." (a) Do they qualify as such according to the Biblical interpretation? (b) What is the significance of the fact that a priest and a Levite ignored the man in need, while a Samaritan stopped and cared for him? (c) What is the answer to the lawyer's question, "And who is my neighbor?"
2. Charles H. Brower has defined a "square" as "a man who never learned to get away with it. A Joe who volunteers when he doesn't have to." Mr. Brower has shown that many of our national heroes would have to be classified as "squares" and has indicated how they might have behaved had they not been:

   Nathan Hale: Me spy on those British! Are you trying to be funny? Do you know what they do with the spies they catch? I'll give you a news flash, chum. They *hang* them.
   Paul Revere: What do you mean—me ride through every Middlesex village and town? And in the middle of the night yet. Why pick on me? Am I the only man in Boston with a horse?
   Patrick Henry: Sure, I'm for liberty. First, last and always. But we've got to be a little realistic. We're a pretty small outfit. If we start pushing the British around, someone is going to get hurt.
   George Washington: Gentlemen, I am honored. But I do wish you would try someone else. Let's say General Gates. I'm just getting things organized at Mount Vernon. You /71/ might say I had already served my time. Against the French, you know.
   Benjamin Franklin: What we really need as Ambassador to France is a young man. I'm 70 years old! It's time a new generation took over. /72/*

   (a) Would the good Samaritan be considered a "square" according to the present values of the American people? (b) Mr. Brower's point was, essentially, that today we are overly concerned for our own safety and comfort, as each of the above "contemporary" responses indicates. Aren't

*Reprinted from *U.S. News & World Report*, April 6, 1964, pp. 71–72.

there, however, situations in which one should consider himself first? When and why? (c) Using the above pattern, indicate what Riccardo and Gerstein of *The Deputy* might have said had they not been "squares."
3. Discuss the opinion held by some people that helping those in need is generally motivated by selfishness: fear of the personal consequences of not helping (spanking by parents, censure of peers, wrath of God); desire to avoid the discomforts of guilt and bad conscience; desire to gain notice, praise, gratitude.

Theme Topics

A Good Samaritan of Our Day
Is the Bible Outmoded as a Daily Guide?
Confessions of a Square
On the Difficulty of Loving One's Neighbor

Library Assignments

1. Using a concordance to the Bible, make a list of all of the citations of the words "Thou shalt love thy neighbor as thyself."
2. In "The Dying Girl That No One Helped," Wainwright states that "Samaritans are very scarce these days." Using the *Oxford English Dictionary*, find out in what sense Wainwright is using the word "Samaritan," what the original meaning of the word was, and how it was given its present meaning.

Henry David Thoreau

CIVIL DISOBEDIENCE

The rights of men invalidate the rights of states.

The Deputy, *Act One, Scene Three*

I heartily accept the motto—"That government is best which governs least"; and I should like to see it acted up to more rapidly and systematically. Carried out, it finally amounts to this, which also I believe—"That government is best which governs not at all"; and when men are prepared for it, that will be the kind of government which they will have. Government is at best but an expedient; but most governments are usually, and all governments are sometimes, inexpedient. The objections which have been brought against a standing army, and they are many and weighty, and deserve to prevail, may also at last be brought against a standing government. The standing army is only an arm of the standing government. The government itself, which is only the mode which the people have chosen to execute their will, is equally liable to be abused and perverted before the people can act through it. Witness the present Mexican war, the work of comparatively a few individuals using the standing government as their tool; for, in the outset, the people would not have consented to this measure.

From "Civil Disobedience," *Selected Writings*, ed. Lewis Leary (New York: Appleton-Century-Crofts. Inc., 1958), pp. 9–32.

This American government—what is it but a tradition, though a recent one, endeavoring to transmit itself unimpaired to posterity, but each instant losing some of its integrity? It has not the vitality and force of a single living man; for a single man can bend it to his will. It is a sort of wooden gun to the people themselves. But it is not the less necessary for this; for the people must have some complicated machinery or other, and hear its din, to satisfy that idea of government which they have. /9/ Governments show thus how successfully men can be imposed on, even impose on themselves, for their own advantage. It is excellent, we must all allow. Yet this government never of itself furthered any enterprise, but by the alacrity with which it got out of its way. *It* does not keep the country free. *It* does not settle the West. *It* does not educate. The character inherent in the American people has done all that has been accomplished; and it would have done somewhat more, if the government had not sometimes got in its way. For government is an expedient by which men would fain succeed in letting one another alone; and, as has been said, when it is most expedient, the governed are most let alone by it. Trade and commerce, if they were not made of India rubber, would never manage to bounce over the obstacles which legislators are continually putting in their way; and, if one were to judge these men wholly by the effects of their actions and not partly by their intentions, they would deserve to be classed and punished with those mischievous persons who put obstructions on the railroads.

But, to speak practically and as a citizen, unlike those who call themselves no-government men, I ask for, not at once no government, but *at once* a better government. Let every man make known what kind of government would command his respect, and that will be one step toward obtaining it.

After all, the practical reason why, when the power is once in the hands of the people, a majority are permitted, and for a long period continue, to rule is not because they are most likely to be in the right, nor because this seems fairest to the minority, but because they are physically the strongest. But a government in which the majority rule in all cases cannot be based on justice, even as far as men understand it. Can there not be a government in which majorities do not virtually decide right and wrong, but conscience?—in which majorities decide only those questions to which the rule of expediency is applicable? Must the citizen ever for a moment, or in the least degree, resign his conscience to the legislator? Why has every man a conscience, then? I think that we should be men first, and subjects afterward. It is not desirable to cultivate a respect for the law, so much as /10/ for the right. The only obligation which I have a right to assume is to do at any time what I think right. It is truly enough said, that a corporation has no conscience; but a corporation of conscientious men is a corporation *with* a conscience. Law never made men a whit more just; and, by means of their respect for it, even the well-disposed are daily made the agents of injustice. A common and natural result of an undue respect for law is, that you may see a file of soldiers, colonel, captain, corporal, privates, powder monkeys, and all, marching in admirable order over hill and dale to the wars, against their wills, aye, against their common sense and consciences, which makes it very steep marching indeed, and produces a palpitation of the heart. They have no doubt that it is a damnable business in which they are concerned; they are all peaceably inclined. Now, what are they? Men at all? or small movable forts and magazines, at the service of some unscrupulous man in power? Visit the navy yard, and behold a marine, such a man as an American government can make, or such as it can make a man with its black arts—a mere shadow and reminiscence of human-

ity, a man laid out alive and standing, and already, as one may say, buried under arms with funeral accompaniments, though it may be—

"Not a drum was heard, not a funeral note,
    As his corse to the rampart we hurried;
Not a soldier discharged his farewell shot
    O'er the grave where our hero we buried."

The mass of men serve the state thus, not as men mainly, but as machines,
with their bodies. They are the standing army, and the militia, jailors, consta-
bles, posse comitatus, etc. In most cases there is no free exercise whatever of
the judgment or of the moral sense; but they put themselves on a level with
wood and earth and stones; and wooden men can perhaps be manufactured
that will serve the purpose as well. Such command no more respect than men
of straw or a lump of dirt. They have the same sort of worth only as horses
and dogs. Yet such as these even are commonly esteemed good citizens. Others—as most legislators, politicians, lawyers, /11/ ministers, and officehold-
ers—serve the state chiefly with their heads; and, as they rarely make any moral distinctions, they are as likely to serve the Devil, without *intending* it, as
God. A very few, as heroes, patriots, martyrs, reformers in the great sense,
and *men*, serve the state with their consciences also, and so necessarily resist it
for the most part; and they are commonly treated as enemies by it. A wise
man will only be useful as a man, and will not submit to be "clay," and "stop a
hole to keep the wind away," but leave that office to his dust at least:

"I am too highborn to be propertied,
To be a secondary at control,
Or useful serving-man and instrument
To any sovereign state throughout the world."

He who gives himself entirely to his fellow men appears to them useless and
selfish; but he who gives himself partially to them is pronounced a benefactor
and philanthropist.

How does it become a man to behave toward this American government today? I answer, that he cannot without disgrace be associated with it. I cannot
for an instant recognize that political organization as *my* government which is
the *slave's* government also.

All men recognize the right of revolution; that is, the right to refuse allegiance to, and to resist, the government, when its tyranny or its inefficiency
are great and unendurable. But almost all say that such is not the case now.
But such was the case, they think, in the Revolution of '75. If one were to tell
me that this was a bad government because it taxed certain foreign commod-
ities brought to its ports, it is most probable that I should not make an ado
about it, for I can do without them. All machines have their friction; and
possibly this does enough good to counterbalance the evil. At any rate, it is a
great evil to make a stir about it. But when the friction comes to have its machine, and oppression and robbery are organized, I say, let us not have such a
machine any longer. In other words, when a sixth of the population of a nation which has undertaken to be the /12/ refuge of liberty are slaves, and a
whole country is unjustly overrun and conquered by a foreign army, and subjected to military law, I think that it is not too soon for honest men to rebel

and revolutionize. What makes this duty the more urgent is the fact that the country so overrun is not our own, but ours is the invading army.

Paley,[1] a common authority with many on moral questions, in his chapter on the "Duty of Submission to Civil Government," resolves all civil obligation into expediency; and he proceeds to say, "that so long as the interest of the whole society requires it, that is, so long as the established government cannot be resisted or changed without public inconveniency, it is the will of God that the established government be obeyed, and no longer. . . . This principle being admitted, the justice of every particular case of resistance is reduced to a computation of the quantity of the danger and grievance on the one side, and of the probability and expense of redressing it on the other." Of this, he says, every man shall judge for himself. But Paley appears never to have contemplated those cases to which the rule of expediency does not apply, in which a people, as well as an individual, must do justice, cost what it may. If I have unjustly wrested a plank from a drowning man, I must restore it to him though I drown myself. This, according to Paley, would be inconvenient. But he that would save his life, in such a case, shall lose it. This people must cease to hold slaves, and to make war on Mexico, though it cost them their existence as a people.

In their practice, nations agree with Paley; but does any one think that Massachusetts does exactly what is right at the present crisis?

"A drab of state, a cloth-o'-silver slut,
    To have her train borne up, and her soul trail in the dirt."

Practically speaking, the opponents to a reform in Massachusetts are not a hundred thousand politicians at the South, but a hundred thousand merchants and farmers /13/ here, who are more interested in commerce and agriculture than they are in humanity, and are not prepared to do justice to the slave and to Mexico, *cost what it may.* I quarrel not with far-off foes, but with those who, near at home, co-operate with, and do the bidding of, those far away, and without whom the latter would be harmless. We are accustomed to say, that the mass of men are unprepared; but improvement is slow, because the few are not materially wiser or better than the many. It is not so important that many should be as good as you, as that there be some absolute goodness somewhere; for that will leaven the whole lump. There are thousands who are *in opinion* opposed to slavery and to the war, who yet in effect do nothing to put an end to them; who, esteeming themselves children of Washington and Franklin, sit down with their hands in their pockets, and say that they know not what to do, and do nothing; who even postpone the question of freedom to the question of free trade, and quietly read the prices current along with the latest advices from Mexico, after dinner, and, it may be, fall asleep over them both. What is the price current of an honest man and patriot today? They hesitate, and they regret, and sometimes they petition; but they do nothing in earnest and with effect. They will wait, well disposed, for others to remedy the evil, that they may no longer have it to regret. At most, they give only a cheap vote, and a feeble countenance and Godspeed, to the right, as it goes by them. There are nine hundred and ninety-nine patrons

1. *Paley,* William (1743–1805), author of the widely read *Principles of Moral and Political Philosophy* (1785). /13/

of virtue to one virtuous man. But it is easier to deal with the real possessor of a thing than with the temporary guardian of it.

All voting is a sort of gaming, like checkers or backgammon, with a slight moral tinge to it, a playing with right and wrong, with moral questions; and betting naturally accompanies it. The character of the voters is not staked. I cast my vote, perchance, as I think right; but I am not vitally concerned that that right should prevail. I am willing to leave it to the majority. Its obligation, therefore, never exceeds that of expediency. Even voting *for the right* is *doing* nothing for it. It is only expressing to men feebly your desire that it should prevail. A wise man will not leave the right to the mercy of chance, nor /14/ wish it to prevail through the power of the majority. There is but little virtue in the action of masses of men. When the majority shall at length vote for the abolition of slavery, it will be because they are indifferent to slavery, or because there is but little slavery left to be abolished by their vote. *They* will then be the only slaves. Only *his* vote can hasten the abolition of slavery who asserts his own freedom by his vote. . . .

It is not a man's duty, as a matter of course, to devote /15/ himself to the eradication of any, even the most enormous wrong; he may still properly have other concerns to engage him; but it is his duty, at least, to wash his hands of it, and, if he gives it no thought longer, not to give it practically his support. If I devote myself to other pursuits and contemplations, I must first see, at least, that I do not pursue them sitting upon another man's shoulders. I must get off him first, that he may pursue his contemplations too. See what gross inconsistency is tolerated. I have heard some of my townsmen say, "I should like to have them order me out to help put down an insurrection of the slaves, or to march to Mexico — see if I would go;" and yet these very men have each, directly by their allegiance, and so indirectly, at least, by their money, furnished a substitute. The soldier is applauded who refuses to serve in an unjust war by those who do not refuse to sustain the unjust government which makes the war; is applauded by those whose own act and authority he disregards and sets at naught; as if the state were penitent to that degree that it hired one to scourge it while it sinned, but not to that degree that it left off sinning for a moment. Thus, under the name of Order and Civil Government, we are all made at last to pay homage to and support our own meanness. After the first blush of sin comes its indifference; and from immoral it becomes, as it were, *un*moral, and not quite unnecessary to that life which we have made.

The broadest and most prevalent error requires the most disinterested virtue to sustain it. The slight reproach to which the virtue of patriotism is commonly liable, the noble are most likely to incur. Those who, while they disapprove of the character and measures of a government, yield to it their allegiance and support are undoubtedly its most conscientious supporters, and so frequently the most serious obstacles to reform. Some are petitioning the state to dissolve the Union, to disregard the requisitions of the President. Why do they not dissolve it themselves — the union between themselves and the state — and refuse to pay their quota into its treasury? Do not they stand in the same relation to the state that the state does to the Union? And have not the same reasons prevented the /16/ state from resisting the Union which have prevented them from resisting the state?

How can a man be satisfied to entertain an opinion merely, and enjoy *it*? Is there any enjoyment in it, if his opinion is that he is aggrieved? If you are cheated out of a single dollar by your neighbor, you do not rest satisfied with knowing that you are cheated, or with saying that you are cheated, or even with petitioning him to pay you your due; but you take effectual steps at once to obtain the full amount, and see that you are never cheated again. Action from principle, the perception and the performance of right, changes things and relations; it is essentially revolutionary, and does not consist wholly with anything which was. It not only divides states and churches, it divides families; aye, it divides the *individual,* separating the diabolical in him from the divine.

Unjust laws exist: shall we be content to obey them, or shall we endeavor to amend them, and obey them until we have succeeded, or shall we transgress them at once? Men generally, under such a government as this, think that they ought to wait until they have persuaded the majority to alter them. They think that, if they should resist, the remedy would be worse than the evil. But it is the fault of the government itself that the remedy *is* worse than the evil. *It* makes it worse. Why is it not more apt to anticipate and provide for reform? Why does it not cherish its wise minority? Why does it cry and resist before it is hurt? Why does it not encourage its citizens to be on the alert to point out its faults, and *do* better than it would have them? Why does it always crucify Christ, and excommunicate Copernicus and Luther, and pronounce Washington and Franklin rebels?

One would think, that a deliberate and practical denial of its authority was the only offense never contemplated by government; else, why has it not assigned its definite, its suitable and proportionate penalty? If a man who has no property refuses but once to earn nine shillings for the state, he is put in prison for a period unlimited by any law that I know, and determined only by the discretion of those who placed him there; but if he should steal ninety times nine shillings from the state, he is soon permitted to go at large again. /17/

If the injustice is part of the necessary friction of the machine of government, let it go, let it go: perchance it will wear smooth—certainly the machine will wear out. If the injustice has a spring, or a pulley, or a rope, or a crank, exclusively for itself, then perhaps you may consider whether the remedy will not be worse than the evil; but if it is of such a nature that it requires you to be the agent of injustice to another, then, I say, break the law. Let your life be a counter friction to stop the machine. What I have to do is to see, at any rate, that I do not lend myself to the wrong which I condemn.

As for adopting the ways which the state has provided for remedying the evil, I know not of such ways. They take too much time, and a man's life will be gone. I have other affairs to attend to. I came into this world, not chiefly to make this a good place to live in, but to live in it, be it good or bad. A man has not everything to do, but something; and because he cannot do *everything*, it is not necessary that he should do *something* wrong. It is not my business to be petitioning the Governor or the Legislature any more than it is theirs to petition me; and if they should not hear my petition, what should I do then? But in this case the state has provided no way: its very Constitution is the evil. This may seem to be harsh and stubborn and unconciliatory; but it is to treat with the utmost kindness and consideration the only spirit that can appreciate or deserves it. So is all change for the better, like birth and death, which convulse the body.

I do not hesitate to say, that those who call themselves Abolitionists should at once effectually withdraw their support, both in person and property, from the government of Massachusetts and not wait till they constitute a majority of one, before they suffer the right to prevail through them. I think that it is enough if they have God on their side, without waiting for that other one. Moreover, any man more right than his neighbors constitutes a majority of one already.

I meet this American government, or its representative, the state government, directly, and face to face, once a year—no more—in the person of its tax gatherer; this is the only mode in which a man situated as I am neces- /18/ sarily meets it; and it then says distinctly, Recognize me; and the simplest, most effectual, and, in the present posture of affairs, the indispensablest mode of treating with it on this head, of expressing your little satisfaction with and love for it, is to deny it then. My civil neighbor, the tax gatherer, is the very man I have to deal with—for it is, after all, with men and not with parchment that I quarrel—and he has voluntarily chosen to be an agent of the government. How shall he ever know well what he is and does as an officer of the government, or as a man, until he is obliged to consider whether he shall treat me, his neighbor, for whom he has respect, as a neighbor and well-disposed man, or as a maniac and disturber of the peace, and see if he can get over this obstruction to his neighborliness without a ruder and more impetuous thought or speech corresponding with his action. I know this well, that if one thousand, if one hundred, if ten men whom I could name—if ten *honest* men only—ay, if *one* HONEST man, in this State of Massachusetts, *ceasing to hold slaves*, were actually to withdraw from this co-partnership, and be locked up in the county jail therefor, it would be the abolition of slavery in America. For it matters not how small the beginning may seem to be: what is once well done is done forever. But we love better to talk about it: that we say is our mission. Reform keeps many scores of newspapers in its service, but not one man. If my esteemed neighbor,[2] the state's ambassador, who will devote his days to the settlement of the question of human rights in the Council Chamber, instead of being threatened with the prisons of Carolina, were to sit down the prisoner of Massachusetts, that state which is so anxious to foist the sin of slavery upon her sister—though at present she can discover only an act of inhospitality to be the ground of a quarrel with her—the Legislature would not wholly waive the subject the following winter.

Under a government which imprisons any unjustly, the true place for a just man is also a prison. The proper place today, the only place which Massachusetts has /19/ provided for her freer and less desponding spirits, is in her prisons, to be put out and locked out of the state by her own act, as they have already put themselves out by their principles. It is there that the fugitive slave, and the Mexican prisoner on parole, and the Indian come to plead the wrongs of his race should find them; on that separate, but more free and honorable ground, where the state places those who are not *with* her, but *against* her—the only house in a slave state in which a free man can abide with honor. If any think that their influence would be lost there, and their voices no longer afflict the ear of the state, that they would not be as an enemy within its walls, they do not know by how much truth is stronger than error, nor how much more eloquently and effectively he can combat injustice who has experienced a little in his own person. Cast your whole vote, not a strip of paper merely, but your whole influence. A minority is powerless while it conforms to the majority; it is not even a minority then; but it is irresistible when it clogs by its whole weight. If the alternative is to keep all just men in prison, or give up war and slavery, the state will not hesitate which to choose. If a

---

2. *my esteemed neighbor*, Samuel Hoare, of Concord, who had been sent to South Carolina to protest imprisonment of free Negro seamen from New England. /19/

thousand men were not to pay their tax bills this year, that would not be a violent and bloody measure, as it would be to pay them, and enable the state to commit violence and shed innocent blood. This is, in fact, the definition of a peaceable revolution, if any such is possible. If the tax gatherer, or any other public officer, asks me, as one has done, "But what shall I do?" my answer is, "If you really wish to do anything, resign your office." When the subject has refused allegiance, and the officer has resigned his office, then the revolution is accomplished. But even suppose blood should flow. Is there not a sort of blood shed when the conscience is wounded? Through this wound a man's real manhood and immortality flow out, and he bleeds to an everlasting death. I see this blood flowing now.

I have contemplated the imprisonment of the offender, rather than the seizure of his goods — though both will serve the same purpose — because they who assert the purest right, and consequently are most dangerous to a corrupt state, commonly have not spent much time in ac- /20/ cumulating property. To such the state renders comparatively small service, and a slight tax is wont to appear exorbitant, particularly if they are obliged to earn it by special labor with their hands. If there were one who lived wholly without the use of money, the state itself would hesitate to demand it of him. But the rich man — not to make any invidious comparison — is always sold to the institution which makes him rich. Absolutely speaking, the more money, the less virtue; for money comes between a man and his objects, and obtains them for him; and it was certainly no great virtue to obtain it. It puts to rest many questions which he would otherwise be taxed to answer; while the only new question which it puts is the hard but superfluous one, how to spend it. Thus his moral ground is taken from under his feet. The opportunities of living are diminished in proportion as what are called the "means" are increased. The best thing a man can do for his culture when he is rich is to endeavor to carry out those schemes which he entertained when he was poor. Christ answered the Herodians according to their condition. "Show me the tribute-money," said he — and one took a penny out of his pocket — if you use money which has the image of Cæsar on it and which he has made current and valuable, that is, *if you are men of the state,* and gladly enjoy the advantages of Cæsar's government, then pay him back some of his own when he demands it. "Render therefore to Cæsar that which is Cæsar's, and to God those things which are God's" — leaving them no wiser than before as to which was which; for they did not wish to know.

When I converse with the freest of my neighbors, I perceive that, whatever they may say about the magnitude and seriousness of the question, and their regard for the public tranquillity, the long and the short of the matter is, that they cannot spare the protection of the existing government, and they dread the consequences to their property and families of disobedience to it. For my own part, I should not like to think that I ever rely on the protection of the state. But, if I deny the authority of the state when it presents its tax bill, it will soon take and waste all my property, and so harass me and my children without end. This is hard. This makes it impos- /21/ sible for a man to live honestly, and at the same time comfortably, in outward respects. It will not be worth the while to accumulate property that would be sure to go again. You must hire or squat somewhere, and raise but a small crop, and eat that soon. You must live within yourself, and depend upon yourself always tucked up and ready for a start, and not have many affairs. A man may grow rich in Turkey even, if he will be in all respects a good subject of the Turkish government. Confucius said: "If a state is governed by the principles of reason, poverty and misery are subjects of shame; if a state is not governed by the principles of reason, riches and honors are the subjects of shame." No: until I want the protection of Massachusetts to be extended to me in some distant Southern port, where my liberty is endangered, or until I am bent solely on building up an estate at home by peaceful enterprise, I can afford to refuse allegiance to Massachusetts, and her right to my property and life. It costs me less in every sense to incur the penalty of disobedience to the state than it would to obey. I should feel as if I were worth less in that case. . . . /22/

Thus the state never intentionally confronts a man's sense, intellectual or moral, but only his body, his senses. It is not armed with superior wit or honesty, but with superior physical strength. I was not born to be forced. I /23/ will breathe after my own fashion. Let us see who is the strongest. What force has a multitude? They only can force me who obey a higher law than I. They force me to become like themselves. . . . /24/

This, then, is my position at present. But one cannot be too much on his guard in such a case, lest his action be biased by obstinacy or an undue regard for the opinions of men. Let him see that he does only what belongs to himself and to the hour.

I think sometimes, Why, this people mean well, they are only ignorant; they would do better if they knew how: why give your neighbors this pain to treat you as they are not inclined to? But I think again, This is no reason why I should do as they do, or permit others to suffer much greater pain of a different kind. Again, I sometimes say to myself, When many millions of men, without heat, without ill will, without personal feeling of any kind, demand of you a few shillings only, without the possibility, such is their constitution, of retracting or altering their present demand, and without the possibility, on your side, of appeal to any other millions, why expose yourself to this overwhelming brute force? You /27/ do not resist cold and hunger, the winds and the waves, thus obstinately; you quietly submit to a thousand similar necessities. You do not put your head into the fire. But just in proportion as I regard this as not wholly a brute force, but partly a human force, and consider that I have relations to those millions as to so many millions of men, and not of mere brute or inanimate things, I see that appeal is possible, first and instantaneously, from them to the Maker of them, and, secondly, from them to themselves. But if I put my head deliberately into the fire, there is no appeal to fire or to the Maker of fire, and I have only myself to blame. If I could convince myself that I have any right to be satisfied with men as they are, and to treat them accordingly, and not according, in some respects, to my requisitions and expectations of what they and I ought to be, then, like a good Mussulman and fatalist, I should endeavor to be satisfied with things as they are, and say it is the will of God. And, above all, there is this difference between resisting this and a purely brute or natural force, that I can resist this with some effect; but I cannot expect, like Orpheus,[4] to change the nature of the rocks and trees and beasts.

I do not wish to quarrel with any man or nation. I do not wish to split hairs, to make fine distinctions, or set myself up as better than my neighbors. I seek rather, I may say, even an excuse for conforming to the laws of the land. I am but too ready to conform to them. Indeed, I have reason to suspect myself on this head; and each year, as the tax gatherer comes round, I find myself dis-

4. *Orpheus,* son of Apollo, the music of whose lyre was said to charm wild beasts, trees, and rocks. /28/

posed to review the acts and position of the general and state governments, and the spirit of the people, to discover a pretext for conformity.

"We must affect our country as our parents,
And if at any time we alienate
Our love or industry from doing it honor,
We must respect effects and teach the soul
Matter of conscience and religion,
And not desire of rule or benefit." /28/

I believe that the state will soon be able to take all my work of this sort out of my hands, and then I shall be no better a patriot than my fellow countrymen. Seen from a lower point of view, the Constitution, with all its faults, is very good; the law and the courts are very respectable; even this state and this American government are, in many respects, very admirable, and rare things, to be thankful for, such as a great many have described them; but seen from a point of view a little higher, they are what I have described them; seen from a higher still, and the highest, who shall say what they are, or that they are worth looking at or thinking of at all? . . .

I know that most men think differently from myself; but those whose lives are by profession devoted to the study of these or kindred subjects content me as little as any. Statesmen and legislators, standing so completely within the institution, never distinctly and nakedly behold it. They speak of moving society, but have no resting place without it. They may be men of a certain experience and discrimination, and have no doubt invented ingenious and even useful systems, for which we sincerely thank them; but all their wit and usefulness lie within certain not very wide limits. They are wont to forget that the world is not governed by policy and expediency. Webster never goes behind government, and so cannot speak with authority about it. His words are wisdom to those legislators who contemplate no essential reform in the existing government; but for thinkers, and those who legislate for all time, he never once glances at the subject. I know of those whose serene and wise speculations on this theme would soon reveal the limits of his mind's range and hospitality. Yet, compared with the cheap professions of most reformers, and the still cheaper wisdom and eloquence of politicians in general, his are /29/ almost the only sensible and valuable words, and we thank Heaven for him. Comparatively, he is always strong, original, and, above all, practical. Still, his quality is not wisdom, but prudence. The lawyer's truth is not Truth, but consistency or a consistent expediency. Truth is always in harmony with herself, and is not concerned chiefly to reveal the justice that may consist with wrongdoing. He well deserves to be called, as he has been called, the Defender of the Constitution. There are really no blows to be given by him but defensive ones. He is not a leader, but a follower. His leaders are the men of '87. "I have never made an effort," he says, "and never propose to make an effort; I have never countenanced an effort, and never mean to countenance an effort, to disturb the arrangement as originally made, by which the various states came into the Union." Still thinking of the sanction which the Constitution gives to slavery, he says, "Because it was a part of the original compact — let it stand." Notwithstanding his special acuteness and ability, he is unable to take a fact out of its merely political relations, and behold it as it lies absolutely to be disposed of by the intellect — what, for instance, it behooves a man to do here in America today with regard to slavery — but ventures, or is driven, to make some such desperate answer as the following, while professing to speak absolutely, and as a private man—from which what new and singular code of social duties might be inferred? "The manner," says he, "in which the governments of those states where slavery exists are to regulate it is for their own consideration, under their responsibility to their constituents, to the general laws of propriety, humanity, and justice, and to God. Associations formed elsewhere, springing from a feeling of humanity, or other cause, have nothing whatever to do with it. They have never received any encouragement from me, and they never will."[5]

They who know of no purer sources of truth, who have traced up its stream no higher, stand, and wisely /30/ stand, by the Bible and the Constitution, and drink at it there with reverence and humility; but they who behold where it comes trickling into this lake or that pool, gird up their loins once more, and continue their pilgrimage toward its fountainhead. . . .

The authority of government, even such as I am willing to submit to—for I will cheerfully obey those who know and can do better than I, and in many things even those who neither know nor can do so well—is still an impure one: to be strictly just, it must have the sanction and consent of the governed. It can have no pure right over my person and property but what I concede to it. The progress from an absolute to a limited monarchy, from a limited monarchy to a democracy, is a progress toward a true respect for the individual. Even the Chinese philosopher was wise enough to regard the individual as the basis of the empire. Is a democracy, such as we know it, the last improvement possible in government? Is it not possible to take a step further towards recognizing and organizing the rights of man? There will never be a really free and enlightened state until the state comes /31/ to recognize the individual as a higher and independent power, from which all its own power and authority are derived, and treats him accordingly. I please myself with imagining a state at last which can afford to be just to all men, and to treat the individual with respect as a neighbor; which even would not think it inconsistent with its own repose if a few were to live aloof from it, not meddling with it, nor embraced by it, who fulfilled all the duties of neighbors and fellow-men. A state which bore this kind of fruit, and suffered it to drop off as fast as it ripened, would prepare the way for a still more perfect and glorious state, which also I have imagined, but not yet anywhere seen. /32/

Topics for discussion

1. In April 1964 the popular folk singer Joan Baez sent the following letter to the Internal Revenue Service explaining her decision to pay only 40 per cent of her 1963 income tax:

> Dear Friends:
> What I have to say is this:
> I do not believe in the weapons of war.
> Weapons and Wars have murdered, burned, distorted, crippled, and caused endless varieties of pain to men, women, and children for too long.
> Our modern weapons can reduce a man to a piece of dust in a split sec-

5. These extracts have been inserted since the lecture was read [Thoreau's note]. The extracts are from Daniel Webster's speeches on the Texas question, Dec. 22, 1845, and on the bill to exclude slavery from the territories, Aug. 12, 1848. /30/

ond, can make a woman's hair fall out or cause her baby to be born a monster. They can kill the part of a turtle's brain that tells him where he is going, so instead of trudging to the ocean he trudges confusedly towards the desert, slowly, blinking his poor eyes, until he finally scorches to death and turns into a shell and some bones.

I am not going to volunteer the 60% of my year's income tax that goes to armaments. There are two reasons for my action.

One is enough. It is enough to say that no man has the right to take another man's life. Now we plan and build weapons that can take thousands of lives in one second, millions of lives in a day, billions in a week.

No one has a right to do that.

It is madness.

It is wrong.

My other reason is that modern war is impractical and stupid. We spend billions of dollars a year on weapons which scientists, politicians, military men, and even the President all agree must never be used. That is impractical. The expression "National Security" has no meaning. It refers to our Defense System, which I call our Offense System, and which is a farce. It continues expanding and heaping up, one horrible kill machine upon another, until for some reason or another a button will be pushed and our world, or a good portion of it, will be blown to pieces. That is not security. That is stupidity.

People are starving to death in some places of the world. They look to this country with all its wealth and all its power. They look at our National budget. They are supposed to respect us. They do not respect us. They despise us. That is impractical and stupid.

Maybe the line should have been drawn when the bow and arrow were invented, maybe at the gun, the cannon, maybe. Because now it is all wrong, all impractical, and all stupid.

So all I can do is draw my own line now. I am no longer supporting my portion of the arms race.

Sincerely Yours,

Joan C. Baez

In your opinion, would Thoreau have approved of this action? Cite portions of the essay in defense of your answer. Is Miss Baez' act likely to be effective? What did Thoreau say regarding the ultimate effectiveness of such protests?

2. In addition to the tax protest waged by Miss Baez and others, the principle of civil disobedience has been much used in our time. Discuss its use in civil rights campaigns in India and in the United States. Discuss its application in cases of internal opposition to totalitarian governments.

3. Consider the following passages from Thoreau's essay:

It is not a man's duty, as a matter of course, to devote himself to the eradication of any, even the most enormous wrong; he may still properly have other concerns to engage him; but it is his duty, at least, to wash his hands of it, and, if he gives it no thought longer, not to give it practically his support.

Action from principle, the perception and the performance of right, changes things and relations. . . . It not only divides states and churches, it divides families; aye, it divides the *individual,* separating the diabolical in him from the divine.

(a) Do these passages contradict one another? Why, or why not? (b) How do the two passages apply to the action of Hochhuth's play, *The Deputy?*

4. Consider the appropriateness of the following description (a) to Biblical times, (b) to the slavery crisis in nineteenth-century America, (c) to the world's attitude towards the destruction of the Jews in World War II, (d) to the civil rights issue in the United States today:

> They hesitate, and they regret, and sometimes they petition; but they do nothing in earnest and with effect. They will wait, well disposed, for others to remedy the evil, that they may no longer have it to regret. At most, they give only a cheap vote, and a feeble countenance and Godspeed, to the right, as it goes by them. There are nine hundred ninety-nine patrons of virtue to one virtuous man.

5. Thoreau states, "If I have unjustly wrested a plank from a drowning man, I must restore it to him though I drown myself. This . . . would be inconvenient. But he that would save his life, in such a case, shall lose it." (a) Discuss the paradox in the last sentence. (b) Do you feel that Thoreau is realistic in placing man's moral obligation above his instinct for survival?

6. It is frequently argued that universal application of Thoreau's ideas would lead not to Utopia but to anarchy. Do you agree or disagree with this argument? Why?

Theme Topics

Thoreau Views the Modern Welfare State
An Answer to Joan Baez
Thoreau's Influence on Gandhi
The Argument for Civil Obedience
The Non-Voter: Consent by Silence?
Utopian Democracy
The Effectiveness of Passive Resistance

Library Assignments

1. Using Bartlett's *Familiar Quotations* (11th ed.), find the source of the following stanza quoted by Thoreau:

> "Not a drum was heard, not a funeral note,
>   As his corse to the rampart we hurried;
> Not a soldier discharged his farewell shot
>   O'er the grave where our hero we buried."

2. Thoreau remains a fascinating and controversial figure in American letters and thought. Consult either Spiller's *Literary History of the United States* or *The Cambridge History of American Literature*, ed. Carl Van Doren *et al.,* for a short biographical sketch and an evaluation of Thoreau's literary position. Do the facts of his life help explain the content of his essay "Civil Disobedience"? Explain.

3. As an index to the increase or decline of interest in Thoreau at various periods in American history, count the number of articles *about* Thoreau

which appeared in nineteenth-century periodicals by consulting *Poole's Index to Periodical Literature*. Then, using the *Readers' Guide to Periodical Literature* for the years 1910, 1920, 1930, 1940, 1950, and 1960, count the number of articles about Thoreau cited in each of these volumes. (a) What do your statistics indicate concerning interest in Thoreau in the nineteenth and twentieth centuries? What are the periods of peak interest? Lowest interest? (b) Why is such a brief statistical survey *not* likely to be an accurate way of determining an author's literary reputation?

Dante Alighieri

HELL: CANTO III

Doing nothing is as bad as taking part.
It is . . .
still less forgivable.

The Deputy, *Act Three, Scene Two*

Argument

Dante, following Virgil, comes to the gate of Hell; where, after having read the dreadful words that are written thereon, they both enter. Here, as he understands from Virgil, those were punished who had past their time (for living it could not be called) in a state of apathy and indifference both to good and evil.

"Through me you pass into the city of woe:
Through me you pass into eternal pain:
Through me among the people lost for aye.
Justice the founder of my fabric moved:
To rear me was the task of power divine,　　　　　5
Supremest wisdom, and primeval love.
Before me things create were none, save things
Eternal, and eternal I endure.
All hope abandon, ye who enter here."
　Such characters in color dim, I marked　　　　　10
Over a portal's lofty arch inscribed:
Whereat I thus: "Master, these words import
Hard meaning." He as one prepared replied:
"Here thou must all distrust behind thee leave;
Here be vile fear extinguished. We are come　　　　15
Where I have told thee we shall see the souls
To misery doomed, who intellectual good
Have lost." And when his hand he had stretched forth.

From "Hell," Canto III, trans. Rev. Henry F. Cary, ed. Oscar Kuhns, *The Divine Comedy of Dante Alighieri* (New York: Thomas Y. Crowell Co., 1897), pp. 53–55. Some footnotes have been omitted.
5. The three persons of the blessed Trinity. /53/
7. The things created before Hell are the angels, the heavens (and the matter out of which the earth is formed); these are eternal. After Hell were created the earth, — as to form, — men, animals, plants, etc., and these are not eternal. /53/
17. *Intellectual good* = knowledge of God. /53/

To mine, with pleasant looks, whence I was cheered,
Into that secret place he led me on.   20
    Here sighs, with lamentations and loud moans,
Resounded through the air pierced by no star,
That e'en I wept at entering. Various tongues,
Horrible languages, outcries of woe,
Accents of anger, voices deep and hoarse,   25
With hands together smote that swelled the sounds,
Made up a tumult, that forever whirls /53/
Round through that air with solid darkness stained,
Like to the sand that in the whirlwind flies.
    I then, with error yet encompast, cried: 30
"O master! what is this I hear? what race
Are these, who seem so overcome with woe?"
    He thus to me: "This miserable fate
Suffer the wretched souls of those, who lived
Without or praise or blame, with that ill band   35
Of angels mixed, who nor rebellious proved
Nor yet were true to God, but for themselves
Were only. From his bounds Heaven drove them forth,
Not to impair his lustre; nor the depth
Of Hell receives them, lest the accursed tribe   40
Should glory thence with exultation vain."
    I then: "Master! what doth aggrieve them thus,
That they lament so loud?" He straight replied:
"That will I tell thee briefly. These of death
No hope may entertain: and their blind life   45
So meanly passes, that all other lots
They envy. Fame of them the world hath none,
Nor suffers; mercy and justice scorn them both.
Speak not of them, but look, and pass them by."
    And I, who straightway looked, beheld a flag,   50
Which whirling ran around so rapidly,
That it no pause obtained: and following came
Such a long train of spirits, I should ne'er
Have thought that death so many had despoiled.
    When some of these I recognized, I saw   55
And knew the shade of him, who to base fear
Yielding, abjured his high estate. Forthwith
I understood, for certain, this the tribe
Of those ill spirits both to God displeasing /54/
And to his foes. These wretches, who ne'er lived,   60

23.   In the earlier circles of Hell Dante is moved to tears at the sufferings of the sinners. Later, however, pity gives way to indignation, and often bitter scorn. /53/
36.   Dante here supposes that in the revolt of Lucifer against God, some of the angels remained
neutral. This idea is probably an invention of his, as it is not found in the Bible. /54/
40.   Lest the rebellious angels should exult at seeing those who were neutral, and therefore less
guilty, condemned to the same punishment with themselves. /54/
50.   The flag represents those who in life were blown about by every wind of doctrine. . . . /54/
56.   Most commentators take this to be the hermit Pietro del Murrone, elected pope under the name
of Celestine V, and induced by fraudulent means to abdicate, thus making way for his successor
Boniface VIII. He was imprisoned by the latter and died in 1295. /54/
60.   That is, who never lived the true life. "The sinful man may truly be called dead."
                                                                Convito, iv. 7. /55/

Went on in nakedness, and sorely stung
By wasps and hornets, which bedewed their cheeks
With blood, that, mixed with tears, dropped to their feet,
And by disgustful worms was gathered there. /55/

Topics for Discussion

1. Why do those who lived without praise or blame, those who did nothing either for or against others "but for themselves/Were only," not really live but merely "pass their time" on earth?
2. Consider these two passages:

   . . . a tumult, that forever whirls
   Round through that air with solid darkness stained,
   Like to the sand that in the whirlwind flies.

   . . . a flag,
   Which whirling ran around so rapidly,
   That it no pause obtained.

   (a) How do these two images help establish the nature of the eternal punishment accorded these praiseless and blameless ones? (b) Does the punishment fit the crime?
3. What is the significance of the fact that the blood and tears of those who had been apathetic throughout their lives is gathered by "disgustful worms"?

Theme Topics

   A Man Must Choose
   Caution or Indifference?
   Flexibility or Cowardice?
   A Punishment to Fit the Crime
   A Living Hell

Library Exercises

1. Many English translations of Dante's *Divine Comedy* have been made. Compare the oldest and the most recent editions of the work in your library with the passage quoted above, *Hell*, III, 1–64. Write an analysis of the differences in text and form that you find. Do these differences give evidence of the date of the work?
2. Dante wrote his *Divine Comedy* in *terza rima*. Using *The Readers' Encyclopedia* or *A Handbook to Literature*, look up this term. Why do most English translators *not* attempt to preserve the form?

George McMillan

SILENT WHITE MINISTERS OF THE SOUTH

Who will, in times to come, respect us still
as moral arbiters if, in this *time,*
we fail so miserably?

The Deputy, *Act Two*

In the White House Rose Garden a few days ago, President Johnson met with 150 leaders of the Southern Baptist Church, in Washington for a leadership seminar. "The leaders of states and cities and towns are in your congregations," he said, "and they sit there on your boards. Their attitudes are confirmed or changed by the sermons you preach and by the lessons you write and by the examples that you set." The President appealed to them to help pass the civil rights bill and to lead the way to the future.

Mr. Johnson's request for help and leadership from the Southern churches is the latest in a long series of such public expressions. Ten years ago, when the Supreme Court ordered an end to school segregation, some observers, particularly in the North, confidently expected the "good people" of the South to step forward and lead the region to a peaceful solution of its racial problems. They looked especially to the churches, both the clergy and the laity, for that leadership.

For the most part, they have been disappointed. From the church hierarchies have come a few broad philosophical statements. Here and there, local ministerial associations have called upon their communities to "observe law and order," though usually only after civil strife and disorder have broken out. Some ministers, of course, have spoken up courageously, often at the cost of their pulpits. And there have been a few martyrs like the Baptist minister in Clinton, Tenn., who was set upon and beaten after he escorted Negro children to high school during the crisis in that city.

But the great majority of the estimated 50,000 white Southern clergymen continue to stand silent about racial matters. They stand silent in the face of racial incidents across the country and even, as on this past Easter Sunday, in the face of incidents right at their front doors—when elders and deacons turn away would-be Negro worshipers. In the fall of 1963, a survey of the 33,000 Southern Baptist churches with their 10 million members, showed that 90 per cent were still segregated, and the percentage would have been greater if the survey had been limited to the Deep South. The record of the Baptists is matched by the Methodists and the Presbyterians, the two other major denominations, and by the rest. There is little or no integration in Southern Protestant churches.

The Roman Catholic Church has steered its own course through the racial crisis. It has usually, though not always, been more liberal in accepting the Negro than the Southern Protestant churches. Many parochial schools are integrated, and the Catholic Church is now working toward desegregation of its hospitals—not only patients but also nurses, laboratory technicians and administrative personnel. In Atlanta, for example, the Catholic hospital is now completely integrated. And today a Negro will find himself welcomed at any Catholic church in the South, even those in Mississippi and Alabama.

"Silent White Ministers of the South," *The New York Times Magazine,* April 5, 1964, pp. 22, 114, 115.

But these relatively more progressive moves have had surprisingly little effect outside the Catholic Church. In the first place, the Catholic Church has not pushed its views on the South. In the second, the South is still a predominantly Protestant environment; it would probably resent it or at best pay very little attention if the Catholic hierarchy tried to take a leadership role in integration.

Many who best understand the situation in the Protestant denominations now have the least hope that the church may prove a progressive factor in the racial crisis. The Rev. Will D. Campbell, an experienced liberal churchman who was race-relations executive in the South for the National Council of Churches for more than a decade, wrote in his "Race and the Renewal of the Church": "Based on past performance, there is little likelihood that white Protestantism will play any significant role in preparing communities for true integration." And the bitter conclusion of Prof. James Sellers of Vanderbilt University's Divinity School, in his book, "The South and Christian Ethics," is that the segregated white church is the "unrepentant Southern Kingdom of God."

The fact is that most Southern churches and their clergymen, particularly in the smaller communities, are still playing out their historic role. They are, as they have always been, conservative Southern institutions defending the status quo, particularly as regards Negroes. In his influential study, "Slavery," Stanley M. Elkins points out that Virginia planters as early as the 17th century fought and won battles with the Anglican Church to keep it from coming between slave and master. From the very beginning, Elkins wrote, "the emergent institution of slavery was in effect unchallenged."

As Southern sectionalism turned into Southern nationalism early in the 19th century, the churches joined wholeheartedly in the movement and clergymen furnished some of the most eloquent defenses of slavery. "God decreed this institution before it existed," thundered the Baptist minister, Thornton Stringfellow, to his congregation in Culpeper /22/ County, Virginia, in 1856. His sermon, "A Scriptural View of Slavery," rang with Biblical chapter and verse in support of his argument.

By changing a phrase here and a word there, Stringfellow's sermon could easily be delivered from a rural Southern pulpit today; in fact, hardly a week goes by that some pastor does not tell his congregation that racial segregation is ordained by God. One minister, quoted by the Mississippi Citizens Council, declaimed: "The Bible does furnish considerable data from which valid inferences may be drawn in support of . . . segregation as an important feature of Divine purpose."

The truth is evident: On the issue of race, the white Southern minister refuses to lead. He follows and parrots the feelings of his congregation. His publicly expressed racial attitudes are very likely to be a good clue to the culture, social and economic make-up of his flock; the more deeply segregationist the minister, the less education he has had. "It's the fellows who never went to seminary or to college who are the fire-eaters," one relatively sophisticated clergyman said.

In a letter to a newspaper last October, a rural minister from South Carolina echoed the feelings of many a small-town churchman: "This thing [integration] is not a Christian issue. It is political and certainly the church has no business supporting it. Unfortunately, there are a number of ministers who seem to think that their supreme duty is to try to ram integration down the throats of the people they are supposed to serve. Our laymen and most of us as ministers and leaders are not going to accept this. In our denomination, many have already pulled out and very, very many more are just waiting."

So intense on the subject are some of these back-country clergymen, and so violent their reaction to those they feel have pushed integration on them, that they are often carried to distasteful extremes, as was the rural clergyman who told his congregation on the Sunday after President Kennedy's funeral: "According to my belief, President Kennedy is not in heaven."

Fortunately, this kind of "preacher" is becoming rarer. But the improvement is only a matter of degree. The typical Southern minister today, though essentially segregationist, is not a "fire-eater." He is a silent, passive conservative, usually Baptist, Methodist or Presbyterian, with a church in a small-to-medium-sized town. "Give him a couple of years to get the highfalutin seminary ideas out of his head, let him get his family started, give him a decent salary and a nice parsonage, and a membership in the local country club, and he's got a good living and knows it," said a prominent businessman and church leader in one town. "And when it comes to dealing with the colored folks, he's as likely to be as conservative as any of us."

"Sure. I'm conservative," one young minister said. "There's not one thing I can do about the race problems anyway, unless my lay leaders go along. Look at it this way: there are five leading churches in my town. Let's say that all five of us clergymen got up and said we were for integration. Why, we'd be crucified!

"And why should we allow ourselves to be? Where would we go? Our training has been in religion and our lives have been spent as Southerners. Why should we have to go off to the North? Frankly, I think our churches should protect us. When they do, then we'll give them leadership in the race issue."

But no matter how deep or shallow the individual Southern clergyman's convictions about racial justice, or injustice, more and more are finding it impossible to avoid the issue. "Don't get the idea these fellas have been sitting around in cloistered studies thinking this one out," said a Tennessee minister. "The Negro has simply besieged us."

Even so, another minister says flatly, "I'll tell you frankly that I'm a moral coward. But the thing reaches me anyway. I can't be neutral."

Though neutrality may be impossible, involvement is often concealed. "We all know that it's all over but the shouting," said a pastor in a small congregation. "In fact, the preachers I know don't even discuss the pros and cons of the big issue at all. We sit around trying to figure out what we can do in our own churches. That's what we talk about."

He didn't add, though he might well have, that they talk about it only among themselves. It is one thing to discuss racial issues in the bosom of the clerical profession and a completely different matter to talk the same way from the pulpit. In fact, few ever do.

"I try to allude to it once in a while," said one Baptist minister; but his allusions are so general they usually fail to have any relevance. "There are an awful lot of sermons these days about 'brotherly love,'" another pastor said, "but darned few of them are specific about who the brothers are."

Still, there are a few who are trying to institute a change. Often their outspokenness leads to trouble for themselves. In the days following the Birmingham riots last year, ministers who expressed themselves on integration were leaving their pulpits at the rate of one a day, and a professional church worker in race relations said, "It is possible that more than 100 [throughout the South] left their pulpits over the race question last year."

To speak out, especially in small rural communities, means conflict with the congregation. A year ago, 28 Methodist ministers in Mississippi signed a "Statement of Conviction." More than half were forced out of or left their churches, and the departure of one, the Rev. James Nicholson of Byram, was accompanied by threats. His church board, he related, "told me they would cut off my salary. When I said I would serve without pay, they said they would see to it that nobody attended services. I said I would hold services for my family and anyone else who wished to come." At that point, the board told Mr. Nicholson that if he tried to hold services, "they would make sure I wouldn't even make it to church."

The battle ended without a final confrontation; the Methodist hierarchy stepped in and named a new pastor, and Mr. Nicholson went off to a small church in Truro, Iowa.

In larger communities, though, it is sometimes possible for a respected minister to advance, at least peripherally, liberal attitudes on race. Not long ago the writer attended a hearing in the chamber of the House of Representatives of South Carolina, conducted by a special committee to test public sentiment on whether to close the state parks or keep them open and integrate them, as a Federal judge had ordered. /114/

Five ministers testified and all spoke in favor of open and integrated parks. The committee paid particular attention to one, the Rev. Roger Harrington, Minister to Youth at the First Baptist Church in Columbia, the largest Baptist church in South Carolina, with more than 4,000 members.

"You're a *Baptist?*" asked one of the committee members incredulously.

"Yes, I am," said Mr. Harrington positively, ignoring the implication that his denomination was more segregationist than others. "We use the parks constantly. We need them for Christian activities. And I feel that the state parks should be open to everyone, anyway."

I called on Mr. Harrington a few days later in his office in downtown Columbia. He is a husky man with wavy hair and clear, smiling blue eyes. I asked whether he had been censured for his testimony. "I've had a bunch of phone calls," he told me. "I kept tab on them and they're running about 7 to 3 backing me up. If you're talking about my job, don't worry!" As proof, Mr. Harrington asked me to meet his superior, the Rev. Archie Ellis, minister of First Baptist.

Mr. Ellis is a thin man with sallow skin but an assured manner. "You were surprised to see Roger down there at the Capitol?" he said to me. "Well, that's all right. Nothing's going to happen to him. Things have changed, you know. You've got to realize that this thing is before people daily now. There is a turn-about of thinking. I can refer to this thing now without any great resistance on the part of my congregation. Why, one of them worshiped here on Sunday and I didn't even know he had been in the congregation until the following Wednesday.

"The time has come," he continued, "when the clergy can do a great deal through a quiet, unsensational approach to the key people in this area."

Mr. Ellis is a new phenomenon—a conservative white clergyman, representing a conservative denomination, who has been called on to operate within the white power structure to help it negotiate, compromise on and work out practical solutions to specific racial situations. (This is, of course, a laggard and disappointing role for the church, when measured against the hopes that have been raised for it by many leading spokesmen, including clergy and laity.)

"Frankly," Mr. Ellis told me, when I asked him about the martyrs of the church, "I believe those ministers who have had trouble with their congregations are the designers of their own trouble."

Mr. Ellis's support of Harrington, his willingness to talk about the race problem to his congregation, and his recent racial activites in Columbia, could, nevertheless, mark a pivotal development in the role of the Southern church and white clergy. For the last 15 months, he has been working on a mayor's committee that has effected integration of lunch counters and some other public accommodations in Columbia.

Ellis's role coincides with the view that the far more liberal Will D. Campbell holds. "The church has always had two edges—a prophetic or pioneering edge and a stabilizing or conserving edge," Campbell wrote. "Critics of the church usually see its conservative nature as its greatest weakness. In the present crisis in race relations, this side of the church may become its strength and the source of the only important contribution the church may make."

But the doubts are strong. The Rev. John B. Morris, executive director of the Episcopal Society for Cultural and Racial Unity, said: "Idealistically, I have to keep telling myself that the church will step out in front, but realistically I don't believe any longer that it will." Mr. Morris recently lost his license to officiate at Episcopal services for his part in the dispute over Atlanta's Lovett School. He, and other critics, charged that the Episcopal Church has not withdrawn its support from the school, once affiliated with the church, even though the school refused admission to the son of the Rev. Dr. Martin Luther King Jr.

Equally disturbed is the Rev. Charles Webster, former Baptist chaplain to the student body of Clemson College. While South Carolina authorities last year made and enforced elaborate plans for preventing violence when Clemson was integrated, Mr. Webster worked to make certain that Harvey Gantt, the Negro student, would not only be accepted but be welcomed by the student body. He did his job well; Gantt has had almost no social or academic difficulties. But Webster was forced out of his post and is today a student working for a graduate degree at Duke University's Divinity School.

The fading of hope for strong leadership from the clergy is perhaps best summed up by Thomas F. Pettigrew, a lecturer in social psychology at Harvard University. In 1959 he and Ernest Q. Campbell published "Christians in Racial Crisis," a study of the behavior of the ministry during the racial crisis in Little Rock. "When I wrote the book I still thought the churches might come through," Pettigrew said recently. "But I'm extremely doubtful now." /115/

Topics for Discussion

1. This article provides a rather interesting present-day parallel to the situation depicted in *The Deputy.* Compare the failure of the white Southern clergy to speak out on the civil rights issue to the failure of high church officials to speak out against the persecution of the Jews.

2. Consider the following passage from Thoreau's "Civil Disobedience":

> Paley . . . resolves all civil obligation into expediency; and he proceeds to say, "that so long as the interest of the whole society requires it, that is, so long as the established government cannot be resisted or

changed without public inconveniency, it is the will of God that the established government be obeyed, and no longer. . . . This principle being admitted, the justice of every particular case of resistance is reduced to a computation of the quantity of the danger and grievance on the one side, and of the probability and expense of redressing it on the other." Of this, he says, every man shall judge for himself. But Paley appears never to have contemplated those cases to which the rule of expediency does not apply, in which a people, as well as an individual, must do justice, cost what it may.

(a) What would Thoreau be likely to conclude from the reasons for their inaction given by Southern clergymen in McMillan's article? (b) In a famous letter to Bishop von Preysing during World War II, Pius XII made the following statement, part of which is used by Hochhuth in *The Deputy* (Act Four, p. 200):

We leave it to the local bishops to weigh the circumstances in deciding whether or not to exercise restraint, *ad maiora mala vitanda* [to avoid greater evil]. This would be advisable if the danger of retaliatory and coercive measures would be imminent in cases of public statements by the bishop. Here lies one of the reasons We Ourselves restrict Our public statements. The experience We had in 1942 with documents which We released for distribution to the faithful gives justification, as far as We can see, for Our attitude.

Compare this statement with that of the Southern clergy. Compare it with Paley and Thoreau as quoted above.
3. McMillan quotes a statement made to him by a professional church worker in race relations: "It is possible that more than 100 ministers [who expressed themselves on integration throughout the South] left their pulpits over the race question last year." This brings up a question frequently introduced in discussions of *The Deputy* and the silence maintained by Pius XII and others: Is it better to remain silent in order to be in a position to work effectively for the desired end, or is one obligated to make his feelings known even when so doing renders one powerless to help the cause he espouses? Comment.

Theme Topics

Some Arguments for Segregation
Some Arguments for Moderation
Expedience Versus Morality
The Role of the Minister in Our Society
Civil Rights and Civil Wrongs
On May 24, 1964, *The New York Times Magazine* published "A Silent Minister Speaks Up," a reply to McMillan's article by Robert Collie, a Methodist minister in the South. Look up the article and write a theme in which you discuss whether Collie's reply effectively counters McMillan's accusations.

Library Exercises

1. In describing the "typical Southern minister today" McMillan says he is not a "fire-eater." A person he interviewed spoke of the "highfalutin" seminary

ideas. Look up the words *fire-eater* and *highfalutin* in *A Dictionary of Americanisms on Historical Principles,* edited by Mitford M. Mathews. What do the words mean in the context of McMillan's essay? What is the earliest known date for each expression?
2. In his article, McMillan refers to a dispute involving the admission of the son of Martin Luther King, Jr., to Atlanta's Lovett School. Look up Martin Luther King, Jr., in *Current Biography.* Would you agree that failure to admit the boy warrants the cutting off of support of the Episcopal Church?
3. In McMillan's article, references are made to three books: Will D. Campbell's *Race and the Renewal of the Church,* James Sellers' *The South and Christian Ethics,* and Thomas F. Pettigrew and Ernest Q. Campbell's *Christians in Racial Crisis.* Using *Books in Print* or *The Cumulative Book Index,* find the information necessary to order the books for your own library (publisher and price).

John Milton

THE TENURE OF KINGS AND MAGISTRATES

. . . I lacked the cynicism
to cite reasons of state when
things like these come to my ears.

The Deputy, *Act Two*

. . . For Divines, if ye observe them, have thir postures, and thir motions no less expertly, and with no less variety then they that practice feats in the Artillery-ground. Sometimes they seem furiously to march on, and presently march counter; by and by they stand, and then retreat; or if need be can face about, or wheele in a whole body, with that cunning and dexterity as is almost unperceavable; to winde themselves by shifting ground into places of more advantage. And Providence onely must be the drumm, Providence the word of command, that calls them from above, but always to som larger Benefice, or acts them into such or such figures, and promotions. At thir turnes and doublings no men readier; to the right, or to the left; for it is thir turnes which they serve cheifly; heerin only singular; that with them there is no certain hand right or left; but as thir own commodity thinks best to call it. But if there come a truth to be defended, which to them, and thir interest of this world seems not so profitable, strait these nimble motionists can finde no eev'n leggs to stand upon: and are no more of use to reformation throughly performed, and not superficially, or to the advancement of Truth (which among mortal men is alwaies in her progress) then if on a sudden they were strook maime, and crippl'd. Which the better to conceale, or the more to countnance by a general conformity to thir own limping, they would have *Scripture,* they would have *reason* also made to halt with them for company; and would putt us off with impotent conclusions, lame and shorter then the premises. In this posture they seem to stand with great zeale and confidence on the wall of *Sion;* but /729/ like *Jebusites,* not like *Israelites,* or *Levites:* blinde also as well as lame, they discern not *David* from *Adonibezec:* but cry him up for the

"The Tenure of Kings and Magistrates," *Complete Poetry and Selected Prose of John Milton* (New York: The Modern Library, n.d.), pp. 729–730.

Lords anointed, whose thumbs and great toes not long before they had cut off upon thir Pulpit cushions. . . . /730/

Topics for discussion

1. Discuss the aptness of the imagery employed by Milton in this brief selection.
2. Discuss the following statement as applied to (a) Pius XII as depicted in *The Deputy,* (b) the Southern white ministers today:

> But if there come a truth to be defended, which to them, and thir interest of this world seemes not so profitable, strait these nimble motionists can finde no eev'n leggs to stand upon: and are no more of use to reformation throughly performd, and not superficially, or to the advancement of Truth (which among mortal men is alwaies in her progress) then if on a sudden they were strook maime, and crippl'd.

Theme Topics

> Hypocrisy in High Places
> Looking Out for "Number One"
> Defenders of Truth
> What Is Truth?

Library Assignments

1. Look up John Milton in *The Cambridge History of English Literature.* To what events that took place in Milton's lifetime does the above passage refer?
2. Using Charles W. Moulton's *Library of Literary Criticism of English and American Authors,* look up John Milton. Write a brief summary of his literary reputation in the *nineteenth* century.
3. Using a *Dictionary of the Bible,* interpret the final sentence of this selection and translate it into your own words.

William James

OBEDIENCE

Your duty is obedience.

The Deputy, *Act Two*

. . . In the ecclesiastically consecrated character three minor branches of self-mortification have been recognized as indispensable pathways to perfection. I refer to the chastity, obedience, and poverty which the monk vows to observe; and upon the heads of obedience and poverty I will make a few remarks. /304/

First, of Obedience. The secular life of our twentieth century opens with this virtue held in no high esteem. The duty of the individual to determine

From *The Varieties of Religious Experience* (New York: The Modern Library, 1929).

his own conduct and profit or suffer by the consequences seems, on the contrary, to be one of our best rooted contemporary Protestant social ideals. So much so that it is difficult even imaginatively to comprehend how men possessed of an inner life of their own could ever have come to think the subjection of its will to that of other finite creatures recommendable. I confess that to myself it seems something of a mystery. Yet it evidently corresponds to a profound interior need of many persons, and we must do our best to understand it.

On the lowest possible plane, one sees how the expediency of obedience in a firm ecclesiastical organization must have led to its being viewed as meritorious. Next, experience shows that there are times in every one's life when one can be better counseled by others than by one's self. Inability to decide is one of the commonest symptoms of fatigued nerves; friends who. see our troubles more broadly, often see them more wisely than we do; so it is frequently an act of excellent virtue to consult and obey a doctor, a partner, or a wife. But, leaving these lower prudential regions, we find, in the nature of some of the spiritual excitements which we have been studying, good reasons for idealizing obedience. Obedience may spring from the general religious phenomenon of inner softening and self-surrender and throwing one's self on higher powers. So saving are these attitudes felt to be that in themselves, apart from utility, they become ideally consecrated; and in obeying a man whose fallibility we see through thoroughly, we, nevertheless, may feel much as we do when we resign our will to that of infinite wisdom. Add self-despair and the passion of self-crucifixion to this, and obedience becomes an ascetic sacrifice, agreeable quite irrespective of whatever prudential uses it might have.

It is as a sacrifice, a mode of "mortification," that obe- /305/ dience is primarily conceived by Catholic writers, a "sacrifice which man offers to God, and of which he is himself both the priest and the victim. By poverty he immolates his exterior possessions; by chastity he immolates his body; by obedience he completes the sacrifice, and gives to God all that he yet holds as his own, his two most precious goods, his intellect and his will. The sacrifice is then complete and unreserved, a genuine holocaust, for the entire victim is now consumed for the honor of God."[1] Accordingly, in Catholic discipline, we obey our superior not as mere man, but as the representative of Christ. Obeying God in him by our intention, obedience is easy. But when the textbook theologians marshal collectively all their reasons for recommending it, the mixture sounds to our ears rather odd.

"One of the great consolations of the monastic life," says a Jesuit authority, "is the assurance we have that in obeying we can commit no fault. The Superior may commit a fault in commanding you to do this thing or that, but you are certain that you commit no fault so long as you obey, because God will only ask you if you have duly performed what orders you received, and if you can furnish a clear account in that respect, you are absolved entirely. Whether the things you did were opportune, or whether there were not something better that might have been done, these are questions not asked of you, but rather of your Superior. The moment what you did was done obediently, God wipes it out of your account, and charges it to the Superior. So that Saint Jerome well exclaimed, in celebrating the advantages of obedience, 'Oh, sover-

---

1. Lejuene: Introduction à la Vie Mystique, 1899, p. 277. The holocaust simile goes back at least as far as Ignatius Loyola. /306/

eign liberty! Oh, holy and blessed security by which one becomes almost impeccable!"

"Saint John Climachus is of the same sentiment when he calls obedience an excuse before God. In fact, when God asks why you have done this or that, and you reply, it is because I was so ordered by my Superiors, God will ask for no other excuse. As a passenger in a good vessel with a good pilot need give himself /306/ no farther concern, but may go to sleep in peace, because the pilot has charge over all, and 'watches for him'; so a religious person who lives under the yoke of obedience goes to heaven as if while sleeping, that is, while leaning entirely on the conduct of his Superiors, who are the pilots of his vessel, and keep watch for him continually. It is no small thing, of a truth, to be able to cross the stormy sea of life on the shoulders and in the arms of another, yet that is just the grace which God accords to those who live under the yoke of obedience. Their Superior bears all their burdens. . . . A certain grave doctor said that he would rather spend his life in picking up straws by obedience, than by his own responsible choice busy himself with the loftiest works of charity, because one is certain of following the will of God in whatever one may do from obedience, but never certain in the same degree of anything which we may do of our own proper movement."[1]

One should read the letters in which Ignatius Loyola recommends obedience as the backbone of his order, if one would gain insight into the full spirit of its cult.[2] They are too long to quote; but Ignatius's belief is so vividly expressed in a couple of sayings reported by companions that, though they have been so often cited, I will ask your permission to copy them once more: —

"I ought," an early biographer reports him as saying, "on entering religion, and thereafter, to place myself entirely in the hands of God, and of him who takes His place by His authority. I ought to desire that my Superior should oblige me to give up my own judgment, and conquer my own mind. I ought to set up no difference between one Superior and another, . . . but recognize them all as equal before God, whose place they fill. For if I distinguish persons, I weaken the spirit of obedience. In the hands of my Superior, I must be a soft wax, a thing, from /307/ which he is to require whatever pleases him, be it to write or receive letters, to speak or not to speak to such a person, or the like; and I must put all my fervor in executing zealously and exactly what I am ordered. I must consider myself as a corpse which has neither intelligence nor will; be like a mass of matter which without resistance lets itself be placed wherever it may please any one; like a stick in the hand of an old man, who uses it according to his needs and places it where it suits him. So must I be under the hands of the Order, to serve it in the way it judges most useful.

"I must never ask of the Superior to be sent to a particular place, to be employed in a particular duty. . . . I must consider nothing as belonging to me personally, and as regards the things I use, be like a statue which lets itself be stripped and never opposes resistance."[1]

1. Alfonso Rodriguez, S. J.: Pratique de la Perfection Chrétienne, Part iii., Treatise v., ch. x. /307/
2. Letters li. and cxx. of the collection translated into French by Bouix, Paris, 1870. /307/
1. Bartoli-Michel, ii. 13. /308/

The other saying is reported by Rodriguez in the chapter from which I a moment ago made quotations. When speaking of the Pope's authority, Rodriguez writes: —

"Saint Ignatius said, when general of his company, that if the Holy Father were to order him to set sail in the first bark which he might find in the port of Ostia, near Rome, and to abandon himself to the sea, without a mast, without sails, without oars or rudder or any of the things that are needful for navigation of subsistence, he would obey not only with alacrity, but without anxiety or repugnance, and even with a great internal satisfaction."[2] /308/

Topics for Discussion

1. William James states that "The secular life of our twentieth century opens with this virtue [obedience] held in no high esteem." As examples of the truth of this statement, we may cite the custom of dropping the word *obey* in favor of *cherish* in the wedding ceremony and the growth of the "family-council" approach to making decisions that were once the sole domain of the father. Has the replacement of obedience by personal responsibility strengthened or weakened (a) family life, (b) religious life, (c) civil life?
2. Riccardo in *The Deputy* had, as an ordained priest in the Society of Jesus, taken a vow of obedience. When accused of breaking his sacred vow, Riccardo replied that he had taken a vow of obedience to God, which, under the circumstances, he could keep only by disobeying his mortal superiors. Discuss Riccardo's position in terms of the definition of religious obedience set forth in James' essay.
3. James mentions that "subjection of [one's] will to that of another finite being" seems to correspond "to a profound interior need of many persons" and that "inability to decide is one of the commonest symptoms of fatigued nerves" so that "it is frequently an act of excellent virtue to consult and obey" someone in whom one has confidence. Discuss these two factors as causes of the rise of dictatorships.
4. In the Nuremberg Trials, the Eichmann trial, and the 1964 Auschwitz trials, the argument that a man was not guilty because he had merely obeyed the orders of his superiors was set forth again and again. Is, as one man states, "obedience an excuse before God," or must a man's conscience intervene between the orders of a superior and his own actions?

Theme Topics

The Breakdown of Authority
The Burden of Self-Reliance
Obedience: How Much and To Whom?
Love, Honor, and Obey
Excuse Before God

Library Assignments

1. Look up Ignatius Loyola in the *Catholic Encyclopedia*. Himmler is said to

2. Rodriguez: Op. cit., Part iii., Treatise v., ch. vi. /308/

have fashioned the SS after Loyola's plans for the Society of Jesus. Point out any similarities and differences you can see in the two organizations.
2. Look up William James in the *Dictionary of American Biography.* What were his major contributions to American philosophy?
3. Using the *Statistical Abstract of the United States,* compare the crime and divorce rates of the nineteenth century to those of the twentieth century. Can you reach any conclusion from these figures concerning the effect of the diminishing authority of the home on American society? Why, or why not?

Samuel Johnson

ON TOLERATION

I understand your ambition to be crucified.

The Deputy, *Act Five, Scene Two*

I introduced the subject of toleration. JOHNSON. "Every society has a right to preserve public peace and order, and therefore has a good right to prohibit the propagation of opinions which have a dangerous tendency. To say the *magistrate* has this right, is using an inadequate word: it is the *society* for which the magistrate is agent. He may be morally or theologically wrong in restraining the propagation of opinions which he thinks dangerous, but he is politically right." MAYO. "I am of opinion, Sir, that every man is entitled to liberty of conscience in religion; and that the magistrate cannot restrain that right." JOHNSON. "Sir, I agree with you. Every man has a right to liberty of conscience, and with that the magistrate cannot interfere. People confound liberty of thinking with liberty of talking; nay, with liberty of preaching. Every man has a physical right to think as he pleases; for it cannot be discovered how he thinks. He has not a moral right, for he ought to inform himself, and think justly. But, Sir, no member of a society has a right to *teach* any doctrine contrary to what the society holds to be true. The magistrate, I say, may be wrong in what he thinks; but while he thinks himself right, he may and ought to enforce what he thinks." MAYO. "Then, Sir, we are to remain always in errour, and truth never can prevail; and the magistrate was right in persecuting the first Christians." JOHNSON. "Sir, the only method by which religious truth can be established is by martyrdom. The magistrate has a right to enforce what he thinks; and he who is conscious of the truth has a right to suffer. I am afraid there is no other way of ascertaining the truth, but by persecution on the one hand and enduring it on the other." GOLDSMITH. "But how is a man to act, Sir? Though firmly convinced of the truth of his doctrine, may he not think it wrong to expose himself to persecution? Has he a right to do so? Is it not, as it were, committing voluntary suicide?" JOHNSON. "Sir, as to voluntary suicide, as you call it, there are twenty /212/ thousand men in an army, who will go without scruple to be shot at, and mount a breach for five-pence a day." GOLDSMITH. "But have they a moral right to do this?" JOHNSON. "Nay, Sir, if you will not take the universal opinion of mankind, I have nothing to say. If mankind cannot defend their own way of thinking, I cannot defend it. Sir, if a man is in doubt whether it would be better for him to expose himself

From James Boswell, *The Life of Samuel Johnson,* ed. Henry Morley (Glasgow: George Routledge and Sons, Ltd., 1891), Vol. II.

to martyrdom or not, he should not do it. He must be convinced that he has a delegation from heaven." GOLDSMITH. "I would consider whether there is the greater chance of good or evil upon the whole. If I see a man who has fallen into a well, I would wish to help him out; but if there is a greater probability that he shall pull me in, than that I shall pull him out, I would not attempt it. So were I to go to Turkey, I might wish to convert the Grand Signor to the Christian faith; but when I considered that I should probably be put to death without effectuating my purpose in any degree, I should keep myself quiet." JOHNSON. "Sir, you must consider that we have perfect and imperfect obligations. Perfect obligations, which are generally not to do something, are clear and positive; as, 'Thou shalt not kill.' But charity, for instance, is not definable by limits. It is a duty to give to the poor; but no man can say how much another should give to the poor, or when a man has given too little to save his soul. In the same manner it is a duty to instruct the ignorant, and of consequence to convert infidels to Christianity; but no man in the common course of things is obliged to carry this to such a degree as to incur the danger of martyrdom, as no man is obliged to strip himself to the shirt, in order to give charity. I have said, that a man must be persuaded that he has a particular delegation from heaven." GOLDSMITH. "How is this to be known? Our first reformers, who were burnt for not believing bread and wine to be CHRIST—" JOHNSON (interrupting him). "Sir, they were not burnt for not believing bread and wine to be CHRIST, but for insulting those who did believe it. And, Sir, when the first reformers began, they did not intend to be martyred: as many of them ran away as could." BOSWELL. "But, Sir, there was your countryman Elwal, who you told me challenged King George with his black-guards /213/ and his red-guards." JOHNSON. "My countryman, Elwal, Sir, should have been put in the stocks: a proper pulpit for him; and he'd have had a numerous audience. A man who preaches in the stocks will always have hearers enough." BOSWELL. "But Elwal thought himself in the right." JOHNSON. "We are not providing for mad people; there are places for them in the neighbourhood" (meaning Moorfields). MAYO. "But, Sir, is it not very hard that I should not be allowed to teach my children what I really believe to be the truth?" JOHNSON. "Why, Sir, you might contrive to teach your children *extrà scandalum;* but, Sir, the magistrate, if he knows it, has a right to restrain you. Suppose you teach your children to be thieves?" MAYO. "This is making a joke of the subject." JOHNSON. "Nay, Sir, take it thus:—that you teach them the community of goods: for which there are as many plausible arguments as for most erroneous doctrines. You teach them that all things at first were in common, and that no man had a right to any thing but as he laid his hands upon it; and that this still is, or ought to be, the rule amongst mankind. Here, Sir, you sap a great principle in society—property. And don't you think the magistrate would have a right to prevent you? Or, suppose you should teach your children the notion of the Adamites, and they should run naked into the streets, would not the magistrate have a right to flog 'em into their doublets?" MAYO. "I think the magistrate has no right to interfere till there is some overt act." BOSWELL. "So, Sir, though he sees an enemy to the state charging a blunderbuss, he is not to interfere till it is fired off!" MAYO. "He must be sure of its direction against the state." JOHNSON. "The magistrate is to judge of that.— He has no right to restrain your thinking, because the evil centers in yourself. If a man were sitting at this table, and chopping off his fingers, the magistrate, as guardian of the community, has no authority to restrain him, however he might do it from kindness as a parent.—Though, indeed, upon more consideration, I think he may; as it is probable, that he who is chopping off his own fingers, may soon proceed to chop off those of other people. If I think it right to steal Mr. Dilly's plate I am a bad man; but he can say nothing to me. If I make an /214/ open declaration that I think so, he will keep me out of his house. If I put forth my hand, I shall be sent to Newgate. This is the gradation of thinking, preaching, and acting: if a man thinks erroneously, he may keep his thoughts to himself, and nobody will trouble him; if he preaches erroneous doctrine, society may expel him; if he acts in consequence of it, the law takes place, and he is hanged." Mayo. "But, Sir, ought not Christians to have liberty of conscience?" Johnson. "I have already told you so, Sir. You are coming back to where you were." Boswell. "Dr. Mayo is always taking a return postchaise, and going the stage over again. He has it at half-price." Johnson. "Dr. Mayo, like other champions for unlimited toleration, has got a set of words.[1] Sir, it is no matter, politically, whether the magistrate be right or wrong. Suppose a club were to be formed, to drink confusion to King George the Third, and a happy restoration to Charles the Third; this would be very bad with respect to the State; but every member of that club must either conform to its rules, or be turned out of it. Old Baxter, I remember, maintains, that the magistrate should 'tolerate all things that are tolerable.' This is no good definition of toleration upon any principle; but it shows that he thought some things were not tolerable." . . . /215/

Topics for Discussion

1. Johnson states that "the only method by which religious truth can be established is by martyrdom." Is dying for a cause an effective means of demonstrating its truth? Consider (a) Jesus Christ, (b) Joan of Arc, (c) John Brown, (d) Medgar Evers, (e) Riccardo in *The Deputy.*

2. According to Johnson, the magistrate or the society for which the magistrate is agent "may be morally or theologically wrong in restraining the propagation of opinions which he thinks dangerous, but he is politically right." Applying the principle, would the following be right or wrong: (a) the arrest and expulsion of "freedom riders" in the South, (b) the outlawing of the Communist party in the United States, (c) the suppression of churches in the Soviet Union?

3. In this selection it is stated that "No man in the common course of things is obliged to carry [duty] to such a degree as to incur the danger of martyrdom, as no man is obliged to strip himself to the shirt, in order to give charity." Is this idea in agreement or disagreement with the thoughts expressed by (a) Rolf Hochhuth in *The Deputy,* (b) Thoreau in "Civil Disobedience"?

Theme Topics

A Martyr of Our Times
Thinking, Preaching, and Acting

1. Dr. Mayo's calm temper and steady perserverance, rendered him an admirable subject for the exercise of Dr. Johnson's powerful abilities. He never flinched: but, after reiterated blows, remained seemingly unmoved as at the first. The scintillations of Johnson's genius flashed every time he was struck, without his receiving any injury. Hence he obtained the epithet of The Literary Anvil. /215/

An Answer to Johnson
Enemies of State

Library Assignments

1. Johnson states, "Why, Sir, you might contrive to teach your children *extrà scandalum. . . .*" In *A Dictionary of Foreign Words and Phrases,* look up the phrase *extrà scandalum.*
2. Writings by and about Samuel Johnson are so numerous that a number of checklists and bibliographies have been compiled to help classify them. Using Besterman's *World Bibliography of Bibliographies,* compile a list of bibliographies on Johnson.
3. What aspects of Johnson's character as described in the *Dictionary of National Biography* are evident in the above selection?

T. S. Eliot

MARTYRDOM SPEECH

I came here with a mission; that must sustain me.

The Deputy, *Act Five, Scene Three*

THOMAS: Unbar the doors! throw open the doors!
I will not have the house of prayer, the church of Christ,
The sanctuary, turned into a fortress.
The church shall protect her own, in her own way, not
As oak and stone; stone and oak decay,
Give no stay, but the Church shall endure.
The church shall be open, even to our enemies. Open the door!

. . . .

Unbar the door!
You think me reckless, desperate and mad.
You argue by results, as this world does,
To settle if an act be good or bad. /211/
You defer to the fact. For every life and every act
Consequence of good and evil can be shown.
And as in time results of many deeds are blended
So good and evil in the end become confounded.
It is not in time that my death shall be known;
It is out of time that my decision is taken
If you call that decision
To which my whole being gives entire consent.
I give my life
To the Law of God above the Law of Man.
Those who do not the same
How should they know what I do?
How should you know what I do? Yet how much more
Should you know than these madmen beating on the door.
Unbar the door! unbar the door!

From Act III of "Murder in the Cathedral," *The Complete Poems and Plays* (New York: Harcourt, Brace & Company, 1952).

We are not here to triumph by fighting, by stratagem, or by
   resistance,
Not to fight with beasts as men. We have fought the beast
And have conquered. We have only to conquer
Now, by suffering. This is the easier victory.
Now is the triumph of the Cross, now
Open the door! I command it. OPEN THE DOOR! /212/

     .   .   .   .

It is the just man who
Like a bold lion, should be without fear.
I am here.
No traitor to the King. I am a priest,
A Christian, saved by the blood of Christ,
Ready to suffer with my blood.
This is the sign of the Church always,
The sign of blood. Blood for blood.
His blood given to buy my life,
My blood given to pay for His death,
My death for His death. /213/

Topics for Discussion

1. This speech is made by the Archbishop of Canterbury, Thomas Becket, as
   he faces martyrdom. (a) Do the words reveal that the Archbishop had, in
   Johnson's words, "a delegation from heaven" in choosing his path? (b) Compare the following two statements, the first from the speech above, the
   second from *The Deputy*. Discuss whether choice is involved or not.

   > THOMAS: It is out of time that my decision is taken
   > If you call that decision
   > To which my whole being gives entire consent.

   > GERSTEIN: I must disillusion you, Father.
   > There was no terrible ordeal,
   > no pangs of conscience, none at all.

2. Compare Becket's attitude toward his martyrdom to Riccardo's in *The
   Deputy*. Consider particularly the following passages:

   > THOMAS: You think me reckless, desperate and mad.
   > You argue by results, as this world does,
   > To settle if an act be good or bad.

   >   .   .   .   .
   >   I am a priest,
   > A Christian, saved by the blood of Christ,
   > Ready to suffer with my blood.

3. Practically all of the selections in this section have brought out the essential
   conflict between the practical man, concerned with his place in this world,
   and the idealist, following a higher authority and seeking a higher reward.
   Perhaps all human conflict has this common origin. Discuss other essays,
   poems, novels, plays, movies which deal with the subject of a practical choice
   vs. a moral one. Is the theme particularly relevant to our day? Explain.

Theme Topics

The Example of the Cross
On Being Practical
The Courage of My Convictions
"As This World Does"
With Conscience As Guide

Library Assignments

1. Using the bibliography volume of the *Literary History of the United States,* find the year in which *Murder in the Cathedral* was first published. Then go to the *Book Review Digest* for the appropriate year and look up the initial reaction to the work. Was the criticism primarily favorable or unfavorable?
2. Using the *Cambridge History of the British Empire* look up the historical background of the martyrdom of the Archbishop of Canterbury, Thomas Becket. Does the speech above fit the historical facts in respect to character and situation?
3. Look up T. S. Eliot in *Who's Who.* What were his major accomplishments?

(though the attempt has been often enough made) ever succeeded in giving rise to a single dramatic work of enduring value, unless the creative force was there to animate the form.

It is therefore the operation of this creative force which we are chiefly interested in noting; and its task begins with the beginning of the dramatist's labours. He must of course start with the choice of a subject; yet it is obvious that the subject is merely the dead material out of which is formed that living something, the action of a play; and it is only in rare instances—far rarer than might at first sight appear—that the subject is as it were self-moulded as a dramatic action. The less experienced a playwright, the more readily will he, as the phrase is, rush at his subject, more especially if it seems to him to possess prima facie dramatic capabilities; and the consequence will be that which usually attends upon a precipitate start. On the other hand, while the quickness of a great dramatist's apprehension is apt to suggest /475/ to him an infinite number of subjects, and insight and experience may lead him half instinctively in the direction of suitable themes, it will often be long before in his mind the subject converts itself into the initial conception of the action of a play. To mould a subject—be it a Greek legend, or a portion of a Tudor chronicle, or one out of a hundred Italian tales, or a true story of modern life—into the action or fable of a play, is the primary task of the dramatist, and with this all-important process the creative part of his work really begins. Although his conception may expand or modify itself as he executes it, yet upon the conception the execution must largely depend. The range of subjects open to a dramatist may be as wide as the world itself, or it may be restricted by an endless variety of causes, conventions and considerations; and it is quite true that even the greatest dramatists have not always found time for contemplating each subject that occurs to them till the ray is caught which proclaims it a dramatic diamond. What they had time for, and what only the playwright who entirely misunderstands his art ignores the necessity of finding time for, is the transformation of the dead material of the subject into the living action of a drama.

What is it, then, that makes an action *dramatic*, and without which no action, whatever may be its nature—serious or ludicrous, stately or trivial, impetuous as a flame of fire, or light as a western breeze—can be so described? The answer to this question can only suggest itself from an attempt to ascertain the laws which determine the nature of all actions corresponding to this description. The first of the laws in question is in so far the most noteworthy among them that it has been the most amply discussed and the most pertinaciously misunderstood. This is the law which requires that a dramatic action should be *one*—that it should possess *unity*. What in the subject of a drama is merely an approximate or supposititious, must in its action be an actual unity; and it is indeed this requirement which constitutes the most arduous part of the task of transforming subject into action. There is of course no actual unity in any group of events in human life which we may choose to call by a single collective name—a war, a revolution, a conspiracy, an intrigue, an imbroglio. The events of real life, the facts of history, even the imitative incidents of narrative fiction, are like the waves of a ceaseless flood; that which binds a group or body of them into a single action is the bond of the dramatic idea; and this it is incumbent upon the dramatist to supply. Within the limits of a dramatic action all its parts should (as in real life or in history they so persistently refuse to do) flow into its current like tributaries to a single stream; or, to vary the figure, everything in a drama should form a link in a single chain of cause and effect. This law is incumbent upon every kind of drama—alike upon the tragedy which sets itself to solve one of the problems of a life, and upon the farce which sums up the follies of an afternoon.

Such is not, however, the case with certain more or less arbitrary rules which have at different times been set up for this or that kind of drama. The supposed necessity that an action should consist of *one event* is an erroneous interpretation of the law that it should be, as an action, *one*. For an event is but an element in an action, though it may be an element of decisive moment. The assassination of Caesar is not the action of a *Caesar* tragedy; the loss of his treasure is not the action of *The Miser*. Again, unity of action, while excluding those unconnected episodes which Aristotle so severely condemns, does not prohibit the introduction of one or even more subsidiary actions as contributing to the progress of the main action. The sole indispensable law is that these should always be treated as what they are—subsidiary only; and herein lies the difficulty, which Shakespeare so successfully overcame, of fusing a combination of subjects taken from various sources into the idea of a single action; herein also lies the danger in the use of that favourite device of the Spanish and other modern dramas—"by-plots" or "under-plots." On the other hand, the modern French drama has largely employed another device—quite legitimate in itself—for increasing the interest of an action without destroying its unity. This may be called the dramatic use of backgrounds, the depiction of surroundings on which the action or its chief characters seem sympathetically to reflect themselves, backbiting "good villagers" or academicians who inspire one another—with tedium. But a really double or multiple action, logically carried out as such, is inconceivable in a single drama, though many a play is palpably only two plays knotted into one. It was therefore not all pedantry which protested against the multiplicity of action which had itself formed part of the revolt against the too narrow interpretation of unity adopted by the French classical drama. Thirdly, unity of action need not imply unity of hero—for hero (or heroine) is merely a conventional term signifying the principal personage of the action. It is only when the change in the degree of interest excited by different characters in a play results from a change in the conception of the action itself, that the consequent *duality* (or multiplicity) of heroes recalls a faulty uncertainty in the conception of the action they carry on. . . . It came to be overlooked that there is nothing in Aristotle's statement to show that in his judgment unity of time and place are, like unity of action, absolute dramatic laws. Their object is by representing an action as visibly continuous to render its unity more distinctly or easily perceptible. But the imagination is capable of constructing for itself the bridges required for preserving to an action, conceived of as such, its character of continuousness. In another sense these rules were convenient usages conducing to a concise and clear treatment of a limited kind of themes; for they were a Greek invention, and the repeated resort to the same group of myths made it expedient for a Greek poet to seek the subject of a single tragedy in a part only of one of the myths at his disposal. The observance of unity of place, moreover, was suggested to the Greeks by certain outward conditions of their stage—as assuredly as it was adopted by the French in accordance with the construction and usages of theirs, and as the neglect of it by the Elizabethans was in their case encouraged by the established form of the English scene. The palpable artificiality of these laws needs no demonstration, so long as the true meaning of the term "action" be kept in view. Of the action of *Othello* part takes place at Venice and part at Cyprus, and yet the whole is one in itself; while the limits of time over which an action — Hamlet's progress to resolve, for instance — extends cannot be restricted by a revolution of the earth round the sun or of the moon round the earth.

In a drama which presents its action as *one*, this action must be *complete in itself*. This Aristotelian law, like the other, distinguishes the dramatic action from its subject. The former may be said to have a real artistic, while the latter has only an imaginary real, completeness. The historian, for instance, is aware that the complete exposition of a body of events and transactions at which he aims can never be more than partially accomplished, since he may present only what he knows, and all human knowledge is imperfect. But Art is limited by no such uncertainty. The dramatist, in treating an action as *one*, comprehends the whole of it in the form of his work, since, to him who has *conceived* it, all its parts, from cause to effect, are equally clear. It is his fault if in the action of his drama anything is left unaccounted for — not *motivé;* though a dramatic *motif* might not always prove to be a sufficient explanation in real life. Accordingly, every drama should represent in organic sequence the several stages of which a complete action consists, and which are essential to it. This law of completeness, therefore, lies at the foundation of all systems of dramatic "construction." /476/

Every action, if conceived of as complete, has its causes, growth, height, consequences and close. There is no binding law to prescribe the relative length or proportion at which these several stages in the action should be treated in a drama; or to regulate the treatment of such subsidiary actions as may be introduced in aid of the main plot, or of such more or less directly connected "episodes" as may at the same time advance and relieve its progress. But experience has necessarily from time to time established certain rules of practice, and from the adoption of particular systems of division for particular species of the drama — such as that into five acts for a regular tragedy or comedy, which Roman example has caused to be so largely followed — has naturally resulted a certain uniformity of relation between the conduct of an action and the outward sections of a play. . . .

The exposition, which may be short or long, but which should always prepare and may even seem to necessitate the action, ends when the movement of the action itself begins. This transition may occasionally be marked with the utmost distinctness (as in the actual meeting between the hero and the Ghost in *Hamlet*), while in other instances subsidiary action or episode may judiciously intervene (as in *King Lear,* where the subsidiary action of Gloster and his sons opportunely prevents too abrupt a sequence of cause and effect). From this point the second stage of the action — its "growth" — progresses to that third stage which is called its "height" or "climax." All that has preceded the attainment of this constitutes that half of the drama — usually its much larger half — which Aristotle terms the . . . tying of the knot. The varieties in the treatment of the growth or second stage of the action are infinite; it is here that the greatest freedom is manifestly permissible; that in the Indian drama the personages make long journeys across the stage; and that, with the help of their under-plots, the masters of the modern tragic and the comic drama — notably those unequalled weavers of intrigues, the Spaniards — are able most fully to exercise their inventive faculties. If the growth is too rapid, the climax will fail of its effect; if it is too slow, the interest will be exhausted before the greatest demand upon it has been made — a fault to which comedy is specially liable; if it is involved or inverted, a vague uncertainty will take the place of an eager or agreeable suspense, the action will seem to halt, or a fall will begin prematurely. In the contrivance of the "climax" itself lies one of the chief tests of the dramatist's art; for while the transactions of real life often fail to reach any climax at all, that of a dramatic action should present itself as self-evident. In the middle of everything, says the Greek poet, lies the strength; and this strongest or highest point it is the task of the dramatist to make manifest. Much here depends upon the niceties of constructive instinct; much (as in all parts of the action) upon a thorough dramatic transformation of the subject. The historical drama at this point presents peculiar difficulties, of which the example of *Henry VIII.* may be cited as an illustration.

From the climax, or height, the action proceeds through its "fall" to its "close," which in a drama with an unhappy ending we still call its "catastrophe," while to terminations in general we apply the term *dénouement*. This latter name would, however, more properly be applied . . . to the whole of the second part of the action, from the climax downwards. In the management of the climax, everything depends upon producing the effect; in the fall, everything depends upon not marring it. This may be ensured by a rapid advance to the close; but neither does every action admit of such treatment, nor is it in accordance with the character of those which are of a more subtle or complicated kind. With the latter, therefore, the "fall" is often a revolution or "return," *i.e.* in Aristotle's phrase a change into the reverse of what is expected from the circumstances of the action . . . —as in *Coriolanus*, where the Roman story lends itself so admirably to dramatic demands. In any case, the art of the dramatist is in this part of his work called upon for the surest exercise of its tact and skill. The effect of the climax was to concentrate the interest; the fall must therefore, above all, avoid dissipating it. The use of episodes is not even now excluded; but, even where serving the purpose of relief, they must now be such as help to keep alive the interest, previously raised to its highest pitch. This may be effected by the raising of obstacles between the height of the action and its expected consequences; in tragedy by the suggestion of a seemingly possible recovery or escape from them (as in the wonderfully powerful construction of the latter part of *Macbeth*); in comedy, or wherever the interest of the action is less intense, by the gradual removal of incidental difficulties. In all kinds of the drama "discovery" will remain, as it was in the judgment of Aristotle, a most effective expedient; but it should be a discovery prepared by that method of treatment which in its consummate master, Sophocles, has been termed his "irony." Nowhere should the close or catastrophe be other than a consequence of the action itself. Sudden revulsions from the conditions of the action—such as are supplied with the aid of the *deus ex machina,* or the revising officer of the emperor of China, or the nabob returned from India, or a virulent malaria—condemn themselves as unsatisfactory makeshifts. However sudden, and even in manner of accomplishment surprising, may be the catastrophe, it should, like every other part of the action, be in organic connexion with the whole preceding action. The sudden suicides which terminate so many tragedies, and the unmerited paternal blessings which close an equal number of comedies, should be something more than a "way out of it," or a signal for the fall of the curtain. A catastrophe may conveniently, and even (as in /477/ *Faust*) with powerful effect, be left to the imagination; but to substitute for it a deliberate blank is to leave the action incomplete, and the drama a fragment ending with a —possibly interesting—confession of incompetence.

The action of a drama, besides being one and complete in itself, ought likewise to be *probable*. The probability or necessity (in the Aristotelian sense of

the terms) required of a drama is not that of actual or historical experience—it is a conditional probability, or in other words an internal consistency
between the course of the action and the conditions under which the dramatist has chosen to carry it on. As to the former, he is fettered by no restrictions
save those which he imposes upon himself, whether or not in deference to the
usages of certain accepted species of dramatic composition. Ghosts seldom
appear in real life or in dramas of real life; but the introduction of supernatural agency is neither enjoined nor prohibited by any general dramatic law.
The use of such expedients is as open to the dramatic as to any other poet;
the judiciousness of his use of them depends upon the effect which, consistently with the general conduct of his action, they will exercise upon the spectator, whom other circumstances may or may not predispose to their acceptance. The Ghost in *Hamlet* belongs to the action of the play; the Ghost in the
Persae is not intrinsically less probable, but seems a less immediate product of
the surrounding atmosphere. Dramatic probability has, however, a far deeper
meaning than this. The *Eumenides* is probable, with all its mysterious commin-
gling of cults, and so is *Macbeth*, with all its barbarous witchcraft. The proceedings of the feathered builders of Cloudcuckootown in the *Birds* of Aristoph-
anes are as true to dramatic probability as are the pranks of Oberon's fairies
in *A Midsummer Night's Dream*. In other words, it is in the harmony between
the action and the characters, and in the consistency of the characters with
themselves, in the appropriateness of both to the atmosphere in which they
have their being, that this dramatic probability lies. The dramatist has to
represent characters affected by the progress of an action in a particular way,
and contributing to it in a particular way, because, if consistent with themselves, they *must* be so affected, and *must* so act.

Upon the invention and conduct of his characters the dramatist must
therefore expend a great proportion—even a preponderance—of his labour.
His treatment of them will, in at least as high a degree as his choice of subject,
conception of action, and method of construction, determine the effect which
his work produces. And while there are aspects of the dramatic art under
which its earlier phases already exhibit an unsurpassed degree of perfection,
there is none under which its advance is more notable than this. Many causes
have contributed to this result; the chief is to be sought in the multiplication
of the opportunities for mankind's study of man. . . . In the matter of comic
as well as of serious characterization—in the individualizing of characters and
in evolving them as it were out of the progress of the action—the modern
drama has not only advanced, but in a sense revolutionized, the dramatic act,
as inherited from its ancient masters.

Yet, however the method and scope of characterization may vary under the
influence of different historical epochs and different tendencies or tastes of
races or nations, the laws of this branch of the dramatic art remain based on
the same essential requirements. What interests us in a man or woman in real
life, or in the impressions we form of historical personages, is that which seems
to us to give them individuality. A dramatic character must therefore, whatever its part in the action, be sufficiently marked by features of its own to
interest the imagination; with these features its subsequent conduct must
be consistent, and to them its participation in the action must correspond.
In order to achieve such a result, the dramatist must have, in the first instance,
distinctly conceived the character, however it may have been suggested to him.
His task is, not to paint a copy of some contemporary or "historical" personage, but to conceive a particular kind of man, acting under the operation of

particular circumstances. This conception, growing and modifying itself with the progress of the action, also invented by the dramatist, will determine the totality of the character which he creates. The likeness which the result bears to an actual or historical personage may very probably, from secondary points of view, affect the immediate stage success of the creation; upon its dramatic result this likeness can have no influence whatever. In a wider sense than that in which Shakespeare denied the charge that Falstaff was Oldcastle, it should be possible to say of every dramatic character which it is sought to identify with an actual personage, "This is not the man." The mirror of the drama is not a photographic apparatus; and not even the most conscientious combination of science and art can bring back even a "phase" of the real Napoleon.

Distinctiveness, as the primary requisite in dramatic characterization, is to be demanded in the case of all personages introduced into a dramatic action, but not in all cases in an equal degree. Schiller, in adding to the *dramatis personae* of his *Fiesco* superscriptions of their chief characteristics, labels Sacco as "an ordinary person," and this, no doubt, suffices for Sacco. But with the great masters of characterization a few touches, of which the true actor's art knows how to avail itself, distinguish even their lesser characters from one another; and every man is in his humour down to the "third citizen." Elaboration is necessarily reserved for characters who are the more important contributors to the action, and the fulness of elaboration for its heroes. Many expedients may lend their aid to the higher degrees of distinctiveness. Much is gained by a significant introduction of hero or heroine—thus Antigone is dragged in by the watchman, Gloucester enters alone upon the scene, Volpone is discovered in adoration of his golden saint. Nothing marks character more clearly than the use of contrast—as of Othello with Iago, of Ottavio with Max Piccolomini, of Joseph with Charles Surface. Nor is direct antithesis the only effective kind of contrast; Cassius is a foil to Brutus, and Leonora to her namesake the Princess. But, besides impressing the imagination as a conception distinct in itself, each character must maintain a consistency between its conduct in the action and the features it has established as its own. This consistency does not imply uniformity; for, as Aristotle observes, there are characters which, to be represented with uniformity, must be presented as uniformly un-uniform. Of such consistently complex characters the great critic cites no instances, nor indeed are they of frequent occurrence in Greek tragedy; in the modern drama Hamlet is their unrivalled /478/ exemplar; and Weislingen in Goethe's *Götz*, and Alceste in the *Misanthrope,* may be mentioned as other illustrations in dramas differing widely from one another. The list might be enlarged almost indefinitely from the gallery of female characters, in view of the greater pliability and more habitual dependence of the nature of women. It should be added that those dramatic literatures which freely admit of a mixture of the serious with the comic element thereby enormously increase the opportunities of varied characterization. The difficulty of the task at the same time enhances the effect resulting from its satisfactory accomplishment; and, if the conception of a character is found to meet a variety of tests resembling that which life has at hand for every man, its naturalness, as we term it, becomes more obvious to the imagination. "Naturalness" is only another word for what Aristotle terms "propriety"; the artificial rules by which usage has at times sought to define particular species of character are in their origin only a convenience of the theatre, though they have largely helped to conventionalize dramatic characterization. Lastly, a character should be directly effective with regard to the dramatic action in which it takes part—that is to say, the influence it exerts upon the progress of the action should correspond to its distinctive features; the conduct of the play should seem to spring from the nature of its characters. In other words, no characterization can be effective which is not what may be called economical, *i.e.* which does not strictly limit itself to suiting the purposes of the action. Even the minor characters should not idly intervene; while the chief characters should predominate over, or determine, the course of the action, its entire conception should harmonize with their distinctive features. It is only a Prometheus whom the gods bind fast to a rock, only a Juliet who will venture into a living death for her Romeo. Thus, in a sense, chance is excluded from dramatic action, or rather, like every other element in it, bends to the dramatic idea.

In view of this predominance of character over action, we may appropriately use such expressions as a tragedy of love or jealousy or ambition, or a comedy of character. For such collocations merely indicate that plays so described have proved (or were intended to prove) specially impressive by the conception or execution of their chief character or characters. . . .

No complete system of dramatic species can be abstracted from any one dramatic literature. They are often the result of particular antecedents, and their growth is often affected by peculiar conditions. Different nations or ages use the same names and may preserve some of the same rules for species which in other respects their usage may have materially modified from that of their neighbours or predecessors. The very question of the use of measured or pedestrian speech as fit for different kinds of drama, and therefore distinctive of them, cannot be profitably discussed except in reference to particular literatures. In the Chinese drama the most solemn themes are treated in the same form — an admixture of verse and prose — which not so very long since was characteristic of that airiest of Western dramatic species, the French *vaudeville*. Who would undertake to define, except in the applications which have been given to the words in successive generations, such terms as "tragi-comedy," or indeed as "drama" (*drame*) itself? Yet this uncertainty does not imply that all is confusion in the terminology as to the species of the drama. In so far as they are distinguishable according to the effects which their actions, or those which the preponderating parts of their actions, produce, these species may primarily be ranged in accordance with the broad difference established by Aristotle between tragedy and comedy. "Tragic" and "comic" effects differ in regard to the emotions of the mind which they excite; and a drama is tragic or comic according as such effects are produced by it. The strong or serious emotions are alone capable of exercising upon us that influence which, employing a bold but marvellously happy figure, Aristotle termed *purification*, and which a Greek comedian, after a more matter-of-fact fashion, thus expressed:

> "For whensoe'er a man observes his fellow
> Bear wrongs more grievous than himself has known,
> More easily he bears his own misfortunes."

That is to say, the petty troubles of self which disturb without elevating the mind are driven out by the sympathetic participation in greater griefs, which raises while it excites the mind employed upon contemplating them. It is to these emotions — which are and can be no others than pity and terror — that actions which we call tragic appeal. *Naïf* as we may think Aristotle in desiderating for such actions a complicated rather than a simple plot, he obviously means that in form as well as in design they should reveal their relative importance. Those actions which we term comic address themselves to the sense of the ridiculous, and their themes are those vices and moral infirmities the representation of which is capable of touching the springs of laughter. Where, accordingly, a drama confines itself to effects of the /479/ former class, it may be called a pure "tragedy"; when to those of the latter, a pure "comedy." In dramas where the effects are mixed the nature of the main action and of the main characters (as determined by their distinctive features) alone enables us to classify such plays as serious or humorous dramas — or as "tragic" or "comic," if we choose to preserve the terms. But the classification admits of a variety of transitions, from "pure" tragedy to "mixed," from "mixed" tragedy" to "mixed comedy," and thence to "pure comedy," with the more freely licensed "farce" and "burlesque," the time-honoured inversion of the relations of dramatic method and purpose. This system of distinction has no concern with the mere question of the termination of the play, according to which Philostratus and other authorities have sought to distinguish tragic from comic dramas. The serious drama which ends happily (the German *Schauspiel*) is not a species co-ordinate with tragedy and comedy, but at the most a subordinate variety of the former. Other distinctions may be almost infinitely multiplied, according to the point of view adopted for the classification. /480/

Arthur Mizener

WHAT MAKES GREAT BOOKS GREAT

Probably the most powerful effect of literature on us is a moral effect, and this effect, rightly appreciated, is what gives literature its unique value. It is something we need, perhaps especially now and in America. Like Rome and France and the British Empire at other times, we have, willy-nilly, had the responsibility of the world thrust upon us and we are anxious not to answer to this thrusting-on of greatness like a nation of Malvolios. Plato may have been right that it is dangerous to trust writers to give us the understanding we need, but men have always done so. The results have sometimes certainly been unfortunate.

For instance, in the spring of 1601 a friend of the Earl of Essex persuaded the Chamberlain's Men, of whom Shakespeare was one, to give a special performance of "Richard II." The day after the performance Essex made his foolish and disastrous attempt to lead a popular rebellion against Elizabeth. He had apparently considered "Richard II," with its representation of the downfall of a weak king, a kind of allegory of Elizabeth's character and deserts. This is an absurd but quite common kind of mistake. In fact, Shakespeare's play sympathizes with Richard because he is human and fallible ("I live with bread like you, feel want * * * need friends"). The tetralogy of history plays of which it is a part is a magnificent imaginative perception of the divine ordination /16/ of established society and the evil consequences of its disruption by violence. Such an insight into a fundamental moral order, while it does not condone the mistakes of a Richard (or of a Bolingbroke), or the frivolity of a Falstaff, does not take any particular instance of them with sentimental moralistic horror. Falstaff is funny and even, like Richard, appealing because his kind of evil is human; among fallen men a certain amount of it is

"What Makes Great Books Great," *Highlights of Modern Literature*, ed. Francis Brown (New York: Mentor Books, 1954), pp. 16–20.

inevitable ("Dost thou hear, Hal? Thou knowest in the state of innocency Adam fell, and what should poor Jack Falstaff do in the days of villainy?").

But though Shakespeare's history plays would be far smaller things than they are without this essentially moral insight into history, they exist because of the intensity of the life in them, because of their apparently inexhaustible wealth of perception of how people talk and act and think. Falstaff and Mistress Quickly, Hal and Hotspur, Bolingbroke and Richard are what make these plays, not Shakespeare's knowledge of The Great Chain of Being. Henry James, who may seem to some people an unlikely man to have made the point, asserted "the perfect dependence of the 'moral' sense of a work of art on the amount of felt life concerned in producing it"; and this is the heart of the matter.

The kind of misreading Essex gave "Richard II" is easy and dangerous. Perhaps the opposite kind of misreading is even more dangerous. We Americans are a practical people, inclined to think that any book about contemporary events of practical or political concern to us is saying something valuable. We read with extraordinary earnestness magazine fiction about anti-Semitism like "Gentleman's Agreement" or mildly perceptive books about contemporary journalism like "The Big Wheel" or almost any novel about the war. Such books have their value. But if they seem to us all there is, we do not read well enough (or even at all) books with real moral perception.

The dangerous thing about the moral effect of literature, then, is that we may, like Essex, ignore the valuable and realized moral insight of good books for some easy and obvious analogy to our immediate, superficial concerns, or suppose that the more nearly a book's subject-matter resembles that of *Time* magazine the more valuable it must be. Like Essex—though not perhaps with such sentimental consequences—we often read great novelists like Jane Austen and Henry James as if they were merely novelists of manners, as if Jane Austen were only a lover of gentility and James only a long-winded snob. But what reader who has got even so far as the first sentence of "Pride and Prejudice"—"It is a truth universally acknowledged that a single man in possession of a /17/ good fortune must be in want of a wife"—can believe in that "Gentle Jane"? Not that her ungentle judgment alone makes "Pride and Prejudice" a great novel, though it would be a much smaller novel without it; the foundation of the novel's greatness is its felt life, a representation of people which is dense, detailed and—as her own age would have called it—"just."

Lady De Bourgh and Mr. Collins, Lydia and Wickham, Elizabeth and Darcy remain for us the standard examples of perennial types because Jane Austen's acute judgment of them emerges for us from a realization of life she had really seen and felt. The same thing is true of Henry James. The grief and terror of such moments as that one in "The Ambassadors" when Strether discovers the Countess de Vionnet, the most magnificent of all grandes dames, is as helplessly in love with Chad Newsome "as a maidservant crying for her young man," would not exist for us had James not made us see and feel, with minute precision, the fineness of that society of which Countess de Vionnet is the finest part.

The kind of failure in apprehension which sees Jane Austen as gentle and James as a snob must also be what makes us see trivial books which deal with fashionable subjects as valuable. Such books seem, decade after decade, to constitute about half of the best-seller list. In the Twenties, for instance, there were the novels about the Younger Generation. The bad ones like Percy Marks' "The Plastic Age" and Dorothy Speare's "Dancers in the Dark" and the moderately good ones like Stephen Vincent Benét's "The Beginning of Wisdom" and James Gould Cozzens' "Confusion" were read with equal earnestness. When a good one like "The Sun Also Rises" came along, it got lumped in with the rest. People still seem to read "The Sun Also Rises" as a period piece about the Lost Generation. But it is much more than that. If it is a novel of manners—as it is—it deals with manners as does Jane Austen or, even better, Congreve.

In all three writers, the ability to feel sharply and finely the way people think and talk and act may appear to be merely an interest in manners for their own sake, but it is actually a kind of moral insight. In "The Way of the World" Congreve may call Mirabell a "wit" and Witwoud "Witwoud," as if to say no more than that one is a fashionable gentleman and the other not, but what he is really doing is making a moral distinction between the man of awareness and genuine feeling and the man of affectation and insensibility. The same thing is true of Jane Austen's contrasts between her pairs of women.

And the same thing is also true of Hemingway's contrast between Jake and Cohn in "The Sun Also Rises." Bill Gorton /18/ says of Cohn: "I like him. But he's just so awful." This may appear to be merely a distinction of manners; it has even been said to be anti-Semitic. But it is really a moral distinction between two kinds of human beings which goes far beyond either manners or race. And it has its effect because it is supported by all the marvelously felt life of "The Sun Also Rises."

In the Thirties, fashionable problem novels about the Younger Generation gave way to fashionable problem novels about the proletariat; and who now even remembers Edward Newhouse's earlier avatar, when he was the author of "You Can't Sleep Here," or Josephine Herbst or Michael Gold? Nowadays we are easily carried away by a novel about the Roman Empire, filled with Roman five-per centers and liberal clergymen disguised as Jesus' disciples; or a novel about E. C. A. administrators in Europe with a Y. M. C. A.-secretary sort of hero struggling against Koestler Communists on the one hand and, on the other, young Americans with crew haircuts and a passion for "irresponsibles" like Hemingway and Eliot; or a novel about the South with a historical love affair between a beautiful colored girl and a Southern aristocrat and a bang-up lynching in the last chapter.

This last kind of novel, about the Negro problem, is perhaps the best illustration of the way a fashionable subject-matter can confuse the issue. Ever since "Uncle Tom's Cabin" there have been inferior novels which create a stir by being sensational in an up-to-date way about the problem. These novels have their moral effect all right, and it is a bad one; they encourage people to enjoy the insidious pleasures of righteousness unearned by understanding. T. S. Eliot once put the effect of such fiction very well when he remarked of Ezra Pound's "Cantos" that they present a hell for other people, not for Mr. Pound or his readers, who are themselves altogether free of the faults which produce the trouble.

Something like this is true of all mediocre fiction which deals with serious moral issues; the author and the reader are Christ harrowing a hell full of all the people who disagree with them. Such fiction does not make us understand our experience better; it even appears to incapacitate some readers for understanding good novels, to teach them to read novels like Faulkner's as if they had the same moralistic intent as "Strange Fruit."

At least this seems the likely explanation of those readers who suppose Faulkner to be the stock Unreconstructed Southerner because of Gavin Stevens' speech in "Intruder in the Dust" or think him "unrealistic" because he does not follow the petty prudential morality of a police court magistrate in "Re- /19/ quiem for a Nun." This is as absurd as Essex' misreading of "Richard II," for Faulkner's hell is obviously not a hell for other people; it is a hell for people like Faulkner and us. We recognize ourselves in its worst inhabitants and of its best we feel that there, but for the grace of God and our own insufficiency, go we. Faulkner makes us see, with something like the awe and terror we feel as we watch the curse on the house of Atreus, the way the terrible curse of slavery breeds in the ordinary lives of generation after generation of Southerners. The evil has been repeated and accumulated like original sin because people, black or white, are human, are lonely and love, try to do right and make mistakes, begin in belief and hope and end by repudiating even grief and despair; it is an evil for which no one and everyone is to blame.

The moral effect of great fiction like this is the nearest thing we have to the moral effect of experience itself under the ideal conditions which experience never provides, when we can understand it fully and face all its moral implications. Only literature can provide this effect, but only when it is great literature and only when we are willing to see its greatness. /20/

Rolf C. Zimmermann

HOCHHUTH'S THE DEPUTY
AND THE TRADITION OF POLEMIC LITERATURE

[In appraising Hochhuth's play] one must try to remove the question from the sphere of arbitrary critical standards, which are generally derived from the literary fashions of earlier days and are more concerned with aesthetics *per se* and the preservation of past values than with contemporary ideology. Let us not lose sight of the fact that taste and culture always represent a passive embodiment of active values. Goethe's *Götz von Berlichingen,* awkward and monstrous, opened the era of romantic individualism and therewith a period of drama which appealed to the senses and the emotions. Nonetheless, even so acute a critic as Lessing considered this initial work of the classic German drama as nothing but a rope of sand. Certainly Hochhuth is not Goethe, nor are there any Lessings among his critics. But, similarly, people time and again view the work from the framework of a long-established eclecticism and condemn it instead of trying to see and understand the play and the spirit which it is trying to express in its own terms. Will this spirit someday create a form of its own? Will it, possibly, introduce a new fashion in literature, a new aesthetic *Lebensraum?* What may not grow from this bud and sprout?

Let us begin by describing it: its pathos grows from an unconditional and unqualified devotion to an idea. Hochhuth's *The Deputy* is centered on an idea and does not, therefore, fit the classic pattern of drama in which the individual is presented in conflict with his environment and in which harmony is achieved by resignation to the will /155/ of God. The very failure to reach a

---

"Hochhuths 'Stellvertreter' und die Tradition polemischer Literatur," in *Der Streit um Hochhuths "Stellvertreter"* (Stuttgart: Basilius Press, 1963), pp. 137–169. Trans. by the editors.

harmonious conclusion is the play's distinguishing characteristic.[1] Riccardo must sacrifice his subjectivity to the objective demands in the foreground of the play; thus, he is not an individual but an instrument through which the ideas of the author are voiced. As a result, dramatic movement is not the outgrowth of internal conflict but the result of an idea expressed in an over-whelming concrete situation. The inner-directed character ceases to have poetic meaning in such a context, and the protagonist becomes, instead, a means to an end. The situation and the material must carry the full weight of the play. But how can they create interest and arouse the emotions? Certainly not in the same way as fiction or invented situations can, evoking a sublime sense of aesthetic satisfaction through the adverse fate of the classic tragic hero. The situation can no longer be merely pleasant, nor of secondary im-portance (a mere vehicle for the characters), nor a means to a purely aesthetic end. Instead it must be actual, concrete, arousing the audience to anger and making it desire to effect a change. Under such circumstances a balancing of reason against emotion is clearly impossible; instead, the material is heavily weighted in one direction and is necessarily contemporary and documentary. The situation is no longer a fictional one, the main character is no longer a unique human being, the audience is no longer permitted to respond as to an aesthetic experience. Instead, it is obliged to participate in the action as jurors in an imaginary courtroom. It is not merely asked to consider the matter, it is forced to do so, for unless the audience is thoroughly caught up in the situa-tion, the play becomes absurd and ineffective. /156/

Subjective feeling and objective reason are combined in Riccardo and can-not, therefore, be balanced against one another; instead, all interest—aes-thetic beauty and human significance—is concentrated on a single point. The attempt to use reason and emotion as a single force lays a foundation for a transformation of poetic materials and poetic form and invests them with new meaning. But it also deprives the work of aesthetic distance and the full-ness of experience which are necessary elements of true art. According to this analysis, then, Hochhuth's work is not a tragedy but a polemic. And it is pre-cisely for this reason that it *is* an important contribution to the contemporary literary scene.

The appeal to the human heart longing for the Good, the True, and the Beautiful, the balancing of reason against emotion expressed thematically in the individual's conflict with nature and society, the concept of human dig-nity—all of which produced a picture of an objectively ordered universe—have not been found on the German stage since the naturalistic dramas of Hauptmann. Rose Bernd's naturalness is just as much of divine origin as are those forces which so blindly destroy that naturalness. As a consequence, the concept of tragedy as requiring no emotional response beyond that to the performance itself, requiring no moral decision or social action from the au-dience, was sustained. Sympathy for the plight of the heroine and intellectual perception of its inevitability are perfectly balanced within the framework of a conflict between Truth and Necessity. But this tragic view, *nihil contra deum nisi deus ipse,* appeared for the last time in Hauptmann. The well-balanced,

---

1.   In this sense, *The Deputy* differs fundamentally from Goethe's *Götz von Berlichingen,* a play in which the conflict between individual desires and external realities demonstrates the human situa-tion. Goethe himself defined the spiritual basis of his play in his Shakespeare Day speech of 1771 by saying that *Götz von Berlichingen,* along with all of Shakespeare's plays, is centered at that point in human experience "at which our individual wills, supposedly free, clash with equally compelling forces outside"—a variable formula which remained basically unchanged and unchallenged in Ger-man drama until well into Hauptmann's era. /156/

self-contained play disappeared from the German stage, and with it went harmony and order. The principles of truth and justice depicted by Hauptmann in his simple-good-hearted man and /157/ inherent in the conflict between a man's rights and the then unreasonable code of society required only the good will of mankind for their realization. With Wedekind, Sternheim, Kaiser, and the young Brecht, the plight of the individual had to be defined in a different ideological context. Modern man, victim to a hostile environment, no longer accepted the fact that there were absolute values of a divine origin operating in an orderly universe. Instead, the natural needs of the individual seemed to be frustrated by a stupid and false social order. These wrongs had to be exposed; hence, subject matter became contemporary, concrete, documentary. As a result, the fire of pure aesthetics was extinguished. The writer became a social critic exposing particular evils and giving little thought to the total human situation: his method was expository; his tone satirical; his characters caricatures. The balance between reason and emotion was lost both as a principle of literary organization for the writer and as a source of aesthetic satisfaction to the audience. With the loss of belief in an objective order, the rapport between writer and audience was weakened. No assumption of shared values could be made. As a result, drama tended more and more towards private jokes and allusions, mysticism, and experimental techniques borrowed from the other arts which few in the audience who were not professional critics or specialists in drama could follow.

That portion of the human heart which longed for happiness and justice and the recognition of the dignity of the individual was rarely addressed from the stage. The result was not only that human responsiveness to dramatic productions declined but also that tragedy and comedy in the classical sense were no longer possible. What remained was a superman /158/ viewed through the distorting lens of the writer's ideology, moving on the pseudo-reality of the stage, and often engaged in grotesque actions. If one unfamiliar with the concepts of Wedekind's human beast, Sternheim's super-citizen, or Kaiser's ego-mania were to chance upon the plays of these writers, he would be simply amused by them.[2] That emotion which springs from a recognition of the human condition—the necessary compromise between inner hopes and outer demands—which Hauptmann so ably evoked had been almost totally replaced by the private dialogue between the author and those ideologically attuned to him. At the same time, the well-rounded, self-sufficient drama had disappeared, having become an impossibility in an irrational milieu. What resulted was the play concerned with an external situation in which the conflict was resolved by the author in a predetermined way, resulting in an untrue picture of both sides. Clever plots, philosophical arguments, distortions of reality, ennui, finally, for intellectually all is relative . . . —these are the characteristics of the German drama which replaced Hauptmann's naturalism. The presentation consists of ideological discussion and satirical portrayal. It does not attempt to move one emotionally but to keep the *mind* occupied, interested in actual problems and motives, and poses psychological, philosophical, /159/ and even theological questions. Creative art is thus reduced to putting a real fact into an artificial form for the purpose of exploring

2.   The periods preceding and following the German classical drama are related in a rather peculiar way. Both, of course, lack the classic synthesis of reason and emotion achieved through the portrayal of the fate of the autonomous individual. Both are characterized by domination of utilitarian minds, pedants, and advocates of distinct religious or philosophical creeds. However, the post-classical period at least retains the possibility of once more achieving what had once been achieved, both by the people and their poets. /159/

an intellectual problem. Drama becomes discussion, if not thesis, and indulges in satire and social criticism, which may be at times witty, penetrating, instructive, even courageous, but which always flees from emotion as from something from the dead past related to a sentimentality whose ideals of the True, the Good, and the Beautiful can never be fulfilled. German drama ceased to recognize the dignity of man, because it no longer believed in it.

As a consequence of a general loss of faith in the values on which romantic individualism and the concept of universal man had been postulated, feeling disappeared entirely from post-naturalistic German drama, and expressionism, skeptical and intellectual, called for a new aesthetic basis. Intensely satirical writing on the overregulated society gave way to hymns to the "uncivilized" man. Great drama cannot emerge from such a subject, and only through its lyrics can expressionism succeed in achieving poetic stature. It is evident that if there has been a loss of faith in the individual and belief in universals, neither an act of volition nor a new aesthetic creed can right the situation. Nonetheless, one cannot fail to recognize that with the expressionists' call for a new aesthetic basis an admission of their own defects was being voiced. And, in addition, one remembers the constant, though faint, cry for a new faith, which alone could lead to a reform in art. It was strongly believed that the basis of a literature and poetry which could deal only intellectually and only with the physical side of man was far too narrow. In all ages, lasting poetry has concerned itself with the whole man. (Nor is it possible for art to remain fixated at a single period of man's development for any length of time.) Usually the beginning or the end of a literary period /160/ concerns itself with a single aspect of human nature: emotional, intellectual, spiritual, physical. If such a period is extended in time, as may happen because of particular sociological conditions, the repressed portions seek their outlet and, however brutally, attempt to bring about a balance. In art, too, repressed energy demands its freedom. (The iconoclasts, the anti-aesthetic Puritans, the anti-Romantic Young Germans, the Nazi and Stalinist persecutions of art — these various movements have one thing in common: each represents a condemnation of elitism in art and a call for greater emphasis on basic concepts of religious, social and human dignity. It always happens when the dreamers and visionaries among artists join together to reassert the integrity of the human being: Grünewald, Milton, Büchner, Brecht. . . .)

In these critical times when art is one-sided and thus unable to fulfill its true function, when man has little belief in his own dignity, a new form has emerged: the polemic of feeling. It emerges from the desire to view man as a totality and to set forth a new concept of human worth. In a sense, polemic literature is as unbalanced as any intellectual form must be, but Luther's and Lessing's polemics were strongly motivated by a sense of humanity, and this feeling is communicated to the reader. A staged polemic certainly differs from a performance of poetic drama, for in the former there is no free play of fantasy and imagination. Instead, concrete reality, the picture of an actual person in a critical situation is presented; /161/ poetic language gives way to that suitable to polemic — specific, impersonal, intellectual, and satirical.

Which language, then, is proper to this new form — that of poetry or that of polemic? For a long time art, in its attempt to deal solely with external realities, had ignored such abstractions as truth and justice. The polemic in art form came into being particularly *because* belief in absolute values had wavered or been abandoned. At a time when art no longer had universal appeal, the new polemic appeared with its emotional appeal calculated to reach the pain and guilt with which modern man is burdened. For despite all else, the craving of the human heart for the True, the Good, and the Beautiful persists, and it is precisely when these values seem most distant that they become most important, much as complementary colors are produced by the eye after one has been staring into strong light. Human sensibility, too, responds according to certain principles: emotions cannot be long repressed without some reaction occurring. When faced with harsh injustice, the human heart remembers its claim to justice, and man acts accordingly. Thus polemics, in a sense, do serve the whole man, though not in the same way that classical literature does. There is a merging of subjective and objective elements, however, and a balancing of one argument against another. In place of aesthetic harmony, there is a peace between tensions, force against force, which finds its analogue in the Mystic Instant and other forms of religious experience. Luther concluded that a polemic had a direct effect not only on one's heart but on one's physical being. In the same way, the polemicist believes that by presenting his cause realistically, he strengthens man's inner consciousness, quickening the intellectual perceptions and awakening him to view life as it is. The dignity of the polemicist arises from his awareness of his function. His sense of mission is communicated to his audience, which is moved to action through it. /162/

But, as has already been stated, the function of poetry and the function of polemic differ: for though a polemic can arouse a spectator to action and make him a socially responsible person, in so doing it sacrifices the quality of aesthetic distance, that quality which permitted a discharge of emotional energy to a made-up situation. To what degree, then, may a polemic also be poetic? Polemic aims at demonstrating something conducive to social action. Obviously, an audience will only be moved in the desired direction if the situation is unequivocal and understood to be so; there can be no alternative. By its very nature the polemic is one-sided, making use of every device to make its point; everyone—even the most simple-minded and unsophisticated—should understand how precious the cause really is, how infamous its opponents and their supporters. Yet when the polemic is primarily concerned with the worth of a personal decision rather than the championing of a cause or the immediate redress of a wrong, the form moves perceptibly closer to poetry, in particular, to lyric poetry. Many of the Luther hymns are of this genre, in contrast to his own polemics. . . .

As we know, in lyric poetry, aesthetic value is dependent on the language, not the content. Thus the problem for criticism /163/ arises when a polemic transcends the merely concrete and creates a character who stimulates the imagination.

To begin with, the writer of polemic, unlike the lyric poet, is not concerned with the expression of his inner being but with some outer reality. So he is not only an artist but a teacher attempting to instruct an audience, and he quite naturally makes his characters instruments of his teaching. Hochhuth's Riccardo is clearly such an instrument. There is one also in Brecht's play, *Saint Joan of the Stockyards,* his Joan Dark, a most polemic character, also a "deputy," though there religion itself is confronted with the suffering it permits. The similarity is further proof that Hochhuth's play is not a mere fortuitous accident but that this *succès du scandale* does require serious consideration as literature. The realistic and satirical literature of social criticism, so highly regarded by most critics, had aroused in man desires it could not itself satisfy. But the moment came when these deep-rooted cravings of the human heart would no longer remain hidden. A comparison of Brecht's *Saint Joan of the Stockyards* and Hochhuth's *The Deputy* reveals another interesting point: the two were faced with similar technical problems. Both had to cope with the questions of how to avoid a tragic denouement and how to evolve a language suitable to the form. Admittedly, Brecht solved both these problems with more genius and expertise; none the less, Hochhuth's play is the more powerful and more stirring one. By all the means at his disposal, Brecht presents his Saint Joan as untragic. Remember, Joan must finally protest and remonstrate against the tragic resignation behind which the hypocritical and unscrupulous tenants conceal the truth from themselves. Nowhere is the fact more clearly demonstrated that polemic literature /164/ is as far removed from real life as is classical tragedy. For in polemics, the situation is not tragic, nor is the protoganist ever swerved from fulfilling his role in the service of the cause by any unforeseen, tragic event. Since the situation is unequivocal, he is never permitted to doubt his own decisions nor to understand the positions of others. One cannot, therefore, expect Hochhuth's play to be a tragedy. If Brecht's Joan were a tragic figure, Mauler and Cridle would be excused; likewise, if Riccardo were a tragic figure, Pius XII would be, too. The motivating indignation would be lost in the understanding of human nature. Therefore, polemics must at all costs avoid tragic elements, if the single point of view is to be retained.

For the same reason, the diction of polemic and the diction of poetry differ in accordance with their different intentions. In classic drama, character is disclosed through speech. To learn of a man through his own voice is to understand him in his tragic dignity. The literary style of classical drama differs from that of everyday speech; nothing is accidental, everything relates to character and its revelation. Post-classical drama abandoned poetic diction, replacing it with naturalistic speech, to stress the new emphasis on a more democratic concept of man. Only rarely was poetry resorted to as a more effective means of stimulating the emotions. It must be kept in mind if one wishes to understand why naturalistic speech is not compatible with polemic drama that such speech tends to define the characters as individuals. Naturalistic drama's emphasis on "unconscious" gesticulation and interjection, the revealing of personality in spite of self, leads one to conclude that *tout comprendre c'est tout pardonner*, a thought, of course, which is pure abomination to the polemicist. On this point the theater of naturalism and the theater of polemics are irrevocably opposed and mutually exclusive. On the other hand, the poetic speech in verse form familiar to classic drama, a speech in which each word reveals aesthetically the worth of the individual /165/ (for every classic hero is also a particular human being) is also forbidden to polemics, since the language itself may thus distract from the main objective.

On the matter of language, Brecht and Hochhuth can once again be compared. Brecht solves the problem of a diction proper to his purpose by resorting to satire. He lets Mauler and Cridle speak in the language of high tragedy, which affords a pitiless contrast between style and content, thus demonstrating the relationship between tragedy and language. By opening with this misplaced diction, the writer achieves a satirical tone; where common everyday speech is expected, high-flown classical diction is found, incidentally affording a comment on modern degradation. For his secondary characters, Brecht's method is very similar to Hochhuth's. In neither Snyder nor Frau Luckerniddle is the least hint of naturalistic plasticity or individual motivation found. They function solely within the author's predetermined framework of right and wrong. The question of their feelings and motives are not subjects for consideration, and it is therefore meaningless to have these characters speak naturalistically. Introducing such elements would have unbalanced Brecht's moral order. And it is exactly the same with Hochhuth. It is rather daring of Hochhuth to have experimented with rhythmic prose; it is also proof that he sensed that naturalistic speech would have been a total contradiction of the polemic character of his play. No individuals were to appear; only the instruments of conscience and of institutions. No character was to react to any situation by being thrown into conflict requiring any reflection or self-questioning on his part. Thus Hochhuth's style leads, above all, to an externalization of the dialogue. The cause itself is so laden with emotional connotations that the characters are not permitted to develop any insight into the views of others or any understanding of their own relations to it. Moreover, the monologues which open Act Five are effective as poetry chiefly because they contradict this principle and do focus on individual responses to a situation. /166/

This should not be misunderstood to mean that Hochhuth has not written an impressive play. However, it is a good theater piece, visually interesting but not deeply touching in the way that a play depicting an individual faced with a human crisis may be. It is a far cry from Hauptmann or Schnitzler. The Cardinal is a stereotype, not an individual with a life of his own. Even the use of a variety of dialects is not intended to give individuality to the characters, but to present a painful contrast between the *Gemütlichkeit* and the horrors under discussion. In fact, Hochhuth's play is characterized throughout by a language which is closer to social comedy than he himself realizes. It has the same consciseness and superficiality except that it is polemic in intent. Though no thesis is proclaimed, the language is that of a morality play. After all, there is a moral intent, and it is set forth in the dialogue.

Having analyzed the work and its relationship to other forms, one concludes that its most distinctive feature is the response it elicits. It is understandable that polemic literature, more than pure poetry, is to be judged by its effect. Generally, one distrusts the "popular" in literature. Still one cannot fail to observe that the widespread discussion of *The Deputy* is at least as much concerned with its literary value as it is with its status as a "hit show." Neither of these subjects are at the center of the discussions, however; they are merely peripheral elements unrelated to the polemic itself. Aesthetics can be discussed only briefly, but a cause can be the subject of endless conversation. Consequently, the effectiveness of the polemic is directly related to the importance of the cause it espouses. Though the play itself has been seen and read by a relatively small number, it is widely discussed on the basis of hearsay. Yet as long as the discussions /167/ are conducted along the lines set by Hochhuth's text, such popularity is not at all contrary to the intentions of the polemic play. We know that the writer's interest lies first and foremost in his subject and only secondarily in the form in which it is presented. In his many appearances at round-table discussions of the play, Hochhuth has stressed the importance of the subject. In this, he stands directly in the tradition of polemics. Luther asserted that he would not regret the disappearance of his booklets as long as their message prevailed. Lessing writes expressly, "I hope I will live to see the time when people will scarcely remember that Lange once translated Horace; and that by this time my criticism* will also have been forgotten. I wish for that." That is not to say that, as writers and poets, Brecht

*Vademecum für Herrn S. G. Lange.—Ed.

and Hochhuth do not have pride in their artistry and interest in form. Still, the polemic character of their plays is so strong that they offer·little opportunity for self-exploration and -expression. Their works are transitional and open a new literary epoch. Brecht, in the unambiguous plays of his mature period, discovered in the paradox of the contemporary twin value system of individual aspiration and social conformity a tragic theme. Hochhuth has merely begun to develop an intellectual problem which must be invested with emotional life, and it is doubtful whether he has succeeded — as Brecht has — in developing the form of his drama to the point where it is more than merely the means to an end, a platform or symbolic framework for his opinions, and becomes instead a symbolic projection of the artist's total personality.

Still, Hochhuth already deserves credit for having turned literature away from the irresponsibility of naturalism and the narrowness of aestheticism and towards the goals of spiritual humanity, spiritual advancement. It is directly opposed to relativism, for in his work everything is clearly defined. A letter from a reader furnished an epigraph for Hochhuth's play in a quotation from the writing of Albert Camus.** /168/ The play is, in fact, a summons to all those who would represent the spirit and to whom the absolute demands of the spirit are a reality (*spirit* here is used in the sense of *soul* rather than *intellect*). That the play has been so widely and favorably accepted in a country in which "the claim of the ideal"[3] has been taboo since the time of Nietzsche and Ibsen and the cult of egotism with its lewdness and vulgarity has so long prevailed is surely cause for wonder. Hochhuth has reversed a trend by postulating higher ideals than personal achievement or the profit motive. He brings forth once again the axiom of universal standards. Though the ethical content and the poetic strain are not well coördinated, there are portions in which the concept of human dignity is translated into art, and that rather more effectively than philosophy has been able to do in this age of science. /169/

Hilde Jaeckel

WHAT ABOUT MODERN GERMAN WRITING?

During the Hitler period and the war years many writers in Germany who opposed the political system either had to cease writing or face having their works remain unpublished. Indeed, some of the greatest authors emigrated and continued writing in exile. In those years literature, like all arts, reached its lowest point in Germany and I am sure some people wondered whether there could or ever would be a revival. If one takes into consideration that after the war most Germans were engaged in a bare struggle for survival, it is almost surprising that as early as in 1947 a group of writers came together. Heinrich Böll and Ingeborg Bachmann, Wolfdietrich Schnurr and Hans Magnus Enzensberger, and other prominent writers of today, belonged to this "Group of 47," as they are now called. Their purpose was not to found a lit-

---

**"Who are we, anyway, that we dare criticize the highest spiritual authority of the century? Nothing, in fact, but the simple defenders of the spirit, who yet have a right to expect the most from those whose mission it is to represent the spirit."   —Albert Camus—*Ed.*

3. To use Ibsen's phrase from *The Wild Duck.* /169/

"What about Modern German Writing?" *The American-German Review,* April–May 1963, pp. 13–16, 33. Hilde Jaeckel is Associate Professor of Modern Languages at Staten Island Community College, New York.

erary school, but rather to acquaint each other with their writing which, they hoped, would have meaning for them, for Germany, and for the world. The emphasis was on the individual and on his creativity rather than on the group as such.

Reading some of their works as well as those of other writers, you realize how difficult it is to discover a definite trend which might characterize this new generation of postwar writers. What seems significant is that the arts, including literature, are not as separate from each other as in former times. Writers, musicians and painters often work together, and at times a writer may express himself in one or the other of the arts. The various literary forms also seem to mingle easily and are less clearly separated from each other than formerly. Novels often resemble essays or journals or diaries; poetry resembles prose, and prose resembles poetry. Many of the literary forms fluctuate, are less rigid, less severely cast into conventional moulds. Literary styles within the period vary also, and as the writer and critic Walter Jens comments: "There are many literary styles but certainly not one which crystallizes from the many." The picture becomes even more complex when you consider that Germany is divided into West and East, with two different philosophies, that produce very different literary works. In addition, we should not forget that there are the Swiss-German and the Austrian worlds whose literary productions also belong to German literature.

The observer of the present disunited literary scene is somewhat at a loss. He realizes that all he can do in a short article is to present a few writers, a few works in the hope of stimulating the reader to plunge into the newest literature and acquaint himself with some of the thoughts that are currently being expressed in German, in a literary form. The emphasis will be on the novel in order to give this short essay unity. /13/

It is not surprising that a large number of works of the postwar period deal with Nazism and War, not surprising because writers have to come to terms with events which had a deep effect on them as well as on their contemporaries.

Although the Swabian writer and clergyman, Albrecht Goes, is perhaps less highly rated now than in the first ten years after the war, his two short works *Unruhige Nacht* (1949) and *Das Brandopfer* (1954) move the reader even today when the Hitler and war periods have receded further into the past. *Das Brandopfer*, which depicts the suffering of the Jews and the deep humanity of a butcher's wife who wants to atone for the cruelties of her fellow men, shows in its structure some of the characteristic features of many short stories and novels in the following years: scenes which seem disconnected and yet are subtly interwoven, conversations, and letters. The small book written in a poetic and somewhat solemn language shows the author's deeply religious and humanitarian attitude towards life and suffering. With all its sadness it has a strangely comforting quality because it contains compassion and love. Perhaps Goes' style, which in this and other works has a Biblical undertone, is disconcerting to a younger generation which may be attracted to books with more objective and detached writing.

While Goes has lost some of his immediate appeal, Heinrich Böll has steadily gained in reputation and is considered nowadays one of the best writers of Germany. In many of his short stories and novels he deals with problems facing Germans of the lower middle classes, social problems of the workers such as poor living conditions that can destroy marriages, problems of young widows and their children, etc. In one of his excellent short stories, "Nicht nur zur Weihnachtszeit," he writes a sharp, witty and devastating satire of bourgeois morale, the decay and hypocrisy of middle class living before and after the war, and includes biting criticism of Nazism, of misunderstood traditions, and wrong values. He uses a strange mixture of humor and seriousness to produce an effect of incredible grotesqueness. His novel, *Wo warst Du Adam?* (1951), is an excellent war book quite different from the literature published after World War I, which depicted realistically the horrors and cruelties of combat. In Böll's work, as in that of many others of his generation, war appears cruel, too, but more than that: completely absurd, and the horrors seem strangely grotesque. The book is called a novel but it is actually composed of nine loosely connected scenes in which people appear and disappear. There is no real plot, no single hero, no development of character — features which in former times were necessary to the novel. Fighting is not actually shown. The soldiers are mostly at the edge of war, suffering from the terrible monotony and dullness of life. The stark realism of senselessness and absurdity is reflected in a staccato style: short, pregnant sentences which render the mood and the actions of the characters. There is great vitality in this writing. Yet despite the sometimes grotesque realism we feel a strange pathos in the moving words spoken by one of the few women who appear in the book: "One must pray to comfort God." Many of Böll's other books reflect the same qualities of writing which I have described here only in connection with *Wo warst Du Adam?*

Heinrich Böll was a great admirer of young Wolfgang Borchert, for whose work he wrote an excellent short epilogue. Borchert's life, like his work, reflects the tragedy of living in the troubled 'thirties and 'forties. He died at the age of twenty-six after having been wounded in the war and persecuted by the Nazis. He had come back to Hamburg a broken man, incurably ill. His writing became a race with death, to which he succumbed in 1947 leaving poems, short stories, and a play entitled *Draussen vor der Tür*. As Böll says, Borchert, already marked by death, wanted to speak in the name of all the dead of the war. History may record the losing or the winning of a battle, but for the dead, "flowers do not bloom, the wind does not exist, bread is not baked anymore."

Draussen vor der Tür (1947), was first only known as a *Hörspiel*, produced on the radio, a form of play which has become more and more popular in Germany. Borchert presents the tragedy of the soldier who comes home after the war. The extreme popularity of the play may be the result of many Germans recognizing themselves in the person of Beckmann, who has become a stranger in his own country without any personal relationships, with a life which no longer has meaning. The despair, the accusation against a world in which wars are possible; against God, who allows them to happen; an outcry against injustice and death are all expressed in passionate and poetic language whose pictures, even in their horror, are beautiful. In the dialogue between Beckmann and a colonel, the former asks for an accounting for the deaths of eleven men among the millions who died uselessly. He wants his superior to take the responsibility for the lost lives, /14/ but actually he himself has to continue bearing the burden of guilt. And as he accuses others of being murderers, he has to recognize that he was a murderer too.

Wer schützt uns davor, dass wir nicht Mörder werden? Wir werden jeden Tag ermordet, und jeden Tag begehen wir einen Mord. Wir gehen jeden Tag an einem Mord vorbei. Und er schreit der Welt ins Gesicht: Ich sterbe!

Und dann liegt er irgendwo auf der Strasse, der Mann, der nach Deutschland kam, und stirbt.

Some of Borchert's short stories — some of them extremely short — are small
masterpieces. The author has the poetic gift of penetrating into the people he
presents and of creating a strongly emotional atmosphere. These people may
be quite ordinary, like the old couple in the beautiful story, "Das Brot," or the
prisoner in "Hundsblume." What makes these stories unique is the emotional
beauty they contain, often beauty of horror and despair. It is no wonder that
Germans mourned Borchert's early death, when so much that he wanted to
say had to remain unsaid. Close to the dead whom he would soon join, he cried
out against indifference, against senseless dying.

In some of Luise Rinser's short stories the themes of war and Nazism play a
role, but in her major novels these topics are in the background. Rinser is one
among several German women who have devoted their lives to writing and
have gained recognition and admiration in literary circles as well as among the
general public. Her well known story, "Jan Lobel aus Warschau," presents the
Jewish tragedy in the lovable person of the prisoner Jan. In "Die rote Katze"
she renders the postwar atmosphere when hunger played such an important
role. *Mitte des Lebens* (1950) was acclaimed as "das ausgeformteste [best constructed and completed] Buch, das die deutsche Literatur heute besitzt."
(*Weltwoche*) It certainly is a novel in content, since the author presents the development and maturing of her heroine, Nina, but in form it illustrates the
trend toward loosening and actually changing the novel by interspersing many
other forms: essays, letters, diaries, conversations, reports. It is written partly
in the first person. Two or three persons relate their experiences and sometimes the same experiences are viewed from different angles. *Abenteuer der
Tugend* (1957) is a continuation of the first book, but with a very definite bent
towards Roman Catholic mysticism. Her heroines, in spite of being independent modern women, never lack the feminine sensitivity which the author pos-
sesses. Luise Rinser's feelings for nature, her presentation of the joys and
sufferings of childhood, her understanding of adolescents, her mystical religi-
osity which becomes more pronounced in her later works, are all reflected in
her light and melodious style and in the carefully chosen words that give some
of her descriptions a delightful charm.

In an essay written for Elisabeth Langgässer's *Mythras, Lyrik und Prosa*, Luise
Rinser tried to bring that writer closer to the reading public. She is well aware
of the great difficulties the reader encounters in Langgässer's most complex
writing. Even Langgässer herself addresses the reader in what she calls
"Statement of Account for the Reader," written in 1949, one year before her
death. Whoever has read her long novel *Das unauslöschliche Siegel* or some of
her poems will have been puzzled by the many symbols she uses, will have
marvelled at her knowledge of the Bible and Greek mythology, at her strange
handling of time, at the interplay of perversity and mysticism, the often
frightening use of nature in formidable storms and strong, sometimes nau-
seating smells and sights. Her work cannot be understood with reasoning and
analysis. All her strange and complex presentations, the struggle between
God and the Devil, are intended to lead to a state of grace, of blind belief. It is
not easy for every reader to follow her on this path.

Luise Rinser and Elisabeth Langgässer, although very different in their
presentation, give /15/ us a Roman Catholic view of life in modern German
literature.

Author Wolfgang Koeppen, who comes from East Prussia, has been repeatedly reproached for the nihilistic attitude toward life that permeates all
his works. In his novel, *Der Tod in Rom* (1954), whose title reminds us of
Thomas Mann's "Tod in Venedig," the atmosphere is utterly depressing. The
members of two German families, who are spending some time in Rome during the postwar period, each embody very different attitudes towards life.One
father, a former Nazi, has adjusted to present conditions, forgotten his past
and become mayor of a German city, while the head of the other family has
remained the convinced and power-lusting Nazi he was. The sons unsuccess-
fully try to escape from their background by turning to music and to Roman
Catholicism. The novel ends on a completely hopeless note of hypocrisy and
cowardice, disintegraton and guilt. The author's satirical gifts and the background of Rome's beauty, heighten the atmosphere of moral decay. Power-
fully written, the form of this novel is most interesting. Like so many today, it
is written in the first person, but in the midst of a paragraph there may be a
sudden switch to the third person. The subject without warning or preparation becomes object, only to become just as suddenly the subject again. We
have become accustomed to a great deal in modern literature: to the inter-
mingling of times, to the inner monologue, to intricate symbols, and we are
asked to accept an interchange of subject and object, shifting the person who
relates closer or further away from the reader. Koeppen's other works also
show his tendency to sharp satire and his merciless presentation of people of
various nationalities and backgrounds.

Hans Erich Nossack, who was discovered by Sartre and whose works have
been translated into various languages, also reveals strong nihilism in his
books, and emphasizes the feeling of deep loneliness which is characteristic
not only of modern German literature but also of modern European and
American. In his well known novel, *Der jüngere Bruder* (1958), Nossack presents
his hero's search for his better self. After a long absence his hero returns to
Europe and we see the Continent through his eyes, a Europe which is only a
reflection of its past adorned with an unreal and feigned culture, where
people play roles and are never themselves. Many of them are *Spiesser,* philis-
tines who lack genuine emotions and live lives of narrow pedantry. After
strange adventures the hero finally dies in an accident, as do many of Nossack's
characters. In this work, as in his others, there is a strange shifting from reality
to imagination, from life to death, and of people changing into others. It is a
life with different dimensions where certainty is lacking and where the ordinary
limits are outdistanced.

Criticism of modern society is also the basis of Gerd Gaiser's very moving
book, *Schlussball (Aus den schönen Tagen der Stadt Neu-Spuhl)* (1958). Gaiser, who
was a painter for a time, wrote among numerous other works, *Die sterbende
Jagd,* which is considered one of the best war novels of modern times. In
Schlussball the author shows us the flourishing city of Neu-Spuhl in Germany,
where people live the "economic miracle" to the hilt and where materialism
and conformity rule and kill the inner life. We hear the voices of some of the
people who were connected with the "Final Ball," even of some who have died.
They are monologues which reveal the lack of relationships between people:
"Sich kreuzende Stimmen, keine, die mit einer anderen redet, jede von sich
und für sich allein. Stimmen noch in der Zeit, Stimmen von aussen, durch die
Zeit stossend, schwebend wie Vögel." Those who do not conform, who feel
and are different, suffer, and those who try to escape from their past and their
guilt cheat themselves out of their real life. The externally separated scenes

represent the separation of people, and yet the common theme gives unity to the work. The book begins with the end and ends with the beginning, a poetically, tenderly written book which shows the author's real gifts for creating stirring moods and unforgettable scenes, for drawing people compassionately and with feeling.

The seriousness of many postwar works is striking, although humor is occasionally found. However, it is often gallows humor, satirical and bitter, a strange mixture of paradoxes and horrors, where past legends and characters of classical literatures are used to interpret modern life. We find this in the plays by Friedrich Dürrenmatt, the Swiss writer. And what could be more paradoxical and grotesque than the hero in Günter Grass's recent novel, *Die Blechtrommel*, a dwarf who looks at the world from an insane asylum and beats his drum as he relates his life. Some of the most recent authors have done some experimenting, especially in creating a new style of writing. Uwe Johnson is one whose constructions are so difficult and so different that his German at times reads like another language. /16/

Many important and representative authors have been omitted here, such as Ingeborg Bachmann, whose gifts were first expressed in poetry but who lately has also published remarkable short stories. There is also Max Frisch, a Swiss who has written plays and a wonderful novel, *Stiller*, and many others whose names cannot even be mentioned here.

As we look back at some of the works and at others which we could not discuss for lack of space, I believe we can discern certain recurring themes: Nazism and guilt, war and absurdity, nihilism and loneliness. In many books Man appears in search of himself in a materialistic world where he is in danger of never knowing who he is. In the handling of many of these themes, especially in Böll's *Wo warst Du Adam?* and in Nossack's *Der jüngere Bruder,* there is intentionally objective and detached reporting, as if the author had not wanted himself to become involved, and the story too personal. There are passages of real beauty, especially in poetry, but the world is certainly not a harmonious and beautiful world. It is an uncertain one which we see reflected in the fluctuating literary forms and changing styles of writing. There are, nevertheless, richness of feeling and thought, pronounced literary gifts in this new Germany which has again and more intensely than ever joined the general cultural life of Europe. It is perhaps as paradoxical as some of the literature, that the reader, in spite of the nihilism and despair expressed by some writers, looks hopefully forward to further promising developments. /33/

Dolores Barracano Schmidt

ROLF HOCHHUTH: THE MAN AND HIS WORK

In 1959 an unremarkable young editorial assistant, up from the provinces via the usual university route, was assigned the unremarkable task of preparing a new edition of the work of Wilhelm Busch, the Edward Lear of the German nursery school set. Though the task itself was hardly one to excite the imagination of a young man with serious literary aspirations of his own, he approached it with his usual conscientiousness and skill. Happily, the new edition was a great success, and his employer rewarded him with three months' vacation with pay. As a result, there is nothing the least bit unremarkable about Rolf Hochhuth's life today.

The bright editorial assistant had a rather unwieldy manuscript in his trunk and used his gift of time to air it out and make it presentable, but, as it happened, this particular trunkful contained somewhat exceptional materials: the facts and fragments out of which *The Deputy* was shaped. By Hochhuth's own admission, an admission definitely supported by the works of his contemporaries in Germany, his interest in the subject of the Nazi destruction of European Jews was perfectly natural: "I was 14 in 1945, and the total collapse of Germany was a great emotional shake-up for me. I considered it my responsibility to study the shameful history of the Third Reich. Again and again I came to think, 'What would you yourself have done if you had been old enough to act?'"[1]—a hypothetical question, perhaps, but one not without practical significance to a generation intent on understanding Germany so that it will never again be the perpetrator of so vile a crime.

Born in 1931, in the small city of Eschwege, of well-to-do parents—shoe-factory owners with no political or intellectual pretensions—Hochhuth's life was secure and orderly. The war affected him little; he was too young and his parents too old to be required to play any very active part in Nazi war efforts, and the city was too remote from the main action to be involved in any serious resistance activity, even if it had occurred to anyone to resist. Young Rolf joined the *Jungvolk* in 1941 as a matter of course. "There was no choice," says the author whose reputation is largely based on his insistence that not choosing is in itself a choice, and "to be absolutely truthful, I didn't mind it too much. We were able to play cowboys and Indians, and we were able to beat each other up without our parents interfering, because the state said that was what we should do."[2] He was already aware of the paradox between moral authority and political power.

Despite his own admission of his delight in the Nazi youth physical training program, his life-long friend, Dieter Vollprecht, remembers him as an indifferent member whose attendance was not regular and whose parents did not encourage his participation: "Literature was already more important to him than pre-military training. . . . We rarely saw him without a book, and the few friends he did have were hardly of the normal, athletic type, which he secretly envied and admired."[3] A description of his childhood is curiously evocative of the childhood of Thomas Mann's *Tonio Kröger* or those other dark, isolated introverts simultaneously scornful and envious of the blond, popular athletes, the childhood of one destined to grow up to become an artist ill at ease with bourgeois values.

Not surprisingly, Hochhuth names Thomas Mann as the foremost influence in his life, artistically and philosophically. Though Rolf Hochhuth has a long way to go to reach the literary height of a Thomas Mann, he resembles his hero in at least one respect: both found themselves in voluntary exile from the Germany they loved so much, because they could not sit back and watch her delude herself and debase herself by honoring false values. Hochhuth, after the appearance of his play on the German stage, felt it necessary to resign from his position at the Bertelsman Verlag, a publishing house and book club, because his presence was an embarrassment to his employer. He now lives in Basel, Switzerland, where he is an assistant director of the Municipal Theater, a position that leaves him much time to write.

1. Quoted in Alfred G. Aronowitz, "The Play That Rocked Europe," *The Saturday Evening Post,* February 29, 1964, pp. 42–43.
2. *Ibid.,* p. 43.
3. Dieter Vollprecht, *Der Streit um Hochhuths "Stellvertreter"* (Stuttgart: Basilius Press, 1963), p. 15.

Particularly ironic, therefore, have been those criticisms that view his play as an apology for Germany. To this charge he has made eloquent answer:

> With the extermination of the Jews, we Germans have brought upon ourselves the greatest guilt and shame of the 20th century, perhaps of all Western history. But I do not concede there is some sort of mark of Cain on the German soul making that people uniquely capable of the Nazi phenomenon. Hitler was the product of a set of circumstances that could conceivably be duplicated elsewhere. This does not mean that I absolve the German people of guilt. Quite the opposite. But there is a hierarchy of guilt. At the top are the people who gave the orders and actually performed the extermination. In the next level is the German people as a whole. It is a simple fact that Hitler came to power legally and that the nation supported him, actively or passively, practically to the end.
>
> But we are not alone. In a sense the whole civilized world shares guilt by association with that deed. It is a fact that a Jewish leader escaped from Poland in 1943 and tried to tell in England and America what was happening. The highest authorities could not or would not believe him.[4]

Hochhuth himself has termed the play a "Christian tragedy," and certainly in intent it is a moral and religious work, an attempt at a personal answer to the question he used as the title of the final act of *The Deputy*, "Where are You, God?" Where was God during the period when Hitler reigned in Germany? Why was His voice not heard? As B. A. Young has pointed out in his review of the London production of the play, "the question asked of God has not been answered,"[5] – not in the play and not in the author's mind. Though he is a member of the German Evangelical Church, who claims, in words which unfortunately belong to the vocabulary of prejudice, that some of his best friends are Catholics, Hochhuth has stated that his belief in religion has been sorely tried "in the face of Auschwitz and Hiroshima."[6]

His view of life tends to be dark. Upon being told of the untimely death of a young woman of his acquaintance, he characteristically remarked, "Probably she has been spared much, certainly, proportionately, far more than life could have offered her, even under the most fortunate circumstances."[7] Like Twain's Mysterious Stranger, Hochhuth believes that early death is the greatest benevolence. Yet if he is pessimistic, skeptical, cynical, he is so with good reason; for hasn't his childhood dream of being a world-renowned writer, discussed by the major critics throughout the western world, come true? And hasn't the dream proved quite empty? For all the discussion, there has been little understanding. "All the uproar, what people refer to as 'fame' is no longer an enticement to me. It has merely proved what I had long suspected – behind the shining appearance, fame is nothing but a mixture of prostitution and hard work."[8]

Certainly no one has worked harder at making his message heard throughout the world than this young playwright, making personal appearances on radio and television, permitting extensive interviews, penning defenses of his historical facts to major newspapers and magazines – even to the Pope him-

4.   Arthur Olsen, "An Interview with Rolf Hochhuth," *The New York Times Book Review*, March 1, 1964, p. 31.
5.   B. A. Young, review of *The Representative*, *Punch*, CCXLV (October 2, 1963), 503.
6.   Quoted in Aronowitz, p. 42.
7.   Quoted in Vollprecht, p. 18.
8.   Quoted *ibid.*, p. 17.

self—personally approving and supervising adaptations to the stage, attending opening performances, watching reactions and reviews from country to country. Yet this public life is completely contrary to the cravings of his personality and to his own needs as an artist. Shy in childhood, he remains a retiring person, conservative and conventional. In 1957 he suffered a nervous illness and partial paralysis, the effects of which are still visible, and this tended to make him draw even more into himself. Significantly, he is not a member of the famed "Group 47," despite the fact that his age and interests so closely correspond with those of the young authors comprising the group. Even his living room reflects his desire for privacy, containing only six chairs, for "do you think I would subject myself to a larger group than that? It is impossible to have any real conversation that way!"[9] Yet he follows his play, like a "bird of prey" as one critic put it, because he believes in the importance of what he has to say. In this connection it is interesting that, though he is an inveterate letter-to-the-editor writer, Hochhuth's defenses have always been of the historical basis of his work, not of its literary value.

Precisely what is Hochhuth's message? What is the sense of mission that motivates him? At Guterslöh he began a serious study of the Third Reich, discovering, among other works, Gerald Reitlinger's *The Final Solution*. As a Protestant, he was particularly struck by Reitlinger's accounts of efforts made by Roman Catholics in behalf of the Jews. A new approach to the question of responsibility for the horrible crime of genocide seemed to suggest itself. "We Protestants," Hochhuth has Gerstein say in *The Deputy*, "depend too much / upon ourselves. One cannot always bear it."[10] But what of those who had a hierarchy to look to—a moral guide whose words could define objectively, amidst all the subjective considerations of wartime, what a man who would serve God must do? Thus Hochhuth turned to a study of the record of Catholicism in World War II and was appalled at what he found. By his own admission, "I have not been the first to think of this question. Camus raised it in 1946. In Germany, many historians have considered it."[11] Hochhuth corresponded with some of the historians, receiving some encouragement for his own views. Reitlinger, for example, spoke of the Pope's obsession with "neutrality and diplomatic immunity" and concluded, "I do not think this need have happened had there been a better Pope."[12] More and more Hochhuth interpreted his sources as meaning that the Vicar of Christ, His deputy on earth, had failed to live up to his moral obligations in an effort to fulfill his political ambitions. "As the Vicar of Christ, he claimed to be the ultimate moral authority on earth. He chose to apply a political measure to the problem. . . . But he was not justified to reject a moral response," the playwright came to believe. He continued to gather materials on the subject, though he had no particular goal in mind. Then, in 1958, with the death of Pope Pius XII, "I came to a decision. . . . He was virtually canonized by world opinion on his deathbed. I felt the record should be put in perspective."[13] His desire to put the record in perspective, implying as it does the exposing of the Pope's true character to the world, though obviously present in the spirit of the play, contradicts some of the author's previous statements. For example, in his interview in Paris with Guy Le Clec'h, Hochhuth said, "I wrote *The Deputy* originally for my wife and some friends, thinking that then I would be through with the subject,

9. Quoted *ibid.*, p. 18.
10. *The Deputy*, p. 83.
11. Guy Le Clec'h, interview with Rolf Hochhuth, *Le Figaro Litteraire*, 18 (December 19–25, 1963), 3.
12. Letter from Reitlinger to Hochhuth quoted in "Sidelights on History," *The Deputy*, p. 304.
13. Olsen, p. 31.

but, unfortunately, the controversy starts anew everywhere the play appears."
In that same meeting, the author was asked to define his "true intention" and
answered: "I wished to show Pius XII, a historical figure, in a specific situation—that which he occupied in October, 1943, in his own city. In the figure
of the Deputy of Christ who remained silent, each spectator—Catholic, Jew,
or Protestant—who did not take a position should see reflected his own guilt.
Each ought to ask himself, 'Where were you? What part of the responsibility
for these happenings is yours?'" Only by depicting "the one most highly
placed in the spiritual hierarchy of the Church" would it be possible "to attack
each Christian to the most profound depth of his being." And, insists Hochhuth, "that is the point: to attack *living* Christians, not solely to criticize Pope
Pius XII, who is dead now and belongs to history."[14]

The fourth act, the act in which Pius XII is actually depicted on stage, has,
of course, been the center of the controversy, though numerous critics have
pointed out that there are many literary precedents for this. Hochhuth's portrait is one of unrelieved villainy, however, and much of the criticism of the
play can be laid to this. "The Pope in Claudel's *The Hostage* suffers himself,"
one French critic has stated; "Hochhuth's Pope makes others suffer."[15] In England it was pointed out that "Brecht allowed some sort of humanity even to
Galileo's inquisitors," but Hochhuth "gives the Pope no moral credit at all."[16]
Hochhuth's lack of knowledge about Catholicism is also partially responsible
for the controversy: the Jesuit, Michel Riquet, has pointed out that the Pope is
not merely another man, he is the spiritual father of millions, and when his
honor is attacked, each child feels himself insulted.[17] His unfamiliarity with
some of the concepts of the Roman Catholic Church have led him to misin-
terpret historical sources. Thus, it has been noted that the evidence cited by
Hochhuth in defense of his accusation that the Pope had a strong interest in
financial matters, an interest far beyond what his role called for, actually had
quite a different significance.

> The aspects of the Pope's scene which may seem least believable to readers
> who know the Pope only from the newspapers were not invented. For in-
> stance, even shortly before his death, irradiated with a vision of Christ,
> Pius XII still went on personally receiving checks. Cardinal Tardini has
> described this.[18]

The situation described by Cardinal Tardini took place four years before the
Pope's death, while he was ill. Two cardinals had brought their "Peter's
pence" checks to the Pope, and Cardinal Tardini hastened to show them to
him in an effort to cheer him and show him in what high regard he was held.
("Peter's pence" is a voluntary gift of the faithful, their contribution to the
direct support of the Holy See, which, consequently, constitutes a personal
tribute to the Pope.[19])

Even more serious charges of historical distortion have been made. In his
own defense Hochhuth has pointed out that he did go to Rome during that
memorable three-month vacation but could not, because of regulations, gain

14. Le Clec'h, p. 3.
15. Andre Gisselbrecht, review of *The Deputy*, *Les Lettres Francaises*, 59–60 (December 12–18,
1963), 8.
16. Reply to Hochhuth in "Letters to the Editor," *The Times Literary Supplement* (London), October
11, 1963, p. 812.
17. R. P. Michel Riquet, "Le Catholique Bafoué," *Le Figaro*, December 19, 1963, p. 6.
18. "Sidelights on History," *The Deputy*, pp. 349–350.
19. *The Brooklyn Tablet*, March 26, 1964, p. 1. I am indebted to Mr. Paul Hallert of the *National
Register*, Denver, for bringing this to my attention.

admission to the Vatican archives, a fact that led him to make the wry observation, "Neither the Vatican nor the Kremlin as yet permit free access to their archives."[20] There is general agreement, however, that Pius XII did not issue any strong, open declaration denouncing Hitler and the extermination policy during the war years, and *that* constitutes the major historical support of Hochhuth's play. By not speaking out, Pius XII made it possible for millions of others to avoid the issue, to go on rationalizing their own inaction. "[A]m I to be more popish than the Pope? / If he keeps his mouth shut till this evening, / I've got to load those trains during the night,"[21] says an SS officer in *The Deputy.* Though his underlying message is a universal one, the writer's own feeling against Pius XII is so strong that he sometimes loses sight of his own higher purpose. Particularly in the stage adaptations of the play, and with the author's express approval, the final effect seems to be more a trial of Pius XII than a challenge to all complacency everywhere. At any rate, as Hochhuth tells it, "I just wrote what I had to write,"[22] which, it seems, was plenty—enough to set off a roaring controversy, to earn the writer two major literary prizes, to warrant twenty-two separate productions in twenty-one cities and ten separate translations of the full text. Two books discussing the work and the historical issues it is concerned with have appeared in German, one in French, and one in Italian, and Grove Press in the United States has published a collection of readings on the subject, edited by Eric Bentley.

The fact that Hochhuth's emphasis has been almost entirely on his subject, a subject made all the more urgent by the fact that his wife's mother was killed at Auschwitz, should not be taken to mean that as a writer Hochhuth considers form unimportant. His supplement to *The Deputy* indicates his understanding of the theater of Lessing, of Schiller, of naturalism, and of Brecht, and of the relationship of his own work to their concepts. Though he failed his university entrance examination, he did spend several years sitting in on classes at Marburg, Heidelberg, Munich, and Guterslöh and, perhaps even more important, using the libraries of those universities to further his study of literary style and contemporary history. His favorite authors, for the most part, are contemporary and realistic: Thomas Mann, Bernard Shaw, Flaubert, Gide, Maupassant, Julian Green. During his university days, Hochhuth experimented constantly to develop a style of his own, though his own uncertainty and his natural reserve kept him from showing these works to anyone. Traditionally, his first literary attempts were autobiographical, and there is an unpublished epistolary novel, *Victoriastrasse 4*, his Eschwege address, still in his trunk. The work, describing life in a town near the East-West dividing line in Germany (Eschwege is five miles from the East German frontier), shows the same concern for defining contemporary issues crucial to an understanding of Germany today as does *The Deputy.* "I shall continue to deal with contemporary issues. In the times we live in, I don't see how a serious writer can avoid it," Hochhuth has said. "Any German who concerns himself with contemporary affairs must engage himself sooner or later with two complexes of events. One is the Nazi period and the other is the present fact of divided Germany."[23] There is already a new play "not in the same vein" under way. Whatever the vein, whatever the subject, one thing is certain: Hochhuth has an audience waiting.

20. "Sidelights on History," *The Deputy*, p. 288.
21. *The Deputy*, p. 188.
22. Aronowitz, p. 43.
23. Quoted in Olsen, p. 31.

Howard Taubman

POTENT PLATFORM AND PULPIT

Forget for the moment which side you take on "The Deputy." Concentrate on the tempest of discussion and debate that the play has aroused, for it is a reminder of the enormous power of the theater as a forum for burning, controversial ideas.

That power has been implicit in the stage for millenniums. Euripides sought to invoke it when his fellow Athenians, intent on dominating the innocuous island of Melos, slaughtered its males and enslaved its women and children. His dramatic cry of outrage in "The Trojan Women" did not change the world, but had it been heeded, it could have.

In medieval times the Mysteries were not only a naive, dramatic narrative of the Bible's stories of man's fall and deliverance but also a vivid warning of the perils of sin and heresy. The lighthearted Latin commedia dell' arte was not merely diverting but used mask and motley as a liberating license to speak cutting truths. The Fool in "King Lear" utters the plainest, most searing words. In Beaumarchais's comedies Figaro, despite his servant's livery, is the precursor of the proud, self-confident democrat.

Although Ibsen is revived these days, it is impossible to bring back with his dramas the sense of resentment and exhilaration they engendered in his belittlers and admirers. Here was a playwright who not only flew in the face of a genteel, empty dramaturgy but also lashed out at outworn shibboleths and putrescent hypocrisies. Ibsenism became a cause, and Bernard Shaw was one of its prophets.

Shaw himself gloried in using the stage as a platform for his prankish, diabolical paradoxes and his intensest convictions. His laughter was serious and his ridicule deadly as he argued that the virtuous people were living on profits earned at the expense of the debased devils they magnanimously pitied and set out to redeem.

The stage has seldom been used more frankly and forthrightly as pulpit and goad than in the Thirties when the Federal Theater Project's Living Newspaper flamed with missionary zeal. It assembled facts in theatrical form about the nation's ill-fed, ill-housed and ill-clothed, about the anguish of the farmer, about the abuse and neglect of the country's resources, and it did not hesitate to editorialize.

Since it was part of a vast Government-supported, make-work program, it did not dare go beyond opinions tolerated by the Administration, and— sometimes not so far. Nevertheless, its opinions were animated in concrete, human terms, and they were a heady experience in the theater.

Off Broadway this season has brought forward two arresting examples of the stage employed to throw light on the racial problem. "In White America" is a furious historical record drawn from letters, documents and books of the exploitation and humiliation of the Negro by the white man. Not a play at all, it throbs with more humanity and greater passion than a host of orthodox dramas.

"The Blood Knot," is a play from South Africa, a transparently simple one for two actors that says more about the ultimate indivisibility of white and black men on this earth than most pamphlets and sermons, and it does so in

"Potent Platform and Pulpit," *The New York Times,* March 15, 1964, Sect. II, p. 1.

the warm, lacerating human terms that are the enkindling language of the theater.

It would be silly, of course, to contend that the stage is the best or only medium to dramatize urgent problems, to fling inflammatory accusations and to spread revolutionary ideas. History abounds in proofs of the potency of other means and forms.

There was a man named Jesus, and He lived and spoke His preachments. There was a stubborn, irascible monk named Luther who by written and spoken word stood up against the power of a monolithic church. The Declaration of Independence articulated the case for an upheaval in measured prose that can be reproduced on one newspaper page as The New York Times proudly does every Independence Day. The Communist Manifesto, which led to later revolutions, was a printed document.

The printed word again and again has been a torch. Harriet Beecher Stowe's sentimental, melodramatic novel, "Uncle Tom's Cabin," had more impact than all the fiery speeches of the Abolitionists. Emile Zola's article, "J'Accuse," concentrated the battle to reverse the decision against Dreyfus and restore France's good name. John Steinbeck's "The Grapes of Wrath" gave disturbing immediacy to the plight of the Okies in a country indifferent to the erosion of its soil and its people. Rachel Carson's "Silent Spring" alerted us to heedless destruction of the balance of nature with our indiscriminate use of baneful pesticides.

Television's power was brilliantly illustrated by Edward R. Murrow and Fred W. Friendly in their bold, blunt program on Senator Joseph McCarthy and his techniques. In a time when fear lurked everywhere, a forthright telecast helped to prove that an ugly dam could be breached.

Yet there are good reasons why the theater, today more than ever, is the most commanding, vibrant medium for the detonation of challenging ideas.

The printed word has become an endless flood which most of us cannot navigate. Has there ever been a time when more books were published and hawked? As the books have increased in number, the theater has shrunk. A play with a thesis has a much better chance of creating a stir than a book.

There is something else about the theater. It is a vivid, communal experience. In the very process of being acted out, a theme becomes tangible and visible. If it conveys shock and excitement, the emotional radiations between stage and audience deepen the group reaction and intensify the individual response.

No one would wish the theater to be only a sounding board for broadsides and polemics. It can be so many other things—escape, laughter, mystery and, most important of all, a high ennobling art that reveals us to ourselves. But it is remarkably hospitable to the expression of overpowering convictions and moral indignation. What a pity that it is not asked more often to be an exhilarating clearing house for daring, searching new ideas, right or wrong. /1/

Ernst Schumacher

PISCATOR'S POLITICAL THEATER

The "proletarian theater" was founded by Erwin Piscator together with Hermann Schüller in March, 1919, in Berlin. Piscator, in his book *The Political*

"Piscator's Political Theater," in *Brecht—A Collection of Critical Essays,* ed. Peter Demetz (Englewood Cliffs, N.J.: Prentice-Hall, Inc., 1962), pp. 86–96. Ernst Schumacher is a German critic best known for his explication, from the orthodox Communist point of view, of Brecht's early work.

Theater, which appeared in 1929, emphasized that his stage had only its name in common with the proletarian theater of the "League for Proletarian Culture" under the direction of Arthur Holitscher, Ludwig Rubiner, Rudolf Leonhard, Alfons Goldschmidt, and Karlheinz Martin. This distinction was inappropriate.

The first version of the "Program of the Proletarian Theater" was just as Messianic and sentimental as that of Rubiner, Goldschmidt, and other left-wing theater people, while the second version proceeded on the following basis: "We banned the word 'art' radically from our program; our 'plays' were proclamations with which we endeavored to intervene in contemporary events, to act 'politically.'"

In the programmatic introductions and commentaries we read, among other things: "The subordination of every artistic intention to the revolutionary goal: conscious emphasis and propagation of the idea of class struggle." In all questions of style the determining question must always be: "Will the gigantic circle of the proletarian audience gain by it? Or will they be bored or confused and infected by bourgeois ideas? *Revolutionary* art can only proceed out of the spirit of the revolutionary working class." They derived from this the demand that the style which was to govern the actor as well as the author and director must be of a "completely concrete nature."

Whatever is said, must be said artlessly, without experimentation, smoothly and not in an "expressionist" manner, determined by a simple, unconcealed revolutionary purpose and will. Consequently all neoromantic, expressionist styles and problems and their like, which proceed out of the individual anarchic need of the artist, are excluded from the very beginning.

The proletarian theater must gradually be able to do without the bourgeois professional actor. The proletarian actor must not become ab- /86/ sorbed in his role. He must make everything an expression of the proletarian idea. The author, on the other hand, must be "the crystallization point of the proletarian cultural will, the catalyst for the worker's urge for comprehension."

The other task of the proletarian theater consists in exercising its propagandistic and educational effect upon the masses of those who are still politically undecided, or indifferent or who have not yet understood that bourgeois art and this kind of "enjoyment" cannot be taken over into a proletarian state.

Here are contained in essence all the theses of the revolutionary "objectivity" (*Sachlichkeit*) which was to govern aesthetics and practice of the [German] radical left in the Twenties. First of all one can here point to the agreement with the international *Proletkult* group, that the task of literature and art lies in "direct action," in the organization of proletarian forces and proletarian life as a whole. A. Lunacharsky made the following restriction in 1919: "Art is above all things the organization of emotional attitudes of individuals or of groups, classes, whole nations, and so forth. Proletarian art is the expression for the process of organizing this emotional life." Correspondingly, as we have noted, the partisans of the "proletarian theater" in Germany had spoken primarily of the task of encouraging the proletarian feeling, of awakening it and developing it. In the *Proclamation of the Executive Committee of the Provisional International Bureau for Proletarian Culture* of September, 1920, we read, on the other hand, that the purpose of the proletarian cultural movement is to arm the proletariat with new knowledge, to organize its movements through the new art, to fill its life with the proletarian, Communist spirit.

A. Bogdanov declared in 1920 in his essay *What is Proletarian Literature?:* "Today poetry and literature are in any case the most widespread and effective means for the education of the urban population, that is, the introduction of the individual into the system of social relations." Correspondingly he characterized the proletarian writers as "organizers," as "representatives of the general tasks, of the *general* will of the community itself, of its *general* power." If the proletarian writer is intimately involved with the community, then he can become "the organizer of its forces and its consciousness in artistic form." In an essay "Art and the Proletariat" in *The Red Banner,* Bogdanov similarly called the artist an "organizer of the living forces of the great community."

These and similar theorems of the *Proletkult* group tended in practice to transfer artistic impulses (in the theater, dramatic impulses) into direct political action under the leadership of the literati and practicing artists. *The Red Banner* in 1919 already had pointed out the dangers of such artistic political activism. It wrote: /87/

> The mistake of the League for Proletarian Culture lies in its pretension of making a revolution by its activity, of being able to lead the fight for freedom of the proletariat by its efforts. . . . But the opinion that the value of art consists in being a part of the proletarian fight for freedom, that in other words it can replace the revolution, the class struggle, is a great error.

Piscator was one of the liveliest and most persistent advocates of the "direct action" of literature, and especially when the "proletarian theater" had finally failed because of the revocation of his license in 1921. Piscator used the expression "direct action" in the theater on the occasion of the staging of the revue *Red Rumble* (*Roter Rummel*) before the Reichstag elections of 1924. Thus it was not the primary task of the theater to create art, but to carry on political propaganda, as had already been stated in the program of 1919. Therefore Piscator pleaded for a "tendentious drama" through which enlightenment, knowledge, and comprehension were to be communicated. "Direct action" demanded a "revolutionary professional theater," the duty of which should be the political enlightenment of the masses (in contrast to the proletarian lay theater which was to penetrate the working class as a whole with propaganda).

But "direct action" could not be satisfied with enlightening the masses politically while they remained purely passive. It was necessary to include the masses actively in the stage action. The boundary between audience and stage had to be removed to a great extent. Piscator believed he could bring this about in two ways. On the one hand, through the stage action; by staging the masses, the masses were to be activated and enlightened. "No longer the individual with his private, personal fate, but the times themselves, the fate of the masses is the *heroic factor of the new drama.*" The intention was to show "the reciprocal effect between the great human and superhuman factors and the individual or class." Piscator called "the basic idea of all stage action the enhancement of private scenes with historical relevance." With this, Piscator continued, "nothing else can be meant but enhancement to political, economic, and social relevance. Through them we brought the stage in contact with life." That this view was undialectical is obvious. The private sphere, taken concretely, contains within it the "political, economic, and social" aspect, or, expressed more precisely, it is an expression of it.

But to the presentation of the masses on the stage was to be added the co-operation of the masses. This was achieved by the direction. We shall speak about the methods later. Piscator saw the ideal of "direct theater" fulfilled in the production of the documentary drama *In Spite of Everything* (*Trotz alledem*), the content of which was the revolution of 1918, describing the fate of Rosa Luxemburg and Karl Liebknecht. This political revue was given in Berlin's *Grosses Schauspielhaus* on /88/ June 12, 1925. The proletarian mass organizations furnished the audience. Piscator claimed: "The masses took over the direction." *The Red Banner* wrote: "The masses began to act, too," and continued: "The theater had become reality for them, and soon it was no longer stage versus audience, but a *single* great audience, a *single* great battlefield, *one single* demonstration. It was this unity which on that evening finally produced proof of the agitative power of political theater." Piscator expressed his goal as follows:

> The removal of the boundary between stage and audience, the hauling in of each individual member of the audience into the action first welds the audience entirely into a mass for which collectivism is not an acquired concept, but an experienced reality, when it is their distresses, their longings, their hopes, their sufferings and joys to which the stage of the political theater gives voice, expression, and form.

In this formulation, the danger of "direct literature" and especially the theater becomes clear: the stage and the experience communicated by it as a substitute for the collectivism lacking in reality, as a substitute for an experience of the masses which in the real world, in political life, does not happen even to the revolutionary party. The stage becomes, as in the bourgeois theater, a place where the inadequacy felt in reality disappears, where the negative complexes can be swept out of sight. The hard, weary skirmishing which is full of sacrifices and often seemingly useless is forgotten, and is replaced by a flight into autosuggestion: everything is going to be all right; it's coming along; we'll make it. It is the substitution for the real class struggle by the demonstration of a copy on the stage. It was certainly not a matter of chance when in September, 1930, *The Left Turn (Die Linkskurve)*, the organ of the League of Proletarian and Revolutionary Writers, impressed by the real effects of this political art, especially the political theater, recalled that the proletarian class must concentrate its energies primarily upon the economic and political struggle. . . .

The dangerous tendencies which lay hidden in the theory of "direct action" in art and literature, namely the claim of being able to enlighten, mobilize, organize, even lead the masses in this way, had been seen by Lenin long before the First World War, when he wrote his essay *Party Organization and Party Literature*. As much as he pleaded for a true party character in literature, he stressed at the same time: "Literature must be a *part* of the general proletarian cause, a little 'cog in the wheel' in the one great unified mechanism which is driven by the whole class-conscious vanguard of the whole working class." To be sure, this essay was not published in German until 1929.

If Piscator saw his task as one of enlightening the masses politically and schooling them for the class struggle, then it was obvious that he /89/ should deal with contemporary materials. Already in the "Proletarian Theater" in 1920–21 Piscator declared: "My idea in those days was a much closer connection with journalism, with day-to-day affairs." He defended his "contemporary theater" as follows: "A contemporization of all mankind has taken place. . . . It [literature] must be real, real to the last detail, true to the point of ruthlessness if it wants only to mirror this life. But how much truer and more real must it be if it wants to intervene in this life as a moving force." And in another place: the theater in all times "stood or fell with its 'contemporaneity.'" The epoch itself, "the times themselves," should become visible on the stage. With Paquet's *Flags* (*Fahnen*) in the Berlin *Zentraltheater* in 1924 Piscator believed he for his part had "crossed the threshold from the theater of art to the theater of the age." *Flags* dealt with the trial of the Chicago anarchists in 1889.

But the content of the times is at its most contemporary in journalistic reporting, in documents. Repeatedly Piscator emphasized his close relationship to journalism. Now the historical drama was to be a "political document of its epoch," not "the tragedy of fate of some hero." Thus—as Piscator wrote—history does not become the background, but political reality does. "It is not the inner arc of the dramatic event which is essential, but the epic course of the epoch from its roots until its last effects are represented as exactly and as comprehensively as possible. Drama is only important to us insofar as it can be documented." Piscator claimed that it was from the document alone that the artistic effect obtained "at the same time an unsuspected intensification." Thus the highest form of the drama was the "documentary drama," in which "the connection between the stage action and the great historically effective forces" was created. Piscator considered the revue *In Spite of Everything* and Alexei Tolstoy's *Rasputin* of 1927–28 successful in this regard.

Here Piscator's efforts resemble those in Soviet Russia during the first years after the revolution. Piscator's theories were anticipated by Kerzhentsev in all essential points. For example, Kerzhentsev was also for a "fusion of audience and stage," which could best take place in a kind of circus. The audience should be included in the action as players. Piscator in his book *The Political Theater* also refers to Kerzhentsev along with Bogdanov, Diebold, Jhering, Kerr, and Anna Siemsen. But while Piscator was endeavoring to create mass theater in Germany in Kerzhentsev's sense, this movement had already passed its peak in Russia. In its place came the mass film of Eisenstein, Pudovkin, and other directors. If the mass theater in revolutionary Russia had a real basis in the masses, in Germany it remained a formal, isolated experiment.

The dramatic form of the representation of historical events and the expansion of every individual fate to a mass fate of the epoch was necessarily epic. The "epic course of the epoch from its roots to its last effects" could only be produced in a juxtaposition and succession of scenes and /90/ tableaux. The dramatic form becomes reportorial. Piscator saw the first success of the "consistent attempt to interrupt the scheme of the dramatic action and put the epic course of the material in its place" in the production of Paquet's *Flags* in 1924. For the first time a play had the subtitle of "Epic Drama." Piscator said that Paquet had attempted "to lay bare the roots of the case in the epic elaboration of the material" and had represented the "essential social and economic background." Piscator summed up: "Thus, in a certain sense, *Flags* represented the first Marxist drama, and that production the first attempt to comprehend the materialistic motive forces." The "scientific penetration of the material" in a Marxist sense could only be brought about in the form of epic theater. To support the claim that "the communication of a certain perception in the philosophy of history, as is provided by the purely historical truths," can only be represented by a succession of stations, episodes, extracts, sketches, and tableaux out of history, Piscator referred to the works and experiences of Döblin, Joyce, and Dos Passos in the field of the novel and to Brecht as well as to his own work in the area of the drama. This is not uninteresting, because here Piscator has unconsciously confirmed his agreement with undialectical, essentially mechanical materialism—with mere sociology.

The philosophical method of these writers at this time was mechanical materialism, or the naïve realism which takes reality as its objective. This view of the world hindered the above-named writers from penetrating to the foundation of the social process. Thus they restricted themselves to reproducing the "thing in itself" as it appears to the undialectical observer. It remained essentially a mere description of the behavior of human beings in certain situations, a spontaneous registration of social or natural phenomena, a journalistic reporting. With even the most exact description of the events, their meaning still remained opaque. The method was at bottom naturalistic, except that it was less primitive.

. . .

Now if Piscator similarly spoke up for the principle of reporting, of an epic succession of tableaux and stations, of the accumulation of documentation, then this is essentially based on the same insufficiency in the philosophical method. Like Dos Passos, who is his closest relative in the epic area, Piscator was unable to grasp concretely the subjective factor of history: the functioning, active human being, the Marxist class fighter in a political sense, both as an individual and as the product of his class and the class struggle. The sociological schematization made him appear only as an abstract in this or that form—above all as part of an anonymous mass. The process itself is no less abstractly comprehended. It was not the result of the action of real living people but something me- /91/ chanical, which therefore could only be developed mechanically in precisely this epic, serial, montage form—not in a living way.

We cannot investigate here how Piscator, in his attempt to justify this theory, could attract Brecht as he did, because first the methodological means which Piscator used to realize his theory must be listed. In Piscator's opinion, contemporization and documentation as well as the epic form called for "montage" in direction and production. For a "release from the petrified architecture of the old naturalist form of the drama," for the expansion and deepening of individual fate into that of the community of the epoch, Piscator required technology. "The new dramatic principle with expansion of materials into space and time required an enlargement and improvement of the apparatus." Against Stanislavsky's naturalism Piscator declared: "It is not accidental that the spiritual metamorphosis of the theater comes at the same time as the technical transformation of its equipment."

According to Piscator only an intensified application of technological means enabled the overcoming of the political problems and their introduction to the masses as a means of agitation. Piscator went in for the "autonomous acting scaffold." "With this construction we hope to show that the problem of the individual's position in society does not have to be represented separate from it, but that his fate is imbedded in its political and social structure."

In this regard, Piscator had the support of *The Red Banner*. It vouched for Piscator in 1927 on the occasion of his production of Toller's *Hurray, We Live (Hoppla, wir leben):*

How can one in our age of proletarian revolution and imperialist reaction make a theatrical presentation? *Only* by exploding the previous bourgeois, private word-theater with the *application of the greatest technological means*, in order to awaken this age of technological achievement to life. Out of this political will of the proletarian, revolutionary director arises the *new content of the theater*. This content, which cannot be presented with the meager means of the traditional bourgeois stage, demands the *new form* and is working it out. Piscator's achievements as a director are determined by the new content, the new theme.

This critique was of course absolutely wrong. The point of it was that only the director creates the play, as Piscator himself later formulated it. According to this critique the content was to be found in the technological form of Piscator's stage, which leads to empty formalism, even if it does have a revolutionary appearance. . . .

The new form first arose through the use of projections. These were initially utilized in the "epic drama" *Flags* in 1924. Boards were set up to the right and left of the stage. The text projected on them, according to Piscator, drew the moral from the action, expanded the material beyond the stage, and illuminated the background of the action. It /92/ turned out to be a "pedagogical principle" which was used in almost all subsequent productions. From the projections came the use of film. Piscator differentiated between the didactic film, which instructed the audience about the material, the dramatic film, which was a scenic substitute, and the commentary film, which according to Diebold had taken the place of the ancient chorus. Through the film, according to Piscator, "the whole drama was lifted out of its original plane onto the higher plane of the didactic drama (tendentious drama)." The film was first used in *In Spite of Everything* (1925), then again in *Rasputin* (1927). Heinz Hilpert and Julius Bab in a discussion in the *Berliner Volksbühne* in November, 1927, declared against the use of the film in the theater, because it weakens the effect of the drama.

In *Rasputin* the segmented globe stage as a "symbol of the world" was used for the first time. "The *idea of the globe* became urgent in me, upon which all events unfold in the closest entanglement and in mutual dependence." In the segments, as they opened, various historical situations with well-known political personalities were shown. At the same time film strips commented on the events. . . . In 1925 already Piscator had used what he termed the *Praktikabel* as a basic form of stage construction—a terrace-like irregular structure which possessed a flat incline on one side, steps and pedestals on the other, and stood on a revolving stage. A further innovation was the moving belt which was used in the dramatization of *The Good Soldier Schweik* (*Der brave Soldat Schwejk*), in order to make Schweik's marches possible. Alongside of it the stage decorations turned in the opposite direction.

As far as the decorations were concerned, it was Piscator's goal that "in place of static decoration the dynamics of a real stage construction should take place before the eyes of the audience." The decorative element was to lose its autonomy by being included in the movement of the stage. Piscator reached this goal best, according to the opinion of *The Red Banner*, in the production of Friedrich Wolf's Chinese play *Tai Yang Awakens (Tai Yang erwacht)* in 1931. Here the "stage-decorations had been divested of their formal character" and become an ingredient of the revolutionary action. The stage constructions of John Heartfield served, as did the whole stage apparatus, for the "reportorial corroboration of the facts" of the revolutionary events in China from 1925 to 1927. In the production of *The Emperor's Coolie (Des Kaisers Kuli)* by Theodor Plivier (performed on August 29, 1930, in the Lessing Theater, Berlin), Piscator had used still another means for the fusion of stage and audience, of theater and reality. He directed "coolies" into the audience who then hurried upon the stage. Besides this he used a "narrator," who commented on the course of the Battle of the Skagerrak, which was illustrated by film diagrams.

These technical innovations, the efforts to bring to the stage the life of reality and to include the masses in the action were actually not as /93/ new as it seemed in Germany. Piscator only imitated extensively what Tairov and Meyerhold had demonstrated years before in the Soviet Union and in Germany itself. While Piscator still celebrated triumphs in Germany, the Russian proletariat had already turned away from this "unchained" and "dynamic" theater because it recognized that it was at bottom only a variation of bourgeois illusionism.

Just as Tairov and Meyerhold remained basically bourgeois directors, Piscator, in the rigorous insistence upon his will as the director and in the subordination of the play as written to the direction, agreed with the formal experimenters of the bourgeois theater in Germany at the beginning of the Twenties. He defended himself by saying that this attitude was not artistically but philosophically determined; indeed, he set his view of directing equal to "scientific analysis" in the Marxist sense. But his practice surrendered the theater to formal technical externalities. The "materialist" Piscator fulfilled the demand of the "idealist" Schiller, that the form must destroy the content.

The primacy of direction was shown most clearly by his treatment of classical works on the stage. Meyerhold and Tairov fulfilled therein the demand of Kerzhentsev for "deformation," a "direct distortion of the author's intention." Piscator is quite their equal, as is shown by his production of Schiller's *The Robbers (Die Räuber,* 1926), which was one of the false, superficial contemporizations well-known from the beginning of the Twenties (Ziegel in Hamburg), even if he dressed it up in a revolutionary costume. The purely mechanical compression of reality in and by the stage apparatus finally led not only to an elimination of the poetic content of a work of art, even to its destruction, but also produced basically the same reaction in the audience as was evoked in the bourgeois theater by other means and other subjects.

Piscator had proclaimed: "The theater should no longer have a merely emotional effect on the audience, no longer speculate on their emotional preparedness—it appeals quite consciously to reason. It should communicate not only uplift, enthusiasm, thrill, but also enlightenment, knowledge, comprehension." But, with the growth of the technical apparatus, the "furioso of action," which had called forth a "human shock" in *In Spite of Everything,* turned increasingly into an intensification of the emotional element, such as the bourgeois theater in its way was no longer able to produce. Under the confusing impression transmitted by the technical stage construction and its functioning, the consciousness of the audience, especially the proletarian audience, had to receive short shrift, despite the mass of material to be communicated. At this point it is not uninteresting that Piscator repeatedly complained about the lack of support from the workers' organizations. This was due not only to a lack of means, but also to the fact that Piscator's theater was basically not a proletarian theater, but like Meyerhold's and Tairov's in Russia a radically left, petty bourgeois theater, which received its ideal /94/ support chiefly from intellectuals and working circles strongly interested in art, but obtained its material aid from the capitalists.

It is precisely the inclusion of the audience in the stage action, the removal of the separation between theater and reality, such as Piscator strove for, which made the illusion of the audience complete. For the spectator no possibility at all remained to think things over correctly, because too much reality, and indeed uncommunicated reality which had not gone through a real artistic medium, stormed in on him. The actor, too, did not have the opportunity to develop that inner distance from the role which Piscator considered suitable to the new age.

Before summing up, let us refer to a few basic pronouncements of Piscator which show the limitations of his Marxist world view. Piscator spoke of an "epoch of classicism" with its correspondence to the "great personality"; of an "epoch of aestheticism," which saw its "eternal plane" in the "intensification into beauty"; of a "moral age" with the absolute value of the "ethical"; of an "epoch of idealism" with its urge toward the "sublime."

To these "epochs" Piscator opposed the "fateful forces of our epoch": "economics and politics and, as the result of both, society." Piscator here has obviously taken over schematic concepts of bourgeois sociology and aesthetics and given them a vulgar-Marxist answer. According to him, history acquires a materialistic basis only in our epoch, but this in Piscator's terms is absolutely mechanical. The basic element of history, the activity of the human being, does not appear in Piscator's thought. Society is presented only as result and product, not as an active element. This coarse, undialectical materialism, which partly transforms itself into idealism, found its fulfillment in the following formulation: "We cannot allow either ideal, ethical, or moral impulses to break into the scene when its real motive forces are political, economic, and social."

In summary, it can be said that Piscator acquired the materialistic, dialectical method only schematically. This failing prevented him from really penetrating into the essence of the history which he wanted to represent artistically. To be sure, he used the terminology of scientific socialism, but numerous pronouncements and his methods of representation on the stage prove that he comprehended class history more as a mechanical construction than as a dialectical process. This proceeded from the negation of his original class position, that of the petty bourgeoisie. Recognizing and feeling the individualism of the bourgeois world as unfruitful, moved by the great revolutionary, collectivist wave which ended the imperialist war, he fell into the extreme of an undialectical view of the masses, and thus of collectivism. The subjective factor of history, the active human being in his effort to come to terms with nature and other individuals—the motor of all history—disappeared behind the sociological concepts community, process, revolution. In adddition he had the genuinely petty bourgeois need to make himself the /95/ schoolmaster of the slowly, incompletely, and wrongly reacting masses, and of the vanguard leading them. The real socialist impetus which animates petty bourgeois people of Piscator's type, became an almost Messianic urge to instruct and lead the masses, which led to an underestimate of the political organization and the fact that the true instruction of the masses and the education of the proletariat take place on the economic and political battlefield of the class struggle. /96/

Ronald Bryden

PSEUDO-EVENT

You face three massive walls of blank grey concrete. In one is a door with a spyhole through which, a voice explains over loudspeakers, guards could watch the naked Jews as the gas took effect. The bodies, the voice adds, were removed to the incinerators through large ports at the other end of the gas-chamber—it is through these that you, the audience, have been looking in. Their huge slabs now roll into place, and on them are projected goose-stepping youths, rolling tanks, a moustached man shouting to a forest of arms, faces peering from cattle-trucks—all the familiar, jerky, chilling imagery of the years which led up to this place. The loudspeaker tells you that this is Auschwitz.

From his stunning opening, by way of Alan Webb's meticulous make-up as Pope Pius XII to the final, flickering films of bodies heaped like cordwood being swept up by a bulldozer, Clifford Williams hammers at you that in watching his production of *The Representative* you are watching not a play but reality—a document. He has borrowed from Piscator, who staged Rolf Hochhuth's play in Berlin, all the techniques of his epic theatre—film cuttings, newspaper extracts, announcers reading statistics—to make it plain that no distinction should be made between what happens on his stage and the world beyond it. This is not to be make-believe, but our own world: the history of our own lifetimes, within which between five and six million Jews were killed in Europe without one word of public protest or condemnation by the head of the largest Church in Christendom.

It ought to be an impressive occasion, and some people have already hailed it as such: as the first use of an English stage to present and discuss real historical fact; as a forum of serious comment on the political actuality of our time. Certainly the audience at the Aldwych came away as Mr. Williams wanted them to, without applauding, bludgeoned into silence by reality. There are only two things wrong. Mr. Williams's importations of documentary actuality have no place or authorisation in Hochhuth's text, nor do they bear any artistic relation to the play he has written. The performance at the Aldwych is two spectacles at war with each other.

'Anyone . . . who does not declare "open and honourable war upon Naturalism in Art,"' writes Hochhuth in the appendix to the published text of his play,*

will have nowadays to give place to any newsreel, if only because it can show 'the raw material of the world' much more drastically and completely than the stage, which only remains true if—as Brecht, the theorist of alienation, was not the first to discover,—'it destroys the illusion which it has itself created'.

The phrases he quotes are from Schiller; the play he has written is a huge Schillerian romantic-historical drama on the lines of *Maria Stuart, Don Carlos* and *Wallenstein*. In its original form, it has five acts, 11 blank-verse scenes; none of these takes place in an Auschwitz gas-chamber. It has 48 characters,

From "Pseudo-Event," *New Statesman*, October 4, 1963, p. 460.
*Translated by Robert Macdonald. *Methuen*. 25s.

three of them historical figures—Pope Pius, Adolf Eichmann and Kurt Gerstein, the Christian SS officer who helped numbers of Jews to escape from concentration camps. The remaining 45, including the main protagonist, an appalled young Jesuit of noble Roman family who tries to persuade the Pope to speak out against the mass-murders, are fictitious. Hochhuth offers in his appendix some parallels between a few of them and living people who performed similar actions in history, but he makes no attempt to pass them off as real personages.

On the contrary, he states explicitly that this is not a work of historical scholarship, nor does it pretend to be. In his stage direction for his last act, set at Auschwitz, he insists:

> The stage setting is throughout ghostly, dreamlike, even if 'reality' is technically possible. A few indications suffice. . . . What happened in the interior of this underworld is not even to be imagined, let alone evoked atmospherically.

And in the appendix again:

> To tie up the already available facts, intuitively, into an artistic and truthful whole, is the high and seldom attained goal of poetry which, in view of *precisely* such a weight of raw material and all the trouble of its compilation, must not allow itself to be robbed of the specific freedom which alone gives primal *form* to the material.

It is all very young, very woollily solemn and very 19th-century-German-High-Romantic. One can see why Mr. Williams and his colleagues wished to ignore it: to produce a Schillerian pseudo-historical drama in mid-20th century is a less noteworthy enterprise than to acculturate Piscator. But the fact remains that this is the kind of play Hochhuth has written, and that he was right. The dramatic bits of *The Representative* are the scenes in which he takes off completely from history to marshal ideas and idealisms; to present not the fact of Auschwitz, which cannot be brought within his experience (he was 14 when the war ended), but the emotion it rouses in a member of his generation. The strongest point of his play is the confrontation of the young Jesuit with 'The Doctor' at Auschwitz, a figure of abstract, poeticised evil who explains his cruelties by revealing that he is a lapsed priest trying to goad God into revealing himself:

> Because I wanted an answer—an answer!
> And so I risked what no man had
> Yet risked since the world began to turn. . . .
> I took an oath that I would provoke
> that Old Man so measurelessly
> So totally beyond measure that he
> would have to give an answer.
> Even if it was only the negative answer, which,
> as Stendhal says, Is all that *can* excuse Him:
> that He does not exist.

Mr. Williams has had the sense to build this into the climax of his evening (he has done so, rather dubiously perhaps, by cutting Hochhuth's own final scene in which the Jesuit is shot down by guards while trying to kill the Doctor). . . . /460/

Renée Saurel

INTERVIEW WITH JORGE SEMPRUN

Tell me, were there many problems involved in cutting and compressing the play?
It certainly wasn't easy. You have read Hochhuth's text and know what problems it poses. I have tried to retain the important elements, those which give the play its flavor, those which are necessary to the main plot. Yet, of course, when it comes to choosing, decisions are always arbitrary. Hochhuth himself had to sacrifice parts of his play for the version now playing in Basel, the only one he himself wrote. He took certain scenes, I took others. That is the case in each country in which the play is produced.

Does your version differ substantially from Piscator's?
Yes. My procedure differs from his. At first, I had a word-for-word translation of Piscator's version in French, but this proved of little use to me. Therefore, I decided to work directly from the Rowohlt edition, the full German text. It seemed best to me to take the original play and then cut out some parts, which I will tell you about in a few minutes. In doing this, the play had to be reworked, tightened. Then, to make up for certain necessary cuts, I introduced a narrator, who is put to a rather unusual use. More exactly there are a series of narrators, for each role is divided into parts. This sounds complicated, but it works out quite well in the staging, as you will see.

In the original there are, if I am not mistaken, forty-three characters, among them, four women and two children. How many have you cut out?
All those I possibly could without sacrificing the main ideas of the play. Notably, all the female roles, since not one is essential to the main action.

Aren't many of Hochhuth's characters historical figures?
That's right. These include Pope Pius XII, the Apostolic Nuncio, Gerstein, Hirt, and Eichmann. As a result, the work required a firm historical basis, precise documentation, almost scientific exactness. I believe that before Hochhuth constructed the work from its multitude of sources, he put in many years of work. He consulted documents and archives throughout Europe, excluding only those of the Vatican and of the Kremlin, to which access is impossible.

The remarkable thing, proving that Hochhuth is something more than a historian and compiler, though, is the manner in which he refashioned all of this material into a work of art. Would you agree?
Yes. The language is beautiful, and that also poses problems for me. Piscator says, in his preface, which you may know, that it is through the use of profound and inspired German free verse that Hochhuth raises his play far above the level of naturalistic documentation. Form is very important here. Hochhuth correctly denied himself the use of metaphor. In striving to re-create a reality in itself so horrible it seemed surrealistic and hallucinatory, he felt a poetic treatment, the attempt to transpose through the use of symbols, could only weaken and cloud the situation.

Have you met Hochhuth? Is he a young man?
He is thirty-one, and he is a Christian, a Protestant — Protestant in the Kier-

Renée Saurel interviews Jorge Semprun [who adapted *The Deputy* for the Paris stage], *Les Lettres Françaises*, December 12 – 18, 1963, p. 18. Trans. by the editors.

kegaardian sense, though that, of course, is revealed through his play. And here—you may look at this—it is the version presented in Basel. [Hochhuth subtitles it] *"Ein christliches Schauspiel,"* "A Christian play."

How many scenes are there in your version?

Eight. There will be a single intermission after the fourth scene. The action covers the period from August, 1942, to October, 1943.

The first scene takes place at the quarters of the Apostolic Nuncio to Berlin, his Excellency Caesar Orsenigo, who was sixty-nine in 1942. Though he had been an eyewitness to the Nazi terror since 1938, he was not moved from his position in support of the Concordat between the Curia and the Reich government. When the Jews were deported, he remained silent. During this scene, Riccardo Fontana, a young Jesuit, is also introduced. Though he is an imaginary figure, he is based on authentic ones: Father Lichtenberg, who asked to be deported with the Jews and died on the way, and the Polish priest, Maximilian Kolbe, who was number 16670 at Auschwitz and voluntarily took the place of a condemned man who was the head of a family. . . . It is to these two priests that the play is dedicated.

Also, in this scene, that unique historical figure, Gerstein, appears.

Is this the same S.S. officer whose name is engraved on a monument dedicated to the victims of fascism which was raised by the Jewish community in Paris?

Yes. The fact that he is an S.S. officer might be misleading to a spectator, so I have taken special pains to make his position clear at the beginning of the play. I make it known that he is a Christian, who had once been imprisoned by Hitler as a suspected enemy of the regime and that, once released, he courageously contrived to be accepted by the S.S. and carry on the dangerous work with which you are familiar. It is believed that the real Gerstein is dead. All trace of him was lost in the German military prison in Paris.

What other scenes are you including?

The second scene takes place at the Jägerkeller in Falkensee, a meeting place and recreation center for S.S. officers and high Nazi officials. It is a very long scene, which Piscator, for one, cut out completely. Though I have retained it, I shortened it considerably. The central figure is Professor Hirt, of the University of Strassburg, a doctor who conducted experiments on human beings, requesting that his "subjects" preferably be live ones. He is given his real name in this play, though today he continues to practice medicine under an assumed name. . . .

The third scene takes place in Gerstein's apartment. You will remember that in this scene the Doctor enters, the diabolic Doctor, who is not even given a name in the play, but who is partially allegorical, the incarnation of Evil itself, a character who might have stepped right out of a mystery play of the Middle Ages. Still, a terribly learned man—lucid, intelligent—and a very elegant one, even a bit of a dandy. Jean Topart has the challenging task of interpreting this role.

I remember that the Doctor enters carrying a jar in which are contained the brains of Jewish twins. I suppose you will omit this somewhat gruesome detail.

I believe it has been omitted in all the stage versions, though I have managed to keep the sense of it by having Gerstein discuss the experiments in the preceding scene, at the Falkensee Jägerkeller. The following scene takes place in Rome in February, 1943, at the house of Count Fontana, Riccardo's father and an aristocrat in the manner of von Papen. He is chamberlain to the Pope and his chief financial advisor.

Financial matters play a very important part in Hochhuth's play, don't they?

Certainly, but other matters are also introduced to explain the Pope's silence: diplomacy, reasons of state, the battle against Bolshevism, the good of the Church. This is the scene, though, in which Riccardo, horrified and distraught, cries out to his father that in his opinion a Vicar of Christ who knows the facts and holds back for a single hour from condemning the executioners is himself a criminal.

In this scene, also, the political Cardinal is introduced.

Following the intermission, a scene between Riccardo and the Father General of a religious order takes place. This is during the time when the Germans are actually arresting and deporting Jews from Rome. The Pope has tried to avert these steps by offering to provide a ransom in gold. Learning this, Riccardo realizes that the Pope had known for some time what was to take place, but had remained silent. It is then that he decides to accompany the deportees himself. Though I have had to cut out the scene depicting the arrest of the Luccani family, I have retained the scene showing the questioning of Italian Jews by Salzer of the Waffen S.S., a scene wherein several of the prisoners identify themselves as Catholics. The climax, of course, occurs in the seventh scene, when Riccardo appeals to the Pope on moral grounds, begging him to protest, and receiving nothing but a *non possumus* and a vague, ineffective, permissive statement. He pins the Star of David to his soutane and departs.

The last scene takes place at Auschwitz. It presented many problems, which I hope I have solved through use of a narrator.

In this scene, do you retain the industrial leaders who are visiting Auschwitz for the purpose of setting up industrial affiliates for Krupp?

I have kept the spirit and meaning of it, for to cut that out would be to violate the author's intention. Auschwitz was also a great production center, operating twenty-four hours a day, and manufacturing, in addition to human corpses, and with the labor of these later victims, all sorts of goods. One of the great virtues of Hochhuth's play is its attempt to denounce *all* those who were in any way responsible: the Wehrmacht as well as the S.S.; the great industrialists—Buna, I. G. Farben, Krupp. I have gone beyond Hochhuth's text here and introduced an authentic document: Document NIK 10746, the statement of Alfred Krupp von Bohlen and Halbech read at the Nuremburg Trial.

And the dénouement?

Riccardo, the Jesuit, and Jacobson, the Jew, die together at the crematory. At this time, the two have exchanged clothing so that Jacobson is wearing the soutane, as he was at the end of the scene in Gerstein's apartment. Before this there is the moving confrontation with the Doctor, the "selector" at the camp. The Doctor's attempts are aimed solely at the destruction of Riccardo's faith, which, though shaken, is not shattered. He forces him to work at the crematories not so much because he is a sadist but because he wishes to extract a confession from the priest that, in the face of so much horror, belief is impossible.

Yes, that scene is excellent. Tell me about the actors.

I am unable to go into details, but here is a list: Alain Mottet (Pius XII), Antoine Bourseiller (Riccardo), Jean Michaud (Fontana Senior), Michel Piccoli (Gerstein), Pierre Tabard (Jacobson), Francois Darbon (the Cardinal), Roland Monot (Eichmann), Jean-Luc Bideau (Commander Fritsche). Some of the actors play two roles: Tabard will also be Salzar, an S.S. officer; Darbon, Professor Hirt; and Roland Monot, the Father General. I hope I haven't left out anyone. When the curtain goes up, all of the actors are sitting in a semicircle, and each steps forward as his turn to speak arrives. This is not just incidental; it has a meaning.

What of the costumes and sets?

They are by Peter Brook with the assistance of Adele Hunkey. Sets are simple and movable; costumes are merely suggested, except for those of church dignitaries. The Peter Brook production has been adapted by Francois Darbon, the director. /18/

Gabriel Marcel

THE DEPUTY *IN PARIS*

Mme. Jacqueline Piatier, in *Le Monde,* was perfectly correct in emphasizing the differences between Hochhuth's complete text and the play presented at the Athénée, differences which cannot be explained as being necessitated by cutting. The style itself has been changed.

How far has M. François Darbon followed the staging of Peter Brook? According to my sources, the play was presented realistically in both London and Berlin, and, certainly, in reading the play, one is overpowered by its realism. On the other hand, at the Athénée, a completely different effect is achieved, which is, in my opinion, the opposite of the author's intention.

Certainly, the emphasis Darbon gives his production is justifiable in itself. He wished to cut out everything that appealed directly to the emotions and senses. Instead, everything must be referred to the intellect and the conscience in such a way that each viewer is forced to question himself, to examine his own culpability, to admit his own sins and omissions in reference to the frightful tragedy depicted in the play.

Jorge Semprun, the adaptor and himself the recipient of a literary award, the Formentor Prize, for his book *Le Grand Voyage,* ably expresses the spirit he sought in these words, appearing in the program notes: "The crime we are concerned with here is a historical fact, and, as is usual in such cases, our social defense mechanisms have attempted to cope with it. A very simple mechanism — it consists of projecting all blame to others: the unbelievers to the Christians, the Protestants to the Catholics, the Catholics to the Pope, the defenders of Pacelli to the vicissitudes of history. But no, *we* are the guilty ones, all of us. In this trial, you are asked to be at one time witness, judge, and the accused."

This is an excellent intention, certainly true to that of the play itself. Yet, it would be interesting to question the audience after the play is over to find out how many actually felt themselves a part of the action, felt themselves on trial. Unhappily, I must state that I do not think many would answer in the affirmative. . . .

In general, the realistic elements have been cut out completely or greatly compressed. For example, the scene showing the Luccani family's plans to seek refuge suddenly interrupted by the Gestapo has been left out. Nonetheless, the frightful scene in which two Jewish Catholics are being questioned by the S.S. and one is forced to spit upon the other has been retained, though it stands out as a blemish.

From a review by Gabriel Marcel in *Nouvelles Litteraires,* December 26, 1963, p. 12. Trans. by the editors. Gabriel Marcel, French dramatist and philosopher, the founder of Christian existentialism, is one of the editors of *Nouvelles Litteraires.*

I am inclined to think that if the play had been presented differently, it would have been more effective, but I can understand, too, that it might have been more offensive. One almost has the sense that he is in the presence of an oratorio without music. Yet music on such a subject is conceivable; there is a music which is next to silence. I am thinking, for example, of certain portions of the dialogues of the Carmelites: that is the tone in which the play should have been written and the style in which it ought to be acted.

I was struck, also, the other evening by the fact that when Gerstein, that paradoxical figure, nonetheless a historical one, appeared in this production, he elicited absolutely no emotional response. Was that the fault of the actor, Michel Piccoli, who is generally quite good? I am not certain of that. More likely it is an error in the direction, for Gerstein is such a singular character he automatically becomes the center of interest. Since he could not be allowed much time in the shortened version, he should have been completely omitted. . . .

Generally, the impression is that the actors are paralyzed; is it through fear of these unaccustomed techniques? I don't think so. I believe the effect is the result of a conflict: the actors are torn between what the production demands and what the play itself dictates as being proper to it. I might, of course, be mistaken.

Yet despite all the faults, which I have made no attempt to ignore, the play is well worth seeing. The other evening the house was packed and the audience extremely attentive. There were no protests and no interruptions. In time, perhaps, the whole controversy will be viewed objectively and unemotionally, as it should be. /12/

John Simon

THE DEPUTY *AND ITS METAMORPHOSES*

When the gifted German novelist and playwright, Martin Walser, hailed *The Deputy* as "a legitimate offspring of the long overdue marriage of Sartre and Brecht," he was only half right. Though *The Deputy* owes much to Sartre's skill in casting political and philosophical polemics in highly stageworthy molds, it has nothing of Brecht's alienation and epic theatre or even didactic satire. Erwin Piscator, who gave the play its first production (in Berlin), was nearer the mark when he called it "a historic drama in the Schillerian sense."

It is certainly true that Hochhuth has all the moral fervor of Schiller, the disciple of Kant, and that the ethical criterion of the play is a categorical imperative that will have no truck with relativist notions of comparative good or comparative evil. However, Schiller's use of the historic in drama is not Hochhuth's. Most patently in *The Maid of Orléans,* but also elsewhere, Schiller was willing to alter historical facts radically to suit his purposes, whereas Hochhuth is at great pains to include all possible historical data and limit his invention to the interstices — sometimes to the detriment of his play.

Actually, among Hochhuth's artistic forebears, two other great German historical dramatists figure more prominently: Kleist and Hebbel. It is Kleist's Romantic passion that largely informs *The Deputy;* its idealistic young Jesuit hero owes something to the Prince of Homburg and even to Michael Kohlhaas, figures whose noble passion makes them politically or socially culpable, but who are more troubled and complex than, say, the hero of Schiller's *The Robbers*. And it is Hebbel's notion of historical drama, based on Hegel rather than Kant, in which protagonists become symbols of their society, their age and the workings of history, that importantly affects Hochhuth's dramaturgy.

This inevitably leads to the question of the role of historicity in historical drama. Does *Richard III* fail as a play because it is unfair to Richard? Does the fact that Anouilh makes his Norman hero into a collaborating Saxon invalidate *Becket*? Does Shaw's cramming *Saint Joan* full of twentieth-century hindsight and Shavian philosophy disqualify it as a historical play? Clearly historic drama can emphasize either half of its name: it can make history subserve the ideas and effects of drama, or use the drama as a vehicle for momentous historical truths. Though either approach is valid, the former is more likely to produce a work of art, the latter a tract in dramatic form. But the importance of the literate tract in the theatre should not be too readily dismissed, whether it is called *The Cradle Will Rock* or *The Exception and the Rule*.

It is equally clear that a major stumbling block is the question of contemporaneity. It is all right to be fiercely critical or freely inventive, or both, where a figure of the distant past is concerned—where our own world and memories are not incriminated and the plea of insufficient evidence can be advanced. Thus *Becket* may grossly caricature a twelfth-century pope and elicit no more than the arching of an isolated eyebrow, whereas *The Deputy* may make a twentieth-century pope less unsympathetic than its author personally considers him and yet provoke outcries of "Caricature!" from critics all over, regardless of race, creed or competence.

Let us consider the main artistic charges (as opposed to political ones) that have been leveled against Hochhuth's Pius XII. We are told that this Pius is not a worthy antagonist for the idealistic hero—in other words, the "caricature" argument in more sophisticated form; and that *The Deputy*, asserting as it does its historical authenticity, has no business imputing motives of a damaging yet unprovable sort to the Pope. Now if you believe in a categorical imperative to do right, as Hochhuth does, Pius can no longer be an equally convincing defender of an antithetical position as Kleist's Elector or Antony in *Julius Caesar* can be. Absolute morality compels a pope to speak up in behalf of six million human beings, dead, dying, or yet to die—even if the consequences, to himself and all Catholics, were more manifestly dangerous than they may have appeared to be. By keeping the Pope as close to absolute silence as dramatically feasible, Hochhuth is actually lending the greatest possible dignity to a position he considers untenable. What makes Shakespeare's Iago a greater figure than Verdi's and Boito's is that, despite minor and inconclusive clues, he remains silent on his ultimate motivation.

Now for that motivation. Hochhuth has indeed put forward all conceivable reasons for the Pope's silence: the safety of Catholics, business and financial considerations, ecclesiastical politics (danger of schism), European politics (Hitler as bulwark against Stalin and communism), a kind of aristocratic hauteur and lack of human warmth, failure of nerve. Hochhuth does not insist on the equal relevance of all—indeed, he allows directors, actors, audiences and readers to consider some of them as irrelevant. If, however, it is objected that the particular juxtapositions are misleading, I reply that the need for compression makes them inevitable. And if it is maintained that there is still too much invention involved, I answer with the words of Lessing from the *Hamburgische Dramaturgie:* "Whoever reasons correctly also invents, and whoever would invent must also be able to reason. Only those believe in the separability of one from the other who are by disposition incapable of either."

Here we come to the crux of the matter. If Hochhuth had written a play about Pius XII and only about him, it is entirely probable that the play would have been, by accepted standards, more dense although not necessarily more substantial: much polemical material that is relegated to the "Historical Side-lights" of the play's appendix could have been set forth in greater detail in the play itself. Hochhuth, however — and here lies what is both the glory and the foredoom of his undertaking — is after something bigger: a historical fresco of the entire complex of events that begat and tolerated Auschwitz. No matter how important the Pope may be to the play, other elements are of equal impor- /270/ tance: the Germans, the Nazi Party, big business and science gone mad, the Catholic Church, other churches, individuals everywhere, and the metaphysics of evil as embodied in the play's one predominantly mythical character, the Doctor. What ultimately drags the play down to some extent is the very opposite of insufficient historical data: the excess of usable, and used, documentation.

We should note, then, that the Catholic Church, for example, is seen in the play not only as the Pope, but also as the Apostolic Nuncio to Berlin (who is a historic figure), the Cardinal (who, I suspect, also has a historic basis), the Ab-bot, three quite different monks, an important lay adviser to the Holy See, and, above all, the young Jesuit, Riccardo Fontana, who stands for not only the two priests to whom the play is dedicated, but also, in Hochhuth's words, "for those priests, mostly nameless, who instantly set love for their neighbor above all utilitarian considerations — ultimately at the price of their lives." It is thus that the entire spectrum of clerical reaction to the plight of the Jews is represented.

So the deputy — or vicar, or representative — of the title is not the Pope, who shirks his duty, but Riccardo, who takes on the Pope's burden and dies for it. Riccardo is a profoundly religious figure, and it is largely because of him that the play can justly call itself "a Christian tragedy." Indeed, it is the only major religious play written since the last war that I know of, and it is perhaps a fit-ting piece of worldly irony which would brand this one, of all plays, as irreli-gious. What makes Riccardo into a Christian tragic hero is not only the fact that he assumes the guilt of his Church and unsolicitedly becomes the vicar's vicar. It is the fact, too, that Riccardo's magnanimous desperation forces him toward two of the gravest sins a priest can commit: insubordination to his spiritual superiors, climaxing in the contemplated political assassination of the Pope; and an attempt to murder the villainous Doctor of Auschwitz. But something prevents him from committing either of these — perhaps salu-tary — sins: is it Providence in its wisdom, or just the weakness of the spiritual arm of this world? In his final despair, Riccardo is forced into something graver yet: doubting the very decency of God. (None of this, by the way, re-mains in the preposterous Broadway version, to list all of whose omissions would require another historical appendix.)

Riccardo's counterpart is Gerstein, who represents the secular hero and the lay sacrifice: the man of moral action who must, in a time of assassins, be-smirch himself by ostensibly joining with evil in order to undermine it, and who, presumably, dies a death which is as anonymous as, but less expiatory than, the priest's. As opposed to these two, there are the two poles of culpa-bility: the scientist whose evil knows no bounds, and the Pontiff whose good-ness, unfortunately, does; or, to put it more abstractly, the sado-satanist doctor whom metaphysical silence drives to unconscionable crimes, and the high-minded trimmer whom unconscionable crimes leave physically silent.

Alfred Kazin has criticized Hochhuth's characterization of the Doctor for not having the horribly vulgar reality of Josef Mengele, the bestial doctor of Auschwitz. And this is, precisely, Hochhuth's problem. There is so much fact in his play that whenever he transcends it into fiction, into art, he seems fated to be immediately pounced upon by one group of partisans or another. Thus Kazin ignores the fact that there are several other characters in the play who quite sufficently body forth the "sadistic clown and frivolous maniac" one might miss in the Doctor.

But if *The Deputy* is too multifariously ambitious to be a complete success, it does not flinch from attempting to pursue a theme into most of its terrible ramifications. In fact, the construction of the play is by no means unskillful in the way it manipulates characters through various scenes — dropping them and picking them up again — toward a final, perhaps somewhat disappointing, showdown. The suspense leading up to the Pope scene is ably handled, and there is also an effective contrapuntal construction: scenes involving individuals alternate with scenes involving larger groups or their typical representatives. (Nothing of this, either, on Broadway.)

Where the play really fails — aside from a certain weakness in some of the characters, partly a consequence of their numerousness — is in its language. Though it is written in free verse, and not at all in blank verse as Susan Sontag asserted in *Book Week,* this free verse makes very little sense in its line breaks, and its rhythms are far from compelling. In truth, it might as well be written out as prose, though even as prose it would be no more than adequate. The one exception is the trio of monologues by representative victims in a freight car on the way to Auschwitz, where the style becomes more unabashedly poetic — not, however, with unqualified success.

What is much less successful, though, is the English translation of the complete text by Richard and Clara Winston. That they were unable to cope with the profusion of juicy dialects enlivening the language and making it ecumenical is understandable and forgivable, although their haphazard attempts at dealing with it are less pardonable. Thus they will Americanize a Nazi doctor who now experiments on "critters," or Eichmann, who now recalls the first "date" he ever undressed, and will turn an ironic reference to the Gestapo from "your friend in need" to "mother's little helper." They can likewise be unidiomatic or overliterate, as when a bowler is told "Take your stance!" or when an importunate visitor is urged by a Bavarian monk "Now please, take yourself off," or when "stir-craziness" emerges as "cabin-fever" and "easier said than done" as "easy to say, but hard to do."

The unfortunate truth is that the translation abounds in errors of taste and judgment, and, every once in a while, even misunderstands the text. Here are a few examples taken from one passage alone. The Winstons, in their prolixity, will turn Gerstein's simple statement, "The souls of the bystanders are also at stake" into a wordy bit of Sunday Christianity: "Those who keep silent are accessories to murder/ and they imperil their immortal souls" (p. 80). They will miss a piece of *humour noir* (p. 79), "people cremated on the family plan," by translating "whole families pushed into the ovens." They reveal ignorance when they refer to "St. Loyola" (p. 76), which is rather like saying "Sir Churchill." When Riccardo (p. 84) uses the conversational *now,* "now don't you go giving up God as well," the Winstons translate it as temporal: "you don't want/ to give up God as well, not now," as if the young priest might condone giving up God later. More serious is the mistranslation of Gerstein's pregnant words (p. 90), "Both of us will not survive this war" (i.e., either Nazi Germany or Western civilization must perish) as "Neither of us/ is going to survive this war."

Some of the worst excesses of the Winstons occur when, for no good rea-/271/ son, they persist in veering toward blank verse: "If you insist on it, you'll die here/ like a snail crushed under an *auto* tire—/ die as the heroes of today *do* die, *namelessly,*/ snuffed out by powers they have never known,/ let alone can fight. In other words, *meaninglessly.*"/ (Italics mine.) But they are fully capable of still more mysterious lapses. Thus when the Pope makes the important statement that he leaves protest against the Nazis to the *Oberhirten* ("chief shepherds," i.e., the episcopate of the respective countries), the Winstons translate, "We leave it to the local parish priest." Again, when the Doctor jeers at a young Jewess who has managed to survive "our recent Feast of Tabernacles, the great autumn wine pressing" (i.e., bloodletting), we read "the Feast of Tabernacles, our harvest-home," which is meaningless. And when Riccardo exclaims, in abhorrence of the Doctor, "What sort of . . . of a devil are you?" we get "What a devil you are!"—straight out of Edwardian farce.

But at least the Winstons try, however clubfootedly, to keep up with the text and respect its integrity. No such thing can be said for the Herman Shumlin-Jerome Rothenberg adaptation we are treated to on Broadway. These two men have cut out, completely or in large part, any scenes of or references to utter horror, Jewish collaboration, Protestant indifference, Catholic inadequacy other than the Pope's. Thus no mention of Himmler's modeling the SS on the Society of Jesus, Cardinal Spellman and Catholic power in the United States, the Holy See acting as bankers for the Italian royal house while also doing business with Mussolini, the Pope's concern with liquidating the Church's Hungarian assets before the Russians march in, the callousness of the German bishops and their active support of the Nazis, and God knows what else. Almost anything beyond a decorous suggestion of Jewish suffering and Papal insufficiency, anything that might really draw blood or tears, is cut. Similarly, finer discussions of philosophy, theology, politics, history, literature—or even just passages where the style is a little more complex and poetic—are all ruthlessly cut.

Inserted, on the other hand, are— . . . besides two scenes which are complete travesties of the original (I, 2; II, 1)—[distorted versions of the textual presentation of speech and character] (I call special attention to Rothenberg's inept translation of German poetry, to say nothing of his own verse). Thus, for example, the Jew Jacobson, an ordinary middle-class person, a teacher perhaps, is turned here into a violent proletarian type continually complaining about his fleas: "They're killing me, the bastards. Look, my navel is raw from them!" and about "pee stains on my underwear . . . what a mess!" The Doctor is reduced to a *Playboy* magazine fan, "You spread their legs apart and read a textbook: hot confessions in the curls of hair," which does not even make sense. Poor Gerstein is obliged to chant incessant litanies—Rothenberg evidently considers the refrain a highly poetic device—and keeps repeating in two separate scenes, "My name is Gerstein!" and "No matter!"

Here are further examples of Rothenbergian poesy: "By the hair and teeth of God! By the plundered hair and teeth of God!" or "Take the star, priest. The light is in the star. The pain is in the star," chanted antiphonally into Riccardo's ears by Jacobson and Gerstein. This at least might stand as a parody of Christopher Fry; but what of "I supplicate, I beg, I grovel, I beseech, I whimper, I demand!" which can only be taken as a parody of Roget's *Thesaurus*. Again, when a young Italian girl is questioned by a Nazi about her fiancé, the text has her reveal that he died fighting in Africa. Here, however, he is made merely a prisoner of war, so that Rothenberg can let the girl scream: "He's blonder than you are! His hair is blond all over his body. It shines in the light." And so it goes. *The Deputy* on Broadway is like one of those comic-strip versions of a literary classic ("My name is Julien Sorel. I just got here!" framed in a balloon above a head) and as the characters bestride the stage you can virtually see the balloons coming out of their mouths.

What makes *The Deputy*, as Hochhuth has written it, important, however, is not so much the political revelation it may have made. Nor technical devices such as having the same actors enact several contradictory parts, to convey that in our age it is merely a matter of "military conscription . . . whether one stands on the side of the victims or the executioners." Nor the elaborate stage directions which bitterly project certain characters into the future, describing, for example, such and such a Nazi as a solid citizen of postwar Germany. What *is* momentous is that in an age which has progressively convinced itself that its significant dramatic form is dark comedy, that, to quote Dürrenmatt, "our world has led to the Grotesque as to the atom bomb, just as the apocalyptic pictures of Hieronymus Bosch are grotesque, too"—that in this era when "the death of tragedy" has become a literary commonplace, *The Deputy* stands as a valid tragedy: not great, but good, and anything but commonplace. /272/

Herman Shumlin

ON ADAPTING THE DEPUTY TO THE STAGE

As you know, the original full play, translated, was published by Grove Press. Whether or not there will be a separate publication of the playing version now being presented at the Brooks Atkinson Theatre I cannot say at this time. I hope that, sooner or later, it will be published but the decision must be made by Grove Press. The basic version as presented here was made by myself and the author, Rolf Hochhuth, translated from the German and then re-adapted by myself and Jerome Rothenberg. The length of the original play of course prohibited its production. Wherever it has been presented it has been presented in a much shortened version and I would doubt that any two have been the same. It has been, more or less, a "director's choice," but as I said before, the basic adaptation from the original for the New York production was made by the author and myself. In editing a play which demanded so much cutting the primary necessity was not to sacrifice any element important to the progress of the play or information important to convey to the audience. In any scene which was eliminated certain elements needed to be retained; since this retention had to appear in other scenes than the particular scene in which they originally appeared, obviously they had to be redramatized since they would have to be used under entirely different conditions.

From a letter written to the editors, July 10, 1964.

Topics for Discussion

1. Mizener defines a great literary work as one that causes us to "recognize ourselves in its worst inhabitants and of its best we feel that there, but for the grace of God and our own insufficiency, go we." Ward defines a great tragedy as one that makes it easier for a man to bear his own misfortunes. (a) Are either of these effects conducive to social or political action? Are they proper to political or polemic theater? (b) Does *The Deputy* fit either of these definitions?

2. Zimmermann, in his essay classifying *The Deputy* as a polemic, claims that "One cannot . . . expect Hochhuth's play to be a tragedy. . . . if Ricardo were a tragic figure, Pius XII would be too." Yet the playwright has referred to his work as a "Christian tragedy." Though he denies that Pius XII is a tragic figure, Hochhuth states: "The tragic figures in my play are the two Fontanas, and the Jews themselves, in other words, the victims; *not* the man whose silence indirectly helped the murderers." Simon, in his review, refers to the work as both a "literate tract" and a "valid tragedy." (a) Discuss the different concepts of tragedy inherent in the three statements. (b) Which of the three men uses the term in the Aristotlean sense defined by Ward?

3. Consider Bryden's description of the London production of *The Deputy*. (a) How does the production reflect the ideas and techniques of Piscator's political theater? (b) Do you agree with Bryden that this treatment violates the author's intentions? (c) Does the treatment accord with Zimmerman's concept of the playwright's intentions?

4. Discuss Hochhuth in relation to the general literary picture in Germany today. (a) To what extent is he typical of his generation? (b) To what extent is his work personal and unique?

5. Zimmerman considers the language of Hochhuth's play in some detail; John Simon dismisses it in a single paragraph, even though he judges its language to be the major failure, the chief weakness, of the play. (a) Does Simon's review make clear what his objections to the language of *The Deputy* are? What particular problems of language the playwright faced? (b) Does he specify what his qualifications regarding the poetic quality of the monologues in Act Five might be? (c) Do you consider Simon a responsible critic? Why, or why not?

6. Compare Bryden's evaluation of the British adaptation, Marcel's evaluation of the Parisian adaptation, and Simon's evaluation of the Broadway adaptation of *The Deputy*. (a) Describe each reviewer's tone and technique. (b) Which review is most constructive? Most convincing? Why?

7. Shortly after the opening of the London production of *The Deputy*, Hochhuth was asked whether he had any objections to the adaptation. The author answered that he had no right to object to cuts being made in a text that would take up to eight hours to read and that he was to blame for having written an unperformable play. The parts of the "unperformable" play that have been performed have varied from country to country. (a) Act One, Scene Two, the Nazi officers at Falkensee, was omitted by Piscator but retained by Semprun. Would you keep the scene or cut it out? Why? (b) Compare Semprun's statements on his efforts to prepare a playable version of *The Deputy* to the author's own statements of his intentions. Do you think Semprun attempted to respect Hochhuth's intentions? (c) Does Hochhuth's approval of a variety of separate acting ver-

sions, most of which have been attacked by critics as being violations of the author's text, strengthen or weaken Zimmermann's opinion of the character of the work? Is there any significance in the fact that the scene in which Pius XII appears has been included in every version?

8. Mizener says that in "all mediocre fiction which deals with serious moral issues, the actor and the reader are Christ harrowing a hell full of all the people who disagree with them." (a) Do you feel that, using this standard, Mizener would classify *The Deputy* as mediocre fiction? Why, or why not? (b) Ward says that "The less experienced a playwright, the more readily will he . . . rush at his subject, more especially if it seems to him to possess *prima facie* dramatic capabilities; and the consequence will be that which usually attends upon a precipitate act." Do you feel that this statement applies in Hochhuth's case? Why, or why not?

9. Ward states that the most important law of drama is that a dramatic action should possess *unity*. (a) Does Hochhuth's play, in its complete text, possess unity? (b) Do the subsidiary actions — Helga's story, the Krupp financial discussions, for example — "contribute to the main action"?

10. Zimmermann urges that we refrain from using old standards to judge new forms and try, instead, "to understand the play and the spirit which it is trying to express in its own terms." Ward, on the other hand, feels that regardless of the age or culture in which a drama originates, it may be judged by a set of standards universally applicable. (a) With which of these views do you agree? Why? (b) Is it possible to apply Ward's rules to Hochhuth's play? Demonstrate.

Theme Topics

Modern Tragedy: An Attempt at Definition
James Baldwin's *Blues for Mr. Charlie* and the Polemic Tradition
Brecht's *Saint Joan of the Stockyards* and Hochhuth's *The Deputy:* A Comparison
How I Would Adapt *The Deputy* for the Stage
Intentions and Achievements: Where Hochhuth Fails and Why
The Responsibilities of a Critic
The Main Function of Theater Today
Messages, Morality, and Art: Some Relationships

Part III
FACT OR FANTASY
The Historical Dimension

Fritz Stern

THE POLITICAL
CONSEQUENCES OF THE UNPOLITICAL GERMAN

Why the German people,
the nation of Goethe, Mozart, Menzel—

The Deputy, *Act One, Scene Three*

For many decades, the course of German politics has puzzled and, at times, terrified the nations of the Western world. How could the Germans, a people of such intellectual eminence and moral intent, endure the blundering authoritarianism of the Empire, the divisiveness of Weimar, the tyranny of Hitler? Why was Germany without a stable political tradition, why had it failed to adopt successfully the political institutions that had become the norms of Western political culture? A frequent answer was that there were two Germanies, the Germany of the educated citizenry, peaceful and potentially democratic, and the official, aggressive Germany, governed by a handful of men. The classic expression of this faith in the other Germany was Wilson's refusal, in October 1918, to deal with the Kaiser's government; he would deal with a democratic Germany or none at all. This idea of the two Germanies—the majority held captive by a small minority—dominated Western historical thinking as well. It encouraged historians to hunt /104/ up villains, to fasten on specific groups or minority interests that may have inhibited Germany's natural bent toward the West.

This view presupposed a far sharper division within Germany than in fact existed; it overlooked the many ways in which the German elite had accommodated itself to its political nonage and had benefited from it. Before 1918 and after 1933, the German *Bürger* did not feel thwarted or enchained; they thought themselves free. Their acquiescence in different political regimes suggests that there was but one Germany, in which the different forces were inextricably mingled. To gain the proper perspective on this Germany the historian must examine German society not at points of obvious divergence or

From "The Political Consequences of the Unpolitical German," *History*, No. 13, September, 1960, pp. 104–134. Fritz Stern is Associate Professor of History at Columbia University.

extremity—such as Nazi Germany—but in periods of apparent normality and quietude. Nor should he concentrate exclusively on some tenacious groups—such as the German army or the much-maligned Junkers. It is not the "bad Germans" that are unique—every Western nation has had its reactionary die-hards, its racists and hypernationalists, its imperialists and fascists—but the "good Germans," the several generations of peaceful and splendidly educated, seemingly Western men. It is to them, to their worship of culture and their depreciation of politics, to their sentiments and ideals, that I shall want to turn.

For a century or more the German term *"Kultur"* had a reverential conno-tation that the simple English word "culture" cannot render. It was invested with the awe and reverence that Germans felt, or thought they should feel, for the diverse creations of the spirit, for the mystery of the arts that to so many possessed a voice as tender and as powerful as religion itself. This ide-alization of culture inspired and guided the great intellectual and scientific achievements of modern Germany; German learning had a great influence on the life of other peoples—as American universities so clearly exemplify. But the ideal of culture, once embodied in institutions, became more and more a passive appreciation of past creativity, and in time it /106/ degenerated into little more than the ritualistic repetition of phrases and pieties. Far more im-portant than the decline was the impact that this veneration of culture had on German society, on politics, religion, and on what may be called the national self-image. As I will try to show, it fostered several political prejudices and positions, none favorable to the development of a democratic society or even to the growth of a cohesive nation. It hastened the rapid and peculiar secular-ization of Protestant Germany and served as a rationalization for a good deal of political and social irresponsibility and iniquity. There is pathos in the fact that the Germans used their greatest achievement, their culture, to augment and excuse their greatest failure, their politics.

The exaltation of culture, the veneration and perfection of learning, had its origins in German Idealism, that extraordinary outburst of artistic and intel-lectual creativity from 1770 to 1830. Diverse, even antithetical, though the several strands of German Idealism were—*Sturm und Drang,* classicism, ro-manticism, and idealistic philosophy proper—together they formed the intel-lectual basis of modern German society. Germany's cultural awakening coin-cided with the democratic revolution of the Western world; the Revolution overwhelmed Germany in its most inexorable and ruthless guise, in Napo-leon, and it is no wonder that German Idealism, which had earlier been in such close dependence on the West, in time absorbed a sharp anti-Western and anti-French strain. It has been said that Idealism was Germany's equiva-lent of the French Revolution, and in some ways at least, Idealism did become a substitute for and a defense against the Revolution. German nationalism, inflamed by Napoleon's triumphs, turned against the political ideals and achievements of the French Revolution. What was exalted by German nation-alism was the cultural achievement and destiny of the Germans, their peculiar gifts for poetry, truth, and music. Consequently German nationalism was less concerned with the political destiny of the Germans, with their practical rights and liberties as citizens. /107/

. . . The German *Burger,* however superbly educated, did not grapple with the precise ideas of Kant or Hegel or even Goethe, but some of the ideas, condensed into a few pat phrases, did mold and perpetuate a vague, elusive, but important *Lebensgefühl,* a cultural stance, a style of life. It is with the polit-ical consequences of these elusive attitudes, with the intellectual or aesthetic presuppositions of politics rarely articulated because so habitual and common, that I want to deal.

Historians have seldom studied this layer of German culture, partly, no doubt, because they took at face value the historical cliché that the German *Bürger* was unpolitical, hence, for the political historian, an object of pity, not of study. Yet the allegedly unpolitical stance of a highly influential class with strong cultural prejudices deserves the closest scrutiny; in it one may find an obstinate condition of Germany's political failure. The self-consciously unpolitical strain in German life has had a profound, and on the whole, an injurious impact on German politics.

It was not accidental that Prussia began its intense institutional concern with culture—the establishment of new universities and the improvement of old ones—at the time of its unprecedented humiliation at the hands of Napoleon. "The State," said Frederick William III, "must replace by spiritual forces what it lost in material strength." Here was the characteristic confusion of spirit and power, and the inchoate assumption that culture could substitute for power. From then on the moral indispensability of education became an article of faith: the self-fulfillment of the individual required the humanistic cultivation of the mind. Under Wilhelm von Humboldt, the Prussian school system was reformed, the ideal of a general education—*allgemeine Bildung*—was embodied, perhaps imprisoned, in those bastions of learning, the German *gymnasia*. /108/

This educational system, with its recruitment and rewards, its gradations and pretensions, was of singular importance in a society that was still far from open, in a society where Guizot's *"enrichissez-vous"* would have been a senseless admonition. Intellectually, the schools sought to prepare the universal man, but not the public-minded citizen; here students gathered their knowledge of the classics, of Christianity, of the Enlightenment, and of Idealism—knowledge often mechanically acquired, but all precious and all conspicuously displayed.[1] The earnest belief in the indispensability of this kind of intellectual and aesthetic education was given practical value as well: the rewards of higher education were enormous and in an economically backward society they continued to be the most important means of climbing the social ladder. An academic degree was a prerequisite for most positions of status and prestige, and in the early nineteenth century the academician or civil servant of humble origin was by no means exceptional. Higher education, moreover, granted the student partial exemption from military service—no mean incentive to culture.

This exaltation of culture had a still more penetrating effect on German society: for the educated classes, especially in Protestant Germany, it brought about the gradual secularization of religion through culture, the substitution in a sense of one for the other. This process, obviously so comprehensive and complex that I can do no more than hint at it, involved the approximation of religion, more accurately of Protestantism, to culture and metaphysics, by stripping religion of the supernatural and the mysterious, of sin and redemption, reducing it to an ethical essence, to a universal core that was immune to higher biblical criticism. It involved as well the elevation of the aesthetic and intellectual aspects of culture, of philosophy, literature, /109/ and art, to be

---

1. The austere intellectualism of the schools and the authoritarianism of the teachers, the remoteness from the workaday world, the absence of sports, helped to mold the typical scholar of the nineteenth century; but at times these also led to sudden outbreaks of youthful irrationalism and anti-intellectualism, of which the Youth Movement before 1914 was the most famous example. /109/

the supreme revelations of the human spirit, and the substitution of the moral commands of German Idealism, of Kant in particular, for older universal and religious commands. The *reductio ad absurdum* of this culture-worship must surely have been the proposal of one German historian that the works of Goethe should be added to the other books of Divine Revelation.

With this veneration of culture there emerged another ideal, a universally accepted tenet of Idealism that persisted as the talisman of the educated classes: the belief in the perfectibility of the aesthetic or rational faculties of the individual, quite independently of political conditions. The inner freedom that Luther preached became secularized, but the state itself, while it must not actively inhibit the pursuit of knowledge, could do little to infringe on the highest good, the unfolding of the personality. To be sure, there were important variations of this belief: the Kantians had a very different sense of the individual's self-fulfillment from the Romantics or from those who cherished Goethe's and Schiller's image of the *Genie*—of the daemonic, asocial genius who in a different guise appears in Hegel's irresistible world-historical figure. This admiration of the self-fulfillment of the individual, in the strictly private sphere, through learning but without good works, proved yet another link between Protestantism and German Idealism. It was in Schleiermacher that the two strains most clearly mingled, and after him this essentially humanistic belief was wrapped in a religious mystique as well. The cultured man, by and large, ceased to be a church man, and his so-called religion of Idealism contributed, as the great Catholic historian Franz Schnabel points out, to the utter secularization of the academically trained classes in Protestant Germany.[2]

This type of individualism had nothing egalitarian about it; here was not the Christian belief in the equality of souls /111/ and sinners nor the beneficial abstraction about a natural man who was created equal "and endowed with inalienable rights to life, liberty, and the pursuit of happiness." This individualism had a distinct aesthetic-aristocratic bent and could, indeed quickly did, degenerate into a cult of the personality. Only the exceptional individual, the great personality, could attain the self-fulfillment, the self-mastery that Idealism prescribed.

This veneration of culture and personality, which became one of the principal pieties of nineteenth-century Germany, was neither exclusively German or in itself culpable. The man of culture has often disdained the grubbiness of politics, has usually been remote from the lower classes. But a difference persisted, a difference well brought out in Matthew Arnold's *Culture and Anarchy*, a book which one would expect to be closely akin to the German ideal. "Culture has one great passion, the passion for sweetness and light. It has one even yet greater! The passion for making them prevail . . . and it knows that the sweetness and light of the few must be imperfect until the raw and unkindled masses of humanity are touched with sweetness and light." The German academically trained person lacked the passion to make it prevail.[3] He often

2. It is significant that in the nineteenth century the formally Protestant groups played the pre-eminent role in German intellectual life, even as the Protestant Church steadily declined. Catholicism, on the other hand, had less impact on intellectual life, and suffered less from the loss of faith in the last century. /111/

3. In 1867, young William James met and reported on this strange, admirable being, the German professor. (It was Wilhelm Dilthey whom he so described, a man far less remote from reality than most of his colleagues.) "He is the first man I have ever met of a class, which must be common here, of men to whom learning has become as natural as breathing. A learned man at home is in a measure isolated; his study is carried on in private, at reserved hours. To the public he appears as a citizen and neighbor, etc., and they know at most *about* him that he is addicted to this or that study; his intellectual occupation always has something of a put-on character, and remains external at least to

felt that the passive enjoyment of culture sufficed, that culture could be tended in almost any society and, finally, that almost any /112/ regime or social injustice could be rationalized or glorified, by reference to German culture. It
was not only that spirit and politics were divorced, as the Germans have always maintained, half proudly and half regretfully; it is that spirit often became a cloak for the politics of callousness and irresponsibility.[4] . . . /114/

It was in the decisive decades between the failure of 1848 and the national
successes of Bismarck that the political implications of unpolitical Idealism
emerged more clearly. For it was in those decades of quickened political life
that several strains of German liberalism capitulated before Bismarck and his
national goals, in effect abandoned, or indefinitely postponed, the demands
for political self-government. But it was the way in which they renounced
their ideals that indicates the critical importance of the Idea of Culture.
When, in 1864, the German liberals lost heart in their own course, which for
once had massive popular strength behind it, they neither accepted nor rejected Bismarck's practical dictum, that blood and iron must decide the great
questions of the day; they were not content to say that this was a necessary sacrifice for the fulfillment of higher national goals. Rather, they repudiated
politics altogether, and asserted that politics—as the then novel term "*Realpolitik*" implied—was necessarily divorced from the realm of ideals and morals,
that spirit and power were distinct, though not necessarily antithetical.

Hermann Baumgarten, a liberal historian and Max Weber's uncle, became
the leading apologist of this retreat from politics: "The *Bürger* is meant to
work, not to rule, and a statesman's primary task is to rule." Referring specifi-
/115/ cally to the *Bürger's* heritage of Idealism, he concluded that in one sense
he was too good for politics and in another not good enough. What better example of this than the immediate past: "We have had the unprecedented experience that our victory would have been a disaster while our defeat has
been an immense blessing." Bismarck had to be accepted, for he was the
master of the practical realm, and in that acceptance emerged fullblown the
unpo- /116/ litical German, the good German who would tolerate and ac-
quiesce in political imperfection, even turpitude, as long as his escape into
Idealism was not blocked by the public authority of the state. They were willing to render unto Caesar what was Caesar's and unto Culture what was Culture's.

But some liberals were not content with the retreat from politics, this escape
to Idealism. Treitschke, for example, took quite a different position; far from
retreating to culture, he provided Bismarck's *Realpolitik* with a spiritual justi-

some part of his being. Whereas this cuss seemed to me to be nothing if not a professor . . . as if
he were able to stand towards the rest of society *merely* in the relation of a man learned in this or that
branch—and never for a moment forget the interests or put off the instincts of his specialty. If he
should meet people or circumstances that could in no measure be dealt with on that ground, he
would pass on and ignore them, instead of being obliged, like an American, to sink for the time the
specialty." (*The Letters of William James*, Vol. I, pp. 110–11.) /112/
4. It is noteworthy that Germans have traditionally exalted those self-images that attested their
nonpolitical, or individualistic, nature. The much-revered image of Tacitus' primitive German, that
self-reliant, robust, and incorruptible barbarian, fighting against the decadent and overcivilized Ro-
mans, hardly fostered the political virtues. In the sixteenth century the legend of the German *Michel*
or of the *Dummer Michel*, the clumsy, charitable boor, sprang up, and by the nineteenth century the
stupid *Michel* was widely and fondly caricatured as the typical German "with his excessive benevolence and political immaturity." Again, the revival of the Siegfried myth: the unsuspecting, naive
hero cut down by the scheming villainous Hagen. The Germans have ever doubted their political
capacities, and their outstanding rulers, from Frederick II to Hitler, and perhaps beyond, have rarely
troubled to disguise their contempt for their people's political sense. The German pantheon, re-
splendent with poets, thinkers, and warriors, contains few, if any, statesmen—a consequence of Germany's political history. /114/

fication, a moral veneer. The decline of Protestantism and the exaltation of culture had gone hand in hand; Treitschke, born into an austere Protestant family, gradually embraced the religion of Idealism, and invested Bismarck's new state with the same passion and absolute moral righteousness that previously had belonged to religion.[5] What Treitschke did rhapsodically, thousands of Germans, organized in the National Liberal Party, did prosaically: they idealized, in Max Weber's phrase, they ethicized, Bismarck's achievement of power. Some eighty years later, Friedrich Meinecke said of the liberal transformation of this period: "Specifically German . . . was the tendency to elevate something primarily practical into a universal world-view theory."

The new Empire was intensely practical. The quaint and quiet nation of poets and thinkers survived only in the nostalgia of the educated classes. After 1871, the material conditions of Germany, though not her politics nor her spirit, rapidly approximated those of the West. For centuries politically divided, Germany was now a nation state, as were her western neighbors; for centuries economically backward, Germany, in her first economic miracle, bounded ahead, surpassed France, challenged Britain, and became the leading industrial nation of the continent; for centuries a weak state, she now became a great military power, a power that by its existence in the heart of Europe posed a threat to Europe. How prophetic was the British M.P. /117/ who, after the battle of Sedan, said: "Europe has lost a mistress and gained a master." But the master's house was divided against itself. Bismarck's semi-absolutistic regime, with its democratic appearances and feudal reality, postponed and embittered the conflict between the aspirations of the democratic forces and the privileges of the nobility and its newly won allies, the captains of industry. Bismarck's political system intensified the class antagonisms, and the newly united nation became socially more divided.

The response of the academic classes to the new Germany was diverse. We have already noted the devastating impact of Bismarck's success on many liberals; no wonder Mommsen charged that Bismarck had broken the moral backbone of the nation and Nietzsche thundered that military victory must not be confused with cultural vitality. After 1871, a small part of the academic class remained critical of imperial Germany even in the face of success and still hoped that Germany would adopt the political institutions of the West. A larger group retired to what came to be called the unpolitical realm, reconciled to their political impotence. A still larger group idealized the existing Germany and its imperialist ambitions and avowed that German culture, superior to that of the West, justified German power as well. Underlying all three positions, blunting the drive of the first and intensifying the jingoism of the last, was the cultured person's fear of the rapidly growing proletariat and his suspicion that culture and democracy, if not incompatible, were certainly opposed to each other. Without surrendering his unpolitical pretensions, the cultured German could, for the sake of his culture, support every conservative measure and oppose every radical move. *Bildung* became as much a conservative bulwark as *Besitz,* and both began to accept the refeudalization of German society. Years later, Friedrich Meinecke, himself an outstanding representative of the intellectual splendor and political fatality of German Idealism, summed up with unmistakable sympathy this fear of the good but unpolitical German: /118/

5. For Treitschke the state was "the most supremely real person, in the literal sense of the word, that exists." For a worshipper of personality, this Hegelian identification meant a still higher aesthetic value for the state. /117/

About the middle of the nineteenth century and later it was the high aim of German culture to preserve from this pressure [by the masses] and from its coarsening and deteriorating effect the sacred heritage of the Goethe period—an almost miraculous gift bestowed upon the German people—and at the same time to support what seemed vital and fruitful in the demands of the new masses.[6]

Certainly the preservation of culture and quality in the face of this coarsening intrusion—which since the 1870's the Germans have chosen to call the threat of Americanization—should engage our sympathetic interest. Critics in the West have argued a similar concern. Still, we must /120/ note that Germany's concern with culture became more and more inimical to the course of German politics itself and soon turned into strong resentment against the West.

At their best the prewar generation of German academics and professionals preserved and enriched the magnificent traditions of German learning. Although no longer the universalists of the early century, they had become erudite specialists, and the creativity of German as well as European thought in the prewar years attested the renewed vigor of that culture. Politically these men had become reluctant adherents of the Empire, often hoping that social reforms would resolve the prevailing antagonisms. The young Weber once likened the Germany of William II to an express train that was roaring ahead without an engineer; the image is apt. Proud of the progress and modernity of Germany, the academic elite of Germany was alarmed /121/ at its political ineptitude and troubled by a premonition of national disaster.

Some of them, unwittingly, hastened the coming of this disaster, for they became exuberant imperialists, justifying Germany's headlong rush into world politics by a kind of cultural Darwinism. Once more, brute force was gilded by idealistic invocations, by reference to Hegel and Fichte and the German Idealist tradition. Similar rationalizations had been propagated in Western countries; the difference, as Ludwig Dehio points out, was that the ideals of the Western powers, of Spain during the Counter-Reformation, of revolutionary France or liberal England, possessed a universal appeal, whereas the "German mission" was parochial and unpersuasive. The Germans were searching for the identity of their mission, in a sense for their own identity; the Kaiser's theatrics were a pathetic instance of this search. To many Germans, with their honest confusion of culture and religion, a superior culture was as much a legitimate reason for ruling others as the Christian missionary impulse had once been. Goethe, after all, was almost as good as god—just as pushpin was always inferior to poetry. The German intelligentsia came to believe that the moral justification of expansion was a guarantee of political success as well, and thus revealed anew the dangers of the unpolitical mind.

The educated bourgeoisie still indulged in the incantations of culture and personality; but material conditions had changed, and these incantations became more and more spurious and less and less disinterested. To pretend to be unpolitical at a time of violent social change and unrest is in itself a support of the existing order. Between 1871 and 1918 a new type of idealism

---

6.   It is curious that intellectuals, and by no means only German intellectuals, often exaggerate the precariousness of intellectual life and of human creativity, protesting that it is doomed to extinction because of the rising masses, because of affluence or poverty, philistinism or creeping conformity. Is the intellectual enterprise really so feeble and intellect so vulnerable or corruptible? /120/

prevailed, one that, because of its wider diffusion and subsequent debasement as well as in recognition of its remoteness and specious descent from the earlier Idealism, I would like to call *Vulgäridealismus.*[7]

These ideals were still propagated in the schools, and many /122/ more Germans were now receiving higher education. Already in 1872, Nietzsche warned that the quality of humanistic education was put in jeopardy by the steady increase in the number of students—a concern not unknown to us. Nietzsche diagnosed the debasing of these ideals as well. It was he who arraigned the culture philistine, that passive consumer of culture who lacked all energy or independence. Still, the pious elevation and conspicuous consumption of culture persisted, attesting sometimes an innocent delight in spirit, frequently representing a claim to an exclusive proprietorship of culture. To carry one's learning lightly is an English phrase that has no German equivalent. The compulsory citation with which all public talks had to begin and end, the indispensable invocation of Goethe and Schiller, became the aesthetic paternoster of the German intelligentsia.

But why not leave the Germans to their pleasing and by no means unique admiration of culture? The answer must be that this Idealism became more and more of a political force, it became in fact the rhetoric with which the unpolitical German denounced the mass society, democracy, liberalism, modernity, indeed all the so-called importations from the West. Treitschke was perhaps the most popular representative of this strain of *Vulgäridealismus.* In the name of Germany's superior national culture he denounced English materialism and utilitarianism, Jewish corruption, Socialist greed, and also the Germans themselves. He attacked universal suffrage because, "our Idealism has always been our strongest national asset; thus it is absolutely un-German to let stupidity and ignorance have the decisive voice." In this way the narrowest class interests could be ennobled and the most aggressive passions cloaked in the rhetoric of Idealism. Men of less bellicose inclinations than Treitschke's appealed to Germany's idealist tradition in order to denounce the forces of modernity and of the West. The deference to culture often bred a condescension for those who had been denied this aristocratic-aesthetic dispensation. Implicit in this attitude was a /123/ disdain for the culturally unpropertied and untitled, and *Vulgäridealismus* could also be defined as a learned attempt at a metaphysics of snobbery.[8]

This vulgar idealism widened and sanctified the social divisions within Germany, yet thought itself unpolitical. It had no concern with practical matters and considered itself dogmatically opposed to realism, pragmatism, and above all to materialism. It is ironic that the German bourgeoisie often hid its massive materialism behind this idealism, while the Socialists hid their passionate idealism behind a façade of scientific materialism. From their Olympian heights, high above the baser struggles, these idealists marshalled the forces of culture against anarchy, in the effort to defend the status quo against the presumption of the lower classes. It is these idealists that recall a remark that President Lowell of Harvard is said to have made: "I don't mind idealists; it is the unprincipled idealist that I find bad."

The tradition of idealism reached a tragic culmination in 1914, when at the beginning of Germany's most exacting collective effort, the unpolitical char-

7. I am, of course, patterning the phrase after the common German terms *"Vulgärmarxismus"* and *"Vulgärliberalismus."* /122/
8. For a satire of the Central European *Vulgäridealist* in the United States, see Jacques Barzun's description of Dr. Schlagobers, the "professional European." (*God's Country and Mine,* Ch. 2.) /125/

acter of its people was glorified and institutionalized. The great exaltation of 1914 has been wrongly interpreted as proving Germany's militarism or chauvinism; actually it was the response of a nation that had for decades searched for "the moral equivalent to war" and now had found in war the equivalent of morality. The heroism and the national unity it had sought for so long had at last been attained. In August 1914 the Germans rejoiced, as they were released from the tensions of the armed peace at home and abroad. With joy they adjourned all politics for the duration; the enfeebled political regime, never so much in need of strengthening, was virtually dismantled, and in 1916 was altogether superseded by the disastrous dictatorship of Ludendorff and Hindenburg. Year by year the cost of this unpolitical rule became heavier, and her final defeat was in no small /125/ measure brought about by the selfish ineptitude of Germany's nonpolitical rulers.

It was during the war that the idealistic tradition was everywhere proclaimed as Germany's superior surrogate for politics. It became a self-conscious doctrine, and writers like Thomas Mann, Weber, Sombart, Troeltsch, and many other of the great German savants, pulled together the various strands of the idealism I have been describing. Immeasurably angered by the West's moralistic invocation of the universal ideals of freedom, and its slogans about Huns and barbarians, the German intellectuals hurled /126/ back a mighty declaration of cultural independence. With the wrath of a Fichte they proclaimed that the German ideals of culture and personality were far more elevated than the selfish, humdrum ideals and institutions of the West. Under provocation, and be it added, often under galling provocation, the German intellectuals developed the anti-Western implications of Idealism to a high pitch.[9]

A few examples of this wartime literature will suffice, important only because even in its exaggeration it was representative of German thought. Ernst Troeltsch, that superb and sensitive historian of the social teachings of the Christian Churches, penned a restrained and moderate disputation against the West's claims that it was fighting for the universal ideals of progressive humanity. In his essay on the spirit of German culture, this unpolitical strain that I have sought to discuss reaches its clearest expression. Troeltsch seeks to examine "the true cultural antagonisms" between Germany and the West, antagonisms that conditioned the political differences as well. After dissecting British and French cultures, pointing to the materialism of the one and the purely formal democracy of the other, Troeltsch defined "German freedom which will never be /127/ purely political, but always linked with the idealistic concept of duty and the romantic concept of the individual." The spiritual-metaphysical essence of the Germans, diffused, as Troeltsch points

9. During the Second World War, when the realities of German atrocities far exceeded the worst fantasies of Allied propaganda during the First World War, the anti-German propaganda was far more subdued. Still, there were regrettable exceptions.

Not a spirited eccentric like Mr. A. J. P. Taylor, but the very sober historian, Sir Llewelyn Woodward, wrote in 1942: "The Teutonic tribes had the standards of other barbarians; they were neither 'better' nor 'worse' than other human beings in this particular cultural stage. Their descendants in Germany have kept barbarian standards of value longer than their descendants in other areas of western Europe. . . . At a time when other countries were slowly outgrowing the 'barbarian' stage, Germany was the only state in western Europe in which, at the beginning of the twentieth century, there had been for two generations something like a large-scale retrogression in social and political standards of value. . . ." (*Short Journey*, pp. 230–1.) This seems rather an absurd interpretation of a people that before 1914 was tiresomely law-abiding, docile, and very much repressed. Before the first war, violence in German society was largely verbal—as witness the personal and political polemics, and perhaps the humor as well. Repression, social and sexual, is an important, obvious, but nevertheless neglected factor in pre-1914 society—as it was in the flamboyant rebellion against it in the 1920's. /127/

out, through the educational system, inhibited the establishment of formal Western institutions. Because of the belief in personality "we Germans are above all a monarchical people." The social divisions of modern Germany needed an independent monarchy as a disinterested arbiter among the competing material interests: "No parliamentary majority can achieve that." The absence of a parliamentary regime "does not in the least impair personal freedom or human dignity . . . in many ways we feel freer and more independent than the citizens of the great democracy." By its thoughtful tone Troeltsch's essay stands out amidst the poisoned literature of the war. By that very token it deserves to be taken seriously, as a manifestation of something deeper than an ephemeral patriotic outburst.

Other writers worked the same theme, more extravagantly and more crudely. Thomas Mann's *Betrachtungen eines Unpolitischen* must rank as the most painful elaboration of the equation of Germany with Idealism and of the German with the unpolitical. "The difference between spirit and politics subsumes the difference between culture and civilization, between soul and society, freedom and suffrage, art and literature; and culture, soul, freedom, art — that is Germanism [*Deutschtum*], and not civilization, society, suffrage, and literature." Mann concluded by accepting not only the existing monarchy but also the authoritarian state in any form, the *Obrigkeitsstaat*, which alone fits the German character. Here the reconciliation of freedom and authority had reached its most unpolitical, its most ethereal form, and a wartime utterance of Meinecke explained how this reconciliation was attained: "By cleansing the idea of the nation of everything political and infusing it instead with all the spiritual achievements that have been won, the national idea was raised to the sphere of religion and the eternal." /129/

The rest is an epilogue in disaster. Many of the men who had proclaimed Germany's imperviousness to politics fathered the Weimar Constitution. Weber helped to draft it — it was he who sought to make the presidency a strong office, because the Germans, he thought, needed a strong authority. With others, Weber founded the Democratic Party, the only nonproletarian group that unreservedly supported Weimar, and the only party that lost in each election; it had begun in 1919 with 18 per cent of the vote, and ended in 1933 with .8 per cent. Despite Weber, Troeltsch, Rathenau, despite Meinecke's brave, if thoroughly unpassionate rallying to the Republic, and despite Thomas Mann's belated recognition of the moral necessity of politics and the virtue of the Republic, the educated classes of Germany remained aloof from the Republic, /130/ seeing in it a shabby, shaky substitute for the imperial regime.[10]

What was the alternative for the university professors, the teachers, the clerics, and civil servants?[11] Many retreated once more to an unpolitical ide-

10. The uneasy antagonism to the West remained as well. In 1925, in his well-known biography of Luther, Gerhard Ritter wrote: "In recent years it has been much disputed whether Luther belonged to the Middle Ages or 'the modern world.' To me the far more important question seems to be whether we ourselves belong to the modern world — or want to belong to it — if by that term one means primarily the spirit of Anglo-Saxon and Romance culture." (*Luther*, 1925, p. 154.) /131/
11. As one illustration of the antirepublican mood, consider Meinecke's attempt, in 1926, together with some colleagues, to organize a few university professors who would be willing to accept the Constitution, either because they thought the Republic an unfortunate necessity or because they were republicans by persuasion. Meinecke explained his intention: "What a misfortune that for our students the present political order is poisoned — not always directly, for few people dare more than an occasional malicious interjection — but indirectly through the whole political attitude of their teachers." He disavowed the founding of a republican group: "For we would only form a rigidly contained minority group that would be rendered ineffectual by all the means of social boycott." (*Die deutschen Universitäten und der heutige Staat*, Tübingen, 1926.) /131/

alism, not as in previous generations to gild the existing regime by a transcendental ideal, but to condemn the existing Republic in the name of an unattainable, mystical ideal. In fact, the simple repudiation of the present was considered idealistic. The educated German went his way, unpolitical, usually utterly contemptuous of the Republic. That attitude itself was inimical to the survival of the Republic.

But a still greater fatality befell this unpolitical German. How was he to respond to the idealism of the nationalist assassins and the Hitler movement, groups clearly in rebellion against reality? In a very real sense, the Hitler movement was idealistic, and that was the condition of its success. Did it not inveigh against materialism and selfishness, defy reality, promise the end of fratricidal conflict and the establishment of social harmony, of unity and leadership, power and confidence? To make it appear that his party's nihilism was really idealism, its resentful and cowardly brutality virile strength—that was Hitler's great propagandistic success. The unpolitical, the /131/ educated German hesitated. It was not the few men of culture that joined the party before 1933 that promoted Hitler's success, but the many that failed to oppose him, failed not out of fear, but out of uncertainty lest this be the untamed Caesar, the real Germanic savior. His anti-Western tirades, his anti-Semitism, uncouth though they were, stirred memories of earlier, more genteel forms of idealistic anti-Semitism. And the way the Jews were mocking culture, were composing cheap three-penny operas, was really intolerable, the *Bürger* thought. If the educated classes floundered, how much more readily would the economically aggrieved, socially disinherited, flock to the Hitler movement. The idealistic appeal of the Nazis must be reckoned with. Dehio was right when he wrote of them and their immediate predecessors: "Idealism was linked to crime, and the nihilistic will to power prepared itself, quite without conscience, to annihilate Occidental ethics."

Even after 1933, many educated Germans were blind to this criminality of the Nazis. So constantly had they depreciated politics that the absence of a free political society troubled them little, if at all. A few were incarcerated, some emigrated, some joined the movement, many retired to the unpolitical sphere;[12] it is no accident that after 1945 the educated Germans argued that their highest achievement had been an "inner emigration," a retirement within the self. A handful of heroes rebounded from this inner emigration and, in a final gasp of genuine idealism, risked their lives in the revolt of the 20th of July. It, too, failed, and the savage vengeance that Hitler visited upon the plotters expressed his hatred for the educated, aristocratic Germans. /132/

In 1946, when all seemed irretrievably lost to the Germans, Meinecke wrote one last summary of German history, concluding with an invocation to the German spirit. His final counsel was:

> In every German city and larger village, therefore, we should like to see in the future a community of likeminded friends of culture which I should like best to call Goethe Communities. . . . The whole idea must start with

12. A German newspaper recently provided an unintentionally amusing illustration. When Hjalmar Schacht was forced out of the presidency of the Reichsbank in 1939, a few unpolitical bureaucrats tried to forestall the appointment of a Nazi, and hence sought to prevail on a young conservative colleague, Karl Blessing, to seek the job. His reply: "Dear friend, When I shave in the morning I have to look at myself in the mirror, and I have to be able to say: 'Blessing, you are a decent chap.' But under this regime, the currency cannot be protected, and hence I would not be a decent fellow if I took the post of president." (*Die Zeit,* January 2, 1958.) At present, Blessing is president of the Bundesbank of the Federal Republic. /132/

individuals, with personalities, the special few who first build among themselves only one such Goethe community, and then let it develop, here in
one form, there in another.

After their disastrous failure, the Germans were to read Goethe to each
other! Was Goethe once more to become the acknowledged legislator of the
Germans, was Germany's great tradition once more invoked for a purpose
that it could not and was not intended to serve? The provisional answer over
the last decade would seem to be no. /133/
The vague idealism of the unpolitical German seems not to have survived
Hitler's excesses, and there appears in progress a gradual *embourgeoisement* of
West German culture, a willingness to be pragmatic, realistic, prosperous.
What so many Germans for so long dreaded and denounced — the Americanization of German culture — seems now to be taking place, quietly and fitfully,
but to the apparent pleasure of the Germans and to the likely benefit of their
still untested democratic regime. /134/

Raul Hilberg

PRECEDENTS

Hitler's legal experts
have drawn up whole collections of new laws
to strip the Jews of civil rights, and now
even physically to annihilate them.

The Deputy, *Act Two*

The destruction of the European Jews between 1933 and 1945 appears to
us now as an unprecedented event in history. Indeed, in its dimensions and
total configuration, nothing like it had ever happened before. Five million
people were killed as a result of an organized undertaking in the short space
of a few years. The operation was over before anyone could grasp its enormity, let alone its implications for the future.
Yet if we analyze that singularly massive upheaval, we discover that most of
what happened in those twelve years had already happened before. The Nazi
destruction process did not come out of a void; it was the culmination of a cyclical trend.[9] We have observed the trend in the three successive goals of
anti-Jewish administrators. The missionaries of Christianity had said in effect:
You have no right to live among us as Jews. The secular rulers who followed
had proclaimed: You have no right to live among us. The German Nazis at
last decreed: /3/ You have no right to live.
These progressively more drastic goals brought in their wake a slow and
steady growth of anti-Jewish action and anti-Jewish thinking. The process began with the attempt to drive the Jews into Christianity. The development was
continued in order to force the victims into exile. It was finished when the
Jews were driven to their deaths. The German Nazis, then, did not discard

---

From *The Destruction of the European Jews* (London: W. H. Allen & Co., Ltd., 1961),
9.   A regular trend is unbroken (for instance, an increase of population); a cyclical trend is observed
in some of the recurring phenomena. We may speak, for example, of a set of wars that become
progressively more destructive, depressions that decline in severity, etc. /3/

the past; they built upon it. They did not begin a development; they completed it. In the deep recesses of anti-Jewish history, we shall find many of the administrative and psychological tools with which the Nazis implemented their destruction process. In the hollows of the past, we shall also discover the roots of the characteristic Jewish response to an outside attack.

The significance of the historical precedents will most easily be understood in the administrative sphere. The destruction of the Jews was an administrative process, and the annihilation of Jewry required the implementation of systematic administrative measures in successive steps. There are not many ways in which a modern society can, in short order, kill a large number of people living in its midst. This is an efficiency problem of the greatest dimensions, one which poses uncounted difficulties and innumerable obstacles. Yet, in reviewing the documentary record of the destruction of the Jews, one is almost immediately impressed with the fact that the German administration knew what it was doing. With an unfailing sense of direction and with an uncanny pathfinding ability, the German bureaucracy found the shortest road to the final goal.

We know, of course, that the very nature of a task determines the form of its fulfilment. Where there is the will, there is also the way, and if the will is only strong enough, the way will be found. But what if there is no time to experiment? What if the task must be solved quickly and efficiently? A rat in a maze, which has only one path to the goal, learns to choose that path after many trials. Bureaucrats, too, are sometimes caught in a maze, but they cannot afford a trial run. There may be no time for hesitations and stoppages. That is why past performance is so important, that is why past experience is so essential. Necessity is said to be the mother of invention, but if precedents have already been formed, if a guide has already been constructed, invention is no longer a necessity. The German bureaucracy could draw upon such precedents and follow such a guide, for the German bureaucrats could dip into a vast reservoir of administrative experience, a reservoir which church and state had filled in fifteen hundred years of destructive activity.

In the course of its attempt to convert the Jews, the Catholic Church had taken many measures against the Jewish population. These measures were designed to "protect" the Christian community from Jewish teachings and, not incidentally, to weaken the Jews in their "obstinacy." It is characteristic that as soon as Christianity became the state religion of Rome, in the fourth century A.D., Jewish equality of citizenship was ended. "The Church and the Christian state, concilium decisions and imperial laws, henceforth worked hand in hand to persecute the Jews."[10] Table 1 compares the basic anti-Jewish measures of the Catholic Church and the modern counterparts enacted by the Nazi regime.[11] /4/

TABLE 1 / *Canonical and Nazi Anti-Jewish Measures*

Canonical Law	Nazi Measure
Prohibition of intermarriage and of sexual intercourse between Chris-	Law for the Protection of German Blood and Honor, September 15,

---

10.   Stobbe, *Die Juden in Deutschland*, p. 2. /4/
11.   The list of Church measures is taken in its entirety from J. E. Scherer, *Die Rechtsverhältnisse der Juden in den deutsch-österreichischen Ländern* (Leipzig, 1901), pp. 39–49. Only the first date of each measure is listed in Table 1. /4/

tians and Jews, Synod of Elvira, 306

Jews and Christians not permitted to eat together, Synod of Elvira, 306

Jews not allowed to hold public office, Synod of Clermont, 535

Jews not allowed to employ Christian servants or possess Christian slaves, 3d Synod of Orleans, 538

Jews not permitted to show themselves in the streets during Passion Week, 3d Synod of Orleans, 538

Burning of the Talmud and other books, 12th Synod of Toledo, 681

Christians not permitted to patronize Jewish doctors, Trulanic Synod, 692

Christians not permitted to live in Jewish homes, Synod of Narbonne, 1050

Jews obliged to pay taxes for support of the Church to the same extent as Christians, Synod of Gerona, 1078

Prohibition of Sunday work, Synod of Szabolcs, 1092

Jews not permitted to be plaintiffs, or witnesses against Christians in the Courts, 3d Lateran Council, 1179, Canon 26

Jews not permitted to withhold inheritance from descendants who had accepted Christianity, 3d Lateran Council, 1179, Canon 26

The marking of Jewish clothes with a badge, 4th Lateran Council, 1215, Canon 68 (Copied from the legislation by Caliph Omar II [634–44], who had decreed that Christians wear blue belts and Jews, yellow belts.)

Construction of new synagogues prohibited, Council of Oxford, 1222

1935 (RGB1 I, 1146.)

Jews barred from dining cars (Transport Minister to Interior Minister, December 30, 1939, Document NG-3995.)

Law for the Re-establishment of the Professional Civil Service, April 7, 1933 (RGB1 I, 175.)

Law for the Protection of German Blood and Honor, September 15, 1935 (RGB1 I, 1146.)

Decree authorizing local authorities to bar Jews from the streets on certain days (i.e., Nazi holidays), December 3, 1938 (RGB1 I, 1676.)

Book burnings in Nazi Germany

Decree of July 25, 1938 (RGB1 I, 969.)

Directive by Göring providing for concentration of Jews in houses, December 28, 1938 (Bormann to Rosenberg, January 17, 1939, PS-69.)

The "Sozialausgleichsabgabe" which provided that Jews pay a special income tax in lieu of donations for Party purposes imposed on Nazis, December 24, 1940 (RGB1 I, 1666.)

Proposal by the Party Chancellery that Jews not be permitted to institute civil suits, September 9, 1942 (Bormann to Justice Ministry, September 9, 1942, NG-151.)

Decree empowering the Justice Ministry to void wills offending the "sound judgment of the people," July 31, 1938 (RGB1 I, 937.)

Decree of September 1, 1941 (RGB1 I, 547.)

Destruction of synagogues in entire Reich, November 10, 1938 (Heydrich to Göring, November 11, 1938, PS-3058.)

Christians not permitted to attend Jewish ceremonies, Synod of Vienna, 1267

Jews not permitted to dispute with simple Christian people about the tenets of the Catholic religion, Synod of Vienna, 1267. /5/

Compulsory ghettos, Synod of Breslau, 1267

Christians not permitted to sell or rent real estate to Jews, Synod of Ofen, 1279

Adoption by a Christian of the Jewish religion or return by a baptized Jew to the Jewish religion defined as a heresy, Synod of Mainz, 1310

Sale or transfer of Church articles to Jews prohibited, Synod of Lavour, 1368

Jews not permitted to act as agents in the conclusion of contracts between Christians, especially marriage contracts, Council of Basel, 1434, Sessio XIX

Jews not permitted to obtain academic degrees, Council of Basel, 1434, Sessio XIX

Friendly relations with Jews prohibited, October 24, 1941 (Gestapo directive, L-15.) /5/

Order by Heydrich, September 21, 1939 (PS-3363.)

Decree providing for compulsory sale of Jewish real estate, December 3, 1938 (RGB1 I, 1709.)

Adoption by a Christian of the Jewish religion places him in jeopardy of being treated as a Jew, Decision by Oberlandesgericht Königsberg, 4th Zivilsenat, June 26, 1942 (*Die Judenfrage* [*Vertrauliche Beilage*], November 1, 1942, pp. 82-83.)

Decree of July 6, 1938, providing for liquidation of Jewish real estate agencies, brokerage agencies, and marriage agencies catering to non-Jews (RGB1 I, 823.)

Law against Overcrowding of German Schools and Universities, April 25, 1933 (RGB1 I, 225.)

No summation of the canonical law can be as revealing as a description of the Rome ghetto, maintained by the Papal State until the occupation of the city by the Royal Italian Army in 1870. A German journalist who visited the ghetto in its closing days published such an account in the *Neue Freie Presse*.[12] The ghetto consisted of a few damp, dark, and dirty streets, into which 4700 human creatures had been packed tightly (*eingepfercht*).

To rent any house or business establishment outside of the ghetto boundaries, the Jews needed the permission of the Cardinal Vicar. Acquisition of real estate outside the ghetto was prohibited. Trade with industrial products or books was prohibited. Higher schooling was prohibited. The professions of lawyer, druggist, notary, painter, and architect were prohibited. A Jew could be a doctor, provided that he confined his practice to Jewish patients. No Jew could hold office. Jews were required to pay taxes like everyone else and, in addition, the following: (1) a yearly stipend for the upkeep of the Catholic officials who supervised the Ghetto Finance Administration and the Jewish community organization; (2) a yearly sum of 5250 lira to the Casa Pia for missionary work among Jews; (3) a yearly sum of 5250 lira to the Cloister of the Converted for the same purpose. In return, the Papal State expended a

12.   Carl Eduard Bauernschmid in *Neue Freie Presse*, May 17, 1870, reprinted in *Allgemeine Zeitung des Judenthums* (Leipzig), July 19, 1870, pp. 580–82. /6/

yearly sum of 1500 lira for welfare work. But no state money was paid for education or the care of the sick.

The papal regime in the Rome ghetto gives us an idea of the cumulative effect of the canonical law. *This* was its total result. Moreover, the policy of the Church gave rise not only to ecclesiastical regulations; for more than a thousand years, the will of the Church was also enforced by the state. The decisions of the synods and councils became basic guides for state action. Every medieval state copied the canonical law and elaborated upon it. /6/ Thus there arose an "international medieval Jewry law" which, in fact, continued to develop until the eighteenth century. The governmental refinements and elaborations of the clerical regime may briefly be noted in Table 2, which shows also the Nazi versions. . . . /7/

TABLE 2 / *Pre-Nazi and Nazi Anti-Jewish Measures*

Pre-Nazi State Development	Nazi Measure
Per capita protection tax (*der goldene Opferpfennig*) imposed upon Jews by King Ludwig the Bavarian, 1328–1337 (Stobbe, *Die Juden in Deutschland*, p. 31.)	
The property of Jews slain in a German city considered as public property, "because the Jews with their possessions belong to the Reich chamber," provision in the 14th-century code *Regulae juris "Ad decus"* (Kisch, *Jews in Medieval Germany*, pp. 360–61, 560–61.)	13th Ordinance to the Reich Citizenship Law providing that the property of a Jew be confiscated after his death, July 1, 1943 (RGB1 I, 372.)
Confiscation of Jewish claims against Christian debtors at the end of the 14th-century in Nuremberg (Stobbe, *Die Juden in Deutschland*, p. 58.)	11th Ordinance to the Reich Citizenship Law, November 25, 1941 (RGB1 I, 722.)
"Fines": for example, the Regensburg fine for "killing Christian child," 1421 (*Ibid.*, pp. 77–79.)	Decree for the "Atonement Payment" by the Jews, November 12, 1928 (RGB1 I, 1579.)
Marking of documents and personal papers identifying possessor or bearer as a Jew (Zosa Szajkowski, "Jewish Participation in the Sale of National Property during the French Revolution," *Jewish Social Studies*, 1952, p. 291n.)	Decree providing for identification cards, July 23, 1938 (RGB1 I, 922.)
Ca. 1800, the Jewish poet Ludwig Börne had to have his passport marked "Jud von Frankfurt," (Heinrich Graetz, *Volkstümliche Geschichte der Juden* [Berlin-Vienna, 1923], III, 373–74.)	Decree providing for marking of passports, October 5, 1938 (RGB1 I, 1342.)
Marking of houses, special shopping hours, and restrictions of move-	Marking of Jewish apartments (*Jüdisches Nachrichtenblatt* [Berlin],

ment, 17th century, Frankfurt
(*Ibid.*, pp. 387–88.)

Compulsory Jewish names in 19th-
century bureaucratic practice (Leo
M. Friedman, "American Jewish
Names," *Historica Judaica* [Octo-
ber, 1944], p. 154.) /7/

April 17, 1942.)
Decree providing for movement re-
strictions, September 1, 1941
(RGB1 I, 547.)
Decree of January 5, 1937 (RGB1 I,
9.)
Decree of August 17, 1938 (RGB1 I,
1044.) /7/

The administrative precedents, however, are not the only historical determinants with which we are concerned. . . .

The picture of the Jew which we encounter in Nazi propaganda and Nazi
correspondence had been drawn several hundred years before. Martin Luther
had already sketched the main outlines of that portrait, and the Nazis, in their
time, had little to add to it. We shall look here at a few excerpts from Luther's
book *About the Jews and Their Lies.* In doing so, let it be stressed that Luther's
ideas were shared by others in his century, and that the mode of his expression
was the style of his times. His work is /8/ cited here only because he was a
towering figure in the development of German thought, and the writing of
such a man is not to be forgotten in the unearthing of so crucial a conceptu-
alization as this. Luther's treatise about the Jews was addressed to the public
directly, and, in that pouring recital, sentences descended upon the audience
in a veritable cascade. Thus the passage:

> Herewith you can readily see how they understand and obey the fifth
> commandment of God, namely, that they are thirsty bloodhounds and
> murderers of all Christendom, with full intent, now for more than fourteen
> hundred years, and indeed they were often burned to death upon the ac-
> cusation that they had poisoned water and wells, stolen children, and torn
> and hacked them apart, in order to cool their temper secretly with Chris-
> tian blood.[15]

And:

> Now see what a fine, thick, fat lie that is when they complain that they are
> held captive by us. It is more than fourteen hundred years since Jerusalem
> was destroyed, and at this time it is almost three hundred years since we
> Christians have been tortured and persecuted by the Jews all over the world
> (as pointed out above), so that we might well complain that they had now
> captured us and killed us—which is the open truth. Moreover, we do not
> know to this day which devil has brought them here into our country; we
> did not look for them in Jerusalem.[16]

Even now no one held them here, Luther continued. They might go whenever they wanted to. For they were a heavy burden, "like a plague, pestilence, pure misfortune in our country." They had been driven from France,
"an especially fine nest," and the "dear Emperor Charles" drove them from
Spain, "the best nest of all." And this year, they were expelled from the entire

---

15. Luther, *Von den Jueden*, p. diii3. /9/
16. *Ibid.*, pp. diii3, diii4. /9/

Bohemian town, including Prague, "also a very fine nest" — likewise from Regensburg, Magdeburg, and other towns.[17]

Is this called captivity, if one is not welcome in land or house? Yes, they hold us Christians captive in our country. They let us work in the sweat of our noses, to earn money and property for them, while they sit behind the oven, lazy, let off gas, bake pears, eat, drink, live softly and well from our wealth. They have captured us and our goods through their accursed usury; mock us and spit on us, because we work and permit them to be lazy squires who own us and our realm; they are therefore our lords, we their servants with our own wealth, sweat, and work. Then they curse our Lord, to reward us and to thank us. Should not the devil laugh and dance, if he can have such paradise among us Christians, that he may devour through the Jews — his holy ones — that which is ours, and stuff our mouths and noses as reward, mocking and cursing God and man for good measure.

They could not have had in Jerusalem under David and Solomon such fine days on their own estate as they have now on ours — which they rob and steal daily. But still they complain that we hold them captive. Yes, we have and hold them in captivity, just as I have captured my calculum, my blood heaviness, and all other maladies. . . .[18]

What have the Christians done, asks Luther, to deserve such a fate? "We do not call their women whores, do not curse them, do not steal and dismember their children, do not poison their water. We do not thirst after their blood." It was not otherwise than Moses had said. God had struck them with frenzy, blindness, and raging heart.[19]

This is Luther's picture of the Jews. /9/ First, they want to rule the world.[20]Second, they are arch-criminals, killers of Christ and all Christendom.[21]Third, he refers to them as a "plague, pestilence, and pure misfortune."[22] That Lutheran portrait of Jewish world rule, Jewish criminality, and the Jewish plague has often been repudiated. But, in spite of denial and exposure, the charges have survived. In four hundred years the picture has not been changed.

In 1895 the Reichstag was discussing a measure, proposed by the anti-Sem-

17. *Ibid.*, pp. diii4, e. /9/
18. *Ibid.*, p. e2. /9/
19. *Ibid.*, p. eii. /9/
20. Emperor Frederick II, excluding Jews from public office, stated, in 1237: "Faithful to the duties of a Catholic prince, we exclude Jews from public office so they will not abuse official power for the oppression of Christians." Kisch, *Jews in Medieval Germany*, p. 149. /10/
21. The following is a passage from a fifteenth-century German lawbook, the municipal code of Salzwedel, par. 83,2: "Should a Jew assault a Christian or kill him, the Jew may not make any reply, he must suffer in silence what the law appoints, for he has no claim on Christendom and is God's persecutor and a murderer of Christendom." Kisch, *Jews in Medieval Germany*, p. 268. Kisch points out that earlier German lawbooks contained no such discrimination.

The poisoned wells legend (fourteenth century) and the ritual murders legend (thirteenth century) were both condemned by the Popes. Scherer, *Die Rechtsverhältnisse der Juden*, pp. 36 – 38. On the other hand, the thirteenth-century Castilian law code "El Sentenario," Partita VII, Tit. 24, Ley 2, makes reference to the capital crime of crucifying Christian children or wax figures on Holy Friday. Scherer, *Die Rechtsverhältnisse der Juden*, pp. 50 – 51. As for the legal view of usury, see Kisch, *Jews in Medieval Germany*, pp. 191 – 97. /10/
22. The Fourth Lateran Council expressly called upon the secular powers to "exterminate" (*exterminare*) all heretics. Kisch, *Jews in Medieval Germany*, p. 203. This provision was the basis for a wave of stake burnings during the inquisitions.

The story of the tenth plague, the slaying of the first-born, has given rise to the ritual murder legend, in accordance with which Jews kill Christian children at Passover time to use their blood in matzos. See also the provision in the "Sentenario" in which the tenth plague is combined with the Gospels to produce the crucifixion of children. /10/

itic faction, for the exclusion of foreign Jews. The speaker, Ahlwardt, belonged to that faction. We reproduce here a few excerpts from his speech:[23]

It is quite clear that there is many a Jew among us, of whom one cannot say anything bad. If one designates the whole of Jewry as harmful one does so in the knowledge that the racial qualities of this people are such that in the long run they cannot harmonize with the racial qualities of the Germanic peoples, and that every Jew who at this moment has not done anything bad may nevertheless under the proper conditions do precisely that, because his racial qualities drive him to do it.

Gentlemen, in India there was a certain sect, the Thugs, who elevated the act of assassination to an act of policy. In this sect, no doubt, there were quite a few people who personally never committed a murder, but the English in my opinion have done the right thing when they exterminated [*ausrotteten*] this whole sect, without regard to the question whether any particular member of the sect already had committed a murder or not, for in the proper moment every member of the sect would do such a thing.

Ahlwardt pointed out that the anti-Semites were fighting the Jews not because of their religion but because of their race. He then continued:

The Jews accomplished what no outer enemy has accomplished: they have driven the people from Frankfurt into the suburbs. And that's the way it is wherever Jews congregate in large numbers. Gentlemen, the Jews are indeed beasts of prey. . . .

Mr. Rickert [another deputy who had opposed the exclusion of the Jews] started by saying that we already had too many laws, and that's why we should not concern ourselves with a /10/ new anti-Jewish code. That is really the most interesting reason which has ever been advanced against anti-Semitism. We should leave the Jews alone because we have too many laws?! Well, I think, if we would do away with the Jews [*die Juden abschaffen*], we could do away with half the laws which we have now on the books.

Then, Deputy Rickert said that it is really a shame—whether he actually said that I don't know because I could not take notes—but the sense of it was that it was a shame that a nation of 50 million people should be afraid of a few Jews. [Rickert had cited statistics to prove that the number of Jews in the country was not excessive.] Yes, gentlemen, Deputy Rickert would be right, if it were a matter of fighting with honest weapons against an honest enemy; then it would be a matter of course that the Germans would not fear a handful of such people. But the Jews, who operate like parasites, are a different kind of problem. Mr. Rickert, who is not as tall as I am, is afraid of a single cholera germ—and, gentlemen, the Jews are cholera germs.

(Laughter)

Gentlemen, it is the infectiousness and exploitative power of Jewry which is involved. . . .

Ahlwardt then called upon the deputies to wipe out "these beasts of prey" (*Rotten Sie diese Raubtiere aus*) and continued . . . that this was no laughing matter but deadly serious business. . . .

23. Reichstag *Stenographische Berichte*, 53. Sitzung, March 6, 1895, pp. 1296 ff. To Paul Massing belongs the credit for discovering this speech and including it in his book, *Rehearsal for Destruction* (New York, 1949). /10/

It is remarkable that two men, separated by a span of three hundred and fifty years, can still speak the same language. Ahlwardt's picture of the Jews is in its basic features a replica of the Lutheran portrait. The Jew is still (1) an enemy, who has accomplished what no external enemy has accomplished: he has driven the people of Frankfurt into the suburbs; (2) a criminal, a thug, a beast of prey, who commits so many crimes that his elimination would enable the Reichstag to cut the criminal code in half; and (3) a plague, or, more precisely, a cholera germ. Under the Nazi regime, these conceptions of the Jew were expounded and repeated in an almost endless flow of speeches, posters, letters, and memoranda. Hitler himself preferred to look upon the Jew as an enemy, a menace, a dangerous cunning foe. This is what he said in a speech delivered in 1940, as he reviewed his "struggle for power": /11/

It was a battle against a satanical power which had taken possession of our entire people, which had grasped in its hands all key positions of scientific, intellectual, as well as political and economic life, and which kept watch over the entire nation from the vantage of these key positions. It was a battle against a power which, at the same time, had the influence to combat with the law every man who attempted to take up battle against them and every man who was ready to offer resistance to the spread of this power. At that time, all-powerful Jewry declared war on us. . . . [24]

A number of Nazis, including the chief of the German SS and Police Himmler, the jurist and *Generalgouverneur* of Poland Hans Frank, and Justice Minister Thierack, inclined to the view that the Jews were a lower species of life, a kind of vermin, which upon contact infected the German people with deadly diseases. Himmler once cautioned his SS generals not to tolerate the stealing of property which had belonged to dead Jews. "Just because we exterminated a bacterium," he said, "we do not want, in the end, to be infected by that bacterium and die of it."[26] Frank frequently referred to the Jews as "lice." When the Jews in his Polish domain were killed, he announced that now a sick Europe would become healthy again.[27] . . . /12/

The twentieth-century Nazis, like the nineteenth-century anti-Semites and the sixteenth-century clerics, regarded the Jews as hostile, criminal, and parasitical. But there is also a difference between the recent writings and the older scripts which requires explanation. In the Nazi and anti-Semitic speeches we discover references to race. That formulation does not appear in sixteenth-century books. Conversely, in Luther's work there is repeated mention of God's scorn, thunder and lightning worse than Sodom and Gomorrah, frenzy, blindness, and raging heart. Such language disappeared in the nineteenth century.

There is, however, a close functional relationship between Luther's references to divine blows and Ahlwardt's reliance upon race characteristics, for both Luther and Ahlwardt tried to show that the Jew could not be changed, that a Jew remained a Jew. "What God does not improve with such terrible blows, that we shall not change with words and deeds."[29] . . . The Jew "cannot help himself" because his racial qualities drive him to commit antisocial acts. . . .

24.   Speech by Hitler, German press, November 10–11, 1940. /12/
26.   Speech by Himmler, October 4, 1943, PS-1919. /12/
27.   Generalgouvernement Health Conference, July 9, 1943, Frank Diary, PS-2233. Remarks by Frank recorded verbatim. /12/
29.   Luther, *Von den Jueden*, p. Aiii2. /13/

Anti-Jewish racism had its beginning in the second half of the seventeenth century, when the "Jewish caricature" first appeared in cartoons.[30] These caricatures were the first attempt to discover race characteristics in the Jew. However, racism acquired a "theoretical" basis only in the nineteenth century. The racists of the nineteenth century stated explicitly that cultural characteristics, good or bad, were the product of physical characteristics. Physical attributes did not change; hence social behavior patterns also had to be immutable. In the eyes of the anti-Semite, the Jews therefore became a "race."[31] /13/

Frank H. Tucker

WAR CRIMES, PEACE CRIMES, AND RACISM

. . . and you can close your eyes to the worst horror
that man has ever inflicted upon man.

The Deputy, *Act One, Scene One*

In modern times, particularly in the nineteenth and twentieth centuries, our world has suffered a remarkable amount of criminal activity on a national scale, and often even on a continent-wide or world-wide scale. By criminal activity, I mean offenses of the sort charged in the Nuremberg Trials of 1946. I would prefer to categorize these offenses as follows: (1) the planning and waging of aggressive war, often unusually extensive or cruel war; (2) such crimes against humanity as genocide, slavery, and other servitude, not omitting many national enterprises of profiteering, plundering, or regimentation; (3) racism—sometimes more accurately labeled nationalism—not always criminal, but seldom a trivial matter, even in its subtle forms of discrimination or presumption of superiority.

Of course, most of these offenses have been with us since ancient times. However, in recent times, they have become much more extensive. Also, they have been vastly aggravated by modern technology, which offers so many new, impressive means of destroying Man and of keeping him under domination and surveillance.

It can be shown that in modern times these major crimes or offenses often have been linked together and that, for example, there are noteworthy connections between nineteenth-century colonialism and the totalitarianisms of Central and Eastern Europe. Not only have these distressing events been related, but their underlying motives seem to be much interwoven. . . .

Now it is notorious that people ignore facts that conflict with their cherished ideas and interests. Even in seeing or hearing, we do not register or observe a thing that does not "fit in," and we forget very quickly those matters which are uncongenial to us. As an example, Martha Gellhorn concludes, after visiting Germany and observing the state of mind there in 1963:

---

30.   Eduard Fuchs, *Die Juden in der Karikatur* (Munich, 1921), pp. 160–61. /13/
31.   For a Nazi discussion of race, including such formulations as "racial substance" (*Rassekern*), "superior race" (*Hochrasse*), and "racial decline" (*Rasseverfall*), see Konrad Dürre, "Werden und Bedeutung der Rassen," *Die Neue Propyläen-Weltgeschichte* (Berlin, 1940), pp. 89–118. /13/
From *The White Conscience* (unpublished manuscript).

The adults of Germany, who know Nazism and in their millions cheered and adored Hitler until he started losing, have performed a nationwide act of amnesia; no one individually had a thing to do with the Hitlerian regime and its horrors. . . . Santayana observed that if a man forgets his past he is condemned to relive it.[1]

In fairness to those who forget their collective crimes, we should add that even the victims of Hitler's horrors were incredulous. Bruno Bettelheim, himself a former concentration camp inmate, writes in his "Dachau and Buchenwald": "The prisoners had to convince themselves that this was real, was really happening and not just a nightmare. They were never wholly successful."[2]

Erich Fromm also notes that people's approach to international relations often causes repression, or an even subtler partial repression. As an example of partial repression, he says:

When one speaks today of the "appeasement" of the thirties, one remembers that England and France, being afraid of a rearmed Germany, tried to satisfy Hitler's demands, hoping that these concessions would induce him not to demand more. What is forgotten, however, is that the conservative government in England under Baldwin as well as that under Chamberlain was sympathetic to Nazi Germany as well as to Mussolini's Italy. . . . Official indignation with Nazi ideology was the result of the political rift, and not its cause.[3]

Fromm also finds appropriate in this connection Nietzsche's famous saying, "My memory says I have done this. My pride says I have not done it; my memory yields." [4] Another Fromm concept of interest here is his "social filter" idea. What he calls the "social filter" is our mental reaction which rejects or deletes the *socially impermissible* contents of experiences. To put it another way, people won't let themselves be *aware* of ideas which would bring them social disapproval or ostracism.[5]

In the sorry record of European and American racism, what common factors can we discern, linking together the manifold brutalities committed by our people, both in Europe and around the world?

First, in virtually all cases, there existed, from the victim's standpoint at least, a monolithic power structure among his oppressors. Their power was not counterbalanced, was not restrained, and was subject to no effective appeal. This is the most obvious, I suppose, in Russia and the rest of Eastern Europe, where a balancing of power has seldom been a feature of society. Also, in that region there has been scarcely any truly indigenous middle class, which could influence, or restrain, the governing class. The Russian peasant traditionally felt that he could turn for relief only to God or to that supposedly benevolent father-image, the Tsar; but the peasants of Imperial Russia also had a coolly realistic proverb, which epitomizes the problem we are discussing here, "God is in heaven, and the Tsar is far away."

1. Martha Gellhorn, "Is There a New Germany?" *The Atlantic Monthly*, 213 (February 1964), 70.
2. U.S. Chief of Counsel for the Prosecution of Axis Criminality, *Nazi Conspiracy and Aggression*, 10 vols. (Washington, D.C.: Government Printing Office, 1946–1948), VII, 824 ff.
3. Erich Fromm, *Beyond the Chains of Illusion* (New York: Trident Press, 1962), pp. 99–100.
4. *Ibid.*, p. 101.
5. D. T. Suzuki, Erich Fromm, and Richard de Martino, *Zen Buddhism and Psychoanalysis* (New York: Harper & Bros., 1960), pp. 103–104.

In Germany, there was certainly a middle class, but it was politically supine, confined to echoing the government ideology.

In the many lands where colonial impositions occurred, there was a lack of counterbalancing or checking power *on the scene.* The politicians far away, in the homeland, might be fine humanitarians, but the actual colonial rule was totalitarian. . . .

Of special interest here, however, are the ideologies of the colonizers, which not only were offensive in themselves, but also helped to produce the totalitarianisms which did so much harm to Europe and, really, to the *world community,* beginning particularly in the 1930's. As Professor Langer wrote in 1935:

> It is now fairly clear, I think, that the Neo-Marxian critics have paid far too little attention to the imponderable, psychological ingredients of imperialism. The movement may, without much exaggeration, be interpreted not only as an atavism . . . but also as an aberration, to be classed with the extravagances of nationalism.[6]

From the same essay, we gather that, quite apart from Marxian economics, Langer did see the inter-relatedness of Europe's round-the-world troublemaking, and the times of troubles within twentieth-century Europe itself. He believed that great domestic crises and outbursts of expansion usually follow one another in history.[7] In calling imperialism a throwback or atavism, he had support from Schumpeter, who applied the same words to it, and from Hobson, who called it "a sociological atavism, a remnant of the roving instinct."[8]

What, then, was the psychology of imperialism and racism? What was their "theology?" Darwin's concepts of "natural selection" and "survival of the fittest" were adapted to provide one source of an ideology for racial dominance, as well as for class dominance. This double capability explains much of the keen interest in Darwinism in Europe and America. . . .

Racialism got a strong boost from the new imperialism, with its urgent desires for the colonizing of Africa, from the 1880's onward. The racism which, by the end of the nineteenth century, was embraced by most of the white regimes in Africa soon influenced the European attitudes toward the Asian peoples. In the nineteenth century, over one hundred thousand Indian laborers had been brought to Natal in South Africa to work on the sugar plantations. There were also thousands of Chinese laborers, imported at about the turn of the century to work in the mines.

From this inter-continental movement of Asian persons, there was apparently a feedback to Asia, causing Europeans in Asia to treat the people of that continent somewhat as they treated the Africans, that is, not quite as human beings. Furthermore, the feedback is likely to have influenced, for the worse, the racist extremists within Europe itself. While this cannot be proven definitely, we do know that the period of exploitation and small-scale genocide by Germans in Africa preceded their genocidal operations in Europe by only about four decades. We know that they found in Africa that racist brutality "worked," that it could be carried out to the accompaniment of orderly, even profitable, colonial administration. We know that the German misdeeds in Africa were given implied approval by the other European colonial powers, since they were engaged in comparable practices at about the same time.

6.   William L. Langer, "A Critique of Imperialism," *Foreign Affairs,* XIV (October 1935), 110.
7.   *Ibid.,* p. 111.
8.   *Ibid.,* p. 109.

In Africa, the European met primitive, tribal people. The pride, dignity, or greed of the newly arrived white man would not allow him to accept these people as fellow men. From this arose brutal enslavement, exploitation, and often massacre — condonable massacre, supposedly, since it did not involve the destruction of one's fellow creatures at all.

Here is a truly central and recurrent misdeed, possibly the worst of all that we could consider: the dehumanizing of Man, the treatment of fellow creatures as *things*, not *men*.

This probably is a throwback to primitive man, who often classified non-members of his group as "non-men." We know that the actual name of many a tribal or national group, to this day, carries the literal meaning of "persons" or "the people." That is the translation of "Bantu" or "Hun," to name two examples. The corollary to this is that outsiders are not to be considered human. Often, in the primitive situation, this also meant that the "non-person" was eligible to attend cannibalistic dinner parties, but as part of the meal, not as a guest.

We also can see that exaggerated nationalism often relates to membership in a group that speaks a common language. For instance, the word for "German" in Polish ("Nemec") and Russian ("Nemets") means, literally, "one who cannot talk," that is, a non-speaker of the in-group's language.

While the literal cannibalization of "non-members" is rare in our day, the lack of human sympathy which it implies has been very much with us. The Russian newspapers have, in fact, somehow picked up the anthropophagous analogy, and their propagandists often hang the label "cannibal" on anyone who is supposed to be exploiting or abusing mankind.[9]

Actually, as Von Mises points out, both the Russian Marxists and the Nazis were quick to label their adversaries, and everything about them, as "alien," "non-proletarian," or "non-Aryan." To many Nazis, "Jewish" meant really anything they disliked, or particularly anything *not serving their ideology*.[10] These "aliens," too, were to be treated as non-human, and their fate ceased, supposedly, to be a matter of human concern. . . .

Now that we have considered dehumanization in general, we should look at some closely related contributions of the colonialists to twentieth-century horrors. The operations of nineteenth-century imperialism actually helped to develop modern bureaucratic standards and techniques.[11] The colonial bureaucrat, building on an even earlier tradition of military discipline and hierarchic power — power phenomenally swollen by Europe's domination of the world — could wield his power with an impersonal detachment that he might call "selfless service of humanity," but which surely did improve the art of report-shrouded, secrecy-encrusted, bureaucratic operations. These were the procedures which, a half century later, in a grim fusion of racism and twentieth-century administrative efficiency, would produce the grotesquely efficient Nazi death camps.

The aloofness of the bureaucracy, whether in Africa or Germany, its rejection of all common ground with the governed, its great dedication to the supposed higher goals or ideals which would justify the use of ruthless means in dealing with the governed, all these made the abuse far worse than a

9. For another facet of the "cannibal" idea, cf. D. O. Mannoni, *Prospero and Caliban: The Psychology of Colonization*, trans. Pamela Towesland (New York: Praeger and Co., 1950), pp. 103–106, 208–209.
10. Ludwig von Mises, *Omnipotent Government: The Rise of the Total State and Total War* (New Haven, Conn.: Yale University Press, 1944), p. 146.
11. Hannah Arendt, *The Origins of Totalitarianism* (Cleveland: World Publishing Co., 1948), p. 186.

merely greedy tyranny would have been. Moreover, the "selfless" bureaucrat, being something of an automaton, does not presume to reflect about intricacies of morals or ideology, when carrying out his instructions. Consequently, his acts are seldom mitigated by any liberal elements in the past traditions of his own people.

Even the laws themselves were seldom allowed to be a restraining, higher force acting on the colonial bureaucrat. If the totalitarian bureaucrat made use of laws, it was usually in the sense of decrees, or laws alterable in short order, in whatever way the "cause" might seem to dictate. Russia's Stalin Constitution of 1936, for example, with its many fine guarantees of human rights, was ignored for decades.

The First World War had helped to bring on, first, the Russian Communist, next, the Italian Fascist, and, lastly, the German Nazi regimes. Naturally, these regimes borrowed much from the old regimes of Czar and Kaiser, which had their own intra-European forms of empire building and bureaucratic callousness. Each of these three postwar revolutionary governments stimulated the next, and each learned useful techniques from the earlier one—the one-party system, the secret police, etc.

The Russian Revolution of 1917 was followed, slowly but inexorably, by the liquidation of many counter-revolutionaries and of "members of classes hostile to the workers' government." The period 1928-1933 saw the liquidation of the "kulak" (well-to-do-peasant) class. Millions of peasants either died in the famines of these years, or were executed, or were dispossessed and exiled to Siberia.

In the years 1935–1938 came the Stalin Purges, in which at least seven million Soviet citizens were put in forced labor camps, while many, many thousands were executed.[12] (Other Soviet oppressions, including the most modern forms of surveillance, interrogation, and brain-washing, have continued to the present in the U.S.S.R. and its satellites. Anti-Semitic persecutions still continue in Russia and, in the Spring of 1964, were, by a coincidence, synchronized with anti-Jewish outbreaks in the Union of South Africa.[13])

The Communist Russian and Nazi German regimes were related to one another in many ways. They were both partial heirs of socialism, they were messianic, and both believed that the higher ends which they served justified the use of any means.

Also in the 1930's, Europe suffered the horrors of the German National Socialist regime, which excelled all others in anti-Semitism, trying with the coldest scientific efficiency to exterminate the Jews of Europe. In this, Germany very nearly succeeded, doing to death millions of Jewish victims, as well as millions of Russians, Poles, and other "enemies of the Third Reich." The fact that the Nazi crimes were part of a greater criminality, which extended beyond Germany and beyond one generation, was well expressed by the late Justice Robert H. Jackson, who represented the United States at the Nuremberg Trials, when he declared at Nuremberg that the Nazi leaders were ". . . symbols of racial hatreds, of terrorism and violence, and of the arrogance and cruelty of power. They are symbols of fierce nationalism and of militarism, of intrigue and war-making which have embroiled Europe, generation after generation."[14] He also brought out the broad implications of the

---

12.   Merle Fainsod, *How Russia Is Ruled* (Cambridge, Mass.: Harvard University Press, 1953), pp. 372–385.
13.   *New York Herald Tribune*, March 30, 1964, p. 6.
14.   Robert H. Jackson, *The Case Against the Nazi War Criminals* (New York: Alfred A. Knopf, 1946), p. 4.

Nazi Epoch when he said, "The cries of [Germany's] victims were heard round the world and brought shudders to civilized people everywhere."[15] "The real complaining party at your bar is civilization."[16]

Hannah Arendt summarizes a number of the inter-related ills of the Western world in this way: "Antisemitism (not merely the hatred of Jews), imperialism (not merely conquest), totalitarianism (not merely dictatorship)—one after the other, one more brutally than the other, have demonstrated that human dignity needs a new guarantee."[17] Erich Fromm feels even more strongly about the process of bureaucratization. He says that both Communist and anti-Communist nations create bureaucracies which transform man into a thing. Thus, the alternative, as he sees it, is not between capitalism and communism, but between bureaucratism and humanism.[18]

Kurt Gerstein

DESCRIPTION OF BELZEC

. . . I have a message
for the Vatican . . .

The Deputy, *Act One, Scene One*

"The next day we left for Belzec, a small special station of two platforms against a hill of yellow sand, immediately to the north of the Lublin-Lvov road and railway. To the south, near the road, were some service houses with a signboard: 'Belzec, Service Centre of the Waffen S.S.'

"Globocnik introduced me to S. S. Hauptsturmführer Obermeyer from Pirmasens, who with great restraint showed me the installations. No dead were to be seen that day, but the smell of the whole region, even from the main road, was pestilential.

"Next to the small station there was a large barrack marked 'Cloakroom', and a door marked 'Valuables'. Next to that, a chamber with a hundred 'barber's' chairs. Then came a corridor one hundred and fifty metres long, in the open air and with barbed wire on both sides.

"There was a signboard: 'To the baths and inhalations'. Before us we saw a house, like a bathroom, with concrete troughs to the right and left containing geraniums and other flowers. After climbing a small staircase, we came to three garage-like rooms on each side, four by five metres in size and 1.90 metres high. At the back were invisible wooden doors. On the roof was a Star of David made out of copper. At the entrance to the building was the inscription 'Heckenholt Foundation'. That was all I noticed on that particular afternoon.

"Next morning, a few minutes before seven, I was informed that in ten minutes the first train would arrive. And indeed a few minutes later the first train came in from Lemberg (Lvov); forty-five cars, containing 6,700 persons, 1,450 of whom were already dead on arrival. Behind the little barbed-wire openings were children, yellow, half scared to death, women and men.

15. *Ibid.*, p. 52.
16. *Ibid.*, p. 90.
17. Arendt, p. ix.
18. Fromm, *Beyond the Chains of Illusion*, pp. 180–181.
"Description of Belzec," *Trials of War Criminals*, Vol. I, Case i, pp. 864–866, as it appears in Rudolf Vrba and Alan Bestic, *I Cannot Forgive* (New York: Grove Press, 1964), Appendix Two.

"The train stopped; two hundred Ukranians, forced to do this work, opened the doors and drove all the people out of the coaches with leather whips. Then, through a huge loudspeaker, instructions were given to them to undress completely and to hand over false teeth and glasses—some in the barracks, others right in the open air. Shoes were to be tied together with a little piece of string handed to everyone by a small Jewish boy of four years of age; all valuables and money were to be handed in at the window marked 'Valuables', without receipt.

"Then the women and girls were allowed to go to the hairdresser who cut off their hair in one or two strokes, after which it vanished into huge potato bags, 'to be used for special submarine equipment, door mats, /278/ etc.', as the S. S. Unterscharführer on duty told me.

"Then the march began. To the right and left, barbed wire: behind, two dozen Ukranians with guns. Led by a young girl of striking beauty, they approached. With Police Captain Wirth, I stood right in front of the death chambers. Completely naked, they marched by, men, women, girls, children, babies, even one-legged persons, all of them naked. In one corner, a strong S.S. man told the poor devils in a strong voice: 'Nothing whatever will happen to you. All you have to do is to breathe deeply; it strengthens the lungs. This inhalation is a necessary measure against contagious disease; it is a very good disinfectant.'

"Asked what was to become of them, he answered: 'Well, of course, the men will have to work, building streets and houses. But the women do not have to. If they wish, they can help in the house or the kitchen.'

"Once more, a little bit of hope for some of these poor people, enough to make them march on without resistance to the death chambers. Most of them, though, knew everything, the smell had given them a clear indication of their fate. And then they walked up the little staircase—and behold the picture:

"Mothers with babies at their breasts, naked; lots of children of all ages, naked, too; they hesitate, but they enter the gas chambers, most of them without a word, pushed by the others behind them, chased by the whips of the S.S. men.

"A Jewess of about forty years of age, with eyes like torches, calls down the blood of her children on the heads of their murderers. Five lashes in her face, dealt by the whip of Police Captain Wirth himself, drive her into the gas chamber. Many of them said their prayers; others ask: 'Who will give us water before our death?'

"Within the chambers, the S.S. press the people closely together; Captain Wirth has ordered: 'Fill them up full.' Naked men stand on the feet of others. Seven hundred to eight hundred crushed together on twenty-five square metres, in forty-five cubic metres! The doors are closed!

"Meanwhile the rest of the transport, all naked, waited. Somebody said to me: 'Naked in winter! Enough to kill them!' The answer was: 'Well, that's just what they are here for!' And at that moment I understood why it was called the Heckenholt Foundation. Heckenholt was the man in charge of the diesel engine, the exhaust gases of which were to kill these poor devils.

"S.S. Unterscharführer Heckenholt tried to set the diesel engine going, but it would not start. Captain Wirth came along. It was obvious /279/ that he was afraid because I was a witness of this breakdown. Yes, indeed, I saw everything and waited. Everything was registered by my stop watch. Fifty minutes . . . seventy minutes . . . the diesel engine did not start!

"The people waited in their gas chambers—in vain. One could hear them cry. 'Just as in a synagogue.' says S.S. Sturmabannführer Professor Doctor Pfannenstiel, Professor for Public Health at the University of Marburg/Lahn, holding his ear close to the wooden door.

"Captain Wirth, furious, dealt the Ukrainian who was helping Heckenholt eleven or twelve lashes in the face with his whip. After two hours and forty-nine minutes—as registered by my stop watch—the diesel engine started. Up to that moment, the people in the four chambers already filled were still alive—four times seven hundred and fifty persons in four times forty-five cubic metres! Another twenty-five minutes went by. Many of the people, it is true, were dead by that time. One could see that through the little window as the electric lamp revealed for a moment the inside of the chamber. After twenty-eight minutes only a few were alive. After thirty-two minutes, all were dead.

"From the other side, Jewish workers opened the wooden doors. In return for their terrible job, they had been promised their freedom and a small percentage of the valuables and the money found. The dead were still standing like stone statues, there having been no room for them to fall or bend over. Though dead, the families could still be recognized, their hands still clasped.

"It was difficult to separate them in order to clear the chamber for the next load. The bodies were thrown out blue, wet with sweat and urine, the legs covered with excrement and menstrual blood. Everywhere among the others were the bodies of babies and children.

"But there is no time!—two dozen workers were busy checking the mouths, opening them with iron hooks—'Gold on the left, no gold on the right!' Others checked anus and genitals to look for money, diamonds, gold, etc. Dentists with chisels tore out gold teeth, bridges, or caps. In the centre of everything was Captain Wirth. He was on familiar ground here. He handed me a large tin full of teeth and said: 'Estimate for yourself the weight of gold! This is only from yesterday and the day before! And you would not believe what we find here every day! Dollars, diamonds, gold! But look for yourself!'

"Then he led me to a jeweller who was in charge of all these valuables. After that they took me to one of the managers of the big stores, Kaufhaus des Westens, in Berlin, and to a little man whom they made /280/ play the violin. Both were chiefs of the Jewish worker units. 'He is a captain of the Royal and Imperial Austrian Army, and has the German Iron Cross, First Class,' I was told by Haupsturmbannführer Obermeyer.

"The bodies were then thrown into large ditches about one hundred by twenty by twelve metres located near the gas chamber. After a few days the bodies would swell up and the whole contents of the ditch would rise two to three metres high because of the gases which developed inside the bodies. After a few more days the swelling would stop and the bodies would collapse. The next day the ditches were filled again, and covered with ten centimetres of sand. A little later, I heard, they constructed grills out of rails and burned the bodies of them with diesel oil and gasoline in order to make them disappear.

"At Belzec and Treblinka nobody bothered to take anything approaching an exact count of the persons killed. Actually, not only Jews, but many Poles and Czechs, who, in the opinion of the Nazis, were of bad stock, were killed. Most of them died anonymously. Commissions of so-called doctors, who were actually nothing but young S.S. men in white coats, rode in limousines through the towns and villages of Poland and Czechoslovakia to select the old, tubercular, and sick people and have them done away with shortly afterwards in the gas chambers. They were the Poles and Czechs of category No. III, who did not deserve to live because they were unable to work." /281/

Rudolf Vrba and Alan Bestic

THERE IS NO GOD

Corpses — a conveyor belt of corpses.
History is a highway paved with carrion . . .
If I knew that He looks on —
I would have to — hate Him.

The Deputy, *Act Five, Scene Three*

. . . I was determined to find out whether Birkenau was fortified equally strongly.

So, when men were needed to work for a day in Birkenau, which, apparently, was getting a little clogged, I volunteered immediately; and half an hour later I was rolling towards the heart of Himmler's biggest extermination centre, happy that I had been able to fiddle the job and quite unaware that I was about to be thoroughly sickened.

All that worried me slightly was the cold, for it was a bitter December day; but even that I was able to tolerate, for underneath my zebra shirt, I wore heavy woolen underwear and a warm sweater. . . .

As we drove slowly into Birkenau, however, all thoughts of the weather, of Auschwitz, for that matter, vanished. Suddenly, about a hundred yards away, in a wired off section of the camp, I saw at least ten thousand naked women, lined up in neat, silent rows.

Around them were dotted the green-uniformed S.S. men; and beyond them, forty or fifty lorries. Distance dulled the harsh outlines of the scene and killed all sound; yet it was even more eerie in its appalling silence, so grotesque that even Unterscharführer Sparsam, in the cabin below us, a man who had seen, perpetrated, and been unmoved by most cruelties, told his driver to slow down while he had a closer look.

We were nearer now and could hear the faint whiplash of commands, see a figure stirring here and there. I gripped the arm of Moses Sonenschein beside me and said: "Those poor bloody girls. They'll /164/ freeze to death. They'll die of exposure in this weather."

Moses, son of a Polish Rabbi and a sincerely religious man, murmured, as he always murmured: "It is the will of God."

I hardly heard him. The full meaning of the horrible vista was slowly becoming clear to my mind which at first had been numbed by the sight.

"Do you know what it is, Moses?" I said. "It's a typhus inspection. If they don't die of exposure, half of them will die in the gas chambers!"

"It is the will of God."

The lorry gathered speed again. The silent naked phalanx, the vast female

From *I Cannot Forgive* (New York: Grove Press, 1964).

army that was going to be cut in half disappeared as we rounded a slight curve in the road.

"Moses," I said, "does God really . . ."

Then I stopped. Somehow the question seemed pointless.

The lorry drew into a small forest and I felt, as I climbed down, that at least everything I would see from now on would be an anti-climax, that we had reached our apex of horror for the day; but I was wrong, for Birkenau still had some reserves.

The air, despite the bitter frost, was slightly warm, I noticed; and it was not difficult to see why. Stretching all around us were ditches vast enough to hold a row of houses, the ditches that spawned that red glow I could see in the sky from the mother camp; great, gaping sores in the forest, not blazing now, but still smouldering.

I moved to the edge of one and gazed in. The heat struck my face and at the bottom of this great open oven I could see bones; small bones. The bones of children.

Moses murmured: "It is the will of God."

I had no time to reply, for we were ordered to work, driven into a huge barracks about sixty yards long. Every inch of its space was packed with clothes of every size, shape and quality; and our job, we were told, was to re-move enough to give the Birkenau prisoners room to work.

I worked blindly, automatically, fast, trying to get the stench of that pit out of my nostrils, to wipe the picture of those naked girls out of my mind; but it was impossible. Every time I picked up a child's overcoat, I thought of those bones. Every time I loaded a bundle of women's clothes, I thought of those who had no clothes.

We worked for three hours in that barracks, like ants burrowing in a graveyard; and when we were finished and were back on our lorry, I suddenly found myself dreading the sight of that women's camp again, yet lured by the awful fascination of it. I felt I had to know what had happened, how many were left, how many would die. /165/

They were still standing there, naked in the frost; but this time the ranks were much thinner; and now the lorries were packed to capacity. Only the si-lence, the overpowering silence, was the same; but as we drew close, it was ripped to pieces.

The engines of forty lorries roared simultaneously, shaking the still air, dominating it; but they were not quite loud enough to cloak the shame of the deed.

From the throats of those thousands about to die came a banshee wail that rose shriller and shriller and became louder and louder and went on and on and on, a piercing protest that only death could stop; and then came the panic that was inevitable.

The trucks started to move. A woman flung herself over the side. Then another . . . and another. The S.S. moved in with their sticks and their whips to beat back those who were trying to follow. Those who had jumped were being beaten too and were trying to clamber back. They fell beneath the quickening wheels while this funeral for the living dead went faster and faster until we could see it no more.

Moses Sonenschein murmured: "There is no God . . ."

Then his voice rose to a shout: *"There is no God! And, if there is, curse Him, curse Him, curse Him!"*

Again I said nothing, for there was nothing to say. Instead I turned my back on Birkenau and hoped I would never see it again. I am glad that at that moment I did not know I was soon to be transferred from the mother camp and was to spend a year and a half there. /166/

Associated Press

AUSCHWITZ CAMP TRIAL TESTIMONY

Unfortunately we cannot reassure ourselves with the thought that a camp like Auschwitz was run by madmen or pathological criminals. Ordinary human beings regarded this as their "place of work."

The Deputy, *Act Five, Scene Two*

FRANKFURT, Germany—A P—Five months of grim testimony have pin-pointed Wilhelm Boger as the main defendant in the long Auschwitz death camp trial.

Witness after witness singles out Boger as the most sadistic of the 21 former SS guards and functionaries accused of participating in Nazi murders at Auschwitz where experts estimate three to four million inmates were killed.

Their minute descriptions of the 58-year-old ex-SS sergeant and Gestapo agent killing adult and child inmates by hanging, beating, kicking, starving, suffocating, shooting and gassing frequently leave Presiding Judge Hans Hofmeyer pale faced and gasping in horror.

Tears invariably trickle down Hofmeyer's cheeks when witnesses describe what they call the "Boger swing" and what the defendant still terms "my talking machine"—a torture apparatus to which inmates were bound and then beaten with such force on their genitals that the victim swung back and forth.

Boger listens intently. He rarely shows any emotion. Sometimes he sneers and smirks, especially when one of his former prisoners breaks down and weeps on seeing him again after nearly 20 years.

Now and then Boger jumps to his feet, jerks his full six feet two inches to rigid attention and screams that the witness is lying.

He once advised Hofmeyer there would be far less juvenile delinquency if his "swing" were used on contemporary German youth "since beating never hurt anyone."

What kind of a person is Boger, the man said to have frequently compared Jews and Slavs to "lice that must be stamped out"?

A former SS colleague in Auschwitz testified that he was an ideal family man—"a father who spent his free time with his wife and children instead of joining his comrades in the camp's club for sergeants."

He is said to have taken great care that his three daughters were reared in the strict Lutheran faith of their parents—"that they all joined hands with their parents in prayer to give thanks for their blessings before every meal."

The vine-covered bungalow inhabited by the Boger family just outside Auschwitz' main gates—they could see from their front windows the camp sign proclaiming "work brings freedom"—was equipped with unpainted wooden furniture issued by the SS quartermaster.

In contrast to this were Boger's interrogation quarters inside the camp.

Associated Press dispatch, Frankfurt, Germany, June 15, 1964.

Former inmates say he furnished them lavishly with rich oriental rugs stolen from wealthy French Jews.

Known at Auschwitz for his spit and polish, Boger shows up at every trial session in a neatly pressed dark suit with a freshly laundered white handkerchief in his breast pocket. But he admits that a normal day's work in Auschwitz left him "in a bit of a mess."

Witnesses say he dripped with the blood of his victims which he washed off with a brisk shower before slipping into a freshly laundered and pressed uniform for the evening's reunion with his family.

Acquaintances of Mrs. Boger report she readily admits Auschwitz was no holiday center, but insists her husband is "too kind hearted" to have ever taken pride—as is charged—in his former title, "the torture master of Auschwitz."

As an example of his kindness, she is reported to have pointed out that he was not at all angry on learning in pre-trial confinement that his oldest daughter had given birth to an illegitimate child fathered by a Sicilian laborer.

Boger gave his blessing to his grandchild, but forbade his daughter to marry the Sicilian as marriage with an Italian "would be a national disgrace."

"As a well brought up German girl, she followed his desires," said the acquaintances.

Boger claims that he merely followed orders in Auschwitz and only reverted to what he calls "sharper methods" when inmates refused to obey his orders.

He insists this was the case when he was "forced to take action" against inmates during the Auschwitz death march to Austria after the camp was partially evacuated in January, 1945.

Survivors of the death march testify that he daily shot hundreds of half starved prisoners who collapsed from exhaustion.

Records of the court show that Boger, son of a Stuttgart drunk, managed to complete about 11 years of school before becoming an apprentice salesman with a hometown firm. A brother, whom Boger refers to as "the black sheep of the family," was a procurer and petty thief who disappeared sometime during the Third Reich.

In 1922 at the age of 16, Boger joined a Nazi youth organization in the fledgling years of the Hitler movement. Eight years later, he became a member of the SS Elite Guard.

He frequently boasts to the court that he is "an old fighter," Nazi terminology for one who joined Hitler when he was still struggling for recognition.

With the Nazis in power in 1933, Boger became a Gestapo detective and, the prosecution says, delivered the first proof that he was a master of third-degree interrogation methods.

In 1941, he donned his SS uniform to join German forces marching on Russia. After nearly a year of fighting, he was wounded and sent to the Gestapo unit in Auschwitz.

After the war, he escaped from an American prisoner of war camp and returned to Stuttgart where he joined under his own name a business firm as an office worker.

Acquaintances say he devoted the postwar years to his job, family and television viewing.

"He lived a typical middle class German life—sober, industrious and adhering to all the outward bourgeois virtues," a member of the prosecutor's staff said.

"He got into trouble only by being on the losing side."

Hannah Arendt

DUTIES OF A LAW-ABIDING CITIZEN

Eichmann orders!
He likes to make himself important, he's always
going on about the Führer's decree—because
on his own hook he wouldn't risk a thing.

The Deputy, *Act Three, Scene Three*

. . . Eichmann's opportunities for feeling like Pontius Pilate were many, and as the months and the years went by, he lost the need to feel anything at all. This was the way things were, this was the new law of the land, based on the Führer's order; whatever he did he did, as far as he could see, as a law-abiding citizen. He did his *duty,* as he told the police and the court over and over again; he not only obeyed *orders,* he also obeyed the *law.* Eichmann had a muddled inkling that this could be an important distinction, but neither the defense nor the judges ever took him up on it. The well-worn coins of "superior orders" versus "acts of state" were handed back and forth; they had governed the whole discussion of these matters during the Nuremberg Trials, for no other reason than that they gave the illusion that the altogether unprecedented could be judged according to precedents and the standards that went with them. Eichmann, with his rather modest mental gifts, was certainly the last man in the courtroom to be expected to challenge these notions and to strike out on his own. Since, in addition to performing what he conceived to be the duties of a law-abiding citizen, he had also acted upon orders—always so careful to be "covered"—he became completely muddled, and ended by stressing alternately the virtues and the vices of blind obedience, or the "obedience of corpses," *Kadavergehorsam,* as he himself called it.

The first indication of Eichmann's vague notion that there was more involved in this whole business than the question of the soldier's carrying out orders that are clearly criminal in nature and intent appeared during the police examination, when he suddenly declared with great emphasis that he had lived his whole life according to Kant's moral precepts, and especially according to a Kantian definition of duty. This was outrageous, on the face of it, /120/ and also incomprehensible, since Kant's moral philosophy is so closely bound up with man's faculty of judgment, which rules out blind obedience. The examining officer did not press the point, but Judge Raveh, either out of curiosity or out of indignation at Eichmann's having dared to invoke Kant's name in connection with his crimes, decided to question the accused. And, to the surprise of everybody, Eichmann came up with an approximately correct definition of the categorical imperative: "I meant by my remark about Kant that the principle of my will must always be such that it can become the principle of general laws" (which is not the case with theft or murder, for instance, because the thief or the murderer cannot conceivably wish to live under a legal system that would give others the right to rob or murder him). Upon further questioning, he added that he had read Kant's *Critique of Practical Reason.* He then proceeded to explain that from the moment he was charged with carrying out the Final Solution he had ceased to live according to Kantian

From "Duties of a Law-Abiding Citizen," *Eichmann in Jerusalem: A Report on the Banality of Evil* (New York: The Viking Press, 1963), pp. 120–134.

principles, that he had known it, and that he had consoled himself with the thought that he no longer "was master of his own deeds," that he was unable "to change anything." What he failed to point out in court was that in this "period of crimes legalized by the state," as he himself now called it, he had not simply dismissed the Kantian formula as no longer applicable, he had distorted it to read: Act as if the principle of your actions were the same as that of the legislator or of the law of the land – or, in Hans Frank's formulation of "the categorical imperative in the Third Reich," which Eichmann might have known: "Act in such a way that the Führer, if he knew your action, would approve it" (*Die Technik des Staates,* 1942, pp. 15 – 16). Kant, to be sure, had never intended to say anything of the sort; on the contrary, to him every man was a legislator the moment he started to act: by using his "practical reason" man found the principles that could and should be the principles of law. But it is true that Eichmann's unconscious distortion agrees with what he himself called the version of Kant "for the household use of the little man." In this household use, all that is left of Kant's spirit is the demand that a man do more than obey the law, that he go beyond the mere call of obedience and identify his own will with the principle behind the law – the source from which the law sprang. In Kant's philosophy, that source was practical reason; in Eichmann's household /121/ use of him, it was the will of the Führer. Much of the horribly painstaking thoroughness in the execution of the Final Solution – a thoroughness that usually strikes the observer as typically German, or else as characteristic of the perfect bureaucrat – can be traced to the odd notion, indeed very common in Germany, that to be law-abiding means not merely to obey the laws but to act as though one were the legislator of the laws that one obeys. Hence the conviction that nothing less than going beyond the call of duty will do.

Whatever Kant's role in the formation of "the little man's" mentality in Germany may have been, there is not the slightest doubt that in one respect Eichmann did indeed follow Kant's precepts: a law was a law, there could be no exceptions. In Jerusalem, he admitted only two such exceptions during the time when "eighty million Germans" had each had "his decent Jew": he had helped a half-Jewish cousin, and a Jewish couple in Vienna for whom his uncle had intervened. This inconsistency still made him feel somewhat uncomfortable, and when he was questioned about it during cross-examination, he became openly apologetic: he had "confessed his sins" to his superiors. This uncompromising attitude toward the performances of his murderous duties damned him in the eyes of the judges more than anything else that was comprehensible, but in his own eyes it was precisely what justified him, as it had once silenced whatever conscience he might have had left. No exceptions – this was the proof that he had always acted against his "inclinations," whether they were sentimental or inspired by interest, that he had always done his "duty."

Doing his "duty" finally brought him into open conflict with orders from his superiors. During the last year of the war, more than two years after the Wannsee Conference, he experienced his last crisis of conscience. As the defeat approached, he was confronted by men from his own ranks who fought more and more insistently for exceptions and, eventually, for the cessation of the Final Solution. That was the moment when his caution broke down and he began, once more, taking initiatives – for instance, he organized the foot marches of Jews from Budapest to the Austrian border after Allied bombing had knocked out the transportation system. It now was the fall of 1944, and

Eichmann knew that Himmler had ordered the dismantling of the extermination facili- /122/ ties in Auschwitz and that the game was up. . . . /123/
    In Jerusalem, confronted with documentary proof of his extraordinary
loyalty to Hitler and the Führer's order, Eichmann tried a number of times to
explain that during the Third Reich "the Führer's words had the force of
law" (*Führerworte haben Gesetzeskraft*), which meant, among other things, that if
the order came directly from Hitler it did not have to be in writing. He tried
to explain that this was why he had never asked for a written order from Hitler (no such document relating to the Final Solution has ever been found;
probably it never existed), but had demanded to see a written order from
Himmler. To be sure, this was a fantastic state of affairs, and whole libraries
of very "learned" juridical comment have been written, all demonstrating that
the Führer's *words*, his oral pronouncements, were the basic law of the land.
Within this "legal" framework, every order contrary in letter or spirit to a
word spoken by Hitler was, by definition, unlawful. Eichmann's position,
therefore, showed a most unpleasant resemblance to that of the often-cited
soldier who, acting in a normal legal framework, refuses to carry out orders
that run counter to his ordinary experience of lawfulness and hence can be
recognized by him as criminal. The extensive literature on the subject usually
supports its case with the common equivocal meaning of the word "law,"
which in this context means sometimes the law of the land—that is, posited,
positive law—and sometimes the law that supposedly speaks in all men's
hearts with an identical voice. To fall back on an unequivocal voice of conscience—or, in the even vaguer language of the jurists, on a "general sentiment of humanity" (Oppenheim-Lauterpacht in *International Law*, 1952)—not
only begs the question, it signifies a deliberate refusal to take no- /132/ tice of
the central moral, legal, and political phenomena of our century.
    To be sure, it was not merely Eichmann's conviction that Himmler was now
giving "criminal" orders that determined his actions. But the personal element undoubtedly involved was not fanaticism, it was his genuine, "boundless
and immoderate admiration for Hitler" (as one of the defense witnesses called
it)—for the man who had made it "from lance corporal to Chancellor of the
Reich." It would be idle to try to figure out which was stronger in him, his admiration for Hitler or his determination to remain a law-abiding citizen of the
Third Reich when Germany was already in ruins. Both motives came into
play once more during the last days of the war, when he was in Berlin and
saw with violent indignation how everybody around him was sensibly enough
getting himself fixed up with forged papers before the arrival of the Russians
or the Americans. A few weeks later, Eichmann, too, began to travel under an
assumed name, but by then Hitler was dead, and the "law of the land" was no
longer in existence, and he, as he pointed out, was no longer bound by his
oath. For the oath taken by the members of the S.S. differed from the military
oath sworn by the soldiers in that it bound them only to Hitler, not to Germany.
    The case of the conscience of Adolf Eichmann, which is admittedly com-
plicated but is by no means unique, is scarcely comparable to the case of the
German generals, one of whom, when asked at Nuremberg, "How was it possible that all of you honorable generals could continue to serve a murderer
with such unquestioning loyalty?," replied that it was "not the task of a soldier
to act as judge over his supreme commander. Let history do that or God in
heaven." (Thus General Alfred Jodl, hanged at Nuremberg.) Eichmann,
much less intelligent and without any education to speak of, at least dimly

realized that it was not an order but a law which had turned them all into criminals. The distinction between an order and the Führer's word was that the latter's validity was not limited in time and space, which is the outstanding characteristic of the former. This is also the true reason why the Führer's order for the Final Solution was followed by a huge shower of regulations and directives, all drafted by expert lawyers and legal advisers, not by mere administrators; this order, in contrast to ordinary orders, was treated as a law. Needless to add, the resulting /133/ legal paraphernalia, far from being a mere symptom of German pedantry or thoroughness, served most effectively to give the whole business its outward appearance of legality.

And just as the law in civilized countries assumes that the voice of conscience tells everybody "Thou shalt not kill," even though man's natural desires and inclinations may at times be murderous, so the law of Hitler's land demanded that the voice of conscience tell everybody: "Thou shalt kill," although the organizers of the massacres knew full well that murder is against the normal desires and inclinations of most people. Evil in the Third Reich had lost the quality by which most people recognize it—the quality of temptation. Many Germans and many Nazis, probably an overwhelming majority of them, must have been tempted *not* to murder, *not* to rob, *not* to let their neighbors go off to their doom (for that the Jews were transported to their doom they knew, of course, even though many of them may not have known the gruesome details), and not to become accomplices in all these crimes by benefiting from them. But, God knows, they had learned how to resist temptation. /134/

William L. Shirer

PROFESSOR AUGUST HIRT

. . . *from the photographs*
and the measurements of the head and finally the skull
our team in Strassburg can carry out exacting
researches in comparative anatomy.

The Deputy, *Act One, Scene Two*

[A] German doctor who had "far-reaching perspectives" was Professor August Hirt, head of the Anatomical Institute of the University of Strasbourg. His special field was somewhat different from those of the others and he explained it in a letter at Christmas time of 1941 to S.S. Lieutenant General Rudolf Brandt, Himmler's adjutant.

We have large collections of skulls of almost all races and peoples at our disposal. Of the Jewish race, however, only very few specimens of skulls are available. . . . The war in the East now presents us with the opportunity to overcome this deficiency. By procuring the skulls of the Jewish-Bolshevik commissars, who represent the prototype of the repulsive, but characteristic, subhuman, we have the chance now to obtain scientific material.

Professor Hirt did not want the skulls of "Jewish-Bolshevik commissars"

From *The Rise and Fall of the Third Reich* (New York: Simon and Schuster, Inc., 1960).

already dead. He proposed that the heads of these persons first be measured while they were alive. Then—

> Following the subsequently induced death of the Jew, whose head should not be damaged, the physician will sever the head from the body and will forward it . . . in a hermetically sealed tin can.

Whereupon Dr. Hirt would go to work, he promised, on further scientific measurements.[73] Himmler was delighted. He directed that Professor Hirt "be supplied with everything needed for his research work."

He was well supplied. The actual supplier was an interesting Nazi individual by the name of Wolfram Sievers, who spent considerable time on the witness stand at the main Nuremberg trial and at the subsequent "Doctors' Trial," in the latter of which he was a defendant.* Sievers, a former bookseller, had risen to be a colonel of the S.S. and executive secretary of the Ahnenerbe, the Institute for Research into Heredity, one of the ridiculous "cultural" organizations established by Himmler to pursue one of his many lunacies. It had, according to Sievers, fifty "research branches," of which one was called the "Institute for Military Scientific Research," which Sievers also headed. He was a shifty-eyed, Mephistophelean-looking fellow with a thick, ink-black beard and at /980/ Nuremberg he was dubbed the "Nazi Bluebeard," after the famous French killer. Like so many other characters in this history, he kept a meticulous diary, and this and his correspondence, both of which survived, contributed to his gallows end.

By June 1943 Sievers had collected at Auschwitz the men and women who were to furnish the skeletons for the "scientific measurements" of Professor Dr. Hirt at the University of Strasbourg. "A total of 115 persons, including 79 Jews, 30 Jewesses, 4 'Asiatics' and 2 Poles were processed," Sievers reported, requesting the S.S. main office in Berlin for transportation for them from Auschwitz to the Natzweiler concentration camp near Strasbourg. The British cross-examiner at Nuremberg inquired as to the meaning of "processing."

"Anthropological measurements," Sievers replied.

"Before they were murdered they were anthropologically measured? That was all there was to it, was it?"

"And casts were taken," Sievers added.

What followed was narrated by S.S. Captain Josef Kramer, himself a veteran exterminator from Auschwitz, Mauthausen, Dachau and other camps and who achieved fleeting fame as the "Beast of Belsen" and was condemned to death by a British court at Lueneburg.

> Professor Hirt of the Strasbourg Anatomical Institute told me of the prisoner convoy en route from Auschwitz. He said these persons were to be killed by poison gas in the gas chamber of the Natzweiler camp, their bodies then to be taken to the Anatomical Institute for his disposal. He gave me a bottle containing about half a pint of salts—I think they were cyanide salts—and told me the approximate dosage I would have to use to poison the arriving inmates from Auschwitz.
>
> Early in August 1943, I received eighty inmates who were to be killed with the gas Hirt had given me. One night I went to the gas chamber in a small car with about fifteen women this first time. I told the women they

73. International Military Tribunal, *Trial of the Major War Criminals Before the International Military Tribunal (TMWC)*, (Published at Nuremberg), XX, 519. /1172/
*And in which he was condemned to death, and hanged. /980/

had to go into the chamber to be disinfected. I did not tell them, however, that they were to be gassed.

By this time the Nazis had perfected the technique.

With the help of a few S.S. men [Kramer continued] I stripped the women completely and shoved them into the gas chamber when they were stark naked.
When the door closed they began to scream. I introduced a certain amount of salt through a tube . . . and observed through a peephole what happened inside the room. The women breathed for about half a minute before they fell to the floor. After I had turned on the ventilation I opened the door. I found the women lying lifeless on the floor and they were covered with excrements.

Captain Kramer testified that he repeated the performance until all eighty inmates had been killed and turned the bodies over to Professor /981/ Hirt, "as requested." He was asked by his interrogator what his feelings were at the time, and he gave a memorable answer that gives insight into a phenomenon in the Third Reich that has seemed so elusive of human understanding.

I had no feelings in carrying out these things because I had received an order to kill the eighty inmates in the way I already told you.
That, by the way, was the way I was trained.[74]

Another witness testified as to what happened next. He was Henry Herypierre, a Frenchman who worked in the Anatomical Institute at Strasbourg as Professor Hirt's laboratory assistant until the Allies arrived.

The first shipment we received was of the bodies of thirty women. . . . These thirty female bodies arrived still warm. The eyes were wide open and shining. They were red and bloodshot and were popping from their sockets. There were also traces of blood about the nose and mouth. No *rigor mortis* was evident.

Herypierre suspected that they had been done to death and secretly copied down their prison numbers which were tattooed on their left arms. Two more shipments of fifty-six men arrived, he said, in exactly the same condition. They were pickled in alcohol under the expert direction of Dr. Hirt. But the professor was a little nervous about the whole thing. "Peter," he said to Herypierre, "if you can't keep your trap shut, you'll be one of them."
Professor Dr. Hirt went about his work nonetheless. According to the correspondence of Sievers, the professor severed the heads and, as he wrote, "assembled the skeleton collection which was previously nonexistent." But there were difficulties and after hearing them described by Dr. Hirt—Sievers himself had no expert medical or anatomical knowledge—the chief of the Ahnenerbe reported them to Himmler on September 5, 1944.

In view of the vast amount of scientific research involved, the job of reducing the corpses has not yet been completed. This requires some time for 80 corpses.

74. Examination of Josef Kramer, Case I of the *Trials of the War Criminals*—the so-called "Doctors' Trial," entitled *United States v. Brandt, et al.* /1172/

And time was running out. Advancing American and French troops were nearing Strasbourg. Hirt requested "directives as to what should be done with the collection."

The corpses can be stripped of the flesh and thereby rendered unidentifiable [Sievers reported to headquarters on behalf of Dr. Hirt]. This would mean, however, that at least part of the whole work had been done for nothing and that this unique collection would be lost to science, since it would be impossible to make plaster casts afterwards. /982/

The skeleton collection as such is inconspicuous. The flesh parts could be declared as having been left by the French at the time we took over the Anatomical Institute* and would be turned over for cremating. Please advise me which of the following three proposals is to be carried out: 1. The collection as a whole to be preserved; 2. The collection to be dissolved in part; 3. The collection to be completely dissolved.

"Why were you wanting to deflesh the bodies, witness?" the British prosecutor asked in the stillness of the Nuremberg courtroom. "Why were you suggesting that the blame should be passed on to the French?"

"As a layman I could have no opinion in this matter," the "Nazi Bluebeard" replied. "I merely transmitted an inquiry from Professor Hirt. I had nothing to do with the murdering of these people. I simply carried through the function of a mailman."

"You were the post office," the prosecutor rejoined, "another of these distinguished Nazi post offices, were you?"

It was a leaky defense offered by many a Nazi at the trials and on this occasion, as on others, the prosecution nailed it.[75]

The captured S.S. files reveal that on October 26, 1944, Sievers reported that "the collection in Strasbourg has been completely dissolved in accordance with the directive. This arrangement is for the best in view of the whole situation."[76]

Herypierre later described the attempt—not altogether successful—to hide the traces.

In September, 1944, the Allies made an advance on Belfort, and Professor Hirt ordered Bong and Herr Maier to cut up these bodies and have them burned in the crematory. . . . I asked Herr Maier the next day whether he had cut up all the bodies, but Herr Bong replied: "We couldn't cut up all the bodies, it was too much work. We left a few bodies in the storeroom."

They were discovered there by an Allied team when units of the U.S. Seventh Army, with the French 2nd Armored Division in the lead, entered Strasbourg a month later.†[77] /983/

---

*Germany had annexed Alsace after the fall of France in 1940 and the Germans had taken over the University of Strasbourg. /983/

75. Sievers' testimony, *TMWC*, XX, 521–525. /1172/

76. *Ibid.*, p. 526. /1172/

†Professor Dr. Hirt disappeared. As he left Strasbourg he was heard boasting that no one would ever take him alive. Apparently no one has—alive or dead. /983/

77. The testimony of Henry Herypierre is in the transcript of the "Doctors' Trial." /1172/

Raul Hilberg

ORGANIZATION OF BYSTANDERS

How can you people go on living, knowing
what day after day, for an entire year,
has been happening here?

The Deputy, *Act Five, Scene Three*

With the onset of the war and the beginning of the "final solution of the Jewish question" in Europe, the problem of migration was fundamentally altered. Before the war the Jews made every attempt to hold on, and the Germans applied every pressure to effect a Jewish mass departure; by 1941 all the Jews of German-dominated Europe wanted to leave, but now the German machinery of destruction held them captive.

On the outside the issue between the world Jewish community and the Allied governments had sharpened. Before the war the Jews could argue only that emigration was necessary for the relief of misery, and the Allied position was correspondingly based on "absorptive capacities" and "political considerations." Now rescue had become for the Jews a matter of life and death. If the Nazi ring could not be sprung open and the Jews brought to a safe destination, they would die in mounting numbers as the catastrophe quickened. The British government and its helpers were not moved to drastic action by this situation. The old reasons for barring the Jews from Palestine were even stronger now, and the old arguments with respect to the political situation were reinforced with the war. Significantly, however, the dichotomy between the Jewish and Allied positions was not from the outset clearly visible. The Jews were slow to react to the challenge; and when the apparatus of Jewish organizations was finally activated in behalf of the victims in Europe, the Jewish leadership, already confronted with millions of dead, was prepared to do little more than save those who were already safe.

We have pointed out repeatedly that the Jews did not anticipate the "final solution." When they woke up to the facts, the disaster was already upon them. By the summer of 1942, however, the volume of deportations and killings had far surpassed the limits within which such an operation could be kept secret from the outside world. Hints, rumors, and reports began to accumulate in information-gathering agencies at widely scattered points.

On August 1, 1942, at a time when about 1,500,000 Jews were already dead, the chief of the Geneva office of the World Jewish Congress, Dr. Gerhardt Riegner, heard through a German industrialist "that a plan had been discussed in Hitler's headquarters for the extermination of all Jews in Nazi-occupied lands." Riegner sent the information via the American and British consulates to Rabbi Dr. Stephen Wise in the United States and M. P. Sidney Silverman in England. Silverman got the information, Wise did not. Silverman then transmitted the message to Rabbi Wise. The rabbi, who was American Jewry's most prominent leader, decided to carry the report to Undersecretary of State Welles. The Undersecretary asked him not to release the story until an attempt could be made to confirm it.[12]

From *The Destruction of the European Jews* (London: W. H. Allen & Co., Ltd., 1961).
12. Stephen Wise, *Challenging Years* (New York, 1949), pp. 274–75. Henry Morgenthau, Jr., "The Morgenthau Diaries VI — The Refugee Run-Around," *Collier's*, November 1, 1947, pp. 22–23, 62, 65. Morgenthau was then U.S. Secretary of the Treasury. In 1942 the Treasury Department was not yet apprised of anything. /718/

The following three months were spent in checking the Riegner report. They were Jewry's bloodiest months. About one million Jews died during this period. The second sweep in Russia was in fullest swing; the Polish ghettos were being emptied out; from the western states and from the Reich itself dozens of transports were converging upon the killing centers. On October 5, 1942, the Jewish Telegraphic Agency reported that mass executions of thousands of /718/ Jews of all ages, including women, were taking place from time to time. Systematic deportations were engulfing the Jews of Lodz. The Lodz Jews, said the telegraphic agency, "are poisoned by gas."[13]

In the meantime, the checking continued. Finally, in November, 1942, the American Legation in Berne transmitted to Washington four affidavits which confirmed Riegner's original report. Welles thereupon told Wise that the information could be made public.[14] On December 17, 1942, the Department of State joined the other Allied governments in a declaration entitled "German Policy of Extermination of the Jewish Race," which stated that the responsible perpetrators "shall not escape retribution."[15]

The Jewish leadership was now confronted with the facts; the issue was clear. What, then, did Jewry's leaders propose to do? On January 6, 1943, Henry Monsky, president of B'nai Brith, called a preliminary meeting of an American Jewish Conference. In his letter of invitation, which was sent to thirty-four Jewish organizations, he wrote:

> American Jewry, which will be required in large measure to assume the responsibility of representing the interests of our people at the Victory Peace Conference, must be ready to voice the judgment of American Jews along with that of other Jewish communities of the free countries with respect to the post-war status of Jews and the upbuilding of a Jewish Palestine.

In this letter no warning to the Germans is proposed, no scheme to put an end to the destruction process is suggested; the destruction of the European Jews is not even mentioned.[16] The European Jews are already given up, and all thoughts turn to postwar salvage. Clearly, the world-wide Jewish action machinery—the network of Jewish pressure groups—was at a standstill. Budgets were at a low point. The holocaust was unopposed. The paralysis was complete.

On January 21, 1943, Undersecretary of State Welles received Cable 482 from the Legation in Berne; the cable contained a message from Riegner reporting that Jews were being killed in Poland at the rate of 6000 a day and that Jews in Germany and Roumania were starving to death. Welles passed on the cable to Wise and instructed Minister Harrison to keep sending full reports from Switzerland. The Jewish organizations now seemed to be jolted. A mass

13. Jewish Telegraphic Agency, *Daily News Bulletin*, New York, October 6, 1942, p. 4, NI-12321. /719/
14. Morgenthau in *Collier's*, November 1, 1947. /719/
15. Department of State press release of December 17, 1942, in *International Conference on Military Trials*, pp. 9–10. For original British draft of declaration, together with U.S. and Soviet amendments, see correspondence, dated December 7–17, 1942, in *Foreign Relations 1942*, I, 66–70. Harold H. Tittmann, assistant to President Roosevelt's personal representative to Pope Pius XII, asked Cardinal Secretary of State Maglione whether there was not something the Holy See could do "along similar lines." The Cardinal replied that the Holy See was "unable to denounce publicly particular atrocities." It could only condemn atrocities in general. For the rest, "everything possible was being done privately to relieve the distress of the Jews." Tittmann report in telegram by Harrison (U.S. Minister in Switzerland) to Hull, December 26, 1942, *ibid.*, pp. 70–71. /719/
16. Kohanski, *American Jewish Conference, First Session*, pp. 15, 319. /719/

meeting was held in Madison Square Garden, relief agencies doubled their efforts, and rescue schemes poured into Washington.[17]

The Jewish restlessness apparently disquieted the State Department, and the department took the position that /719/ the question had to be "explored." Some of its political experts then decided to suppress the flow of information. A cable, numbered 354, was dispatched under the signature of Undersecretary Welles to Harrison in Berne. It referred to "Your cable 482, January 21." The text then proceeded as follows:

> In the future we would suggest that you do not accept reports submitted to you to be transmitted to private persons in the United States unless such action is advisable because of extraordinary circumstances. Such private messages circumvent neutral countries' censorship and it is felt that by sending them we risk the possibility that steps would necessarily be taken by the neutral countries to curtail or forbid our means of communication for confidential official matter.[18]

The cable was initialed by four officers of the Foreign Service. The message was handled only by the European Division and the political adviser of the State Department; the Undersecretary is believed to have signed the document without full awareness of its contents.[19] It appears, then, that the career men were attempting to withhold the information not only from the Jewish community but also from the men who directed the affairs of the United States government.

In March, 1943, the British Foreign Secretary, Anthony Eden, arrived in Washington for conferences with American leaders. During one of these discussions the American Secretary of State Hull brought up the problem of rescuing the Jews, in the presence of President Roosevelt, Harry Hopkins, Undersecretary Welles, British Ambassador Halifax, and the Assistant Undersecretary of State in the British Foreign Office, William Strang. Hopkins' summary of that exchange of words was:

> Hull raised the question of the 60 or 70 thousand Jews that are in Bulgaria and are threatened with extermination unless we could get them out and, very urgently, pressed Eden for an answer to the problem. Eden replied that the whole problem of the Jews in Europe is very difficult and that we should move very cautiously about offering to take all Jews out of a country like Bulgaria. If we do that, then the Jews of the world will be wanting us to make similar offers in Poland and Germany. Hitler might well take us up on any such offer and there simply are not enough ships and means of transportation in the world to handle them.

17. Morgenthau in *Collier's*, November 1, 1947. DuBois, *The Devil's Chemists*, pp. 184, 187. DuBois was then in the Foreign Funds Control Division of the Treasury Department. /719/
18. Text of cable 354, dated February 10, 1943, in Morgenthau, *Collier's*, November 1, 1947. /720/
19. Josiah DuBois reports that "the 'political boys' had ordered that Treasury was not under any circumstances to have a copy." DuBois, *The Devil's Chemists*, p. 187. Neither Morgenthau nor DuBois believes that Welles signed the message with intent to suppress information about the Jewish catastrophe. The attitude of the European Division in Jewish matters appears to have been recorded before the end of 1941, upon receipt of a suggestion from the Turkish Minister in Bucharest that the Roumanian Jews be brought across Turkey to Palestine. Cavendish Cannon wrote at that time to the acting chief of the division (Atherton) and the adviser on political relations (Dunn) that no formal note should be sent to the British. The arguments against tackling the problem included, among others, "ships," the "Arab question," the possibility of "pressure for an asylum in the western hemisphere," and a possible request for similar treatment of the Jews in Hungary "and, by extension, all countries where there has been intense persecution." Memorandum by Cannon, November 12, 1941, *Foreign Relations 1941*, II, 875–76. /720/

Eden said that the British were ready to take about 60 thousand more Jews to Palestine but the problem of transportation, even from Bulgaria to Palestine is extremely difficult. Furthermore, any such mass movement as that would be very dangerous to security because the Germans would be sure to attempt to put a number of their agents in the group. They have been pretty successful with this tech- /720/ nique both in getting their agents into North and South America.

Eden said that the forthcoming conferences in Bermuda on the whole refugee problem must come to grips with this difficult situation.

Eden said he hoped that on our side we would not make too extravagant promises which could not be delivered because of lack of shipping.[20]

During the following months two abortive rescue schemes were considered in London and Washington. The British government, through the Swiss Legation in Berlin, offered to accept 5000 Jewish children from the *Generalgouvernement* and the occupied eastern territories in Palestine. The German Foreign Office agreed to deliver the children to Britain in exchange for interned Germans. The British refused to release any Germans on the ground that the children were not nationals of the British Empire. That was where the matter rested.[21]

The second rescue scheme evolved when Undersecretary of State Welles cabled to Berne for more information about the destruction of the European Jews. In reply he received what appears to be the Antonescu plan for the release of some 60,000 Jews in exchange for money. The State Department experts were not enthusiastic about a ransoming attempt; they had to be worn down by the department's economic adviser Dr. Herbert Feis, the weighty intervention of the Treasury Department's Foreign Funds Control Division under John Pehle, and an appeal by Rabbi Wise to President Roosevelt himself. After eight months the State Department issued a license enabling Jewish organizations to deposit money to the credit of Axis officials in blocked accounts in Switzerland. The license was issued over the opposition of the British Foreign Office, which—in the words of a note delivered to the American Embassy in London by the British Ministry of Economic Warfare—was concerned with the "difficulties of disposing of any considerable number of Jews" in the event of their release from Axis Europe.[22]

The rescue effort was failing. Within the State Department there was disinclination to undertake large-scale action; within the Foreign Office there was fear of large-scale success; and within Axis Europe fewer and fewer Jews remained. The frustrations inherent in this situation finally resulted in an establishment of special rescue machinery in the American Jewish community and in the United States government itself.

From August 29 to September 2, 1943, the first session of the American Jewish Conference, which had been called seven months before, met in deliberation. The destruction of the European Jews was still not on its agenda. In the preliminary meeting only two substantive points had been drawn up for discussion: "rights and status of Jews in the post-war world" and "rights of the

20. Memorandum by Hopkins on meeting between Roosevelt, Hopkins, Hull, Welles, Eden, Halifax, and Strang, on March 27, 1943, in Robert E. Sherwood, *Roosevelt and Hopkins* (New York, 1948), p. 717. /721/
21. Wagner to Müller (RSHA), July 13, 1943, NG-4747. Wagner via *Staatssekretär* to Ribbentrop, July 21, 1943, NG-4786. Von Thadden to Wagner, April 29, 1944, NG-1794. /721/
22. Morgenthau in *Collier's*, November 1, 1947. DuBois, *The Devil's Chemists*, pp. 185–88. /721/

Jewish people with respect to Palestine." In the words of the B'nai Brith delegate David Blumberg, the purpose of the conference was the formulation of a program to be heeded "by the proper authorities after the war is over." Rabbi Dr. Stephen Wise, as delegate of the American Jewish Congress, then declared that the conference would have to deal immediately with the problem of rescuing European Jewry. /721/

An observer, the chairman of the British section of the World Jewish Congress, Dr. Maurice L. Perlzweig, proposed that the conference urge the Allied nations to demand from the Axis the release of its Jewish victims and to proclaim the right of asylum for any Jews who should succeed in escaping. The conference thereupon adopted a resolution calling for a "solemn warning" to the Axis and the establishment of a "temporary asylum" for the Jews.[23] The delegates then adjourned and left the business of the conference in the hands of an interim committee which established, on October 24, 1943, a rescue commission.[24]

One of the commission's efforts was directed towards the creation of a parallel agency in the government. Such an agency was finally set up by executive order after considerable agitation in Congress and a "personal report" by Morgenthau to President Roosevelt on the State Department's conduct in the refugee question. The date of the executive order was January 22, 1944. The title of the agency was the War Refugee Board. Its membership consisted of the Secretaries of State, the Treasury, and War (Hull, Morgenthau, and Stimson); the executive director was John Pehle of the Treasury Department. The board maintained its own network of special representatives abroad.[25]

The rescue program had thus been centralized. A specific agency had been created for the task. That agency had centers for the receipt of information, means of communication, and powers of negotiation. Moreover, it could call upon private Jewish organizations for detailed knowledge, age-old experience, and—in the event of ransom possibilities—"quickly available funds."[26] The challenge came soon, for in the spring of 1944 Hungarian Jewry was threatened with destruction.

We have already seen what happened in Hungary: on March 19, 1944, the Hungarian government was overthrown, and the line to Auschwitz was cleared. For the Germans there was no further barrier; for Jewry there was

23. Kohanski, *American Jewish Conference, First Session*, particularly pp. 15, 18–19, 25–26, 33, 73, 115–17, 127–30. /722/
24. American Jewish Conference, *Report of Interim Committee*, November 1, 1944, pp. 13 ff. /722/
25. The following is a list of the posts:
United Kingdom: Josiah E. DuBois, Jr., general counsel of the board, from the Treasury Department
Turkey: Ira A. Hirschmann, department store executive
Portugal: Dr. Robert C. Dexter, Unitarian Service Committee
Sweden: Iver C. Olsen, Treasury
Switzerland: Rowell McClelland, American Friends Service Committee
Italy: Leonard Ackerman, Treasury
Another post was established in North Africa. American Jewish Conference, *Report of Interim Committee*, 1944, pp. 19–22. Executive Director, War Refugee Board (William O'Dwyer), *Final Summary Report* (Washington, D.C., 1945), pp. 1-6. Morgenthau in *Collier's*, November 1, 1947. DuBois, *The Devil's Chemists*, pp. 15, 31, 188, 198. /722/
26. The War Refugee Board collected a considerable amount of information. In April, 1944, two Slovak Jews escaped from Auschwitz and made their way to Switzerland. They brought with them many details about transport arrivals and gassings in the camp. Not clear is the date on which the statements were received, when they were transmitted to Washington, and what action was based on them. See affidavit by Pehle, November 13, 1947, NI-12545. Further, DuBois, *The Devil's Chemists*, pp. 183–84. Also, the report itself, published by the War Refugee Board in November, 1944, under the title, "The Extermination Camps of Auschwitz and Birkenau" (mimeographed). The War Refugee Board could not spend much money. Under the U.S. Constitution federal expenditures must be authorized by Congress; agencies established by congressional statute are usually provided with necessary funds, but the War Refugee Board was set up by the President in an executive order. /722/

no more protection. Between the Jews and the gas chambers there remained /722/ only a series of predetermined bureaucratic steps. However, the activation of these steps required a certain amount of preparation, and the Germans did not have very much time. They were losing the war. Every day the German position was becoming more difficult. The steady buildup of this destructive operation was the work of an administrative machine in which the bolts were already beginning to loosen. Everything therefore depended on the ability of outside forces to recognize these weaknesses and to immobilize the machine before it could deliver its blow.

The outside world was in a position to attempt a rescue effort on two levels, the physical and the psychological. Physical action could be implemented from the air. We have already noted that a Slovak official furnished to the Jewish Bratislava rescue committee the routes over which the Jews were to be carried to their death. That information was transmitted to Switzerland, but it brought no results. The railway junctions were not bombed. When the transports arrived in Auschwitz, no bombers appeared over the gas chambers. The opportunity was lost. The notion of stopping the killings by physical means apparently occurred to no one. The outside Jews were not accustomed to think about rescue in terms of physical force, and the outside Christians were not thinking about force for the purpose of rescue. The Hungarian Jews thus had to be saved with psychological methods alone.

We know that in the psychological sphere the Allies possessed a potent weapon. At a time when Hungary was gripped with the fear of Allied air raids, the Hungarian government was concentrating the Jews in cities of 10,000 people or more. Today one might easily question why no one thought then about the possible consequences of an Allied promise of immunity that would have been honored as long as the Jews remained in those cities. The answer appears to be that the Jews could not think in terms of "interfering" with the war effort, and the Allies on their part could not conceive of such a promise. They could no more take the Jews into account to refrain from bombing than they could think of Jews in planning their missions. The Allied bombers roared over Hungary at will, killing Hungarians and Jews alike.

The world outside was inert. The War Refugee Board and the Jewish offices at its service had posted a receiving organization at the perimeter of the destructive arena. There the rescuers waited for openings, opportunities, and offers. Incredibly enough, an offer was to come.

We have had previous occasion to note that on April 6 and 7, at a time when the German momentum in Hungary was approaching its climax, the Armaments Ministry secured from Hitler himself an authorization to remove 100,000 of the expected Jewish deportees from Auschwitz to construction projects which were then being planned by the Pursuit Planes Staff.[27] Two and a half weeks after this diversion had been authorized, Obersturmbannführer Eichmann called to his office in the Budapest Hotel Majestic a leader of the Jewish rescue committee in Hungary, Joel Brand.[28] Eichmann received Brand with words in the following vein:

Do you know who I am? I have carried out the *Akionen* in the Reich — in Poland — in Czechoslovakia. Now it is Hungary's turn. I let you come here to talk business with you. Before that I investigated you — and your people.

27. See pp. 599–600. /723/
28. Except as indicated otherwise, the entire account of the Brand mission is taken from Alexander Weissberg, *Die Geschichte von Joel Brand* (Cologne-Berlin, 1956). /723/

/723/ Those from the Joint and those from the Agency.[29] And I have come to the conclusion that you still have resources. So I am ready to sell you—a million Jews. All of them I wouldn't sell you. That much money and goods you don't have. But a million—that will go. Goods for blood—blood for goods. You can gather up this million in countries which still have Jews. You can take it from Hungary. From Poland. From Austria. From Theresienstadt. From Auschwitz. From wherever you want. What do you want to save? Virile men? Grown women? Old people? Children? Sit down—and talk.

Brand was a careful negotiator. How was he to get goods, he asked, that the Germans could not confiscate on their own? Eichmann had the answer: Brand was to go abroad; he was to negotiate directly with the Allies and bring back a concrete offer. With these words Eichmann dismissed Brand, warning him in parting that the discussion was a Reich secret that no Hungarian was allowed to suspect.

Sometime in the beginning of May, following the railway conference in Vienna, which determined the routing of the transports, Eichmann called Brand again. "Do you want a million Jews?" If so, Brand was to leave immediately for Istanbul. He was to bring back an offer to deliver trucks. "You deliver one truck for every hundred Jews. That is not much." The total would be 10,000 vehicles. The trucks had to be new and suitable for winter driving. "You can assure the Allies that these trucks will never be used in the West. They will be employed exclusively on the eastern front." In addition, the Germans would be pleased if the Allies would throw in a couple of thousand tons of tea, coffee, soap, and other useful items.

Cautiously, Brand replied: "Mr. Obersturmbannführer, I personally can believe that you will keep your word, but I do not possess ten thousand trucks. The people with whom I must negotiate in Istanbul will demand guarantees. Nobody is going to deliver ten thousand trucks in advance. What assurance can you offer that these million Jews will actually be freed?"

Eichmann thereupon gave a decisive answer. "You think we are all crooks. You hold *us* for what *you* are. Now I am going to prove to you that I trust you more than you trust me. When you come back from Istanbul and tell me that the offer has been accepted, I will dissolve Auschwitz and move 10 per cent of the promised million to the border. You take over the 100,000 Jews and deliver for them afterwards one thousand trucks. And then the deal will proceed step by step. For every hundred thousand Jews, a thousand trucks. You are getting away cheap."

Brand had to conceal his excitement. For the first time he saw a way out. If the verbal assurance could be given in time, the Jews could, without delivering a single truck, score a major breakthrough. To be sure, the Germans could change their conditions. So far they had made no concessions, but if Brand could return with a promise, the Germans could not kill so long as they wanted the trucks. Without blood, no merchandise.[30]

The rescue committee now telegraphed to Istanbul that Brand would be arriving there; the answer came quickly, "Joel should come, Chaim will be there." To the committee this could mean only that Chaim Weizmann him-

29. Reference here is to the American Jewish Joint Distribution Committee and the Jewish Agency for Palestine. /724/
30. Brand did not know of the German plan to use up to 100,000 Jews for forced labor in any case. /724/

self, the president of the Executive of the Jewish Agency, would be on hand.

On May 15 Brand saw Eichmann for the last time. It was the day on which the deportations began. Eichmann /724/ warned Brand to return quickly. If the offer came in time, Auschwitz would be "blown up" (*dann sprenge ich Auschwitz in die Luft*), and the deportees now leaving Hungary would be the first to be sent to the border.

On the following day, Brand secured "full powers" from the *Zentralrat der Ungarischen Juden;* he also received a companion: a Jew who had served the *Abwehr*, Bandi Grosz. The two went to Vienna and, paying for their fare in dollars, left by special plane to Istanbul.

When Brand landed at the Istanbul airport, he made a disturbing discovery. The Jewish Agency had not processed an entry visa for him, and "Chaim" was not there. The man to whom Jerusalem had referred was not the agency's chief executive, Chaim Weizmann, but the chief of its Istanbul office, Chaim Barlasz, and that man was riding around in the city at the very moment of the plane's arrival to obtain a visa for Brand. Fortunately, Brand's counterintelligence companion, Grosz, had many connections in Istanbul. After a few telephone calls by Grosz, the two men were allowed to move into a hotel. There the Jewish Agency representatives were waiting for the emissaries.

Brand was angry and excited. "Comrades, do you realize what is involved?. . . We have to negotiate. . . . With whom can I negotiate? Do you have the power to make agreements . . . ? Twelve thousand people are hauled away every day . . . that is five hundred an hour. . . . Do they have to die because nobody from the Executive is here? . . . I want to telegraph tomorrow that I have secured agreement. . . . Do you know what is involved, comrades? The Germans want to negotiate. The ground is burning under their feet. They feel the coming of the catastrophe. Eichmann has promised us an advance of a hundred thousand Jews. Do you know what this means? . . . I insist, comrades, that a man come here whom all the world knows. The Germans are observing us. They will know at once that Weizmann is here or Shertok. Even if you cannot accomplish anything concrete with the Allies while I am here, I can go back and tell Eichmann that the Agency has accepted. Then Auschwitz can be blown up. . . ."

To the representatives of the Jewish Agency the matter was not so simple. They could not be sure, they said, that a telegram sent to Jerusalem would arrive there without mutilation. No one had enough influence to obtain a plane. No representative of the War Refugee Board was on the scene. Brand wanted to reach Steinhardt, the American Ambassador in Ankara. "Steinhardt," he said, "is supposed to be a good Jew. And besides that, a good man." But no plane seat could be bought for a trip to Ankara. The hours began to pass, then the days. Brand, still waiting for someone to arrive in Istanbul, gave the Jewish Agency representatives some important data. "I gave the comrades an accurate plan of the Auschwitz concentration camp. I demanded the bombing of the gas chambers and crematories insofar as this was technically possible. I demanded diversions and air strikes against the junctions on the railway lines which led to Auschwitz. I gave our comrades accurate information about places where parachute troops could land, and I gave them a list of documents and other things that the parachutists absolutely had to have to get through. I named a number of addresses of reliable helpers on the roads to Budapest."

Brand had exhausted his mission, and it was exhausting him in turn. In repeated discussions with the Jewish Agency representatives he gained the distinct impression that they did not /725/ quite realize what was at stake. "They did not, as we did in Budapest, look daily at death."

As Brand waited for a reply, a number of unexpected things began to happen. For a few days he was in danger of deportation. The Turkish authorities had ordered his apprehension, together with Bandi Grosz, although the latter was a "director" of a Hungarian transport corporation engaged in discussion with the director of a Turkish state transport company. Why the deportation of Grosz? Already Brand suspected that the British were controlling the "main switch," but he dismissed the thought. "I could not believe," he states, "that England—this land which alone fought on while all other countries of Europe surrendered to despotism—that this England which we had admired as the inflexible fighter for freedom wanted simply to sacrifice us, the poorest and weakest of all the oppressed."

Soon, however, another curious situation arose. Moshe Shertok, the chief of the political department of the Jewish Agency, its second in command, was unable to obtain a visa to Turkey. The agency decided to bring Brand to Aleppo in British-occupied Syria; there Shertok was to meet him. On June 5, 1944, after fifteen fruitless days in Istanbul, Brand, with a British visa in his German passport, boarded the Taurus express train. When the train passed through Ankara, a representative of the Jewish Revisionists (*Irgun*), accompanied by an Orthodox Party man, got on to warn him that he was moving into a "trap." Shertok had not obtained a visa because the British wanted to lure Brand into British-controlled territory, where they could arrest him. Britain was in this matter no "ally" (*Die Engländer sind in dieser Frage nicht unsere Verbündeten*). They did not want his mission to succeed. If he continued on his journey, he would never be able to return; he would be arrested.

Brand was confused. The train was about to pull out, and he decided to stay on it. On June 7, 1944, he arrived in Aleppo. A porter entered the compartment and took off Brand's luggage. Brand wanted to follow the porter when an Englishman in civilian clothes blocked his way.

"Mister Brand?"

"Oh, yes."

"This way, please."

Before Brand knew what was happening, two plainclothesmen had pushed him into a waiting jeep whose motor was already running. Brand tried to resist, but it was too late.

After two days of arrest the British brought Brand to a villa where Shertok was waiting. Shertok invited Brand to tell about his mission again. In the presence of the British, who were listening silently, Brand talked for ten to twelve hours. When the session was over, Shertok went into a huddle with the British representatives. Then he turned to Brand. "Dear Joel, I have to tell you something bitter now. You have to go south. The British demand it. I have done everything to change this decision, but it is a decision of the highest authorities. I could not alter it."

For a second Brand did not understand what had been said to him. When finally he caught on, he screamed: "Do you know what you are doing? That is simply murder. That is mass murder. If I don't return our best people will be slaughtered! My wife! My mother! My children will be first! You have to let me go! I have come here under a flag of truce. I have brought you a message. You can accept or reject, but you have no right to hold the messenger. . . . I am here as the messenger of a million people condemned to death. . . . What do you /726/ want from us? What do you want from me . . . ?"

Brand was brought to Cairo for exhaustive intelligence interrogations. He was henceforth a prisoner. Shertok, at the behest of Foreign Minister Eden, flew to London for more "discussions." The War Refugee Board's representative, Ira Hirschmann, chased after Brand in Istanbul and, not finding him there, moved on to Cairo. In Cairo the ranking British official, Deputy Minister of State Lord Moyne, tried to persuade Hirschmann to fly to London too. Hirschmann, a New York department store executive not given to diplomatic niceties, told Moyne that he would be ready to take orders from Eden whenever Moyne decided to follow the instructions of Secretary of State Hull. Finally Hirschmann managed to talk to Brand. By that time it was July.[31]

The almost impossible had happened. An incredible German offer had been met with the most unlikely refusal. There were to be no negotiations; there was to be no bombing. Not even the parachutists had been landed in the right places. Those Jewish volunteers from Palestine were dropped over military targets where most of them could die for England.[32]

By the beginning of July most of the Hungarian Jews were dead. The Jews of Budapest were waiting for their turn. They were saved at the last moment, when the Regent Horthy and the Sztojay government, wearied by the protests of neutral states and the Church and frightened by intercepted Anglo-American teletype messages containing among other things the Jewish requests for target bombings of Hungarian government offices as well as the names of seventy prominent officials, decided to stop the operation in its tracks. Two days after the deportations had come to a halt outside the Hungarian capital, Prime Minister Churchill wrote the following letter to Eden:

> There is no doubt that this is probably the greatest and most horrible crime ever committed in the whole history of the world, and it has been done by scientific machinery by nominally civilised men in the name of a great state and one of the leading races of Europe. It is quite clear that all concerned in this crime who may fall into our hands, including the people who only obeyed orders by carrying out the butcheries, should be put to death after their association with the murders has been proved. . . . There should therefore, in my opinion, be no negotiations of any kind on this subject. Declarations should be made in public, so that everyone connected with it will be hunted down and put to death.[33]

This letter reveals a great deal about the British Prime Minister's thoughts. In these instructions Churchill was not particularly concerned with the safety of the Jews; he was worried about the reputation of the German nation. The culprits had disgraced their race.

The Jews continued to be gassed. Outside Hungary the operation was not over. The Jews were being deported from Italy; they were shipped out from the islands of Greece; they were hauled out of the ghetto of Lodz; they were thinned out in Theresienstadt; they were moved out of the Polish labor camps. In the fall came the turn of the remaining Slovakian Jews. Once more, ransom negotiators were sent out from Germany; this time the associate president of the Zionist Organization in /727/ Hungary, Kastner, accompanied by Standartenführer Becher, arrived in Switzerland. They too were negotiating with the wrong party. On the opposite side stood the president of

31.   Ira A. Hirschmann, *Lifeline to a Promised Land* (New York, 1946), pp. 109–32. /727/
32.   Marie Syrkin, *Blessed Is the Match—The Story of Jewish Resistance* (Philadelphia, 1947), pp. 19–35. Veesenmayer to Ritter, July 8, 1944, NG-5616. /727/
33.   Churchill to Eden, July 11, 1944, in Winston S. Churchill, "The Second World War," Vol. VI: *Triumph and Tragedy* (Boston, 1953), p. 693. /727/

the Jewish community in Switzerland, Saly Mayer. He disliked the negotiations and refused to promise the Germans anything.[34] If Saly Mayer reflected upon his negotiating tactics after the war, his only consolation must have been the circumstance that the SS and Police were determined to destroy the Slovak Jews in any case. The negotiators on the German side had not been the right party either.[35]

In Cairo Joel Brand remained in custody. His mission had failed, and his wife and children in Budapest had almost paid the penalty for the failure. He was constantly afraid that they might still have to pay, but the British would not let him go. He was now invited to clubs and hotels, more as an object of curiosity than a source of intelligence information. One day at the British-Egyptian Club Brand was engaged in conversation by a man who did not introduce himself but who, Brand believes, may have been Lord Moyne. The Englishman asked once more about the Eichmann offer and how many Jews were involved. Brand replied that the offer encompassed a million people. "But Mr. Brand," the British host exclaimed, "what shall I do with those million Jews? Where shall I put them?"[36] There were no longer a million; from the moment of Brand's departure from Budapest 500,000 Jews had been killed in the gas chambers of Auschwitz. The entire network of standby organizations had become a vast organization of bystanders. /728/

Raul Hilberg

STATISTICS ON JEWISH DEAD

Your Excellency, daily,
every single day in those places,
ten thousand Jews, more
than ten thousand,
are being murdered. . . .

The Deputy, *Act One, Scene One*

Statistical Recapitulation of Jewish Dead (by operation)

Area of mobile killing operations		1,400,000
Tabulated dead	900,000	
Untabulated dead	500,000	
Unreported by *Einsatzgruppen*	150,000?	
Higher SS and Police Leaders and BdS GG	100,000	
Army killings, PW killings, and operations by anti-partisan units	100,000	
Ghetto dead	100,000?	
Death of fleeing Jews	50,000?	

From *The Destruction of the European Jews* (London: W. H. Allen & Co., Ltd., 1961), Appendix III, p. 767
34.   Dr. Rezsö Kasztner (Kastner), *Der Bericht des jüdischen Rettungskomitees aus Budapest*, pp. 91–99. /728/
35.   See pp. 472–73. /728/
36.   Weissberg, *Brand*, pp. 214–15. Lord Moyne was shortly thereafter assassinated by two *Irgunists*. Brand speculates that the conversation had been reported in Palestine and that the *Irgun* struck at Moyne in anguish. *Ibid.*, p. 216. Long afterwards, Eichmann said: "The plain fact was that there was no place on earth that would have been ready to accept the Jews, not even this one million." *Life*, December 5, 1960, p. 148. /728/

Area of deportations		3,700,000
Killed in camps (including Transnistria)	3,000,000	
Ghetto and aggravated deaths	700,000	
Total		5,100,000

*Statistical Recapitulation of Jewish Dead (by territory)**

250,000	Reich-Protektorat area		250,000
	USSR		700,000
3,900,000	Baltic states		200,000
	Poland		3,000,000
	Mobile operations	500,000	
	Ghetto dead	550,000	
	Killed in camps	1,950,000	
	North	(less than a thousand)	
200,000	The Low Countries		130,000
	France and Italy		70,000
	Yugoslavia		60,000
	Greece and Rhodes		60,000
750,000	Slovakia		60,000
	Roumania		270,000
	Hungary and Carpatho-Ukraine		300,000
5,100,000	Total		5,100,000

*Borders refer to August, 1939.

Jacques Gommy

CRIMES AGAINST HUMANITY

. . . human wreckage
strewn upon the oceans, upon
the countries of the earth. Men sacrificed
on every front, slain in the fire,
on the gallows, in the gas —

The Deputy, *Act Two*

Hochhuth's play has put Hitler's inhuman destruction of millions of innocent Jews into the limelight. The crime is certainly an adequate reminder of the guilt and shame of an entire people, yet it should be remembered that the Jews were not the only ones to be deliberately massacred in droves, nor was Nazi Germany the only nation guilty of such horror. Nazi Germany was neither the first nor the last nation to perpetrate crimes against nature itself.

The First Deportees: Political Enemies

On January 30, 1933, Hitler became Chancellor of the Reich. On February 27, he had fire set to the Reichstag and then accused the German Communists of having done it. On the 28th, on the basis of the crime and the accusation, he ordered the Chief of State, Hindenburg, to suspend all civil liberties in Germany. During the next few days, six to seven thousand Communists, Social Democrats, and Liberals were arrested. For those prisoners who were not immediately slaughtered, the first concentration camps were set up. A few of these prisoners managed to survive until 1945, but very few. These arrests

"Pie XII devant les massacres de Hitler," *L'Homme Nouveau*, No. 372 (a special issue entitled "Le Vicaire du Christ"), April 19, 1964, pp. 12–13. Trans. by the editors.

came as no surprise to those outside Germany, but the world was stupefied with horror when it learned of the butchery which took place on June 30, 1934. During the night of that Saturday, more than a thousand people were arrested without warning and executed without trial. Many of them were Nazi extremists, Roehm and the other leaders of the S.A., but among the victims were also General von Schleicher and Erich Klausener, the head of Catholic Action. In addition, all the "collaborators," among them Klausener's widow, were sent to concentration camps. Not long after, Gustav von Kahr, the former head of the Bavarian government, and many others joined them there.

The Nuremberg laws depriving Jews of legal rights were enacted on September 15, 1935. Thirteen decrees putting further restrictions upon them followed. These were intended to force the Jewish population to leave Germany by making life totally intolerable for them there. They were not yet, however, threatened with imprisonment and extermination. That was to come in 1941. In the meantime the Nazis concentrated on persecuting Catholics and Protestants.

Anti-Christian Persecution

When the Catholic Youth League was dissolved in July, 1933, thousands of Catholics, priests, members of religious orders, and practically all the directors of Catholic groups were arrested and sent to concentration camps. The encyclical "Mit brennender Sorge" of Pius XI refers to these persecutions. Despite the papal protest, abuses continued until the time of the war and even during the war years.

At the end of 1935, the Gestapo arrested 700 Lutheran clergymen of the Confessional Church. In May 1936, that church, then headed by Pastor Niemoller, issued a firm but courteous protest mentioning the anti-Christian and anti-Semitic policies of the regime. Immediately, hundreds of ministers were arrested and interned at Sachsenhausen, where Pastor Weissler, one of the signers of the protest, was executed. On February 12, 1937, Dr. Kerrl, Nazi Minister of Ecclesiastical Affairs, declared pointedly, "Positive Christianity *is* National Socialism. National Socialism is the will of God revealed through German blood. Dr. Zoelener (a Lutheran clergyman) and Count Gallen (the Catholic bishop at Münster) would have you believe that Christianity is founded on the faith of Jesus Christ, who is the Son of God. That is nonsense. The true, the only, Christianity is represented by the National Socialist Party. The Führer has brought a new 'Revelation.'" On May 1, 1937, Dr. Niemoller was arrested and imprisoned first at Sachsenhausen and then at Dachau. 800 members of his church, both clergy and laity, joined him there that same year. Bormann, one of Hitler's intimates, declared, "National Socialism and Christianity are irreconcilable." So they were. A look at some of the articles from a plan for a National Church of the German Race drawn up by Rosenberg at Hitler's request in 1942 confirms the plot to abolish Christianity in Germany:

Article 5: The National Church of the German Race categorically claims the exclusive right and the exclusive power to control all churches within the borders of the Reich: it declares these to be national churches of the German Reich.

Article 7: The National Church has no pastors, chaplains, or priests, but only orators of the Reich who will speak in its name.

Article 13: The National Church demands that the printing and distribution of Bibles in Germany be halted immediately.

Article 14: The National Church declares that for it, and thus for the German nation, the Führer's book *Mein Kampf* is the greatest of all works. In it is contained the truest and purest ethic whereby our nation will be guided in the present and in the future.

Article 19: On the altars will be found only two items: A copy of *Mein Kampf*, the book most sacred to the German race and, therefore, to God, and, to the left of the altar, a sword.

Article 30: From the day of its establishment, all churches, cathedrals, and chapels must remove the Christian cross . . . and replace it with the invincible symbol, the swastika.

The First Genocide Program

The first act of genocide was not directed against the Jews. On September 1, 1939, the opening day of the war, Hitler, through a secret decree, initiated his euthanasia program. He ordered that *all* the mentally ill classified as incurables in all the hospitals in Germany be put to death with carbon monoxide fumes. Between 1939 and 1942, more than 100,000 Germans were thus wiped out for the good of the German race. This particular phase of the Nazi massacres was then postponed until after the war, since the secret had leaked out, and a protest by the bishops and the families of the unfortunates had followed.

Objectives and Methods of Hitler's War

The task that the Nazi leaders had undertaken was the extermination of thirty million *Untermenschen*, inferior beings, mainly Jews and Slavs.

From a report of General Heinrich, who was second in command of Bohemia-Moravia, it is known that by October 15, 1940, Hitler decided that half the Czechs were to be deported to Germany, where they would be assimilated, and the others, "the intellectuals in particular," were to be "eliminated." From a report by Bormann, Hitler's secretary, it is known that during the same period Hitler reminded Frank, Gauleiter of Poland: "It must be remembered that the Polish nobility, however cruel it may seem, must be eliminated in its entirety. We are going to exterminate all representatives of the Polish elite."

At the beginning of March 1941, Hitler called together the Chiefs of Staff of the German army and gave orders regarding the war against Russia which was to begin the following June 22: "This is a matter of a struggle between two ideologies, two racial concepts. We must be relentless /12/ in our severity. All of you must free yourselves of every scruple. I know that this type of warfare may be distasteful to some of you, but I wish to have my orders obeyed without question. The Soviets must be liquidated. German soldiers who break the international laws of war will be guiltless." On September 18, 1941, Hitler ordered that Leningrad should be abolished from the face of the earth with its entire population of 3 million persons. A year later he told his assistants,

"Anyone who speaks of showing love toward the people of this country (Russia) or of attempting to civilize them will be sent straight to a concentration camp." These general directives were interpreted into specific measures by Keitel for the army, by Rosenberg in the administration of occupied territories, and by Goering in planning economic exploitation of conquered lands. The latter two forbade the distribution of food to Russian civilians, a policy which was responsible for the deaths of millions of innocent people.

Surprising as it may seem, Rosenberg himself wrote to Keitel on February 28, 1942: "The conditions of the Russian prisoners of war in Germany are truly tragic. Of the 3,600,000 prisoners taken, only a few hundred thousand are still fit to work. . . . The camp commanders have refused to feed them, preferring to see them starve to death. . . . In some camps *all* the 'Asiatics' have been executed." Of the 5 million Russian prisoners, barely a million survived to the end of the war.

Four portable extermination units, the *Einsatzgruppen,* under the direction of the S.S., had the task of assassinating all Soviet officials and Russian Jews. These executions of men, women, and children, hallucinations of horror, took place in the occupied territories. When inquiries were made about these victims at Nuremberg, Ohlendorf, the chief of *Einsatzgruppe D,* declared: "All the Jewish and Communist officials were ordered removed from camps and exterminated. To my knowledge, this order was followed throughout the war with Russia." At Kiev, on September 29 and 30, 1941, 33,771 people were killed. The four units managed to "eliminate" approximately 800,000 Jews and Communists during the war.

The Death Camps

High as that figure might seem, it is nothing in comparison to the number who disappeared in the extermination camps, the *Vernichtungslager* of Himmler, from 1941 on. These camps became the symbol of the martyrdom of the Jews, who were sent to them by the trainload, those unable to work and children being immediately gassed. According to Reitlinger *(The Final Solution),* 600,000 people were destroyed in the gas chambers in Auschwitz alone, the best equipped plant for "the final solution to the Jewish problem," to use the Nazi phraseology. An additional 300,000 died there of hunger and illness or were shot to death. In 1944, 20,000 Gypsies were gassed there within a few days, some of them wearing the decorations they had earned in the German army during the Polish campaign! The gas chambers were also used on Russian prisoners. At Auschwitz, as at all the death camps, both soldiers and civilians from Russia, Poland, France, Holland, Belgium, and Germany were confined. In the camps elsewhere, civilian deaths during the war reached a grand total of 5 million Jews, 5.4 million Poles, and 10 million Russians. (In addition, Russia also lost 7 million men in the military.)

Treatment of Allied Prisoners

In general, the treatment accorded Allied prisoners was not as harsh as that received by the Russians and the Poles. Nonetheless, an "ultra-confidential" order from Hitler dated October 19, 1942, condemned to death *all* the members of the Allied commandos: "Armed or not, captured in combat or arrested in flight, they will be executed, *without exception.*" In May 1944, Hitler ordered the execution of Allied pilots. Many of these were victims of a "special treatment" popular at Matthausen: "Forty-seven officers were led barefooted to a quarry. . . . The guards loaded stones on the backs of these unfortunates and ordered them to carry them to the top. When they had completed the first trip, carrying stones weighing 30 kilograms and being flogged all the way by the guards, they were loaded with heavier stones for the second trip. By evening, there were 21 bodies lying in the quarry; the remaining 26 officers died the following morning."

It stood to reason that any attempt at resistance was met by immediate reprisals. In France alone 30,000 hostages were executed. On December 7, 1941, Hitler issued the *Nacht und Nebel Erlass*, the "night and fog decree," whereby "all people representing any danger to Germany" were to be not merely executed but "caused to vanish without a trace" under cover of the night and fog: the very place of their burial was to remain a mystery forever.

Medical Experiments

This was another phase of man's inhumanity to man, a true dungeon of horrors, a hell on earth! Jews were not the only victims. Nazi doctors used many Russians, Poles and other Slavs, and even Germans could be counted in the final tally. Experiments were of different types. In one, human guinea pigs were shut in hermetically sealed containers. Then the air was removed bit by bit to test at what point the victims would stop breathing. Others were inoculated with typhus germs or the organisms of other infectious diseases. Poison gas was tested on these victims. At Ravensbruck, hundreds of Poles, referred to as "lapines," were infected with gas gangrene and died after horrible suffering. At Dachau and Buchenwald, Gypsies were kept on nothing but salt water as observations were made to see how long they would last. Also at Dachau, "Doctor" Rascher pursued his studies on cold tolerance, preferring Russian subjects for his work as they were believed to have developed greater resistance to cold. "Thank God," wrote this singular doctor to Himmler in 1943, "Thank God we have had a cold spell. Some naked subjects were left outdoors for a period of fourteen consecutive hours when it was −6°. Their body temperatures fell to 25° and there was peripheral frost-bite." . . . In addition, he had a refrigeration chamber in which the temperature could be lowered to −40°; it was in that chamber that two Russian officers, under the watchful eyes of the doctor, took five hours to die. Many victims lost their minds in the course of these experiments.

Atrocities Committed by the Other Side

These were some of the sins with which the conscience of mankind became burdened during the period 1939–1945. No, the martyrdom of the Jews should not be forgotten; neither should the martyrdom of countless others. Most particularly, we should not forget those victims whose suffering continues to this very day. For, though genocide in Poland and Central Europe was introduced by the Nazis, it had been and continues to be practiced by the Communists. The western world today does not like to be reminded of Hungary, concerning which it has a bad conscience: though it had spoken with indignation and determination about the martyrdom of Hungary, when the Hungarians sought help, none was offered.

Yet if the Soviet leaders have shown themselves so well able to continue the policies of the Nazis, it may be because they had had previous experience in such techniques. Hitler had not yet come to power in 1929–1930 when the Russians liquidated the kulaks and uprooted small land owners, whole families being deported by the trainload and sent to Siberian camps. More than ten million men, women, and children, according to some historians, were thus sent to the cold, barren land where they died of hunger, fatigue, physical and mental torture. Indeed, by many death was welcomed. Nor has it yet been learned whether these camps are still in existence.

Germany and Japan ignored the basic principles of humanity, but their adversaries, too, proved that they could ignore them. A million and a half German civilians perished during the war, many of them burned alive, enveloped in phosphorus flames from bombs dropped by British and American airplanes. Was it not a display of cruelty and inhumanity to use the atom bomb on two large cities in a country which had already been virtually defeated? As a result of that act, 200,000 civilians were immediately destroyed, and thousands of others took years to die, years during which they suffered horribly and constantly.

What was there, then, for Pius XII to do? He had warned that the unspeakable horrors of technological warfare could destroy the world. No one listened. Pius XII, consequently, denounced all atrocities, all, including the extermination of the Jews, though he could not condemn only one side when both were equally guilty. In addition, Pius XII did what the West did not in the Hungarian situation: he acted. He did everything in his power to stop human suffering and to save human lives, that is, he did far more than anyone else did. And though in this world we tend to ignore the power of prayer, surely his constant prayers and fatherly concern for all mankind touched the infinite mercy of God and helped bring an end to the homicidal folly. Surely that counted above all. /13/

Pope Pius XI

MIT BRENNENDER SORGE

The old Chief was a fighter. . . .

The Deputy, *Act Two*

VATICAN CITY, March 22.—The official English abstract of the encyclical epistle from Pope Pius to German Bishops, including some textual excerpts, follows:
The encyclical which the Holy Father, under date of March 14, Passion Sunday, directed to all Bishops in Germany in regard to the situation of the Catholic Church in the Reich is a document of high doctrinal value because it reaffirms with admirable clarity the doctrine of the Catholic Church against the errors which have been widely diffused in Germany and raises its voice against the persecutions to which the church has been subjected.

But it is also a document inspired by true and understanding benevolence toward the German people. The accents of the Holy Father reveal the sorrow of one who, placed at the head of the church, sees his beloved children reduced to a condition of living which grows constantly more difficult; it is the word of a father who admonishes and comforts and because it is necessary

Official English abstract of the encyclical epistle "Mit brennender Sorge," from Pope Pius XI to the German bishops, as it appeared in *The New York Times*, March 23, 1937, p. 5.

protests, but who is moved by sentiment, charity and compassion, even toward those who offend and persecute.

The Holy Father declared: "We have weighed every word of this encyclical in the balance of truth and love."

In the introduction of his encyclical letter, the Holy Father treats at length with the concordat which the Reich concluded with the Holy See and in which it assumed the obligations which, unfortunately in a large part, have not been fulfilled.

"When in the Summer of 1933, at the request of the government of the Reich, we agreed to resume negotiations for a concordat on the basis of the project elaborated some years earlier and thus reached a solemn accord which succeeded in satisfying you all, we were moved by duty and of solicitude to safeguard the freedom of the church's mission of salvation in Germany and to assure the welfare of souls entrusted to it and at the same time we were, by a sincere desire, rendering service of capital interest to the pacific development and well-being of the German people.

"In spite of many and grave misgivings, we came then, though not without effort, to a determination not to deny our consent. We wished to spare our faithful and our sons and daughters of Germany in so far as it was humanly possible the trials and tribulations which otherwise they would have had to expect in view of the conditions of the tie.

"We desired to demonstrate, indeed, to all that we were seeking only Christ and things that belong to Christ and do not refuse to extend to any one, if he himself does not spurn it, the peaceable hand of the mother church.

"If the tree of peace, planted with pure intent in German soil by us, has not borne the fruit which we desired in the interests of your people, there will be no one in the whole world with eyes to see and ears to hear who can say today that the fault is with the church or with its supreme head."

The Holy Father, recalling what he had done for the observance of pacts freely entered into, adds:

"We have done everything to defend the sanctity of the solemnly plighted word and the inviolability of obligations voluntarily contracted against the theories and practices which, if officially admitted, would have destroyed all confidence and rendered intrinsically valueless every pledged assurance for the future.

"If the time ever comes to expose to the eyes of the world these efforts which we have made, all right-thinking men will know where to seek the guardians of peace and where (to seek) its disturbers.

"Whosoever has preserved in his soul a vestige of love for truth and in his heart even a shadow of a sense of justice will have to admit that in the difficult years so charged with incident which followed the concordat, each one of our words and each of our actions had as its norm fidelity to sanctioned accords.

"But he will have to recognize also with amazement and inward repulsion how, from the other side, there arose as an ordinary rule, distortion of facts, their evasion, their voiding and finally their more or less open violation."

Confronted with this state of affairs which is constantly getting worse, His Holiness has not found it possible to remain silent.

"Even today when the open fight against confessional schools protected by the Concordat and suppression of liberty of choice for those who have a right to Catholic education reveal, in a field particularly vital to the church, the tragic seriousness of the situation and a condition of spiritual oppression such as never before has been witnessed, paternal solicitude for the good of souls counsels us not to leave out of consideration any prospect, however slight, of a return to the fidelity of contracts and to an understanding such as our conscience will permit."

The Holy Father, therefore, does not wish to exclude the hope, small though it may be, that the situation may improve. He even declares openly:

"God, who searches hearts and minds, is our witness that we have no desire more intimately cherished than that of restoring true peace between the church and State in Germany.

"But, if through no fault of ours, peace is not to be, then the church of God will defend its rights and liberties in the name of the Omnipotent Whose arm, even today, is not shortened."

On the other hand, to the children who are suffering, the Pope cannot refrain from saying a word of comfort after reports made to him by their excellencies, the bishops, some of whom came to visit him recently during his illness.

"In this hour when faith is tried as true gold in the fire of tribulation and persecution, both treacherous and open, when they are hemmed in by thousands of forms of organized restriction of their religious liberties, and when they are oppressed by the impossibility of receiving true information and defending themselves by normal means, they have a double right to a word of truth and moral encouragement from him, to whose predecessor the Saviour directed those words so full of meaning: 'I have prayed for thee that thy faith fail not and that thou, being converted, might confirm thy brethren.'"

Among the many points of Catholic doctrine touched upon by the encyclical, it is possible in a brief résumé to indicate but few.

After recalling the correct notion of God as "Creator of the Universe, Lord, King and ultimate end of the story of the world, Who does not and cannot permit other gods beside Him," the Pope adds:

"If a race or people, if a State or one of its determinate forms, if a representative of civil power or other fundamental elements of human society have in the natural order an essential place and one worthy of respect, whosoever removes them from this scale of earthly values to elevate them as supreme ruler of all, even of religious values, and to deify them with an idolatrous cult, perverts and falsifies the order created and imposed by God and is far from true faith in God and from the conception of life in conformity with true faith."

After reaffirming the redemptive mission of Jesus Christ as announced beforehand by the sacred books of the Old Testament, the Pope continues:

"He, therefore, who with sacrilegious disregard for the essential difference between God and the creature, between God-man and simple man—dares place beside Christ, or, worse still, above Him or against Him, a simple mortal, even though the greatest of all time, let him know that he is a senseless prophet of absurdity to whom is to be applied with terrible apposition the word of the Scriptures: 'He who dwells in the heavens laugheth at them.'"

Further on the Pope says:

"Those human laws which are in irreconcilable opposition to natural rights are tainted with original defect which cannot be healed either by coercion or by any form of external force. By this criterion is to be judged the principle: 'Right is that which is useful to the nation.'"

The Pope brings out into particular relief the mission and work of the Catholic Church which, "founded by the Saviour, is one for all people, and for all nations, and under whose roof as an arched firmament of the whole universe, all people and all tongues find a place and all properties, qualities, missions and purposes which have been assigned by God, the Creator and Saviour, to individuals and to human societies can be developed."

The Pope, while reiterating to priests, religious (organizations) and the laity the most urgent recommendations to fulfill better and better "the sacred duty of bringing faith and conduct into that harmony required by the law of God and demanded with untiring insistence by the church," observes human shortcomings, which unfortunately are found also among members of the church, are not to be exaggerated or estimated according to an unjust measure by forgetting the numberless merits of the church and closing the eyes to numerous and more grievous shortcomings which are found among those hostile to the church.

"The divine mission which the church fulfills among men and which she must fulfill by means of men cannot be obscured by the human, at times all too human, which at certain times grows as a cockle amid the wheat of the Kingdom of God.

"Those who know the word of the Saviour in regard to scandal and those who give scandal know how the church and each individual should be the judge of that which is sinful.

"But those who, basing their judgment upon those lamentable differences between faith and living, between word and action, between external conduct and internal conviction of some—even if there were many—forget or knowingly pass over in silence the immense capital of genuine effort toward virtue, the spirit of sacrifice, fraternal charity, and heroic sanctity in so many members of the church, show evidence of injustice which is blind and blameworthy.

"And when, then, we see that this severe standard, by which such a one judges the hated church, is set aside when there is a question of other societies, near to him because of sentiments or interest, it becomes evident that, while proclaiming himself hurt in his presumed sense of purity, he reveals himself similar to those who, in the cutting phrase of the Saviour, see the mote in the eye of their brother but are not aware of the beam in their own."

The Pope sends to the religious of Germany, men and women, an expression of gratitude which is joined with intimate understanding and sympathy because, as a consequence of measures against religious orders and congregations, many of them have been torn away from fields of activity blessed and dear to them.

"If certain ones have been found wanting and have shown themselves unworthy of their vocation, their faults, condemned also by the church, do not diminish the very great merit of those who with the most disinterested and involuntary poverty have served with complete dedication their God and their people."

After other doctrinal explanations, the Holy Father deplores the opposition in Germany to confessional schools of Christian education and obstacles which have been placed in the way of liberty and the right of parents in regard to the education of their children.

The Holy Father shares with all his soul the sorrowful condition in which good and faithful German Catholics live.

"With pressure veiled and open, with intimidation, with promises of economic, professional, civil and other advantages, the attachment of Catholics, especially of certain classes of Catholic government employes, to faith is exposed to violence as illegal as it is inhuman.

"With paternal emotion, we feel and suffer profoundly with those who have paid such a great price for their attachment to Christ and to the church; but the point has now been reached where there is a question of the final and highest end, of salvation or of perdition, and therefore the only way to salvation for the believer is that of generous heroism."

Finally, the Pope addresses his affectionate appeal to young people, to the clergy, secular and religious, and to the faithful of the laity, particularly to the millions in the ranks of Catholic Action.

In expressing the hope and desire that erring children and persecutors of today recognize their errors and that there may soon sound for them an hour of repentance, he affirms "that hastening of that hour is the object of our unceasing prayers."

The encyclical concluded with the apostolic benediction. /5/

Guenter Lewy

THE ROLE OF THE PAPACY

I have *already asked the Pope to protest.*
But he is playing politics.

The Deputy, *Act Five, Scene Two*

In April 1933 a communication reached Pope Pius XI from Germany expressing grave concern over the Nazis' anti-Semitic aims and requesting the Supreme Pontiff to issue an encyclical on the Jewish question. The letter was written by the philosopher Dr. Edith Stein, a Jewish convert to Catholicism and later known as Sister Teresia Benedicta a Cruce of the Order of the Carmelites.[73] Edith Stein's request was not granted and nine years later, in August 1942, she was seized by the Gestapo from a Dutch monastery in which she had sought refuge, and sent to Auschwitz to be gassed. The debate over whether the Papacy could have prevented or should at least have vigorously protested the massacre of the Jews of Europe, of which Edith Stein was one of the victims, has been going on ever since and has acquired new vigor as a result of the Hochhuth play.

In response to Hitler's anti-Semitic drive, Pius XII's predecessor, Pius XI, like the German episcopate, seems to have limited his concern to Catholic non-Aryans. At the request of Cardinal Bertram, the Papal Secretary of State in September 1933 put in "a word on behalf of those German Catholics" who were of Jewish descent and for this reason suffering "social and economic difficulties."[74] In the years that followed the Holy See often took issue with the Nazis' glorification of race, but the Jewish question specifically was never discussed. In 1934 the influential Jesuit magazine *Civiltà Cattolica*, published in Rome and traditionally close to Vatican thinking, noted with regret that the anti-Semitism of the Nazis "did not stem from the religious convictions nor

From "Pius XII, The Jews, and the German Catholic Church," *Commentary*, February 1964, pp. 23–35. For further discussion, see Lewy, *The Catholic Church and Nazi Germany* (New York: McGraw-Hill Book Co., 1964).

73. Cf. Hilda Graef, *Leben unter dem Kreuz: Eine Studie über Edith Stein* (Frankfurt a.M., 1954), p. 130. /35/

74. Note of the Papal Secretariat of State to the German government, September 9, 1933, *Documents on German Foreign Policy*, C, I, doc. 425, p. 794. /35/

the Christian conscience . . . , but from . . . their desire to upset the order of religion and society." The *Civiltà Cattolica* added that "we could understand them, or even praise them, if their policy were restricted within acceptable bounds of defense against the Jewish organizations and institutions. . . ."[75] In 1936 the same journal published another article on the subject, emphasizing that opposition to Nazi racialism should not be interpreted as a rejection of anti-Semitism, and arguing—as the magazine had done since 1890—that the Christian world (though without unChristian hatred) must defend itself against the Jewish threat by suspending the civic rights of Jews and returning them to the ghettos.[76]

Pius XI's encyclical *"Mit brennender Sorge"* of March 1937 rejected the myths of race and blood as contrary to revealed Christian truth, but it neither mentioned nor criticized anti-Semitism *per se*. Nor was anti-Semitism mentioned in the statement of the Roman Congregation of Seminaries and Universities, issued on April 13, 1938, and attacking as erroneous eight theses taken from the arsenal of Nazi doctrine.[77] On September 7, 1938, during a reception for Catholic pilgrims from Belgium, Pius XI is said to have condemned the participation of Catholics in anti-Semitic movements and to have added that Christians, the spiritual descendants of the patriarch Abraham, were "spiritually Semites." But this statement was omitted by all the Italian papers, including *L'Osservatore Romano*, from their account of the Pope's address.[78]

The elevation of Cardinal Pacelli to the Papacy in the spring of 1939 brought to the chair of St. Peter a man who, in contrast to his predecessor, was unemotional and dispassionate, as well as a master of the language of diplomatic ambiguity. "Pius XII," recalls Cardinal Tardini, "was by nature meek and almost timid. He was not born with the temperament of a fighter. In this he was different from his great predecessor."[79] But whether, as Hochhuth has speculated, Pius XI /30/ would have reacted to the massacre of the Jews during World War II differently from Pacelli, is a question to which no definite answer is possible.

That the Holy See had no intrinsic objection to a policy of subjecting the Jews to discriminatory legislation again became clear when in June 1941 Marshal Pétain's Vichy government introduced a series of "Jewish statutes." The Cardinals and Archbishops of France made known their strong disapproval of these measures, but Léon Bérard, the Vichy ambassador at the Holy See, was able to report to Pétain after lengthy consultations with high Church officials that the Vatican did not consider such laws in conflict with Catholic teaching. The Holy See merely counseled that no provisions on marriage be added to the statutes and "that the precepts of justice and charity be considered in the application of the law."[80] In August 1941 the consequences of this discriminatory policy could not yet be clearly seen, but when mass deportations from France got under way in 1942, the Papal Nuncio, without invoking the authority of the Holy See, requested Laval to mitigate the severity of the

75. *Civiltà Cattolica*, no. 2024, quoted in Daniel Carpi, "The Catholic Church and Italian Jewry under the Fascists (to the Death of Pius XI), *"Yad Washem Studies*, IV (1960), p. 51. /35/
76. *Ibid.*, pp. 51–52. /35/
77. Cf. Yves M.—J. Conger, *Die Katholische Kirche und die Rassenfrage*, trans. W. Armbruster (Recklinghausen, 1961), p. 69. /35/
78. The statement was first reported by *La Croix*, no. 17060, September 17, 1938. It is accepted as accurate by Luigi Stutzo, *Nationalism and Internationalism* (New York, 1946), p. 47. /35/
79. Domenico Tardini, *Pius XII*, trans. Franz Johna (Freiburg, Br., 1961), p. 59. /35/
80. Léon Poliakov, *Harvest of Hate* (London, 1956), p. 300. /35/

measures taken against the Jews of Vichy, France.[81] By that time, however, such pleas could no longer halt the machinery of destruction.

Meanwhile, there was growing criticism of the Pope's failure to protest publicly against Nazi atrocities, and especially against the murder of the Jews in the Polish death factories. In July 1942, Harold H. Tittmann, the assistant to Roosevelt's personal representative at the Holy See, Myron C. Taylor, pointed out to the Vatican that its silence was "endangering its moral prestige and is undermining faith both in the Church and in the Holy Father himself."[82] In September 1942, after authorization by Secretary of State Hull, Tittmann and several other diplomatic representatives at the Vatican formally requested that the Pope condemn the "incredible horrors" perpetrated by the Nazis. A few days later Taylor forwarded to the Papal Secretary of State, Luigi Maglione, a memorandum from the Jewish Agency for Palestine reporting mass executions of Jews in Poland and occupied Russia, and telling of deportations to death camps from Germany, Belgium, Holland, France, Slovakia, etc. Taylor inquired whether the Vatican could confirm these reports, and if so, "whether the Holy Father has any suggestions as to any practical manner in which the forces of civilized opinion could be utilized in order to prevent a continuation of these barbarities."[83] On October 10 the Holy See, in reply to Taylor's note, said that up to the present time it had not been possible to verify the accuracy of reports concerning the severe measures that were being taken against the Jews. "It is well known," the statement added, "that the Holy See is taking advantage of every opportunity offered in order to mitigate the suffering of non-Aryans."[84]

After the Western Allies in December 1942 had vigorously denounced the cold-blooded extermination of the Jews, Tittmann again asked the Papal Secretary of State whether the Holy See could not issue a similar pronouncement. Maglione answered that the Holy See, in line with its policy of neutrality, could not protest particular atrocities and had to limit itself to condemning immoral actions in general. He assured Tittmann that everything possible was being done behind the scenes to help the Jews.[85]

Two days later, in the course of a lengthy Christmas message broadcast by the Vatican radio, Pope Pius made another of his many calls for a more humane conduct of hostilities. Humanity, the Pope declared, owed the resolution to build a better world to "the hundreds of thousands who without personal guilt, sometimes for no other reason but on account of their nationality or descent, were doomed to death or exposed to a progressive deterioration of their condition."[86] Again, addressing the Sacred College of Cardinals in June 1943, the Pontiff spoke of his twofold duty to be impartial and to point up moral errors. He had given special attention, he recalled, to the plight of those who were still being harassed because of their nationality or descent and who without personal guilt were subjected to measures that spelled destruction. Much had been done for the unfortunates that could not be described yet. Every public statement had had to be carefully weighed "in the interest of those suffering so that their situation would not inadvertently be made still

81. Abetz to Foreign Ministry, August 28, 1942, *Politisches Archiv des Auswärtigen Amtes* (Bonn), *Staatssekretär, Vatikan, Bd. 4.* /35/
82. Tittmann to Secretary of State, July 30, 1942, *U.S. Diplomatic Papers 1942*, III, p. 772. /35/
83. Taylor to Maglione, September 26, 1942, *ibid.*, p. 776. /35/
84. Tittmann's summary of Holy See statement of October 10, 1942, *ibid.*, p. 777. /35/
85. Tittmann to the Department of State, December 22, 1942, Department of State Papers, 740.0016 European War 1939/689. /35/
86. Corsten, *Kölner Aktenstüke*, doc. 220, p. 280. The message was mimeographed and distributed in Germany by the diocesan chanceries. I have seen a copy in Diocesan Archives Eichstätt. /35/

more difficult and unbearable." Unfortunately, Pius XII added, the Church's pleas for compassion and for the observance of the elementary norms of humanity had encountered doors "which no key was able to open."[87]

The precise nature of these interventions has not been revealed to this day. We do know, however, that Nuncio Orsenigo in Berlin made inquiries several times about mass shootings and the fate of deported Jews. (Ernst Woermann, the director of the Political Department of the German Foreign Ministry, recorded on October 15, 1942 that the Nuncio had made his representation with "some embarrassment and without emphasis."[88] State Secretary Weizsäcker told Monsignor Orsenigo on another such occasion that the Vatican had so far conducted itself "very cleverly" in these matters, and that he would hope for a continuation of this policy. The Nuncio took the hint and "pointed out that he had not really touched this topic and that he had no desire to touch it."[89] /31/

The Pope's policy of neutrality encountered its most crucial test when the Nazis began rounding up the 8,000 Jews of Rome in the fall of 1943. Prior to the start of the arrests, the Jewish community was told by the Nazis that unless it raised 50 kilograms of gold (the equivalent of $56,000) within 36 hours, 300 hostages would be taken. When it turned out that the Jews themselves could only raise 35 kgs., the Chief Rabbi, Israel Zolli, asked for and received a loan from the Vatican treasury to cover the balance. The Pope approved of this transaction.[90] But the big question in everyone's mind was how the Supreme Pontiff would react when the deportation of the Jews from the Eternal City began.

The test came on the night of October 15/16. While the round-up was still going on, a letter was delivered to General Stahel, the German military commander of Rome. Bearing the signature of Bishop Hudal, the head of the German Church in Rome, it said:

> I have just been informed by a high Vatican office in the immediate circle of the Holy Father that the arrests of Jews of Italian nationality have begun this morning. In the interest of the good relations which have existed until now between the Vatican and the high German military command . . . I would be very grateful if you would give an order to stop these arrests in Rome and its vicinity right away; I fear that otherwise the Pope will have to make an open stand which will serve the anti-German propaganda as a weapon against us.[91]

A day later, Ernest von Weizsäcker, the new German Ambassador at the Holy See, reported to Berlin that the Vatican was upset, especially since the deportations had taken place, as it were, right under the Pope's window:

> The people hostile to us in Rome are taking advantage of this affair to force the Vatican from its reserve. People say that the bishops of French cities, where similar incidents occurred, have taken a firm stand. The Pope,

---

87. Pius XII to the Cardinals, June 2, 1943, excerpts in *Amtsblatt für die Erzdiözese München und Freising*, August 12, 1943. /35/
88. Memo of Woermann, *Politisches Archiv des Auswärtigen Amtes* (Bonn), Staatssekretär, Bd. 4. /35/
89. Weizsäcker to Woermann etc., December 5, 1941, quoted in Raul Hilberg, *The Destruction of the European Jews* (Chicago, 1961), pp. 441. /35/
90. Hilberg, *op. cit.*, p. 427. /35/
91. Gumbert (of the German Embassy at the Quirinal) to the Foreign Ministry, October 16, 1943, *Politisches Archiv des Auswärtigen Amtes* (Bonn), Inland II g, 192. /35/ Bishop Hudal had signed this letter at the urging of several anti-Nazi officials in the German legations at the Quirinal and Holy See, who had composed it. I have used the English translation of Hilberg, *op. cit.*, p. 429. /35/

as supreme head of the Church and Bishop of Rome, cannot be more reticent than they. They are also drawing a parallel between the stronger character of Pius XI and that of the present Pope.[92]

Contrary to Hudal's and Weizsäcker's apprehensions, however, the man in the Vatican palace remained silent. On October 18, over one thousand Roman Jews—more than two-thirds of them women and children—were shipped off to the killing center of Auschwitz. Fourteen men and one woman returned alive. About 7,000 Roman Jews—that is, seven out of eight—were able to elude their hunters by going into hiding. More than 4,000, with the knowledge and approval of the Pope, found refuge in the numerous monasteries and houses of religious orders in Rome,[93] and a few dozen were sheltered in the Vatican itself. The rest were hidden by their Italian neighbors, among whom the anti-Jewish policy of the Fascists had never been popular. But for the Germans, overwhelmingly relieved at having averted a public protest by the Pope, the fact that a few thousand Jews had escaped the net was of minor significance. On October 28 Ambassador Weizsäcker was able to report:

> Although under pressure from all sides, the Pope has not let himself be drawn into any demonstrative censure of the deportation of Jews from Rome. Although he must expect that his attitude will be criticized by our enemies and exploited by the Protestant and Anglo-Saxon countries in their propaganda against Catholicism, he has done everything he could in this delicate matter not to strain relations with the German government, and German circles in Rome. As there is probably no reason to expect other German actions against the Jews of Rome, we can consider that a question so disturbing to German-Vatican relations has been liquidated.
>
> In any case, an indication for this state of affairs can be seen in the Vatican's attitude. *L'Osservatore Romano* has in fact prominently published in its issue of October 25–26, an official communiqué on the Pope's charitable activities. The communiqué, in the Vatican's distinctive style, that is, very vague and complicated, declares that all men, without distinction of nationality, race, or religion, benefit from the Pope's paternal solicitude. The continual and varied activities of Pius XII have probably increased lately because of the greater sufferings of so many unfortunates.
>
> There is less reason to object to the terms of this message . . . as only a very small number of people will recognize in it a special allusion to the Jewish question.[94]

Since the end of World War II, Pius XII has often been criticized for his silence. It has been argued—and most recently by Hochhuth—that the Pope could have saved numerous lives, if indeed he could not have halted the machinery of destruction altogether, had he chosen to take a public stand, and had he confronted the Germans with the threat of an interdict or with the excommunication of Hitler, Goebbels, and other leading Nazis belonging to the Catholic faith. As examples of the effectiveness of public protests, it is possible to cite the resolute reaction of the German episcopate to the euthanasia pro-

---

92. Weizsäcker to the Foreign Ministry, October 17, 1943, *Politisches Archiv des Auswärtigen Amtes* (Bonn), Inland II g, 192. The translation is that of Poliakov, *op. cit.*, p. 297, n. 16. /35/
93. Cf. Robert Leiber, S.J., *"Pius XII und die Juden in Rom 1943–1944,"* Stimmen der Zeit, CLXVII (1960–61), pp. 429–430. /35/
94. Weizsäcker to the Foreign Ministry, October 28, 1943, *Politisches Archiv des Auswärtigen Amtes* (Bonn), Inland II g, 192. The English translation is that of Poliakov, *op. cit.*, pp. 297–298, n. 16. /35/

gram. Also, in Slovakia, Hungary, and Rumania, the forceful intervention of
Papal nuncios, who threatened the Quisling governments with public condemnation by the Pope, was able, albeit temporarily, to stop the deportations.[95] At
the very least, it has been suggested, a public de- /32/ nunciation of the mass
murders by Pius XII, broadcast widely over the Vatican radio, would have revealed to Jews and Christians alike what deportation to the East actually
meant. The Pope would have been believed, whereas the broadcasts of the
Allies were often shrugged off as war propaganda. Many of the deportees
who accepted the assurances of the Germans that they were merely being re-
settled, might thus have been warned and given an impetus to escape; many
more Christians might have helped and sheltered Jews, and many more lives
might have been saved.

There exists, of course, no way of definitively proving or disproving these
arguments. Whether a papal decree of excommunication against Hitler would
have dissuaded the Führer from carrying out his plan to destroy the Jews is
very doubtful, and revocation of the Concordat by the Holy See would have
bothered Hitler still less. However, a flaming protest against the massacre of
the Jews coupled with an imposition of the interdict upon all of Germany or
the excommunication of all Catholics in any way involved with the apparatus
of the "Final Solution" would have been a more formidable and effective
weapon. Yet this was precisely the kind of action which the Pope could not
take without risking the allegiance of the German Catholics. Given the indifference of the German population toward the fate of the Jews and the highly
ambivalent attitude of the German hierarchy toward Nazi anti-Semitism, a
forceful stand by the Supreme Pontiff on the Jewish question might well have
led to a large-scale desertion from the Church. When Dr. Edoardo Senatro,
the correspondent of *L'Osservatore Romano* in Berlin, asked Pius XII whether
he would not protest the extermination of the Jews, the Pope is reported to
have answered, "Dear friend, do not forget that millions of Catholics serve in
the German armies. Shall I bring them into conflicts of conscience?"[96] The
Pope knew that the German Catholics were not prepared to suffer martyrdom
for their Church; still less were they willing to incur the wrath of their Nazi
rulers for the sake of the Jews, whom their own bishops for years had casti-
gated as a harmful influence in German life. In the final analysis, then, "the
Vatican's silence only reflected the deep feeling of the Catholic masses of Europe."[97]

Some Catholic writers have suggested that a public protest by the Pope
would not have been unsuccessful in helping the Jews but might have caused
additional damage—to the Jews, to the *Mischlinge*, to the Church, to the terri-
torial integrity of the Vatican, and to Catholics in all of Nazi-occupied Europe. So far as the Jews are concerned, it is tempting to dismiss this argument
by asking what worse fate could possibly have befallen them than the one that
actually did. But in any case, the Catholic bishops of Holland tried the gamble
and failed. In July 1942, together with the Protestant Churches, they sent a
telegram of protest against the deportation of the Dutch Jews to the German
Reichskommissar (commissioner) and threatened to make their protest public
unless the deportations were halted. The Germans responded by offering to
exempt from deportation non-Aryans converted to Christianity before 1941 if

95. Cf. Hilberg, *op. cit.*, p. 539; Gerald Reitlinger, *The Final Solution* (New York, 1953), pp. 431–432.
The successful intervention of the Papal Nuncio in Rumania was attested to by the former Chief
Rabbi of Rumania at the Eichmann trial (cf. New York *Times*, May 24, 1961, p. 12). /35/
96. Statement of Dr. Senatro on March 11, 1963, at a public discussion in Berlin (Fritz J. Raddatz,
ed., *Summa iniuria oder Durfte der Papst schweigen?*, Reinbek bei Hamburg, 1963, p. 223). /35/
97. Poliakov, *op. cit.*, p. 302. /35/

the churches agreed to remain silent. The Dutch Reformed Church accepted the bargain, but the Catholic Archbishop of Utrecht refused and issued a pastoral letter in which he denounced the wrong done to the Jews. The Germans retaliated by seizing and deporting all the Catholic non-Aryans they could find, among them Edith Stein.[98] There was thus some basis for the fear that a public protest, along with any good that could come of it, might make some things worse, if not for the Jews, at least for the *Mischlinge* and the Catholics themselves.

The Pope had other, perhaps still weightier, reasons for remaining silent. As Mr. Tittmann was told by highly placed officials of the Curia, the Holy See did not want to jeopardize its neutrality by condemning German atrocities, and the Pope was unwilling to risk later charges of having been partial and contributing to a German defeat.[99] Moreover, the Vatican did not wish to undermine and weaken Germany's struggle against Russia. In the late summer of 1943, the Papal Secretary of State declared that the fate of Europe depended upon a German victory on the Eastern front;[100] and Father Robert Leiber, one of ✦Pius XII's secretaries, recalls that the late Pope had always looked upon Russian Bolshevism as more dangerous than German National Socialism.[101]

Finally, one is inclined to conclude that the Pope and his advisors—influenced by the long tradition of moderate anti-Semitism so widely accepted in Vatican circles—did not view the plight of the Jews with a real sense of urgency and moral outrage. For this assertion no documentation is possible, but it is a conclusion difficult to avoid. Pius XII broke his policy of strict neutrality during World War II to express concern over the German violation of the neutrality of Holland, Belgium, and Luxemburg in May 1940. When some German Catholics criticized him for this action, the Pope wrote the German bishops that neutrality was not synonymous "with indifference and apathy where moral and humane considerations demanded a candid word."[102] All things told, did not the murder of several million Jews demand a similarly "candid word"? /33/

Joseph J. Lichten

A QUESTION OF JUDGMENT: PIUS XII AND THE JEWS

The Pope, daily contending
with the world, with God, knows what he is doing.
He knows why he must be silent.

The Deputy, *Act Two*

There is considerable documentation in support of Pope Pius' fear that a formal statement would worsen, not improve, conditions for the persecuted.

98.   Louis de Jong, "Jews and non-Jews in Nazi-Occupied Holland," Max Beloff, ed., *On the Track of Tyranny* (London, 1960), pp. 148–149. /35/
99.   Tittmann to the Department of State, October 6, 1942, *U.S. Diplomatic Papers 1942*, III, 777; Tittmann dispatch of September 8, 1942, Department of State Papers, 740.00116 European War 1939/573, 1/2. /35/
100.   Reported by Weizsäcker, September 23, 1943, *Politisches Archiv des Auswärtigen Amtes* (Bonn), *Staatssekretär, Vatikan, Bd. 4*. /35/
101.   Robert Leiber, S.J., "Der Papst und die Verfolgung der Juden," Raddatz, *op. cit.*, p. 104. /35/
102.   Pius XII to the German bishops, August 6, 1940, copy in Diocesan Archives Regensburg. /35/

Ernst von Weizsäcker, the German ambassador to the Vatican during World War II, wrote in his memoirs:

"Not even institutions of worldwide importance, such as the International Red Cross or the Roman Catholic Church, saw fit to appeal to Hitler in a general way on behalf of the Jews or to call openly on the sympathies of the world. It was precisely because they wanted to help the Jews that these organizations refrained from making any general and public appeals; for they were afraid that they would injure rather than help the Jews thereby."

Pius XII's "silence," let us remember, extended to persecutions of Catholics as well. Despite his intervention, 3000 Catholic priests were murdered by the Nazis in Germany, Austria, Poland, France, and other countries; Catholic schools were shut down, Catholic publications forced out of print or strictly censored, Catholic churches closed. The possibility of a public statement from the Vatican moved German Foreign Secretary Joachim von Ribbentrop to wire Von Weizsäcker on January 24, 1943:

"Should the Vatican either politically or propagandistically oppose Germany, it should be made unmistakably clear that a worsening of relations between Germany and the Vatican would not at all have an adverse effect on Germany alone. On the contrary, the German government would have sufficient effective propaganda material as well as retaliatory measures at its disposal to counteract each attempted move by the Vatican."

Pius learned precisely how firm this German threat was from the protest of the Dutch bishops against seizures of the Jews, for immediately following that protest and, as later confirmed by an S.S. officer, in direct answer to it, the Nazis stepped up their anti-Jewish activities in the Netherlands: a week after the pastoral letter was read at all the masses in Holland, the S.S. rounded up every priest and monk and nun who had any "Jewish blood" whatever, and deported them to concentration camps. Pius and his bishops and nuncios in Nazi-occupied or -dominated countries knew that, like a sane man faced with a gun-carrier threatening to shoot, Hitler and his cohorts could not be considered civilized human beings. As Archbishop Andrea Cassulo, papal nuncio in Roumania, said in June, 1942, "I must proceed cautiously /660/ because [my actions] could ruin, instead of being useful to, so many wretched persons whom I must often listen to and help."

The Pope's decision to refrain from a formal condemnation of the Nazis' treatment of Jews was approved by many Jews. One Berlin couple, Mr. and Mrs. Wolfsson, came to Rome after having been in prison and concentration camps. They took shelter in a convent of German nuns while Pius himself, whom they had seen during an audience, arranged for them to escape to Spain. Recalling those terrible days, the Wolfssons recently declared:

"None of us wanted the Pope to take an open stand. We were all fugitives, and fugitives do not wish to be pointed at. The Gestapo would have become more excited and would have intensified its inquisitions. If the Pope had protested, Rome would have become the center of attention. It was better that the Pope said nothing. We all shared this opinion at the time, and this is still our conviction today. . . ."

Pius XII's defenders in print—among others Sir D'Arcy Osborne, Msgr.

"A Jewish Defense," *The Commonweal*, February 28, 1964, pp. 660–662. Lichten, director of the Intercultural Affairs Department of B'nai B'rith's Anti-Defamation League, is the author of a 35-page booklet entitled *A Question of Judgment: Pius XII and the Jews* (National Catholic Welfare Conference, 1963), from which the *Commonweal* excerpts were taken.

Alberto Giovannetti, Father Robert Leiber, and Harry Greenstein, who represent three faiths and four nationalities—point to two elements of the Pope's personal philosophy in addition to the pragmatic reason for his decision to refrain from an explicit condemnation of the Nazis. First, he considered it his paramount duty to be pastor of the universal Church, and in his eyes this position required the strictest impartiality. Second, as an experienced diplomat, he knew full well that the days when a Vatican sanction carried weight were long since past, as Sir Alec Randall points out: we have already seen just how correct this appraisal was. The era of renewed spiritual and moral leadership introduced by the pontificate of John XXIII had not yet dawned. . . .

It is a matter of record, of course, that Pope Pius XII did not launch a verbal attack directly against the Third Reich; the statements he did make during World War II, with rare exceptions, were general expressions of sorrow and sympathy for all victims of oppression of any kind, and did not name names. As Von Weizsäcker wrote in a report to the Minister of Foreign Affairs in Berlin on October 28, 1943:

"Regardless of the advice of many, the Pope has not yet let himself be persuaded to make an official condemnation of the deportation of the Roman Jews. Despite the fact that he must expect his attitude to be criticized by our enemies and attacked by the Protestants in Anglo-Saxon countries, who will use it in their anti-Catholic propaganda, he has thus far achieved the impossible in these delicate circumstances in order not to put his relations with the German government and with its representatives at Rome to the test. Since it is currently thought that the Germans will take no further steps against the Jews in Rome, the question of our relations with the Vatican may be considered closed.

"In any case, it appears that such is the viewpoint of the Vatican. *Osservatore Romano* of October 25–26, however, published an official statement on the Pope's charitable activities. The statement, which was couched in the usual abstract and vague Vatican terminology, said that the Pope expressed his paternal solicitude for all men without regard to race, nationality, or religion. The many activities of the Pope would be increased because so many were suffering so much misfortune.

"One could not raise any objection to this statement because few will recognize a direct reference to the Jewish problem in it."

According to the March, 1961, article "Pius XII and the Jews, 1943–1944" in the Jesuit publication *Civiltà Cattolica*, by Father Robert Leiber, Pius XII's personal assistant from 1924 to 1959, the Pope directly denounced an illegal procedure only once during the entire war: the German invasion of Holland, Belgium, and Luxemburg on May 10, 1940, prompted the now famous telegrams to the heads of the three invaded states. These messages aside, Pope Pius XII followed the policy of Pope Benedict XV during World War I, and protested in general terms against injustices and violence wherever these might be found.

But is it correct to say that Pius XII was otherwise silent on the subject of Nazi atrocities? Had he utterly ignored the plight of the Jews, the term would be appropriate; had he spoken directly in their cause, he might today be called foolhardy—if we are to carry even his accusers' admissions to their logical conclusion. In effect, he chose a third course, one dictated by his long experience as a Vatican statesman and his great desire to save lives. . . .

That the Pope was deeply antagonistic to the racism the National-Socialists advocated is evident from his work prior to his election to the papacy. The famous *Mit brennender Sorge* shows the hand of Pacelli, then Vatican secretary of state; more directly, as papal legate, Pacelli spoke these scathing words to 250,000 pilgrims at Lourdes on April 28, 1935:

"They [the Nazis] are in reality only miserable plagiarists who dress up old errors with new tinsel. It does not make any difference whether they flock to the banners of the social revolution, whether they are guided by a false conception of the world and of life, or whether they are possessed by the superstition of a race and blood cult."

Pacelli had obviously established his position clearly, for the Fascist governments of both Italy and Germany spoke out vigorously against the possibility of his election to succeed Pius XI in March of 1939, though the cardinal secretary of state had served as papal nuncio in Germany from 1917 to 1929 and had been instrumental in the signing of a Concordat between Germany and the Vatican. The day after his election, the Berlin *Morgen-* /661/ *post* said: "The election of Cardinal Pacelli is not accepted with favor in Germany because he was always opposed to Nazism and practically determined the policies of the Vatican under his predecessor. . . ."

Early in the German occupation of Italy, the S.S. began their persecution of the Jews. On September 27, 1943, one of the commanders demanded of the Jewish community in Rome payment of 100 pounds of gold in 36 hours, failing which 300 Jews would be taken prisoner. The Jewish Community Council worked desperately, but was able to gather together only 70 pounds of the precious metal. In his memoirs, the then Chief Rabbi Zolli of Rome writes that he was sent to the Vatican, where arrangements had already been made to receive him as an "engineer" called to survey a construction problem so that the Gestapo on watch at the Vatican would not bar his entry. He was met by the Vatican treasurer and secretary of state, who told him that the Holy Father himself had given orders for the deficit to be filled with gold vessels taken from the Treasury. There is some disagreement today among some of the principals involved—Zolli, other prominent Jews of Rome, and Father Robert Leiber—over the amount of gold demanded as ransom and whether the Community Council actually borrowed the gold; but there is no question that the Vatican did make the offer.

From the first days of the war, Pope Pius distributed untold sums to aid Jews all over Europe. The Vatican's own refugee agencies and the St. Raphael Verein gave financial and other material help in amounts we cannot begin to guess until the Vatican archives are opened, but the sums which passed through the hands of the Pallottine fathers, who administered the St. Raphael Verein and who kindly gave me materials from their own records, were very large. In addition, Pope Pius supervised the receipt and disposition of funds sent in his care by various sympathetic individuals and groups in Europe and the Americas, notably the Catholic Refugee Committee of the United States. American Jews put large sums into the hands of the Pope, who distributed them according to the wishes of the donors; Father Leiber estimates that Pius received some 2½ billion lire from Jews in the United States by the end of 1945. . . .

Ten years after his address to the pilgrims at Lourdes, Pope Pius returned full circle to the theme of brotherhood which, contrary to playwright Hochhuth's allegations, inspired his unflagging help to persecuted Jews. After the liberation of Rome, while there was apprehension over the fate of Jewish prisoners in the hands of the Axis powers in northern Italy and Germany, he said: "For centuries the Jews have been most unjustly treated and despised. It is time they were treated with justice and humanity. God wills it and the Church wills it. St. Paul tells us that the Jews are our brothers. Instead of being treated as strangers, they should be welcomed as friends."

The tangible evidence of Pius' real character—his love for all men, and his particular concern for "justice and humanity" toward Jews—lies in the fact that throughout the war Jewish leaders from all over the globe approached him for help. One of the foremost of these was Chief Rabbi Isaac Herzog of Jerusalem, to whom the Pope gave the message that he would do everything in his power to help the persecuted Jews. Rabbi Herzog traveled to Constantinople to seek financial and other assistance for his Jewish Aid Fund, and, true to the Pope's word, found in the apostolic delegate in Istanbul, Archbishop Angelo Roncalli, an uncommonly dynamic collaborator in the rescue operations carried out for the Balkan Jews. A letter dated February 28, 1944, which the future John XXIII wrote the Vatican to transmit a plea from Rabbi Herzog for help for the Jews of Roumania, began: "Chief Rabbi Herzog of Jerusalem . . . came to the Apostolic Delegation personally in order to thank the Holy Father and the Holy See officially for the many forms of charity extended to Jews in these last years. . . ."

No one who reads the record of Pius XII's actions on behalf of Jews can subscribe to Hochhuth's accusation. However, though the evidence moves against the hypothesis that a formal condemnation from Pius would have curtailed the mass murder of Jews, this is still a question of judgment. /662/

Father Robert Leiber, S. J.

ON HOCHHUTH'S HISTORICAL SOURCES

Let us not judge him.

The Deputy, *Act Five, Scene Two*

Where did Hochhuth obtain the information on which his conclusions are based? Nowhere, really, for one would have to have access to the Vatican Archives to be able to formulate any new, valid account of these matters. Hochhuth himself admits this (p. 288). However, it must be observed that the Vatican Archives are not opened beyond the year 1846! Hochhuth, therefore, relies on statements of "high church officials," "anonymous eye-witnesses," and, as he has stated (Frankfurter *Allgemeine Zeitung*, Vol. XXVI, No. 48, February, p. 16), "in addition, I was also received in a one-hour audience with the Secretary of State of the Holy See," a meeting of which there is no record at the Vatican. At one point, Hochhuth quotes from my own book, *Hausprälaten Pius' XII*, implying that the statement was made directly to him by "one of the prelates of the Papal household" in Rome (p. 351). At the same time, he asserts that I made a number of statements which I never made (p. 349). A news item he quotes from *Spiegel* is also a falsehood. The author of *The Deputy* has based his work on such published accounts as are generally available, taking particular care to emphasize anything derogatory to the late Pius XII.

From "Der Papst und die Verfolgung der Juden," *Frankfurter Allgemeine Zeitung*, March 27, 1963, as it appears in *Summa iniuria oder Durfte der Papst schweigen?*, ed. Fritz Raddatz (Hamburg: Rowohlt, 1963), pp. 101–107. Trans. by the editors. Page references to the Grove Press edition of *The Deputy* have been substituted for Father Leiber's references to the Rowohlt edition.

His generally low estimation of Pius XII is made clear in a number of ways in *The Deputy*. In presenting this derogatory picture, the author makes a number of specific charges, which we will now examine.

In Act Four, as well as in the historical appendix, Hochhuth refers to the financial transactions of the Jesuits, giving an article from the *Spiegel* as his source. All of this information is false.* The statements to the effect that the Pope's nephews held personal fortunes of 123 million marks are likewise false. Yet on these "facts" Hochhuth bases the entire weight of the act, as the Pope is shown to remain silent in order not to jeopardize the investments of the Vatican and other aristocrats. /102/ The entire meaning of the act would collapse without this false foundation.

There are a number of errors and misrepresentations in the author's discussion of the Concordat (pp. 295–298). It was *not* Cardinal Pacelli who pressed for a Concordat with Hitler's government in 1933. The initiative, as well as the desire for a hasty conclusion, came from the Berlin government. Even less true is the statement that Cardinal Pacelli "fell into a trap" (p. 298). The Holy See rejected the first offer of a pact and did not agree to sign a concordat until it became apparent that National Socialism was slowly destroying the Catholic philosophy of life in Germany. The Catholic bishops in Germany rejoiced in 1933 that the pact had been concluded and their position clearly defined. From the moment Pius XI signed the Concordat, Cardinal Pacelli himself made every effort to see that its provisions regarding the religious life of Catholics were upheld, and, in this connection, he addressed over fifty-five notes to Berlin, some of them quite sharp. All of these matters are public knowledge, as studies of the conference were made and published in the post-war years, yet Hochhuth seems to be ignorant of them. It is also made clear in the encyclical "Mit brennender Sorge" of Pius XI that there were no provisions for legal recourse in the event of violations of the Concordat. There is certainly nothing that is in any way damaging to the reputation of Pius XII revealed in an analysis of that encyclical.

Shortly after the Polish campaign in 1939 and throughout the winter of 1939–1940, an anti-Hitler resistance group developed in Germany. The group, composed of diverse elements, hoped to gain enough support to overthrow Hitler and oust the National Socialist Party from power. It then hoped to enter into negotiations with the Western Allies. Before attempting to use its power against Hitler, however, it wished some assurance that the Western powers would deal with the new government. The Pope was asked to mediate, and he agreed to do so, mediating successfully despite the obvious difficulty of his position. The *coup d' état* did not take place because of internal disagreements among the various elements of which the resistance movement was composed. Accounts of the affair have been published in both English and German, the most recent, "Pius XII," *Stimmen der Zeit*, Vol. 163, November 1958, pp. 98–99. In 1944, a high British officer, remarking on the Pope's involvement in this matter, said, "The Pope went as far as he possibly could for a man in his position." So much, then, for the theme of the alliance between Pius XII and Hitler, which is sounded over and over again in Hochhuth's play.

Nor is it true that Pius XII ever considered Hitler's war a war against Bolshevism.

---

*In the American edition of the play, Hochhuth cut sixty-eight lines from the discussion between the Pope and Count Fontana on this subject in deference to Father Leiber's criticism. See note, *The Deputy*, p. 350.—*Ed.*

Pius XII viewed the "unconditional surrender" terms which the Allies demanded in the Casablanca conference in 1943 as a great calamity. /103/

Throughout the war, he never changed his mind on that point. What other position, after all, was there for him to take? Time and again he had repeated his hopes and ardent desires for a lasting peace built on terms both sides could live with.

The Vatican had done its best, throughout the war, to assure the fact that the peace terms would not be left to mere chance. Pius XII put forth a number of proposals indicating his sincere and honorable efforts in the direction of establishing and maintaining peace.

On the other hand, he knew he had to cope with both Bolshevism and National Socialism and that a victory for either would be dangerous. It wasn't until June, 1944, that the Pope's views were confirmed by the western Allied statesmen, military leaders, and politicians. By that time, the destruction of the Nazis was assured, and the problem for the Western world was to build a strong and lasting peace unthreatened by Communism. Unfortunately, the Pope's views were not understood soon enough.

But let us turn to the main theme — Pius XII and the Jewish emergency: Were the Jews offered any assistance during their distress? Hochhuth states that they could not hope to receive support and that they did not, not even from the Vatican. "That is the horrifying truth," he writes (p. 317). The Vatican had extended aid to the Jews long before Hitler's "final solution" had been evolved and put into operation, and the effect of the persecutions was to strengthen, not lessen, the feeling of fellowship between Christians and Jews. Significantly, the first intervention on the part of the Holy See in behalf of the German Jews was made just before Easter 1933 (April 10, 1933), in the form of an urgent plea to Hitler to cease his anti-Semitic practices and policies. Needless to say, this plea did not alter his course in any way.

Pacelli, once he became Pope, carried on the work of his predecessor in the rescue of the Jews. Through the Vatican Registers, beginning in 1939, one is able to trace some of the work of papal intervention in behalf of the Jews, particularly the German Jews. Many of the details of this work were personally handled by Pius XII. (See my own article, "Pius XII. und die Juden in Rom 1943/44," *Stimmen der Zeit,* Vol. 167, March 1961, p. 431.) During the occupation of Rome by the Germans, the Pope issued an official statement on his readiness to assist the Jews in the event that ransom demands were made, and the demand was made. Other relief work was carried on: men, women, and children were hidden in religious houses and schools to protect them from the Gestapo; the Vatican information service conducted a search to seek out Jews in need of assistance; the cooperative efforts of the papal workers of St. Raphael and the Jewish Delasen made it possible for many Jews to go overseas to safety. The cooperation of these two groups was so close that it would have been difficult to tell the members of one from the members of the other. Anton Weber, Pallatin father, was in charge of this phase of the work for the Vatican. The Registers show that /104/ over a three-year period the equivalent of 16,700,000 marks was spent on this work alone. Many other efforts and additional financial expenditures were unrecorded.

The Jews themselves thanked the Pope for his help. Elio Toaff, the Chief Rabbi of Rome, described the work of Pius XII as follows, "Every Jew in Rome is filled with praise for the good and spiritual Pope who did so much for them during those unfortunate years."

Let us consider the main question: Why did the Pope remain silent?

The ideas shared by Pius XI and Pius XII on the subject of war is made clear in their writings. They believed, as had Benedict XV, that the Church should stand on the side of Providence, denouncing war in all its forms as evil, cruel, and brutal. This is the position the Church took in both world wars, and the position which it maintains today. Consequently, it would have been impossible for the Pope to declare himself to be on either side. . . . /105/

. . . Would a strong papal protest at this time have produced any positive results? In order to answer this question one must know both the official position of the Church during those years and the madness and destructiveness of Hitler. In 1942, when the Dutch bishops issued a protest against the persecution of the Jews, a Nazi reply was not long in coming. They retaliated by deporting to the extermination camps not only the Dutch Jews, but also all Catholic converts of Jewish blood, among them, Edith Stein. For the sake of saving human lives, was it not better to remain silent? Pius XII considered that the wiser course, though he did not insist that the papal nuncios abide by it.

The best expert on this subject, the Jewish scholar, Léon Poliakov, confirms the wisdom of this policy. On the question of what would have been the effect of a solemn papal protest on the destruction of Jews, he states: "Had the Pope issued a solemn public protest putting the Church in direct opposition to the Nazi government by opposing the destruction of the Jews, it is unlikely that the deportations would have ceased. . . ."

The Deputy, despite what the most informed opinion maintains, declares that a papal protest against Hitler's Jewish policy would have brought about an immediate cessation of the atrocities. In clinging to this fantasy, Mr. Hochhuth ignores all facts, substituting opinion for knowledge. The papal nuncios in the Balkans, as he himself notes, were successful in their protests to end the deportation of the Jews (pp. 299–300), but he fails to note that they were successful because they dealt with the local regents and governments, not with Hitler. No one with first-hand knowledge of that terrible period could possibly believe that a public protest by Pius XII would have brought an end to the atrocities. . . . /106/

It is reasonable to assume that a papal protest would not have changed matters. The Roman Jews themselves were thankful that the Pope had remained silent during the period of German occupation. The Pope based his decision, as Poliakov has indicated, on the fact that any protest meant further reprisals and more lives lost. He preferred to remain silent. It is presumptuous to condemn this silence. /107/

Father A. Martini, S. J.

THE HISTORICAL TRUTH
AND ROLF HOCHHUTH'S THE DEPUTY

What is offered here is not scholarly work and is not meant to be.
The Deputy, *"Sidelights on History"*

Since the evening of February 20, 1963, when *The Deputy* first appeared on the Berlin stage, it has been seen in many theaters throughout Germany, and

"La vera storiá e *Il Vicario* di Rolf Hochhuth," *La Civiltà Cattolica,* June 6, 1964, pp. 437–454. Trans. by the editors.

in London, Stockholm, Basel, Paris, Vienna; since February, 1964, it has been playing in New York.

The extraordinary interest and passionate polemics the play has evoked everywhere, even in Italy and Rome, are adequately explained by the fact that it centers on the person and role of Pope Pius XII, who is accused, tried, and condemned by the author. The Pope, in fact, in the face of positive knowledge of the destruction of six million Jews, in the face of a crime against fundamental principles of morality and justice, is moved neither by human compassion nor by the call to conscience demanded by his position as supreme custodian of divine law and its highest embodiment on Earth. Instead, he abandons the Jews to their destiny, shutting himself in a silence demanded by his concern for worldly matters.

The enormity and impiety of this accusation are further emphasized by the staging of the play and the historical documentation the author provides at the end of his text. It is also interesting that though the length of the author's original work makes extensive cutting necessary for stage presentation, whatever interpretation has been given the work, the fourth act has always been retained in its entirety, the act in which the Pope is bodily present on stage. Some have gone further by presenting a ridiculous amount of pomp and posturing and ornate settings to accentuate the Pope's aloofness, aristocracy, and distance from reality. The author, in his historical supplement, declares that he wished to compile a reconstruction of the man and his work from authentic documentation and primary sources and that the extensive study required took almost three years to complete. /437/

To some, three years might seem a rather short interval in which to complete a deep historical investigation and to rework the materials into a creative literary form. The author presents his "Christian tragedy" in the dual role of drama and history, thus allowing himself the artistic freedom to go beyond merely historical data. Nor have critics had to contend with the accuracy of the historical picture, a problem they avoided by reviewing the work as literature.

Thus the question of whether Rolf Hochhuth has succeeded in his intention of compiling a historical work in support of his opinon that Pius XII was responsible for the extermination of six million Jews by not having stopped Hitler through his personal intervention remains unanswered. Hochhuth is convinced that Pius XII's inaction renders him fully guilty, "a criminal."

Such a peremptory condemnation has understandably excited violent reactions, particularly from Catholics. To see a contemporary Pope, known and loved by millions, put on stage and given a trial by theater without possibility of defense, to see a matter which should be examined with serenity and objectivity treated so profanely, touches the emotions of the faithful and inspires hostility towards the author. The result is that the impassioned attack is answered by equally emotional defenses.

Though such reactions are understandable, they are not really necessary. A serious and dispassionate examination of Hochhuth's research methods and an analysis of his historical reconstruction will permit a true judgment to be made.

The Personality of Pius XII

As the fourth act unfolds in the audience room of Pius XII, the point to which all the preceding action was leading is revealed. From Berlin, where a

young Jesuit priest, Riccardo Fontana, makes the acquaintance of an S.S. officer, Gerstein, and is horrified to learn of the atrocities taking place at Nazi
extermination camps; from Germany, where all of the action and interest is
intended to provide information of the destructive policies of the Nazis and
the general passivity of the world, Hochhuth directs the movement toward
Rome, toward the Pope. In the third act, the young priest makes a final decision to have an encounter with the Pope; it is the only hope. Once he can
make the Pope understand the reality of the situation, he will undoubtedly
speak the words and assume the role consonant with his responsibility,
thereby /438/ stopping Hitler and rescuing the Jews from the infernal machinery of death.

In the actual encounter, however, the personage who confronts him is a
lofty, distant aristocrat who, with obvious irony, shows himself to be preoccu-
pied "mit brennender Sorge," with burning concern, for the industrial, min-
ing, and other investments of the Holy See which, at the moment, are
threatened by the Allied air invasions in Germany and North Italy. To his
avid economic interests, and perhaps of even greater importance, is added a
coldly calculating and shrewd concern for the political implications of each
phase of the war and of his own position as negotiator. To the young Riccardo, who has come to disclose the atrocities of Auschwitz, the Pope speaks
only in terms of the future of Europe and the world, and of the Bolshevist
threat, to which Hitler offers the only valid resistance, an end which, in effect,
excuses the means. Riccardo finally has no recourse but to appeal on moral
grounds: he reproaches the Pope for permitting a great injustice to take place
underneath his very windows, urging him to protest in behalf of the persecuted innocents, to participate in their martyrdom, and to stop uttering insin-
cere condolences and ambiguous statements or offering such partial remedies
as the opening of religious houses and schools. But, supreme irony, the Pope,
whose anger at this act of criticism and rebellion in his presence can hardly be
restrained, responds by expressing his sorrow for Riccardo's nervous condition and advising him to take a restful vacation and long, solitary walks.

Having seen the Vicar of Christ resolutely refuse to assume his duties in the
face of all the facts, nothing remains for Riccardo, the idealist, but to pin the
Star of David to his soutane and announce that he will go with the Jews to
the extermination camp as the vicar's vicar. And the Pope, having soiled his
hands with ink while signing the offensive statement, calls for a bowl of water
and washes his hands.

Such is the Pius XII in Rolf Hochhuth's historical reconstruction, a characterization documented with references of three kinds: first, the descriptions
of Cardinal Tardini and Father Robert Leiber, and of Galeazzi Lisi, /439/ the
Pope's personal physician; secondly, the confidences received from high
church officials while he was on a visit to Rome but whose names he has promised not to reveal, at least until the time of their deaths; and, thirdly, a number of publications and photographic documents containing scattered references to conversations with the Pope, primarily material from newspapers,
magazines, diaries, and memoirs of contemporary figures.

The search for documents and an objective, critical examination of them to
determine their true significance are primary duties of a historian. Hochhuth
has recognized these obligations and attempted to fulfill them, for in his
historical supplement he deplores the fact that he was unable to attain access
to the archives of the Vatican and the Kremlin, as he felt certain the materials therein would have confirmed his interpretation of history. On the

other hand, it is noteworthy that he uses no other archive material of any kind.

It seems, also, that in his examination of various sources he has seen only what he wished to see, omitting anything which might contradict his thesis and distorting other portions to fit his needs. For example, the works of Father Leiber and Cardinal Tardini, two men who were intimates of Pius XII for thirty to forty years, are noteworthy for their serene detachment and judiciousness, qualities which are amazing considering that the books were written only a short while after the Pope's death. From these works emerges a picture of a man different in every way from the Pope in Hochhuth's play, a man to whom money and the amassing of riches were of no interest and in whom moral and spiritual considerations were uppermost. These writers admired the intellect and insight of the Pope, his far-reaching vision and interest in contemporary affairs, his understanding of worldly problems and his attempts to approach them from the spiritual and religious viewpoint, and his sensitivity to the obligations accompanying his high position. Had Hochhuth examined his documents carefully, he could not have failed to find within them the evidence he required for a reconstruction of the Pope's personality, for the question of the strength of his conscience is clearly answered in these books: Pope Pius XII did not lack inner courage; he stood ready to meet whatever sacrifice, even martyrdom, for his beliefs.

Unfortunately, Hochhuth chose to give undue weight to the rumors and tales he picked up in Rome. Too many of his "facts" are in the sly whisper of the malicious gossip-monger and self-important "insider." Such people and stories gather about every important personage and have gathered about all popes, Pius XII not excepted. Used judiciously, such disclosures may reveal certain insights into personality, but certainly they require comparison and collation with statements contained in works known to be based on solid fact and verified information. /440/ For example, in addition to the nameless "eye-witnesses" and the two sources named above, Hochhuth may well have consulted Monsignor Montini, Cardinal of Milan at the time of Hochhuth's visit to Italy, who had been for so many years, and particularly during the war years, an intimate of Pius XII. Yet he did not choose to interview him, and it was not until June 29, 1963, in a letter to the British Catholic weekly, *The Tablet*,[1] that the present Pope had an opportunity to correct the playwright's misconstructions. Pope Paul VI also took the opportunity to present an accurate and positive picture of Pius XII in his oration on March 12 of this year [1964] at the unveiling of a monument at St. Peter's erected to Pius XII.

Again, in his reconstruction of the personality of the Pope, Hochhuth has relied heavily on the statements of career diplomats, men whose very positions required them to meet the Pope and view him through a double standard: with unbiased objectivity and with regard for the success of their own particular assignments and political fortunes. First of all, the playwright has seized on passages from the memoirs of Weizsäcker, the German ambassador assigned to the Vatican during the war years, whose book was published in 1951. He also quotes widely from Weizsäcker's associate, von Kessel. In March, 1963, Osborne, the British ambassador to the Vatican during World War II, issued a statement which was published in *The Times;* Häggelöf, the Swiss ambassador in London, wrote an article which appeared in Stockholm on September 29, 1963; Gripenburg, the ambassador from Finland assigned

---

1. "Pius XII and the Jews" reprinted in *Civiltà Cattolica*, 1963, III, 160–162. /441/

to the Vatican, wrote an article for a Helsinki newspaper, published in that city on December 5, 1963, and translated into English in April of this year [1964]. These statements are unanimous in acknowledging very different qualities in Pius XII than those attributed to him by Hochhuth. Sir Osborne says: "Pius XII was the warmest, gentlest, most generous (and in a word, saintliest) character whom I have had the privilege to encounter in the course of my long life." Häggelöf lists Pius' purity of heart, the characteristic of a religious person, and his political foresight, which he felt surpassed that of any other statesman he had met. Gripenburg sums up his impression of his meeting with the Pope in the following words: "spiritual, affable, wise, impartial, of the highest sentiments, sickened by the inhuman horror of the war."

Pius XII and the Jewish Problem

We have already described Hochhuth's characterization of Pius XII. On the basis of these personality weaknesses, he explains Pius' refusal to act in behalf of the Jews. Pius' main sin, according to the young author, was a sin of omission: he chose silence when he ought to have spoken. He failed to protest openly, to excommunicate Hitler and his henchmen, to break off the Concordat with the Reich government, to incite the Catholics of Germany and the occupied /441/ countries to rebellion, to send the faithful to their martyrdom in extermination camps with the Star of David pinned to their chests—all actions which would have forced Hitler to desist from his madness and cease the executions.

Failures. Sins of omission, sins imputed to the Pope's own personality deficiencies: he was cold, skeptical, egotistical; he cared only for the financial and economic manipulations of the Church and the enhancement of his own political and diplomatic role in the destiny of Europe. Finally, his character was such as to naturally dispose him favorably towards totalitarian regimes, towards the German people and their government, and to make him fear Bolshevism to such an extent that he could visualize Nazi Germany as the sole hope of Europe.

For these very serious charges, Hochhuth offers no documentary proof. I say *none* since he makes no attempt to uphold or verify his charge of the supremacy of the Pope's economic interests, and, despite his references to American, British, and German documents in regard to the political charges, the papers, all of which were published after the war, do not support his statements. Of the latter the most important are the Tittmann papers, State Department, Washington, D. C., stating Tittmann's impressions of the common interests of the Allies in persuading the Pope to issue a statement condemning the Nazis (see particularly the selections pertaining to August—September, 1942); the report of Bérard, ambassador from Vichy, France, on the anti-Semitic legislation of that government, issued in September, 1941; and two telegrams from the German ambassador, Weizsäcker, October 17 and 20, 1943, immediately following the deportation of Roman Jews on October 16, 1943.

Putting aside for the moment the significance of the American documents, let us examine in their historical context both Bérard's report and the Weizsäcker telegrams.

On August 7, 1941, Marshall Pétain entrusted Bérard to probe the Secretary of State of the Vatican as to whether the Church would react unfavorably to the anti-Semitic policies recently enacted by the Vichy government. He replied by citing the long history of racism within the Church, speculating on its relation to the legislation under discussion, and declaring that no protest would be /442/ forthcoming from the Vatican. His report, which was found among the Vichy papers, was published in *Jewish Documents* in 1945 and included in Poliakov's book on the Nazi extermination of the Jews. These anti-Semitic laws had been enacted by the French government at the instigation of the Germans and went so far as to define matrimonial relationships between Jews and Christians. Had the Church let them pass without protest, it would have been guilty of a serious failure to act. Poliakov reveals with historical accuracy that Bérard's information had been elicited from two assistants to the Secretary of State to whom he had not given full particulars. Also, that in reporting their reactions, he interpreted his material in such a way as to make it precisely what he felt his superior would most want to hear. The actual response of the Church to the anti-Semitic policy of the Vichy government was something quite different.

On the 13th of September, 1941, Marshall Pétain, in a meeting with Monsignor Valeri, the Papal Nuncio, and the ambassadors from Spain and Brazil, casually referred to the laws and asked the Nuncio's opinion of them. Monsignor Valeri immediately denounced them and, in reply to Pétain's statement that his superiors might think differently, pointed out that the principles which inspired the laws were those of racism, a philosophy unequivocally condemned by the Catholic Church. The Marshall offered to let him see Bérard's report on Vatican reaction, but the Nuncio insisted that every article was totally inadmissable and left a strongly worded protest based on specific ecclesiastical principles violated by the legislation. He immediately referred the matter to Rome and was given full approval and support for his action. He was also informed that had Bérard given full and accurate information to the two prelates of the Secretary of State from whom he had elicited his information, he would not have received the bland assurances to which he referred.

The Nuncio, as witnessed by the two ambassadors present, had stated the Church's position clearly and strongly. Shortly afterwards, Radio London and other Allied broadcasting systems reported the news of a protest from the Holy See to the Vichy government. Though Bérard's report was widely publicized in France, perhaps in an effort to counteract the decisive reproval of the French episcopacy, it in no way corresponded to the facts of the case [*The Deputy*, p. 345–346].

Let us turn now to the Weizsäcker telegrams of October 16 and October 23, 1943 [*The Deputy*, pp. 325–328, 284–285].

Those who lived in Rome throughout those weeks of autumn, 1943, remember well the chaotic situation when raids were the order of the day and one did not dare to venture into the streets. Generally, the first indication that a deportation was going to take place was the compiling of lists of able-bodied men in the Jewish community. A little later /443/ a ransom demand was made: 50 kilograms of gold was to be raised by the Roman Jews in 36 hours. The Pope immediately offered his assistance by promising to provide whatever portion of the ransom was lacking. His response was immediate and unqualified, and if, in the end, there was no need for the Jews to take advantage of the offer, that does not lessen the value of his gesture.

During the dark days leading up to the deportations, the German ambassador had reason to fear a *coup de main* by the Gestapo to take the Pope prisoner and cut him off from the Church. Marshal Kesselring and Ambassador von

Rahn shared Weizsäcker's fears and, knowing the Pope's firm intention not to leave Rome unless compelled by force to do so, they tried to avert disaster.

These were the circumstances in the Holy City at the time the Gestapo conducted its first round-up of Jews in Rome, the morning of October 16. They had been given orders to take all—the aged, the ill, the women, the children—and they were taking no chances and showing no pity. More than a thousand had been gathered at the military school at Lungara and nothing could induce the Gestapo to release them. The news was spread throughout Rome, reaching the Vatican and St. Peter's.

Immediately, two actions were set in motion: Bishop Hudal was assigned by the Pope to protest to the military commander of the city, General Stahel; concurrently, Cardinal Maglione, the Secretary of State, met with the ambassador from Germany, Weizsäcker. While Hudal was demanding the immediate cessation of the arrests, the Cardinal Secretary of State was strongly and directly condemning the injustice and sinfulness of what was taking place in Rome. Both the military head and the ambassador would no doubt have acted in response to these demands. However, the action was being conducted by the secret police, which received its orders from the Security Service of the Chancellor of the Party (after Himmler, Eichmann was the power behind this phase of Nazi policy). In those days in Rome, the number of men in the secret police was reckoned in thousands, and they were not noted for releasing victims who had fallen into their clutches.

It was under these conditions that Weizsäcker sent his telegram of October 17, which had as its primary aim the stopping of the arrests and deportations. He gave the most forceful reason he could, the threat of a papal protest in the event that the action continued. By the time he sent his second telegram, October 28, the arrests had, in effect, been concluded, and his primary purpose /444/ was to ward off any reprisals and, most particularly, to discourage that most-feared measure, the deportation of the Pope. Again, thinking in terms of the most effective arguments he could give, he stated that the Pope had no desire to come to an open break in relations with Hitler's government and would not offer an open protest to his policies. Thus was Weizsäcker forced to play both ends against the middle.

A third action at this time, approved, supported, and sustained by Pius XII, was the opening up of religious houses, churches, and schools as refuges for all Jews who had had to flee from their homes. The granting of sanctuary to the oppressed Jews constitutes one of the most beautiful chapters of the spirit of Christianity.

The actions described can hardly be interpreted as evidence that the Pope was deaf to the cries of anguish of the Jews of Rome, or that he wished to remain free of any involvement in their affairs, or that he did nothing to stop the Gestapo from rounding up Jews under his very windows.

Hochhuth's main hypothesis, which he supports with some statements, none of which are arranged in any semblance of orderly history, is that *if* the Pope had protested publicly, Hitler would have ended his extermination policy. But history is not built on *if*'s. Nor is it possible, even if it were true, to suppose that because Goebbels, in his diary, had bemoaned the fact that during the war he was not permitted to carry on his program of liquidating the Catholic Church, the Church was aware that it had nothing to fear from the Nazis [*The Deputy*, p. 304]. It is, after all, equally easy to document the fact that Hitler, in his *Table Talk*, spoke boastfully and with great confidence of the way he had broken a resistance movement and put down a revolution. There is further confirmation of the confidence in their power and the lack of effectiveness of threats and protests displayed by the Nazis in a document described by the American prosecutor, Jackson, at the Nuremberg Trials. He affirmed that among the papers of the German Foreign Office, he discovered a copy of the noted declaration made by Churchill and Roosevelt in 1942 on the sanctions to be taken at the war's end against all those who participated in the destruction of the Jews and other atrocities. The copy was heavily annotated with arguments strongly supporting the continuation and total execution of the prepared plan. The Jews themselves were thoroughly convinced of the irreversible decision made by Hitler and the Nazis in regard to their extermination policy. A. L. Kubowitzki, at the World Jewish Congress, held in Atlantic City, November, 1944, said: "We know that the Germans will not be dissuaded from their project by warnings; we are convinced that their striving for world domination could not have been halted by any power. More likely, protests will cause them to step up their activities."

Again, it is not true that the Pope had a formidable weapon in the Concordat or that, had he wished to, he might have called upon the Catholics in Germany and other countries under Nazi power to rise up *en masse* against the barbarities being committed. The facts reveal that both these notions are completely erroneous.

Renouncing the Concordat would only have strengthened Hitler's position. The fact is /445/ that the Concordat referred specifically to the conditions of life and the activity of German Catholics. Its renunciation by the Holy See would have given Hitler two advantages: an immediate propaganda weapon and a free hand to abolish Catholicism wherever his power extended. Hitler and his propaganda division, headed by Goebbels, had stressed the role of the "international Jewish conspiracy" in the fight against Germany, blaming the Jews and their organizations for all of Germany's ills since the time of the Versailles treaty. In this way, they had shifted the blame for starting a world conflict from themselves to the Jews. Breaking off the Concordat would have been interpreted as positive proof of the Vatican's close association with a criminal group to whom the worst kind of tyranny and exploitation had been imputed, not as an indication of the Catholic world's sympathy for an oppressed people. In addition, the renunciation of the Concordat would have meant an end to whatever contact was still possible between the faithful in Germany and the hierarchy of the Roman Catholic Church. Not only would diplomatic relations between Germany and the Vatican have ended, but all relations between the Holy Father and his children would have been affected. This situation already existed in Poland and other occupied countries. In Warsaw the Papal Nuncio and the entire diplomatic corps had been expelled and not permitted to return throughout the period of German occupation. When Monsignor Orsenigo of Berlin attempted to protest over the treatment of the Church in Poland, he was curtly reminded that his accreditation limited him to Church affairs in Germany, specifically in Germany proper and not in the occupied territories. Clergy and laity in Polish territories were forbidden to communicate with Rome, so that the churches became a series of independent communities completely outside the reach of the Vicar of Christ and at the mercy of the despotic totalitarian regime. Even in Germany itself, where the Concordat had been in force since 1933, the threat of a similar treatment weighed heavily. In June, 1942, at the conclusion of the Bishops' Conference at Fulda, a statement was made grieving over the latest oppressive measures of the German government and predicting that worse were yet to come. From the beginning they had feared that the war against the Church would be waged to its "final solution," and in that statement they used the still secret word by which the Germans referred to their Jewish policy, *Endlösung*.

Obviously, it would have been far easier to abolish the Church if its communication /446/ with the outside world and with the center of Catholicism had been cut off. History shows that whenever a government has wanted to take over the churches, it has first isolated them by prohibiting them to contact the mother church. Consider the fate of the Church under Elizabeth I, Napoleon, or Nicholas I of Russia, or, in our own century, in Mexico and in countries behind the Iron Curtain. In each instance the dismissal and expulsion of the Papal Nuncio constituted the first step in the persecution of the Church. Voluntarily breaking off the Concordat, then, could only have given Hitler the opening he was seeking to wage a total war on the Christian churches.

It is evident that the Pope could not hand him such a weapon. Even less could he incite the German Catholics to rebellion, regardless of how much admiration and inspiration such a demand might have generated throughout the world. The Holy See had been obliged to enter into negotiations with Germany in 1933, but there were no guarantees or means of forcing the Reich government to uphold the provisions of the Concordat. Cardinal Pacelli, however, knew he could not rely on the good faith of the Nazis, and he did not. Between 1933 and 1939 he addressed more than ninety notes of protest to Germany enumerating violations of the Concordat. Once he became Pope, he was well aware of the rather shaky basis on which stood the German Catholic Church and of how much chance a rebellion or strong resistance movement had. In addition, the Church was not and ought never to be an organized party or a center of revolution and armed resistance. Again, looking to historical analogies, the effectiveness of a threat of excommunication is greatly to be doubted. Did the excommunication of Elizabeth I cause her to release her subjects from vowing obedience to her church?

These are all facts which must be recognized, considered, and accepted as valid explanations for the Pope's behavior during the war years.

The Actions of Pius XII

Essentially, Pius XII believed that all evil, regardless of which side committed it, ought to be clearly and openly condemned. Only by recognizing and denouncing evil wherever it existed could a just social order emerge. Hochhuth is concerned solely with the Jewish tragedy and emphasizes it in such a way as to distort the actual situation. Surely the extermination of millions of Jews, the Nazi policy of genocide, was an abomination of the most unjust and disgusting kind. Seen in its true perspective, this policy was a consequence of racism, of concession to atheism, of a materialistic view of life and of the world; in short, the destruction of the Jews was the result of man's having turned away from the laws of God. /447/ Pius XII, from the time of his first encyclical in October, 1939, through the moving Christmas messages of the war years (particularly the message of 1942), in all of his public and private letters, and in public addresses (especially that of June 2, 1943) expressed his concern for the rebuilding of a world and a social order firmly based on spiritual principles of the brotherhood of man and the fatherhood of God. He condemned all evil; he spoke out many times protesting the extermination of unarmed civilians and defenseless prisoners. His thoughts on and attitudes toward all the crucial events taking place in the world were clearly stated and well known to all who cared to know. It is true that he was constantly being urged by politicians and statesmen to make more explicit statements condemning specific acts, as the letter of Sir Osborne cited by Hochhuth indicates [*The Deputy*, p. 332]. Yet the New York *Times* of December 27, 1943, stated that the Pope's Christmas message contained an explicit condemnation of the Jewish massacres, adding that the Pope had denounced all injustice without seeming to show favoritism towards either side. It is unfortunate that the same newspaper, in 1964, in flat contradiction of its own earlier and more accurate statement, should take up the accusation made by Hochhuth and entitle an article about Pius XII "Silence."

Pius XII, out of consideration for his position and duties, spoke only when he was certain of his facts. During the war years, information was not always readily available, nor were many of the reports which were issued entirely free from bias. No one, of course, knew until after the war that a total of six million Jews had been exterminated by the Nazis. It was only after Germany's defeat that the details, partially known and certainly suspected since the middle of 1942, of the policy and method of "the final solution" were made known. Even the World Jewish Congress through its posts for gathering and disseminating information on the Jewish situation had only approximate figures, which were wrong by hundreds of thousands according to the final verification. The Polish government in exile was a main source of information, the one from which the Jewish agency received much of its news. Naturally, prime importance was given to news concerning Poland. Some of the facts thus received were essentially accurate: the locations of the camps, the exact methods of extermination, the approximate number of victims executed daily. The Pope did have additional sources of information, though these were infrequent and often inaccurate: the clergy in occupied countries, military chaplains passing through Rome, civilians and military men on official business. For the most part, /448/ it was impossible to verify this information, and without confirmation little could be said or done. No international organization, not even the International Red Cross, of those groups dedicated to the relief of civilians and military prisoners was ever permitted entry into a civilian camp. Even in areas where the Red Cross was permitted to go to the aid of prisoners of war, insurmountable obstacles were found in the approaches to concentration camps. It was even forbidden to forward packages of food, toilet articles, and medical supplies to such places. Nor were denials that extermination camps existed issued only by German Nazis. Even after 1945, many denied that such camps had ever existed, citing the Reich government's declaration of July, 1944, that the atrocity stories were merely Allied propaganda.

All sides, of course, attempted to get the Pope to make an energetic statement in their favor. It is in such a light that the Tittmann-Department of State papers of July-September, 1942, alluded to above, must be looked at [*The Deputy*, p. 332]. In them are contained the Allied attempts to urge Pius XII to issue "a public protest against the Nazi atrocities." It should be noted that no specific mention is made of the suffering of the Jews and the desire to alleviate that suffering. The plight of the innocent victims was not the main consideration; political advantage was. Undoubtedly, such a protest would have had tremendous propaganda value and would have been amply exploited by the Allies, perhaps being distorted in the process. It would also have compromised the Pope for no good reason, restricting his movements and limiting his effectiveness.

Those most directly concerned with the Jewish situation, the Jews subjected to persecution and the personnel of the International Jewish Congress, certainly disagreed with Hochhuth's position regarding the effectiveness of open protest. Though the Jews frequently turned to the Pope for help, not one request for such an action was made. C. Barlas, who represented the Jewish Agency in Palestine, wrote to the Apostolic Delegate for Egypt and Palestine on January 20, 1943:

The highly humanitarian act of the Holy See in having expressed its indignation at the present racial persecutions has given considerable comfort to our brothers. If it is ever possible, may I request that you extend our public gratitude for all the good work of the Church in our behalf? Perhaps our appreciation for all those Catholics who, how we do not know, manage to help Jews escape from the occupied territories to safety will be of some encouragement to them. Certainly, we do not underestimate the great difficulty this work involves. /449/

The real and constant possibility of reprisals was well understood by the Jews themselves. In a special meeting of the World Jewish Congress at Atlantic City, November 26–30, 1944, A. Leone Kubowitzki defended the organization from charges of timidity and failure to act by recalling Nazi retaliations: "Perhaps we ought to have acted more forcefully, perhaps we ought to have dared more, perhaps we ought not to have hesitated, but we feared that any attempt would have proved more detrimental than inaction." And Herzog, the Chief Rabbi of Jerusalem, made a radio appeal to the world on December 2, 1942, in which he said: "Remember, all of you, that protests and warnings, important though they may be, are not enough. What is needed is practical support, assistance to help the Jews weather this storm. Create an international corps specifically assigned to find ways and means of helping the Jews. Open the doors, especially the doors to the land of our fathers, to all those who seek refuge from Nazi tyranny." Perhaps even more significant are the letters addressed to the Pope by the Roman Jews in October and November of 1943, the period immediately following the deportations from that city. They did not ask him to make any grandiose gestures in their behalf; quite simply, they requested assistance in obtaining information about those who had been arrested and deported, so that they might find ways to help them.

It is evident that all those who had witnessed Nazi reprisals did not desire a public protest.[2] The case of Poland is typical. Though the refugees abroad, far from the day-to-day encounter with the situation, took violent exception to the Pope's alleged silence, aiming particularly barbed criticism at the Archbishop of Cracow, Monsignor Sapieha, no one inside Poland could fail to realize what the reaction to open protest would be on the part of the Nazis. Sapieha, certainly the embodiment of the ideal priest and patriot, had himself written to the Pope that the faithful among the people in Poland needed to be reassured of his interest in their plight. On March 23, 1943, the Pope asked

2. See on this subect the full text of a letter to the bishops of Germany, September 13, 1942, sent to Cardinal Bertram by Pius XII and now in the Breslavia archives. In reply to the cardinal's request for a word of encouragement for the clergy and the German people, the Pope sent a magnificent letter on January 3, 1943, in which he reassured them of his knowledge of their situation. He left to the judgment of the bishops whether the letter should be read to the people from the pulpit. Bertram could not risk asking them by letter and therefore waited until the conference at Fulda (August 17–19, 1943) to raise the issue. Almost all present agreed not to read the letter in order not to provoke the terrible anger of the government and the party. /450/

him whether it would be opportune to have a new letter from him read from the pulpit; he was refused for fear /450/ that immediate and harsh reprisals would be forthcoming. As early as August 28, 1942, Sapieha had written, "We are already victimized for being suspected of having had contact with Rome." The bishops of Holland, too, had shown their courage, only to regret it. On Saturday, July 11, 1942, they, in conjunction with the leaders of various Protestant churches, had addressed a telegram of protest against the threat of deportation of the Jews to the east to Reichkommisar Seyss-Inquart. On July 20, the telegram was included in a pastoral letter scheduled to be read in all Catholic churches on the following Sunday, July 26. On August 2, General-Komissar Schmidt accused the bishops of having broken their promise not to publicize the telegram and ordered that, in reprisal, Jewish Catholics would also be arrested and deported. Jewish Protestants were spared because none of the Protestant churches had made the contents of the protest known to their followers. Schmidt was lying, as the bishops had never promised silence on the matter, but his threat of reprisal was only too true. The Catholic Jews of Holland, among them Edith Stein, the famous Carmelite nun, were arrested, deported, and exterminated.

There was good reason, then, for Pius XII to take the position he did in a letter to the Bishop of Berlin, von Preysing, on July 30, 1943, a letter rendering homage to Monsignor Lichtenberg, a martyr of World War II, and approving the initiative taken by the various dioceses in extending help to the Jews, a dangerous, complex, but widespread practice:

> We leave to each diocese the decision of whether danger of reprisal and repression would make unwise, despite the best of intentions, an open protest. A prudent reserve *ad maiora mala vitanda*. It is for this reason that we do not ourselves go as far as we might like, as far as we had hoped in 1942 it would still be possible to go, in our pontifical messages.
>
> For non-Aryan Catholics and those of the religion of Israel the Holy See has done everything in its power to offer both spiritual and physical assistance. We have spoken about that which is presently being done in Germany against non-Aryans in our Christmas message. Though our reference was brief, it has been well understood. But no matter what happens, let us assure all, Catholics, both Aryan and non-Aryan, the children of the Church, as well as others, that throughout their tribulations our fatherly affection and interest has been with them. At the present time, the only direct aid I can give them is through prayer, but the time will come when circumstances will once more permit my voice to be raised in their favor.

Thus we see the figure of a man whose course of action had been decided after full understanding and consideration of the realities. /451/ He acted in the full light of his responsibilities to God and to man, not as a diplomat or a politician would have done, but honestly and directly. There has been full documentation of the perseverance and effectiveness with which Pius XII acted in Slovakia and Roumania.[3] Most authorities agree that the papal protest was the decisive influence in causing the Regent of Hungary, Horthy, to act to save the remaining Hungarian Jews from the personal destructive operation of Eichmann. The Jewish refugees, in Southern France and those on

3.   F. Cavalli, S. J., "La S. Sede contra la deportazione degli ebrei della Slovacchia durante la seconda guerra mondiale," in *Civilatà Cattolica*, 1961, III, 13 – 18; A. Martini, S. J., "La S. Sede e gli ebrei della Romania durante la seconde guerra mondiale," in *Civiltà Cattolica*, 1961, III, 449 – 463. /452/

the Dalmation coast knew that, for them, the presence of the Italian army was a source of security. Yet the Italian army had to be directed and sustained by the Ministers of the Interior and of Foreign Affairs, and it was the solicitude of the Pope and of Cardinal Maglione, their untiring efforts to keep alive the sense of humanity of these men and to obtain pledges, remind them of their promises, and impel them to prohibit injustice and criminal acts, which rendered the Italian army an effective safeguard against Nazi atrocities. Their work in this connection was unrelenting and unceasing. A few of the practical measures taken as a result of Vatican intervention may be cited. Monsignor Borgongini Dura and Father Tacchi Venturi, two faithful servants of the Holy See, and Cardinal Maglione, the Secretary of State of the Vatican, obtained a pledge from Buffarini Guidi in 1942 that no new restrictions against Jews would be passed and that all existing legislation would be reviewed. On January 22, 1943, a promise was made that the Jews in Southern France would no longer be under police surveillance. On March 18, when it was suspected that the Gestapo was getting ready to act, the Nuncio was ordered to request an audience with the Minister of Foreign Affairs and to speak to him "strongly and pointedly." On the following morning, the Minister gave deep assurances of his own good faith, though he added that the situation was a difficult one and explained the obstacles he had encountered. The papal delegate, Monsignor Marcone, was engaged in similar work in Zagab, where he had been sent with express orders to work for the aid of the Jews.

Though these were *ex officio* actions, they nonetheless required patient and persevering daily work, sending dispatches, reports, diplomatic notes, and, at the end, their results could be counted in individuals and groups snatched from death. In the final analysis, what counted above all else was the saving of human lives. Nor should it /452/ be forgotten that throughout this period the Reich government, inaccessible to any direct intervention in its dogged determination to continue the execution of its infernal design of destruction, had before it as a constant reminder a man whose presence and attitude constituted an admonishment and a condemnation. Faced with a similar dilemma, the International Red Cross made the same choice for the same reasons. According to testimony presented by its president in Toronto in 1952, the organization had preferred the choice of day-to-day drudgery, the undramatic work of collecting and disseminating information and collecting and distributing emergency supplies, work which might mean the saving of human lives, rather than the momentary glory and journalistic acclaim it might have had by engaging in spectacular denunciations.

The saving of lives! Throughout this period, this was Pius XII's chief concern. He well remembered how much had been accomplished by Benedict XV during World War I and wished to follow his example. That his efforts were understood and appreciated by those most directly concerned has been amply illustrated.

On January 2, 1940, Chicago's United Jewish Appeal for Refugees and Overseas Needs offered the sum of $125,000 in memory of Pius XI to Pius XII to establish a fund for the assistance of all those persecuted because of race or religion. This was an eloquent testimony of the belief of responsible Jewish leaders in the Pope's impartiality and in his charity. On April 12, 1944, a request from President Roosevelt came asking whether it would be possible for the Holy See to transmit financial aid to Polish Jewish Refugees and to the organization to aid Jewish children. On April 25, the Vatican answered that it would continue as it had in the past to render aid to all those in need.

These then were the ways in which Pius XII acted during the war years in behalf of the Jews and all the other persecuted peoples.

The direct testimony of all those who had contact with him, clergy or laymen, Catholics or non-Catholics, unanimously /453/ declares that the Pope, confronted with the horrors of war, was a truly tragic figure. To the Bishop of Berlin, who had written "rarely since the beginning of the pontificacy has so heavy a burden been placed by God on the shoulders of a Pope," he replied on April 30, 1943: "One must always be cautious when comparing the present and the past. . . . Yet it is probably true that seldom has a Pope had to subdue his own innermost desires to the extent that is true at present. And what is even a greater source of sorrow to me is the war with all the pain and guilt it engenders. The inhuman ferocity of modern technical warfare, the growth of which has no comparison, makes it seem almost unbearable that the mutual murders should continue for any length of time."

The above references will suffice as honest verification of the Pope's clear conscience in regard to the manner in which he executed his duties during the war years. His actions continued forceful and direct in clear response to the various events and emergencies then facing the world. A less able person would certainly have buckled under the strain and pressure of that immense burden. Surely Pope Paul VI, in the lecture on March 12 referred to above, spoke justly when he said:

Whatever the circumstance, he considered it justly and conscientiously, so that he might truly say that he never ceased to speak and act so as to uphold the laws of justice, to defend the weak, to succor the suffering, to prevent great ills, to smooth the way for peace. The numerous evils without equal which devastated humanity during his reign cannot be imputed to any cowardice, egotism, or aloofness on his part. Whoever maintains the contrary is guilty of ignoring truth and justice. If the results of his studies, efforts, endeavors, prayers, work for humanity and peace did not suffice to meet all his own wishes and the needs of others, it was not because he was unmoved by the world conflict, the injustice, pain, and blood seen everywhere in a war-torn world, over-run by the furor and oppression of totalitarianism.

I do not wish to deny to anyone the right to believe in the efficacy of open protest or to write apocalyptics. These roads are open to whoever wishes to travel them. But as an honest historian seeking the truth, I cannot accept as accurate the characterization of Pius XII set forth by Hochhuth and utterly opposed to the documentary evidence. There is no basis for his historical "reconstruction" of the "silence" maintained by the Pope in the face of Hitler's massacre of the Jews. Still less do I understand the words of one who professes to be a Catholic, "*il fallait que le scandale éclatât!*," because all of the charges are false, and there is no greater sin for a historian than to contradict the truth. /454/

Interpretation and Analysis of Sources

Anyone who has read the articles in this section and Hochhuth's own "Sidelights on History" has had ample opportunity to observe that facts do *not* speak for themselves. The same fact may be used to support different, even opposite, opinions. Consider the ten items in the chart below, checking the page references given. A *"D"* in front of a page number refers to page numbers in *The Deputy,* Grove Press edition (paperback or hardbound); other page references are to this section of the text.

A. *Fact:* Throughout the war, Pius XII, though condemning racial injustice and persecution of the innocent, never once mentioned the Jews or Hitler's atrocities specifically.

   View I: Pius XII was unmoved by the plight of the Jews; he supported Hitler and did not want to criticize him. *Ref.: D299; D329; D332; D349;* pp. 153–154, 157.

   View II: Pius XII condemned the roots of evil, not specific acts. Pius XII as head of a universal church could not take sides in a world conflict. He condemned *all* injustice on both sides: Jews were not the only victims, Nazis were not the only persecutors. *Ref.:* pp. 142–147, 152, 164, 165, 172–173.

B. *Fact:* Pius XII did not abrogate the Concordat with Hitler.

   View I: Even when Catholic priests and nuns were being persecuted, Pius XII showed that he desired to be allied with Hitler. The Concordat with the Catholic Church had first made Hitler's government "respectable," and its continuation was a great propaganda advantage to him. *Ref.: D296–297; D* Act Two.

   View II: Abrogating the Concordat would have given Hitler an opening to destroy churches throughout Nazi territory. Hitler would have used the breaking of the Concordat as a basis for propaganda against the Catholic Church. Pius XII was concerned for the welfare of German Catholics; this was the reason for the Concordat in the first place and the only reason he chose to continue it. *Ref.:* pp. 158, 170–172.

C. *Fact:* On October 16, 1943, Jews were deported from Rome and sent to Auschwitz. Among them were many Catholics.

   View I: Even when Jews were rounded up under the very windows of St. Peter's, Pius XII remained silent and did nothing. *Ref.: D* Acts Three and Four; *D324;* pp. 154–156.

   View II: Upon learning of the arrests, the Pope immediately launched a three-fold action: military protest, diplomatic protest, rescue efforts. Protests were ineffective; therefore, a policy of quiet, continuous relief and rescue work was followed by the Church. *Ref.:* pp. 154–155, 158, 159–161, 163, 170, 176.

D. *Fact:* Strong, open protests from the Church in Rumania, Czechoslavakia, and Hungary succeeded in halting Jewish deportations in those countries.

   View I: These examples proved that open protest could be successful and that Hitler feared the power of the Church. *Ref.: D40; D299–301; D328;* pp. 151, 155–156.

   View II: Protests were effective only when the Church dealt with regional governments, not when protests were made directly to Hitler. *Ref.:* pp. 163, 164.

E. *Fact:* The Vatican knew about anti-Semitism in Germany as early as 1933.

   View I: Edith Stein had written a letter to Pius XI telling of the terror against the Jews in Germany, but he ignored it. *Ref.: D297;* p. 151.

   View II: Pius XI made his first protest against anti-Semitism in Germany in April, 1933, but Hitler ignored it. *Ref.:* p. 163.

F. *Fact:* Dr. Edith Stein, a Jewish philosopher who later converted to Catholicism and became a Carmelite nun, was deported from Holland and killed by the Nazis at Auschwitz in 1942.

View I: Dr. Stein died because the Church chose to remain silent about Nazi persecutions. *Ref.:* D81–82; p. 151.

View II: Dr. Stein was one of the Dutch Catholic Jews murdered in reprisal because the Dutch bishops had dared to make a public protest. *Ref.:* pp. 164, 175.

G. *Fact:* Pius XII feared that the spread of Communism would be detrimental to the future peace of the world.

View I: Pius XII saw Hitler as the defender of Europe and thus the lesser evil. *Ref.:* D Acts Two and Four; D305; D332–335; p. 157.

View II: Pius XII knew that a victory for either Communism or National Socialism would be a disaster; he never viewed Hitler's war as a crusade against Communism. *Ref.:* pp. 160, 162–163.

H. *Fact:* The International Red Cross, though aware of the existence of the Nazi death camps, did not issue a denunciation throughout the war.

View I: This is proof of the world attitude toward the Jews and of the fact that they could not expect help from any outside group. *Ref.:* D317–318; p. 158.

View II: This proves that every responsible group concerned with the welfare of others knew that quiet, diligent work to save lives was more effective than spectacular statements, which might have made further rescue work impossible. *Ref.:* pp. 163–164, 176.

I. *Fact:* Pius XII disapproved of the Allied demand for "unconditional surrender" defined at Casablanca.

View I: Pius XII had always been sympathetic towards Germany; he had hoped to be the mediator of peace terms. *Ref.:* D111; D208–209: D303.

View II: Pius XII thought that such terms were not conducive to building a lasting peace; he wished the war to end as soon as possible but believed that such humiliating terms would mean a fight to the end. *Ref.:* p. 163.

J. *Fact:* Bérard, after speaking to assistants of the Secretary of State of the Vatican, reported to Pétain that the Church would issue no protest against the anti-Semitic legislation of Vichy, France.

View I: The statement is proof that the anti-Semitism long prevalent in high Vatican circles remained unchanged during the Jewish emergency. *Ref.:* D331; D345–346; pp. 152–153.

View II: Though Bérard did make these statements, his report was false; he did not give full information to the Vatican, and he reported to Petain only what he felt Pétain would like to hear. The Church did protest immediately upon learning of the legislation. *Ref.:* p. 169.

1. For each fact in the above list, determine which view, if either, is the "truth." Is it always possible to determine the validity of an interpretation of a fact? What, then, is history?

2. Borrowing a term from psychoanalysis, historians sometimes speak of a certain event or movement as being "overdetermined," having more than one determining factor. Consider the three articles by Stern, Hilberg, and Tucker describing the conditions and feelings preceding the Nazi extermination policy; the three articles discuss some of the determinants of that historical fact. Though the world reacted with disbelief and has yet to assimilate fully the reality of "the final solution," it is apparent that the road to the crematories was built over a long period of time in full view of the world. The *inevitability* of an Auschwitz, the disclosure that the world might have acted two hundred, or twenty, or two years earlier to prevent it, but did not, is far more horrifying than the comfortable conviction that Auschwitz was

a sudden whim of a few madmen. What, then, are some of the uses of history? Do the three articles complement or contradict one another? Explain.

3. Using the materials in this section, particularly the three articles referred to in question 2, write a paper on "The Road to Auschwitz." Document your paper, using the original pagination provided.

4. As an exercise in overdeterminism and research writing, choose any work of art with which you are thoroughly familiar and write a paper indicating how the artist's life and personality, the historical period in which he lived, and the dominant aesthetic theory of his day influenced the particular work.

5. Classify all of the materials in this section according to whether they are primary or secondary sources. Give reasons for each of your classifications.

6. In examining the articles to determine whether they were basic or derivative, you may have come across several that defied simple classification. Lewy's article is clearly derivative: he had no first-hand experience of the events he discusses but depends upon books, articles, and documents for his information. Gerstein's report is clearly basic: he reports only what his own senses had witnessed. But what of Father Leiber's essay? He is a writer, scholar, and recognized authority on the subject under discussion, and he documents his statements in several cases with specific references to articles, books, and documents. On the other hand, he was a personal assistant to Pius XII from 1924 to 1958, and much of his report is based on personal knowledge of the attitudes and actions of the Pope. His article, therefore, must be viewed as providing two different types of information. Does a primary or a secondary source provide greater accuracy? Greater objectivity? Why? (Remember the chart above when formulating your answer.)

7. Every campus has its tale of the professor who doesn't read research papers but weighs them or counts the number of footnotes and items on the bibliography. Though the tale is mythical, it has its origin in the hopes and fears of the myth-makers, as all myths do. Many students believe that quantity rather than quality determines excellence in research writing. Yet one needs to be wary of how, when, and what documentation is used. In a sense, in order to be able to evaluate a secondary source competently, one must verify the documentation. Martini (p. 169) discloses, for example, that Lewy's conclusions (pp. 152–153), essentially the same as Hochhuth's (*D*345–346), although Lewy cites two additional sources for his information, are erroneous because they are based on false statements about the situation he discusses. Lewy's paragraph gives exact dates, names, and quotations, and it has the additional respectability of two footnotes, one to original archive material. At one point Lewy quotes from the article by Leiber also included in this section. Check his statement against the original. Is he justified in using Leiber as an authority on the statement he makes? On pp. 151–152 Lewy describes the tone and policy of the publication *Civiltà Cattolica*. Do his notes indicate that he has had first-hand experience with this publication? How much weight do his statements on the subject carry? Lewy, Hochhuth, and Father Leiber all quote from Léon Poliakov, and Father Leiber praises him highly as the most authoritative voice on the subject of the effectiveness of open protest in World War II. Yet Poliakov himself wrote a letter of protest shortly after Leiber's article appeared, stating that the latter had quoted him out of context and distorted his meaning. What Poliakov actually said amounted to a regret that Pius XII did not speak out in protest against the persecution of the Jews, even though the results may

not have been to halt the whole process. In many cases, then, the author may quote exactly but interpret falsely.

Conclusions and implications must be examined with particular care: When Lewy says "Finally, one is inclined to conclude that the Pope and his advisors—influenced by a long tradition of moderate anti-Semitism so widely accepted in Vatican circles—did not view the plight of the Jews with a real sense of urgency and moral outrage," has he arrived at this conclusion logically? Check Lewy's article for facts that uphold his conclusion. Check other sources to see whether *they* support or contradict it.

Part IV
THE CRITICS SPEAK
Response from Two Continents

Erwin Piscator

TOWARD MASTERING THE PAST

Rolf Hochhuth's *The Deputy* is one of the few substantive contributions toward mastering the past. Relentlessly it calls things by their names; it shows that no tale can be out of date when it was written with the blood of innocent millions; it apportions to the guilty their measure of guilt; it reminds all the participants that they could have made their decision, and that in fact they did make it even when they thought they did not.

The Deputy makes liars of all those who assert that a historical drama as a drama of decision is no longer possible because, given the faceless anonymity of socio-political patterns and pressures in an absurd construct of human existence that sees everything as predetermined, decisions as such are no longer possible for man. Such a theory, which blots out historic action, recommends itself to those who would like to escape the truth of history, the truth of their own historic acts.

Hochhuth's play aims at objectivizing, exploring the total human attitude, not in story but in history. It is an epic play for epic "political" theater, the theater for which I have fought for more than thirty years. It is a historical drama in Schiller's sense. It sees man as acting and, in his acting, representative ("deputy") of an *idea*—free in its fulfillment, free in his insight into the necessity of categorically ethical, essentially human behavior. This freedom that we all possess, that we all possessed under the Nazi régime as well, must be our point of departure if we wish to master our past. To disclaim this freedom would be to disclaim the guilt each took upon himself if he did not make use of his freedom to decide *against* inhumanity.

I hope that attack and defense of the play will reach *all*, as they have the few who have read it to date; I hope that the value of such a work lies not only in the artistic, the formal, the esthetic, but first and last in its words with and its reach into life; I hope this play will be a force *for change*. My anti-Schopenhauer optimism, despite natural wear through resignation, is still strong enough to believe in a change in human history through understanding—a peaceful change, not a violent material change that admits evolution

Statement by Erwin Piscator, director of the original West Berlin Volksbuhne production of *The Deputy*, translated by Clara Mayer, *Saturday Review*, March 14, 1964, p. 16.

henceforth as evolution exclusively toward catastrophe. But from objective recognition a passionate avowal of values can develop, for which Hochhuth attempts a new formulation in this play. This new author seems to me not only a good playwright and poet, but also a man confessing. The discovery of such a man is healing and consoling in a world of silence—silence that is empty, without content, useless. /16/

German Bundestag

LETTER TO THE MINISTER OF FOREIGN AFFAIRS

Bonn, May 2, 1963

We ask the federal government:

Must it not seem strange to the friends of our nation that Pius XII, a person who not only actively helped the Jews during the period of Nazi persecution but also remained on good terms with Germany throughout his pontificate, is attacked, and that by Germans?

Majonica	Dr. Kanka
Lemmer	Dr. Kliesing (Honnef)
Arndgen	Krüger
Balkenhol	Nieberg
Bausch	Dr. Seffrin
van Delden	Dr. Stecker
Draeger	Dr. Freiherr von Vittinghoff-Schell
Dr. Gradl	Vogt
Dr. Hauser	Wagner
Heix	

Schröder

REPLY TO THE GERMAN BUNDESTAG

Bonn, May 3, 1963

I answer your inquiry as follows:

The German nation, through her official representatives, has fully and repeatedly admitted its responsibility for the persecution and mass destruction of Jews under the Third Reich. Through internal legislation and international agreements, it has sought to make whatever reparations were still possible.

The federal government deeply regrets that, in reference to this matter, accusations have been directed against Pope Pius XII. On many occasions the

"Antwort der Bundesminister des Auswärtigen auf die Kleine Anfrage," May 3, 1963, as it appears in *Summa iniuria oder Durfte der Papst schweigen?*, ed. Fritz Raddatz (Hamburg: Rowohlt, 1963), p. 230. Trans. by the editors.
"Kleine Anfrage der Abeordneten Majonica, Lemmer und Genossen an den Deutschen Bundestag," May 2, 1963, as it appears in *Summa iniuria oder Durfte der Papst schweigen?*, ed. Fritz Raddatz (Hamburg: Rowohlt, 1963), p. 229. Trans. by the editors.

Pope's voice was raised against racial discrimination and persecution in the Third Reich, and he saved many Jews from the grasp of their persecutors.

Now as ever the federal government is gratefully aware of the fact that after the collapse of Hitler's regime, Pope Pius XII was one of the first to use his influence towards the reconciliation of Germany and other nations. All this makes the degradation of his memory, particularly by Germans, incomprehensible and regrettable.

Schröder

Ewart E. Turner

NO LETUP FOR DER STELLVERTRETER

On my recent visit to Germany I found that the vehement discussion about Rolf Hochhuth's play *Der Stellvertreter* which Bert Stoop reported in these pages earlier (Aug. 7) is waxing rather than waning. On Sept. 15 Rowohlt of Hamburg, publishers of the play, brought out a paperback entitled *Summa Iniuria, oder Durfte der Papst Schweigen?* (The Height of Injustice, or Should the Pope Have Remained Silent?). It contains 90 commentaries selected from the more than 3,000 major articles, addresses and brochures dealing with the play. They represent opinion both in Germany and abroad. I had an opportunity to look over most of the material from which the selection was made.

The opinions reflected in the compilation are about evenly divided for and against Hochhuth's thesis. In the preface the compiler, Fritz J. Raddatz, notes that no German work since Erich Maria Remarque's *All Quiet on the Western Front* has attracted such great ideological interest and literary response. Among the 14 foreign entrepreneurs who have acquired production rights to the play are Ingmar Bergman in Stockholm, Peter Hall in London (for the Royal Shakespeare Company), Billy Rose in New York and Julius Gellner (for the Habimah National Theater) in Tel Aviv. Publishing rights have been granted to firms in eight countries, and the play is being filmed.

I

Protestant opinions quoted in the Rowohlt paperback range from Bishop Otto Dibelius' thundering that the play "renders no good service" to Prof. Helmut Gollwitzer's "The pope should have spoken." Dibelius points out that never having experienced life in a totalitarian state, the young author does not know that "public protest means sudden death." But he does identify those guilty for the extermination of the Jews: "The Germans come first for they let Hitler come to power; the Allies have responsibility for they helped produce Hitler and they knew the facts about the gas chambers yet didn't widely protest them; our appeal to the neutral nations to do something fell on deaf ears."

Some close comrades of Bishop Dibelius in the church struggle against the nazis, however, express an opposite point of view. Prof. Günther Harder recalls that when in the blackest days of the Hitler terror a council of the Confessing Church was discussing the weakness and silence of the bishops of Bavaria and Württemberg, Dibelius, then in enforced retirement, defended their inactivity "in view of their responsibility for thousands of pastors and congregations." Writes Harder: "We younger men of the council were of another opinion. We believed—all honor to responsibility—that situations arise when a bishop must not calculate consequences but is called to give a witness for divine truth." He notes that the Confessing Church of the Old Prussian Union did speak out in 1943 ("but much too late"), citing the commandment "Thou shalt not kill" and explicitly mentioning the extermination of the Jews.

Those Protestant churchmen who suffered in Hitler's concentration camps tend to support Hochhuth's thesis that no one did enough, and that the one who is called Christ's vicar on earth should above all others have spoken out. Writes Gollwitzer: "Many would have been saved, and many others would not have had to be caught up in the guilt of participation." Martin Niemöller wrote to Hochhuth: "I am grateful that the book . . . has aroused such disquietude. The critics consciously refrain from attempting to dispute the facts presented. Future generations will see in this a proof of how factually justified and necessary your work was and remains." Heinrich Gruber, the only German to testify at the Eichmann trial, the man whose rescue work on behalf of the Jews won him torture at Sachsenhausen, points out: "The issue in the book is not Pius XII but the guilt of all of us. Guilt is not only the bad we do but the good we neglect." Gruber notes that many who have seen the play report that one of its implications is that if a man like the pope remains silent, there is excuse for "little people" not to invite trouble.

Roman Catholic opinion as reported in the compilation is also divided. Personal friends of Pius XII are wounded by Hochhuth's handling of Pacelli as a person. A typical comment: "The actor who portrays Pacelli should recall that His Holiness is less a person than an institution." Catholic Action in Berlin has issued an extensive documentation of the papal help extended to the Jews — help which Hochhuth acknowledges in his play. The head of the West Berlin hierarchy has written a book refuting the thesis that protest from the Vatican would have aided the Jews. The Jesuit Robert Leiber, who was secretary to Pius XII, defends the pope at length, denies that he "loved" the concordat with Hitler, and quotes expressions of thanks extended by Roman Jews after the war.

II

On the other hand, the noted Roman Catholic drama critic Friedrich Heer sees in the wide discussion the play has elicited an opportunity for church leaders to reflect on what political effect the church might now exert on a world threatened by nuclear war. Reporting after the premiere of the play in an article published in the *Munich Review* under the title "The Truth Is Frightful," Heer points out that Hochhuth's daring to criticize the church's shortcomings is not new in literary history "but is nearly as old as higher Christian literature itself." He recalls that Walter von der Vogelweide inveighed against the pope of Rome and the princes of the church, that Dante in his *Divine Comedy* elevated only one pope to heaven (and even there he was superceded by the apostles), and that in modern times Catholic laymen have continued such "utterance of conscience": Giovanni Papini, Georges Bernanos, Reinhold Schneider. "A layman speaks his word," he concludes. "His word is prophecy, promise, and court of justice."

"All Catholics, from the uppermost summit to the lowliest (and anti-Semitic) priest and layman, participate in the guilt of Jewish extermination," writes Heer. "Not only Catholics, of course. Not only the thousands of baptized, confirmed and church-married Christians who participated directly in the exterminations. Not only the bishops who (as in Poland and Hungary) wrote and released anti-Semitic pastoral letters. The days seem far away when Catholic publications in France rejoiced over the pogroms in Algeria and openly incited to murder in the Dreyfus case. /1269/ Near at hand, skin near, is the terrible denial in Rome from 1933 to 1945."

Heer reports that when he was in Rome in 1945 he found that the view presented by Hochhuth is similar to that held by many "serious" priests at that time in the holy city. The general tenor of their comments to him was "under Pius XI this would not have been possible."

III

As I left Berlin's Freie Volksbuehne after seeing *Der Stellvertreter* I realized that what remained above the theatrical weakness of the production and the controversy the thesis has aroused was the awful fact that millions of human lives had been exterminated because of racial origin. Here was a plea for continuing manifestation of contrition and reconciliation from *all* men, from the lowliest to the proclaimed vicar of Christ. *Der Stellvertreter* seeks to fix guilt and responsibility, to wrest from Christ's vicar, whose succession claims infallibility in morals as well as in doctrine, a confession of shortcoming as a basis for a new era of Christian effectuality. As precedent for such acknowledgment Friedrich Heer cites the gripping confession of guilt made by Hadrian VI as the Reformation began. The question confronting one as he leaves the theater has to do not with Pius XII but with oneself, one's own country, one's own church.

A number of correspondents at the U.S. press center in Berlin told me that they had heard the play likened to *Hamlet*. But as Friedrich Luft, dean of the Berlin drama critics, has pointed out, it is the very lack of any Hamlet quality in Pius XII as Hochhuth has depicted him that removes the portrayal from the realm of tragedy. Hochhuth's Pius experiences no great inner struggle, no anguish of soul; he is rather the skilled, calculating diplomat, the prince of compromise, the anticommunist who sees in Hitler a Cyrus of the Lord's instrumentality.

Taken as a whole, however, the play is—as its subtitle notes—a Christian tragedy. And the Hamlet quality is indeed found in the nature of certain Catholic and Protestant Christians who play a major part in the action. It is the Jesuit Riccardo Fontana and the Protestant undercover worker Kurt Gerstein who represent the conscience of the church pitted against the demons of this world. /1270/

German Television Symposium

SHOULD THE POPE HAVE REMAINED SILENT?

On May 29, 1963, Alfred Andersch moderated a round-table discussion on German television to consider a question raised by Hochhuth's play, "Should the Pope have remained silent?" Though space does not permit a full transcript here, we quote below some of the significant answers.

Provost Grüber: In matters of morality, how useful an act would be is not a consideration. We do know that the Nazis were fearful of arresting German bishops, as is made clear by the correspondence between Bormann and

"Durfte der Papst schweigen?" *Der Streit um Hochhuths "Stellvertreter"* (Stuttgart: Basilius Press, 1963), pp. 92–94. Trans. by the editors.

Goebbels concerning the arrest of Bishop Wurm and Bishop von Galen. I do think that open protest, in deed as well as word, would have led to martyrdom, but such martyrdom could not have failed to make its point. If on a Sunday, all the bishops in Germany had appeared in their pulpits with Jewish stars pinned to their vestments in place of their gold and silver crosses, that would have been an act understood not only by the persecuted Jews, but by all the faithful in Germany and elsewhere.

Father Oscar Simmel: From our present perspective, the question of why Pius XII remained silent during the persecution and murder of the Jews is probably unanswerable. Only Pius XII could have told us what motivated him not to try to bring his influence to bear on behalf of the Jewish victims. We can only speculate and attempt to explain his motives to our own satisfaction, but whether the motives we thus attribute to him are valid is another matter. The Pope remained silent because he knew that any protest would have been useless. One can believe that. Yet, the question that confronted him was far more complicated, namely: whether a protest on his part might not have destroyed the last hope existing for many Jews. He had to choose the lesser evil and do what could be done. Whether his reasoning was right or wrong cannot be determined, not now and not ever. Yet in remaining silent, he was not an accomplice in guilt. We may sincerely believe, we may be firmly convinced, even, that Pius XII could have spoken and acted differently in the situation, but it would be impossible, as I have already said, to prove that this were so.

Bishop Dr. Otto Dibelius: I find it exceedingly difficult to answer the question [should the Pope have remained silent?]. It is not for me to decide what a Pope ought to do or is permitted to do. I can only say that I knew Pius XII, and I cannot agree that Mr. Hochhuth's opinion /92/ of him, as expressed in his play, is correct. In addition, I find it in bad taste to put a man of the stature of Pius XII on the stage, particularly so soon after his death. Certainly the persecution of the Jews was in no way related to what Pius XII did or did not do; he was in no way responsible for that situation, and it ought not to be discussed on the stage so shortly after his death. Instead, it ought to be dispassionately considered by those who have examined all the sources after a decent interval. I cannot say more. A word from the Pope would have been welcomed by the Christians in Germany, but I cannot imagine how the Pope could have spoken out, considering his responsibility for all Catholics, the world over. Therefore, I cannot give a simple yes or no answer. I can only repeat that for those of us who were in Germany and could not speak, a word from outside would, naturally, have been encouraging.

Father Willehad Eckert: I believe that Pope Pius XII and the German resistance movement were in a similar dilemma. He could not support nor wish for either a Bolshevist victory or a Nazi victory. In either eventuality he foresaw only unending misery for Europe and its people. Instead, he kept in close contact with German resistance groups and hoped that they would succeed in overthrowing the Nazi regime and effecting an honorable peace with the Allies.

Carl Amery: The Pope had to remain silent if he did not wish to repudiate completely the entire series of agreements with the Third Reich, from the Lateran Treaty of 1929 to the Concordat. All these agreements were made with the full approval of the German Catholics, who desired their continuance. Whatever serious Catholic opposition there was centered upon the Concordat, and some individuals among the clergy and the laity worked towards applying political and moral pressure for a change in future Church policy. Some of this opposition was directly aimed at the Concordat. Yet, had the Pope and the Curia issued an official protest against the extermination of the Jews, the Nazis would have totally repudiated the Concordat.

In 1943 the Pope and the Curia had only two alternatives: to keep silent and honor the agreements or to protest and risk the loyalty of German Catholics. Thus in 1943 Rome was faced with the same dilemma /93/ German Catholicism had faced in 1933. And in both situations, the same question arose: in view of the growing schism between the laws of God and those of the ruling powers, shouldn't the Church change its policy on political intervention? But Catholicism remained rooted in nineteenth century attitudes far too long; as a result the grim problems of the twentieth century were approached, faced, and solved only by a few isolated heroic individuals. /94/

Friedrich Heer

THE NEED FOR CONFESSION

No play since the end of World War II has scored such a direct hit as Rolf Hochhuth's "The Deputy." Catholics, Protestants, Jews and "neutrals" have vociferated against the play and its staging. Catholics, Protestants, Jews and "neutrals" have also supported it. But the loudest and most violent protests have come from Catholics, including Catholic journalists, who have neither read nor seen the play but who are mesmerized and shocked by its theme. The play, they feel, is a monstrous insult to the Holy Father and to our Mother, the Church; anti-Christ has stepped before the footlights!

But Hochhuth's play, which dares to violate some of the most cherished taboos, is neither anti-Christian nor anti-Catholic. Hochhuth, a young German Protestant, made an exhaustive study of the question, not least in Rome, where he was advised by an elderly and experienced German-speaking bishop. Moreover, "The /656/ Deputy" is dedicated to the memory of two Catholic priests: Father Maximilian Kolbe, prisoner No. 16670 at Auschwitz, and Father Bernhard Lichtenberg, provost of St. Hedwig's cathedral in Berlin — two courageous opponents of Hitler who suffered martyrdom. Thus we have to realize, in this connection, that many of the Catholics of German-speaking regions who attack Hochhuth are actually defending not so much Pope Pius XII as themselves, their own attitude, their collaboration with Hitler to the — literally — bitter end. Two Catholic writers — Gordon Zahn in *German Catholics and Hitler's Wars* and Carl Amery in *Die Kapitulation — oder deutscher Katholizismus heute* [*The Surrender — or German Catholicism Today*] — have shown the well-nigh total integration of a certain type of German Catholicism in Hitler's war machine.

"The Need for Confession," *The Commonweal*, February 28, 1964, pp. 656–660. Friedrich Heer is Professor of Catholic History at the University of Vienna, a noted church historian and hagiographer, and director of the Vienna city theatre.

Hochhuth was interviewed by the editors of the *Züricher Woche* (27 September 1963) at the time his play opened in Basle. He was asked: "You are accused, for instance, of anti-clerical bias. . . . Do you personally have any anti-clerical sentiments? Do you perhaps bear some personal grudge against Catholics?" To which he replied: "My best school friend is a Catholic. In fact, so strict a Catholic that his parents were very much afraid that he would enter the priesthood. He is now in the Federal Department of Justice at Bonn. He is also my son's sponsor. That would not indicate anti-clerical or anti-Catholic bias on my part, though I make no secret of the fact that I find the silence of the higher clergy about what happened absolutely reprehensible—in contrast with the lower clergy. Three thousand European Catholic priests fell victim to Hitler, without the Pope so much as raising a finger on behalf of any one of them."

Now let me quote the letter which a German Catholic cleric wrote to Mr. Hochhuth and which expresses openly what a number of distinguished Catholic theologians and high-ranking churchmen have admitted to me in private conversation, but without making their sentiments public:

"Since I consider the attacks made upon you by certain groups of Federal German Catholics on account of your play as exaggerated and unjustified, I feel impelled to take this means of expressing to you my appreciation and admiration for your work. I rejoice that you have dared to scatter the artificial mists which had been raised in order to obscure the past. The Pope's silence about those crimes was and remains painful to me. On 12 July 1943, at a clerical conference, I sharply criticized the Pope's silence, after an eye-witness had given me an unforgettably detailed description of the mass execution of Jewish persons. After the war, therefore, I could never understand how the Catholic press could positively idolize Pius XII. Your work has a cleansing and liberating effect, and gives grounds for hope for the future. Those who think it harms the Church are mistaken. Moreover, I could complete and confirm your 'historical spot-lights' in certain points from my own experience, and I am sending you today the photostat of an English leaflet which the RAF dropped over northern Germany in the summer of 1943. The original is in my possession. I wish you every success in your further labors. Do not lose heart in the face of the massive attacks launched against you."

This letter, written by Dr. Gökhen of Lingen/Ems on May 18, 1963, appears on pages 81–82 of the miscellany entitled *Summa Iniuria, oder: Durfte der Papst schweigen? —Hochhuth's Stellvertreter in der öffentlichen Kritik* ["Summa Iniuria, or: Should the Pope Have Kept Silence? Hochhuth's 'Deputy' in the light of public criticism"]. This work, together with the volume put out by the Basilius Presse of Basle, *Der Streit um den Stellvertreter* ("The 'Deputy' Controversy"), constitutes a good introduction to the discussion of Hochhuth's play in German-speaking Europe.

Dr. Gökhen hopes that Hochhuth's Christian tragedy will have a cleansing and liberating effect—precisely on Catholics. But this calls for an important qualification: the play can have such an effect only on Catholics who have acquired a certain degree of twentieth-century consciousness.

American Catholics are reproached—unjustly, in my view—for cultivating an immature, infantile Catholicism, informed by a primitive group egotism, incapable of so much as perceiving spiritual problems. They are alleged to be incapable of discussion, of objective argument with friend or foe; to be vain, egocentric, wrapped up in themselves, nationalistic, inclined to react with annoyance to anything they do not like. Personally I do not believe that these characteristics apply to American Catholics; but they do apply to many European Catholics, who now sit in judgment upon Hochhuth.

This is where one has to take a personal stand. Pius XII treated me, personally, with the greatest friendliness, kindness and cordiality. It was in the consciousness of that fact that I wrote, in my frequently quoted statement on "The Deputy" of 17 March 1963:

"Anyone who ever approached the impressive figure of Pope Pius XII and looked into his careworn features, his bloodshot eyes, anyone to whom he extended his hand, finds it hard to 'judge' this Pope. I cannot do it, I do not want to do it, but I have to confess that all Catholics, from the highest to the lowest – priests, chaplains, laymen (anti-Semitic to this day) – are co-responsible for the mass-murder of the Jews. Not only the thousands of baptized, confirmed and religiously wedded Christians who took a direct part in the mass murders. . . . Not only bishops who, as in Poland and Hungary, drew up anti-Semitic pastoral letters and /657/ permitted their publication. . . . We have present to us the frightful failure of Rome from 1933 to 1945. There were many reasons for this. One of the principal reasons for the terrible error of Pope Pius XII should be looked for in the circumstance that this Pope – who was not well disposed toward democracy, as he himself admitted to Heinrich Brüning, and not a few members of the Curia, more unconsciously than consciously – regarded Hitler's war against Russia as a possible liberation from Communism."

I concluded that statement with the following lines: "One word more as a Catholic. For years I have been haunted by the thought of the confession of sins – *Confiteor Deo omnipotenti* – recited by millions of Catholics in thousands upon thousands of Holy Masses. . . . The Confiteor is ritualized thoughtlessly, without understanding, mechanically; whereas if it were actualized, it could mobilize tremendous energies and powers of the soul. The great potential of inner powers – the real armament which is needed within the Church and throughout Christendom – will be released only when the daily confession of sins is in the best sense of the term politicized, actualized, concretized. Then it will mean: 'I confess to God the almighty Father . . . that I have sinned . . . through my fault, through my most grievous fault in the persecution of the Jews . . . (for "Jews" you can substitute, as occasion arises, the next best hated "enemy").' Rolf Hochhuth's "Deputy" is a clear invitation to such an actualization of the Confiteor."

That seems to me the chief point, for Catholics, about this provocative play. I am using "provocative" in the positive sense of a call, a challenge, a calling forth to personal responsibility. Catholicism will become believable again, in the family of man, only when it takes its place squarely in the world's solidarity in guilt. We Catholics do not live in the beyond, but right in the middle of this world, and we are united in multifarious ways with all our brethren, black, red, yellow, brown. The preconditions for Hitler's "solution" of the Jewish question were, on the one hand, a thousand-year Christian, and also Catholic, anti-Semitism, and, in the nineteenth and twentieth centuries, a close alliance between leading churchmen and authoritarian, totalitarian, Fascist men and powers.

Pope Pius XII was a prisoner of the nineteenth century. The promulgation of papal infallibility made the Pope a prisoner of the integralist party. The integralists locked the Pope up in the Vatican and raised him – for the masses – to the position of a fetish surrounded by taboos (hymns to the Holy Ghost, for instance, were directly applied to the Pope). The Pope, "the Holy Father," became a protective shield for the intrigues of the "officials," as Lord Acton and Friedrich von Hügel called similar men in their day, who loudly invoked the authority of the papacy in their hard struggle for mastery over the Church and over those objectionable Catholics whose views differed from their own. They were always talking of the Holy Father, but they listened to him only when his words suited them. What is the function of the Holy Father for these integralists? Quite simply to defend the fortress of the Church against anti-Christ, in the person of the bad liberals, etc. How is he to do this? By concluding agreements, pacts, concordats with princes, kings, emperors, statesmen, by issuing pastoral letters and encyclicals fulminating against innovators and modernists. In addition, there must be no conversation with the "enemy," no dialogue, no sober and objective discussion with adversaries.

The nineteenth-century popes sought alliances with the Czars, and sacrificed Poland to them—Poland, the ancient bastion of Catholic Christendom in eastern Europe. On the eve of Hitler's invasion of Poland, Pius XII made arrangements with Hitler's Government through his nuncio in Berlin for the protection of the rights of the Church in Poland after the occupation. Shortly before the outbreak of the Second World War, at the Eucharistic Congress in Budapest (near Vienna, already under Nazi occupation, where a good number of Catholics were imprisoned), Cardinal Pacelli, as the legate of Pope Pius XI, made a statement which at the least could be interpreted as a call to arms against the godless Bolsheviks. On the eve of the German invasion of the Soviet Union, and during that invasion, Pius XII made arrangements concerning the ecclesiastical "new order" in the occupied territories. Pius XII, prisoner of the nineteenth-century curial mentality, concluded agreements with Hitler, Franco, Mussolini. . . . The many thousands of sheets of paper which constitute the encyclicals, addresses and radio messages of Pope Pius XII contain no reference to the Jews—nor to the thousands of Orthodox Serbs murdered by the Catholic Croats.

This leads us to an extremely important conclusion: up to the time of Pius XII it was not considered self-evident that the Catholic Church should champion the rights of those outside its fold—Jews, Protestants, and /658/ others were "overlooked." Suffragan Bishop Kampe, discussing the Hochhuth play, emphasized the point: "It is not customary," he said, "for ecclesiastical pronouncements explicitly to take up the cause of groups adhering to a different philosophy." But that is precisely where Catholics who believe in an open Catholicism come in: for them it is intolerable not to be responsible before God and man; for them, the *Pontifex maximus*, as chief shepherd and bridge-builder, must identify himself with all the persecuted, with all who are threatened with extermination.

The great Copernican revolution in the Church set in only *after* Pius XII. Under John XXIII and Paul VI the Church has begun to see itself as involved in discussion, in dialogue: discussion among Catholics of greatly differing viewpoints on politics and spirituality; and discussion between the Church and the rest of the world. A Council under Pius XII would have been unthinkable; so would a statement by the Church about its share in guilt for what has happened in the twentieth century; and so would a statement by the Church on a matter which has long been necessary—a new encounter between Christians and Jews. It is no accident that to this day, in Rome, integralist Catholics can campaign against the presentation of a schema to the Council which would reformulate the relations between Christians and Jews—after fifteen hundred years of Christian murder and persecution of Jews.

Pius XII himself was neither a friend of Hitler nor an enemy of the Jews, but his political ideas were such that he considered it more important not to "stab Hitler in the back" by diplomatic means (diplomatic negotiations, *in camera*, would have sufficed to postpone Hitler's "solution" of the Jewish question to the day of victory!) because he regarded the Wehrmacht as the strong bulwark against Bolshevism. He was therefore opposed to the policy of unconditional surrender. Father Robert Leiber, S.J., who for many years served as his confidant and secretary, expressed it thus on March 27, 1963: "The Pope regarded the policy of unconditional surrender declared at Casablanca in January, 1943, as a calamity."

Yet the abandonment of the principle of unconditional surrender would have meant a peace treaty with Hitler! And that would have meant the elimination of all "objectionable" Christians and Catholics, or at least their deportation to the East (the plans had already been worked out).

The *Neue Jiddische Zeitung* of Munich stated on March 8, 1963: "Pius XII's attitude is a sad historical reality, confirmed by secret diplomatic papers which the American Department of State has made public. These papers tell of Washington's efforts to alleviate the plight of the European Jews by soliciting the support of the Vatican on their behalf. The American ambassador in Switzerland approached the Vatican on a number of occasions to urge the Pope to protest publicly against the horrors committed by the Nazis—in vain. A similar intervention by Brazil was equally unsuccessful. Nevertheless, the United States Secretary of State, Cordell Hull, ordered his ambassadors to continue their efforts. Finally, on October 16, 1942, Cordell Hull was officially informed that the Vatican had rejected America's diplomatic endeavors. Mr. Myron Taylor, President Roosevelt's representative at the Vatican, reported to Washington that the Vatican was seeking to circumvent the problem on the grounds that it was impossible to verify the accuracy of the documents concerning the murder of Jews. This answer was made after Myron Taylor had presented to the Vatican documents containing precise details of that frightful murder."

We know now that Hitler, Himmler and the S.S. were very careful to show regard for the Pope, at least until the day of "final victory." Pius XII did not once protest when in Rome itself, literally at his doors, thousands of Jews were herded off to extermination. This is attested by a Catholic member of a resistance group in Rome, Hans Kühner-Wolfskehl: "A public appeal should have been made at the latest on the day when the first thousands of Jewish Roman citizens departed for their agonizing death. The death trains, as we believed at the time on the basis of our immediate knowledge of the situation, would not have left Rome, with all that that entailed, had the Pope personally intervened, and the arrests would, in addition, immediately have been called off.

"When he wished, as in connection with the two bombardments of Rome, Pius XII could act astonishingly fast. But in the case of the deportation of the Jewish citizens, we of the resistance waited in vain for the appearance of even a single cardinal. It must be clearly stated today—and in this respect Hochhuth is right—the threat of an interdiction and the denunciation of the ill-starred concordat which bound up papal history with Hitler Germany and which Hitler constantly violated, would have had a not insignificant effect. During the difficult months of terror prior to the liberation of Rome, we repeatedly discussed this with responsible personalities."

The editors of the *Züricher Woche* also put this question to Hochhuth: "Have you not been accused of attacking a Pope for an individual failure, and thereby by implication of attacking the whole Church?" Hochhuth answered: "No, I wish people would finally understand. But they don't. Pius is not regarded as one of 260 pontiffs; people identify themselves so completely with Pius, or rather, they identify Pius with the Catholic Church, with the whole institution of the papacy, as though there had been no other popes, as though there were no other possibilities, as though all this had not taken place eighteen long years ago. And I believe that /659/ a change will come. Recently, here in Basle, a Jesuit father visited me. He told me that in a group of clergy in Cologne an old, very distinguished Jesuit had said that what Hochhuth said about Pius was not so important after all. Pius was a historical figure, he was not the Church. This surprised me very much. It was the first time anyone had reacted in that way. Yet that is how people should react. This old Jesuit in Cologne was much more concerned about the reference to God in Act 5 of 'The Deputy'."

The controversy about "The Deputy" leads, for Catholics, to the very heart of the necessary discussion of the firmly-entrenched tradition of the Church: Should the Church continue to regard itself, as it has since the Counter-Reformation, as a fortress which, in defending its own "holy interests," ignores the life, suffering and death of people of different views? Or should the Church — Mother Church — be conceived of as the matrix of mankind, open, protective of all the children of men, Buddhists, atheists, Negroes, etc?

There is something else which Rolf Hochhuth's creative provocation should and could call forth among Catholics: a really adequate presentation of the life and suffering of Pope Pius XII. Thus far he has been surrounded by taboos, glorified as a plaster saint, dehumanized — and thus made to appear inhuman. But this would be a task for a truly Catholic investigation and historical writing, conscious of the duty of the *Pontifex Maximus* since Auschwitz, Maidanek, Mauthausen and Hiroshima: to portray the Pope bearing the cross of human guilt, of common guilt, up until his frightful agony, his solitary death, deprived of human communication.

To such a pope, bearing the cross of human guilt, Christians and non-Christians would not give a false aura of holiness, but neither would they deny him a crown — the crown proper to a mortal man who, in times of Copernican revolution, where Catholicism seeks to shake off the shackles of centuries, has to carry a burden which (as he admitted himself, in a note found in an envelope before his death) was beyond his strength. /660/

Father Michel Riquet, S. J.

AN INSULT TO CATHOLICS

When one has followed to its natural conclusion the skillful — too skillful — dialectic of Hochhuth's play, *The Deputy*, he is left with the opinion that in World War II, the Jews were Hitler's only victims and the Russians Hitler's only active opponents. Only then can he applaud the play with good conscience. A Catholic, however, can feel only insulted by such a view.

All that which so many Catholics, clergy and laity, bishops and cardinals, did both before and during the war to round up, shelter, hide and save from

"Le Catholique Bafoué," *Le Figaro*, December 19, 1963, p. 6. Trans. by the editors.

death thousands of Jews, frequently at the peril of their own lives and freedom; all the protests and interventions by the French, Belgian, Dutch, German, Czech and Polish episcopates, which can be read about in detail in Abbé Toulat's book, *The Jews, My Brothers,*—all *that* is forgotten, or, at the least, brushed aside as a mere palliative. That which is alone important, assailing the conscience of the viewer like an obsessive hallucination, is the Pope's silence, his refusal to speak the words which would have, it is alleged, stopped everything, or, at any rate, unburdened the conscience of mankind. The rest does not count.

Hence the struggle of German Catholics and Christians against the Nazis, the actions of such men as Faulhaber and Bertram, of von Galen and von Preyssing, as well as those of the Christians of France, Belgium, Holland, Poland, Austria and Czechoslovakia are not to be taken seriously. Nonetheless, throughout those terrible years, as we listened to Radio Vatican and the messages of Pius XII, we felt ourselves to be in alliance with the Pope in succoring the persecuted Jews both by fighting against Nazi violence and by repeating loudly and frequently his solemn condemnation, promulgated once and for all by Pius XI with the complete accord of his Secretary of State, the future Pius XII, and referred to many times throughout the war, notably in *L'Osservatore Romano* of January 22, 1942.

What was the result in 1937 of the vigorous encyclical, *Mit brennender Sorge*, which condemned anti-Semitism and racism and denounced all of Hitler's violations of the famous Concordat, with which Hochhuth is so obsessed? Did it put an end to the persecution of the Jews? Not at all. Instead, it set off an exceedingly brutal persecution of German Catholics and a long series of trials and arrests of priests, of whom several hundred were found still at Dachau in December, 1944, when two thousand priests from all over Europe were sent to join them, leaving behind, at various camps from Buchenwald to Auschwitz and Mauthausen, some few survivors and hundreds of dead. *There* is decisive proof that the Nazis did not fear having trouble with the Church. Didn't we have with us in those camps even bishops and abbots?

In those times, we never thought for a moment that a simple appeal by the Pope could have changed the bestial fury of our torturers the least bit. They would have continued notwithstanding. We were still at their mercy when, on March 18, 1945, Pius XII declared, with finality, *urbi et orbi*, from the balcony of St. Peter's: "For those who have let themselves be misled by the advocates of violence, and who, after having followed them uncritically, have begun at last to awaken from their illusions, dismayed to see where their docile following has led them, for those there is no other way to salvation than to repudiate fully the idolatries of nationalism, racism, and materialism and to turn resolutely towards a sincere spirit of brother-hood." That did not stop Himmler from telegraphing the commander at Dachau a short time afterwards: "No concentration camp prisoner should fall into the hands of the enemy alive. Liquidate all of them, *alles liquidieren*." The reality was far more horrible and far more complicated for the Pope, as for all of us who lived through it, than Mr. Hochhuth imagines.

Lacking in Hochhuth, as in most of those who applaud him, is the actual experience of the situation. And, more particularly, he lacks an understanding of the solidarity in which the members and the head of the Church of Christ are united, whereby an insult to their leader is resented by all, just as all loving and faithful children rally to the defense of an injured father whom they have been taught to honor.

Despite his intentions and sincerity, despite all the special apparatus and historical references and the talents of the actors interpreting his work, his play will be resented as a bitter derision of their efforts and sacrifices by all those who once risked their lives to save the Jews and are still today actively working for Judeo-Christian friendship and the reconciliation of faiths. /6/

André Gisselbrecht

A YOUNG MAN'S POLEMIC AGAINST WHOM?

The young author of this epic play, unrivaled in our time, outshining even the *Last Days of Humanity* by the Austrian Karl Kraus, is a Christian: and precisely for this reason he could not make *The Deputy* simply an anticlerical polemic. For despite the central characters and the climactic scene so reminiscent of *Don Carlos*, *The Deputy* is not primarily the tragedy of a Pope. In West Germany, where Catholicism is so prevalent as to be almost a forbidden subject — East Germany is no longer Ultramontanist — its anti-Catholicism was all many people chose to see. Criticisms of the play were almost entirely written along denominational lines: the Pope's aloofness, the financial manipulations of the Vatican, the emphasis on good works rather than faith, the rebellion against authority, the idea of being a "substitute" — the Pope is a deputy for God, the frail Jesuit is a deputy for the Pope — all of these make it only too clear: Hochhuth is a Protestant! But let us ignore all that, for that is not the proper tone for criticism.

It is, in the author's own opinion, a "Christian drama." Yet it lacks grace. It is unlike Claudel's *The Hostage* or *The Humble Father*, wherein the Pope suffered; here, he makes others suffer. There is a certain parallel, as pointed out by some critics, between the situation of Pius VII and Napoleon and that of Pius XII and Hitler. Just as Pius VII risked death and imprisonment, Pius XII, in denouncing the Concordat with Hitler, in rising up against the final solution, might have been imprisoned or put to death; yet, though Pius VII dared to act and excommunicated the followers of Napoleon, throughout the period when a great part of the Jewish population of Europe disappeared into the furnaces of the extermination camps, not a single German bishop went to his martyrdom, and Hitler, the fascist beast, did not die excommunicated. . . .

This is a Christian play in still another sense, for it pits the Doctor, Lucifer himself, an incarnation of the essence of mocking atheism, against Riccardo, an embodiment of the first martyrs of the Church. It is questionable, though, whether the analogy is valid, for atheism was not essentially a part of the Nazi philosophy, nor does Riccardo's sacrifice serve any greater purpose than to provide a bold contrast to the deficiencies of the Pope. Perhaps the question asked at the end of Albrecht Goës' novel, *The Sacrificial Fire*, might well be asked here: "Can the sacrifice of an individual — a butcher's wife, who, in despair, sets fire to her house — atone for the terrible guilt of an entire people?"[1]

Certainly the attitude of the Catholic Church and its hierarchy towards fas-

"Après qui en-a-t'il, ce jeune homme?" *Les Lettres Françaises*, December 12–18, 1963, p. 8. Trans. by the editors. André Gisselbrecht is a member of the Faculty of Letters and Human Sciences at the National School of Fine Arts and Applied Arts, University of Nancy, France.
1. From Goës' novel, which deals with a similar subject. /8/

cism is one of the blackest periods of its history. Who was to blame? All Catholics? The Vatican? The Pope alone? It is a fact that Pius XI had himself condemned anti-Semitism *expressis verbis* and had mentioned the name of the Jews. It is also a fact that Hochhuth, a Protestant, seems to have a much stronger belief in the weight of the moral authority of the Pope than do most Catholics, though as he uses the Pope in his play, he represents the record of Christianity. The play poses the very problem which Pope John XXIII was trying to solve by calling for *l'aggiornamento*, an effort to overcome the heritage of his predecessor. Must Catholicism forever remain in conflict between its worldly and diplomatic concerns and its spiritual and moral obligations? Must its allegiance to a social order which is already dead forever prevent it from extending its hand, showing love of neighbor, condemning all atrocities?

Pope Paul VI's letter to the editors of a London magazine indicates that these problems are far from being solved.

In order to give a fair hearing to *The Deputy*, it is necessary first of all to dispel some of the misconstructions of the West German critics. Hochhuth does *not* attempt to relieve the guilt of the German people by making Pope Pius XII a scapegoat.[2] Seeing or reading the play is likely to increase, not relieve, one's sense of guilt. A German could not say, "If the Pope himself did nothing, what could I have done, insignificant as I was?" Those who have charged Hochhuth of this never consider the fact that there was a hierarchy of guilt; the very importance of this work is that the author clearly and with few exceptions enumerates, as has never been done on the German scene (and particularly not by Zackmayer), all those who must share the blame for the destruction of the Jews. He does not hesitate to question the characters and motives of von Rutta, of Müller, of Siemens, I. G. Farben, Buna, Krupp. . . . Also, Hochhuth does not accuse the Pope of anti-Semitism, nor for that matter, the Cardinal,[3] nor does he attribute Nazi sympathies to them (they simply consider Hitler "useful" in the war against Communism). For Hochhuth, Pope Pius XII was simply "the grand neutral," yet he was the only person who, had he spoken, would have been believed by all. In sum, the author would have wished that the papal infallibility used in interior theological decisions had been projected to exterior social matters. After all, this opinion is not without value. Nor does he affirm that Pope Pius XII was responsible for the massacre of the Jews, nor that his intervention would have stopped at a moment's notice the vast machinery of destruction set up by the Nazis; he says only that he ought to have tried, and he did nothing. What might have happened remains forever unknown. Has he, perhaps, overestimated the Church's power in the affairs of men?

There is no doubt that Hochhuth overemphasizes the Nazi fear of having trouble with the Church during the war. The Church was not that important then, though the present Vatican Council does indicate that the successor of Pius XII desired to reinforce it as a power in the world, a power certainly diminished by its sorry record during the dark days of fascism. Did it not take the appalling fact of six million innocent deaths to make the Church drop its references to "the perfidy of the Jews," to make the Church realize to where the anti-Semitism it had encouraged since the Middle Ages could lead? How could a Pope who exalted Franco, who raised Hitler to respectability by signing a Concordat and never protested his violations of it, even when the faith-

---

2. J. Nobécourt in *le Monde* adopts this erroneous point of view, so widely held by both clergy and laity in Germany. /8/

3. These passages have been deleted from the French version. /8/

ful themselves suffered, have been a proper leader for a twentieth-century church?

But it is not, after all, a Pope against whom this young man rages; it is the basis of the problem. It is significant that in Germany clergymen who were part of the Resistance movement have rallied to Hochhuth's defense. The Protestant Provost Gruber[4] has said, "We older ones recognize ourselves in the mirror which this young man holds up to us; we see that we had failed in our duties, not only during the twelve years, but *before*." The theologian Göllwitzer said, "Pius XII represents all of us; the question posed is this: 'Could we not have done more?'" Rolf Hochhuth puts on trial all authority— officials, ministers, teachers—all those who have been lying to themselves since 1945. Above all, he unmasks the miracle of "the grand revision."

What makes Hochhuth's play so unbearable to so many people is that he has pierced the armor of modern-day Germany and Western Europe. His crime is not that he attacks a Pope—the literature of the Western world is full of such attacks—but that he, a young German who cannot be called a Communist, has given the most complete, the most truthful, the most undeniable picture of what his country was like twenty years ago. He has provided his own generation with a picture of what their fathers were like at that time, with an idea of what the tone of their speech was then, they, who are today peaceable citizens, supporters of democracy. The very basis of the political thought of the German Federation today, its emphasis on joining the Western world in the common cause of fighting Communism, is the very antithesis of Roosevelt's intention in calling for an "unconditional surrender," in desiring a Europe which could never again be threatened by an armed Germany. Yet a whole network of rationalizations, of lies and noble poses have accompanied the reconstruction of Germany: Hitler was, in spite of himself, the sword of Christianity against Communism; in the light of this noble role, his delirious anti-Semitism may be passed off as a venial sin. This, of course, is a condemnation of western democracy. Hitler the lesser evil, Hitler wrong in his means but not in his ends, an attitude shared by Pius XII and Father Przynara. An attitude shared, too, by those who undertook the reconstruction of Europe of which the German Federation is today the pillar. This, then, is the secret that an imprudent young man has divulged. He has concerned himself with far more important things than a Pope's reputation.

Some critics have grumbled, "A German ought to sweep in front of his own door and not be accusing non-Germans." Yet international responsibilities do not lessen national ones. Hochhuth is just as critical of the official hypocrisy characterizing his country since 1947. And again, Pius XII was precisely "the German Pope," about whom the Christian Democrat answering the imprudent question of the Bundestag could say, "He was the first to use his influence towards the reconciliation of Germany and other nations." Did he support the Germany of *before* or *after* 1945? Hochhuth demolishes all the pretexts that have grown in the past fifteen years: the common man knew nothing about Auschwitz (but the smell alone would have been enough); a German soldier was not defending Hitler but Germany (Gerstein answers, "The traitors, they alone, today / are saving Germany's honor"); suppose that one can pass off as trivial the death of millions of Jews, which seems to be the case beyond the Rhine today; in forgetting, one builds not a better life, but a far worse one.

The new Simplicissimus, Rolf Hochhuth, thirty-two years old, set out naively

---

4. Gruber testified at the Eichmann trial. /8/

in quest of the troublesome truth which had been hidden, which had been sugar-coated, which had been carefully edited from the textbooks, which, since 1947, had reduced year by year the number of pages on the extermination camps. He went beyond the textbooks to the sources themselves, which he cautiously appended to his play. Then he dropped the enormous paving stone into the stagnant pool of the good German conscience. It created quite a splash. Hitler might have been written off the ledger as a balance of credits and debits, but the bodies of six million noncombatants — not even Lady Macbeth had quite so much to wash off her conscience.

Hochhuth is not alone, today, in Germany. Max Frisch has done the same thing in *Andorra,* a tragi-comedy about anti-Semitism, implicating in its accusations both Germany and his own country, Switzerland. In this novel the young Andri no longer wishes to be the son of his father; he prefers to identify himself with the Jews, though he is not one. Another novelist of Hochhuth's generation, Christian Geissler, has also looked into the past of his father's generation, seeking to make them say something more than "it was a great tragedy," or "one was powerless to do anything," or "time covers a multitude of sins." Like Hochhuth, he uses the documentary method to unmask: chants, slogans, scholarly articles. (It is interesting to note that Hochhuth can point to documents as the basis of three fourths of the dialogue of his play.) Yet today the revolution of the sons against the fathers, against a satisfied cowardliness and forgetfullness, differs from the "literature of the ruins," those writings immediately following the war. Then everything was chaotic, nightmarish, belief was no longer possible. Hochhuth believes in courage, in social responsibility, in fighting evil. It has taken fifteen years for West Germany to produce a work of art which speaks loudly to all of us and which brings nothing but honor to the author's own country. /8/

Times Literary Supplement

THE POPE AS TRAGIC FIGURE

The Critic Writes

. . . By a smart piece of theatre the note of contempt for the Pope is struck in his first words, in which he expresses his "burning concern" (his "brennende Sorge", the title of Pius XI's famous encyclical against the Nazis). For what? His stocks and shares! Riccardo confronts him and says he will wear the Star of David until the Pope has done his duty. Pius then dictates a statement like one he actually made in 1943, denouncing crimes against people because of their nationality or race, but not specifically attacking Hitler. As he signs this he gets some ink on his fingers, and is shown washing his hands like Pilate. After this act it is no surprise to find that, in his notes, the author calls the Pope a hypocrite, a cold sceptic, cold, callous, a careerist, a "neutrum", in short, a criminal. Such unrelieved denigration, apart from its truth, fairness or otherwise, is a dramatic weakness, for it is hardly a tragedy to show the central character not struggling as Pius XII may with good reason be conceived as doing, between the terrible duty of saying too much and saying too little, but as entirely contemptible, like the stock figure of Stalinist propaganda. What could have been a true tragedy is turned into a mere denigration. Far

From a review of *The Representative, The Times Literary Supplement,* September 27, 1963, p. 722, and from "Letters to the Editor," *The Times Literary Supplement,* October 11, 1963, p. 812.

more effective are the ensuing scenes, in which Riccardo, forced to go and work in the crematoria, is confronted with the sinister Doctor, and eventually killed—his faith destroyed by the scenes of horror he has had to witness. These concentration-camp scenes, in fact, bring to dramatic life the awful horrors of the whole extermination procedure.

The "Historical Sidelights" . . . are a collection of documents, often interesting and useful, but clearly selected to exclude anything which might modify or disturb the writer's notion of Pius's action—which is an historical fact, in the sense that he never denounced Hitler, or indeed anyone else, by name—and his motives, on which there is room for much argument. It is legitimate to point to the paucity of material from the Vatican archives; some has been produced since the play was first staged, and it might, had it been known to Herr Hochhuth, have enabled him to lighten his black portrayal. There are other partisan features in the play, side-hits at Krupps, at Chancellor Adenauer, minimizing the Allies' part in the defeat of Hitler. Much of this is ephemeral journalism. But the writer must be given the credit for an illustration, of true dramatic power, of the almost incomprehensible story of the Nazi obsession against the Jews and the cold inhumanity of the scientific exterminators. Whole chapters of the Nuremberg trial documents have been used to distil this concentrated essence of a prodigious crime which was in some danger of being forgotten or belittled. It is unfortunate that the searchlight is so much diverted from the chief villains to the figure of the Pope, a fault, not only of taste and injustice, but, especially, so it would seem, in the stage-version, of dramatic construction. Quite truly, at the end, Herr Hochhuth says that "without freedom of choice there can be no dramatic conflict". But his Pope's inaction is determined by an innate and unrelieved villainy. What might have been a tragic drama is turned, in this respect at least, into nothing more than a propagandist indictment. /722/

The Author Replies

Sir,—With your reviewer's estimate of the literary value of my play, *The Representative*, I have, of course, no quarrel. It does, however, seem necessary to me to take him up on one or two points of historical accuracy.

(1) It is not true, as your reviewer states, that, since the play was first staged, material has been produced, either by the Vatican itself or by historians, which, had it been known to me, "might have enabled [me] to lighten [my] black portrayal", or which confutes my argument. The fact remains: neither did the Pope protest publicly against the massacres, nor did he attempt, through diplomatic channels, to suggest to Hitler that the massacres be stopped—whereas he did, for example, address himself, repeatedly and in writing, to Roosevelt, when it was a question of protecting Rome from further bombing.

(2) On the first page of the "Historical Sidelights" I state expressly that neither the Vatican nor the Kremlin open their archives to researchers. It may, however, be assumed that the Vatican does not possess any document which exonerates them in this matter, since, in the seven months since the play appeared, they have neither produced nor published any such document. I shall not presume to judge the objective value of Pope Paul's statement against my play; but it should be remembered, in this context, that the attitude of Under-Secretary of State Montini to the deportations of the Roman Jews was made clear only after discussions on the subject with Hitler's diplomatic representative to the Vatican at the time.

(3) Your critic writes that, in Act IV, I make Pius dictate "a statement *like* one he actually made in 1943" on the occasion of the deportation of the Roman Jews. I would like to point out that the text of the statement in my play is that of the *actual* statement which appeared in the *Osservatore Romano,* and that it is quoted uncut.

(4) Your critic also writes that I imply Pius's silence to be based on "concern for the Vatican investments". This is not true; I have put into the Pope's mouth serious and statesmanlike arguments and apprehensions—apprehensions that were translated, in great part, during the period 1944–1947, into an unfortunate reality, which was more clearly foreseen by Pius XII than, for example, by Roosevelt. This political argument should characterize him as a statesman of some standing, and it is in this context alone that Riccardo's demand that a Pope should not simply be a diplomat is fully justified. Each feels his attitude to be entirely right, and from this arises the unresolvable conflict. Anyone who reproaches me for mentioning stocks and shares in this scene should, in fairness, not conceal the fact that I also mention the half-hundred-weight of gold which the Pope was prepared to pay the Nazis as ransom for the Jews of Rome.

(5) Your critic suggests that I have failed to make a tragic figure out of Pius XII. This has at no time been my intention, as no single document from the fifteen years during which Pius continued in his pontificate after the deportation of the Roman Jews has ever persuaded me to regard him in this light.

There is no word in all the twenty-two volumes of speeches and writings which he left behind him which suggests that he suffered retrospectively about the questions of the deportations from his own diocese and of his own silence regarding them. The tragic figures in my play are the two Fontanas, and the Jews themselves, in other words, the victims; *not* the man whose silence indirectly helped the murderers, in that he did not even fulfil the Christian duty of warning the Jews. Countless families in Western Europe demonstrably allowed themselves to be registered for the death-journeys, completely unaware of the purpose of these journeys, because not even the Pope, the great neutral figure, the one man whose word could be trusted in those times, not even he informed these people that the terrible rumours from Poland were *not* Allied horror-propaganda.

To attribute tragic stature to Pius XII is a blasphemy: he did not even once make personal intervention for any one of the 3,000 nameless priests whom Hitler, his partner in the Concordat, caused to be murdered. It is these priests, however, who are the true martyrs, in Kierkegaard's sense, of the Church in our century. In Riccardo Fontana, abandoned by his superiors, like the rest of the 3,000, I have tried to portray one of them. . . .

To your critic's reproach that Pius is made "the stock figure of Stalinist propaganda" I can make no further comment. Nor can I make much of his claim that Chancellor Adenauer is attacked in my play. Before reading *The Times Literary Supplement* I had no idea that Adenauer's name was ever mentioned either in the play or in its appendix. On which page had your reviewer discovered it?

Rolf Hochhuth /812/

The Critic Answers

Our reviewer writes:—My reply to Herr Hochhuth is that he and I are talking about two different things. He asserts—and I do not contradict him—that Pius XII made no specific protest or public denunciation of Hitler during the war. I may remark that he did protest about the Poles at the very beginning, and was asked not to, as it merely increased the Nazi terrorism. My concern was, however, with the motives attributed to the Pope. Putting reasonable political arguments in the Pope's mouth, or mentioning his offer of gold for the Roman Jews is heavily outweighed by the setting in which Herr Hochhuth introduces the Pope; the words "mit brennender Sorge" (title, of course, of Pius XI's vigorous and, unhappily, ineffective encyclical of 1937) are followed by some three pages of discussion about investments. The gold episode is history; the chat about investments in this context is invention. Then when the dramatist makes the Pope dictate a short protest—making no use of his two long, moving statements about atrocities, with their clear allusion to racial persecution—he interrupts it with talk of Hungarian railway shares, and tops it with the hand-washing scene.

I am sorry Herr Hochhuth should feel it necessary to condemn in such extravagant terms my idea that, with more knowledge, he might have moderated his presentation. I was alluding chiefly to Pius XII's letter to Bishop Preysing of Berlin, of April 30, 1943. To the impartial reader this, I think, reveals the Pope as deeply troubled about what worse things his more specific public action might provoke. When I wrote my review I did not know that Herr Hochhuth, writing to the *Frankfurter Allgemeine Zeitung* on May 30, 1963, said that he would, in future productions, put messages from this letter in the Pope's mouth. This leaves me even more puzzled.

Someone lately has pointed out that Brecht allowed some sort of humanity even to Galileo's inquisitors. Herr Hochhuth, in the book, gives the Pope no moral credit at all, calls him "a criminal", "a cold sceptic", "a neutrum", "an introverted mystic" and so on. He also says "never perhaps in the whole of history have so many paid with their lives for the passive attitude of one man". Taken literally, this seems to "let out" Hitler, Himmler and all the rest, which I am sure was not Herr Hochhuth's intention. The view he gives of the Pope's character has been decisively contradicted by people who knew him well. It is a pity Herr Hochhuth, in his researches in Rome, could not find material for a better balanced portrayal. As for Pius XII's writings, full of religious and moral guidance and laying down Christian principles on which the late Pope built his last encyclical—they are dismissed as "trivialities".

I named Dr. Adenauer because I took the sarcastic references to Bonn politicians and "Germany's economic miracle" as pointing at his government. It is unimportant compared with the fact that, by exhibiting in such a contemptible light a recent Pope known to millions the play becomes a rather lopsided piece of propaganda. /812/

Mary Zavada

HOCHHUTH IN LONDON

Der Stellvertreter, Rolf Hochhuth's theatrical indictment of Pius XII, was recently added to the repertory of the Royal Shakespeare Company, stationed

From "Hochhuth in London," *America*, January 25, 1964, pp. 139–140.

at the Aldwych Theatre, in London. The original six-hour opus has been translated by Robert David MacDonald and shortened and prepared for the stage by him in collaboration with Clifford Williams. The production received a great deal of press coverage—the *Observer* printed the scene in which Pius appears—and tickets for it were hard to obtain. At the Lord Chamberlain's request for an authoritative Catholic opinion, the Aldwych programs printed a letter written to the editor of the *Tablet* by Cardinal Montini just before his election to the papacy. His Holiness defends Pius XII and suggests, among other things, that "playwrights insufficiently endowed with historical discernment . . . forbear from trifling with subjects of this kind." The quarrel over the late Pope continues and shows no sign of subsiding. It might be interesting to shove the controversy aside and review the work purely on the basis of dramatic value.

The Representative, as the work is called in London, is divided into two acts, of three scenes each. These scenes are separated from each other by film clips. Some of these clips are innocuous; there is one, for instance, of Pope Pius smiling at a crowd. But others are repulsive. The most gruesome—that of a bulldozer pushing piles of naked, decaying corpses—is the last thing one sees before leaving the theatre. The immediate response is strong and painful, but it is elicited not by the author's creativity; it is the natural reaction to the diabolism of the Nazi concentration camps.

The essence of theatre is the audience-actor relationship, a relationship impossible in a movie house, where the screen performers are not at all affected by the audience—be it enthusiastic, bored or asleep. *The Representative* is not the first drama to include film snatches. Like its predecessors, it should be judged *in toto*. Nevertheless, dissociation of the film clips from the author's work is here astoundingly easy. Ralph Koltai compiled the film sequences; but he was too interested in polemic to be attentive to such a requisite of art as unity. The film material and the live drama result in separate reactions, and thus separate judgments can be made. When one has said that the shots of the atrocities are horrible, he has not made a statement on the author's creation. Since *The Representative* purports to be theatre, the bulk of one's attention should be given to the text of the play.

The Representative, sans film clips, is tenuously held together by the figure of Riccardo Fontana, S. J. . . . /139/

Alec McCowen, in the role of Fontana, is so strident that one responds—but only with the impulse to suggest a remedy for his pain. Warm milk? A cold shower? What is the treatment for hysterical young men? Surely the author doesn't mean that Fontana is the preferable alternative to the fictional complacent Pope. It is true that inaction, as well as action, can induce calamity; but Fontana's frenzies are at least as alarming as the mumblings of this Pope.

In the last scene—overly long, but the only instance when actual drama flickers through Hochhuth's doling out of guilt to past and present—Fontana engages in debate with a German officer in the ghostly dawn of bestial Auschwitz. Faced with a lunatic German who looks upon mass murder as a test of the existence of God—so many months and not even a thunderbolt to show that He exists—Fontana surprisingly summons wisdom and charity and duels with the monster verbally. The author cannot sustain this *débat* between allegorical good and evil without resorting to his version of history. The Inquisition and other skeletons are jangled again.

For the drama reviewer, historical accuracy is by no means the primary question. Any character, with or without a historical genesis, must be fully developed, believable, human—though, of course, not necessarily humane. He must not be a caricature, a grotesque inflation of a single thesis in the author's mind.

Hochhuth's Fontana is simply and shrilly antipope. Three sentences of the play flirt with psychology. (We learn that Pius' image had hung over Fontana's bed since he was twelve; that because of this influence, he had become a priest; and that his mother had begged him not to enter the priesthood.) But these lines are pushed aside by the mass of statistics and vituperations that Fontana exclaims. On the other hand, Hochhuth's Pius is a simpleton, a doddering bore. When he spills ink on his hands while signing his document of sorrow, the papal aide hurries in with a basin of water, and the author presents Pius, the new Pilate, attempting to wash his guilt away. This gross symbolism is typical of the author's lack of finesse.

The Aldwych production shows a corresponding lack of taste and theatrical skill. Hitler's picture hangs in the Nazi common room in the second scene, as Pius' picture dominates the walls of clerical establishments. The cardinal and priests in the play are crude ignoramuses who belt down glasses of wine and entangle themselves in coy little dances as they extend their rings to be kissed.

Such satire is heavy-footed indeed. It is particularly out of place here, where the author's intention is to win approval for the supposedly noble Fontana. Is that his intention? Or is he simply spewing out his hatred of Hitler and the Pope, of nazism and the Church? The latter seems the correct answer; but what a pity that the author chose the tedium of negation instead of the excitement of a more positive view.

Drama must be the aggregation of significant plot, vital characters and the mature sympathies of the author. The new dramatists want to shake man to an awareness of his condition. They should make certain they are not substituting fantasy for fantasy. Ranting is permissible in Hyde Park, but good theatre demands the expression of a more refined sensibility. Playwrights insufficiently endowed with a dramatic sense should forbear from wasting our time. /140/

Pope Paul VI

LETTER ON THE DEPUTY

This letter on "The Deputy" was one of the last written by Pope Paul VI as Cardinal Montini, Archbishop of Milan. It was received by the *Tablet*, an English Catholic Weekly, June 21, 1963, the date of Cardinal Montini's election to the papacy, and printed by that periodical in its issue of July 6, 1963. The full text follows:

Dear Sir,

It gave me much pleasure to read the article entitled "Pius XII and the Jews," which appeared in your excellent periodical on May 11th, 1963: it was a most welcome defense not only of Pope Pius XII, of venerated memory,

"Letter from Pope Paul VI," *The Commonweal*, February 28, 1964, pp. 651–652.

and of the Holy See, but also of historical truth and sound logic, not to speak of common-sense.

It is not my intention here to examine the question raised by the author and the producer, Rolf Hochhuth and Erwin Piscator respectively, of the play "The Deputy": namely, whether it was Pius XII's duty to condemn in some public and spectacular way the massacres of the Jews during the last war. Much, to be sure, might still be said on this point, even after the very clear and cogent article in the *Osservatore Romano* of April 5th; for the thesis of Herr Hochhuth's play—that, to quote Mr. George Steiner's review in the Sunday *Times* of May 5th, "We are all accomplices to that which leaves us indifferent"—bears no relation whatever to the personality or the work of Pope Pius XII.

I cannot myself conceive how anyone could bring such a charge (let alone make it the subject of a play) against a pontiff who might well, had he wished, have declared with a clear conscience to the whole world: "No effort on our part was lacking, nothing that anxious solicitude could suggest was left untried to prevent the horrors of mass deportation and exile; and when despite our just expectations this proved impossible, we set ourselves to do everything in our power to mitigate, at least, the cruelties of a state of affairs imposed by brute force." But history—a very different thing from such artificial manipulation of facts to fit a preconceived idea as we see in "The Deputy"—will vindicate the conduct of Pius XII when confronted by the criminal excesses of the Nazi regime: history will show how vigilant, persistent, disinterested and courageous that conduct must be judged to have been, when viewed in its true context, in the concrete conditions of that time. /651/

For my part I conceive it my duty to contribute to the task of clarifying and purifying men's judgment on the historical reality in question—so distorted in the representational pseudo-reality of Hochhuth's play—by pointing out that the character given to Pius XII in this play (to judge from the reviews in the press) does not represent the man as he really was; in fact, it entirely misrepresents him. I am in a position to assert this because it was my good fortune to be drawn into close contact with Pius XII during his pontificate, serving him day by day, from 1937, when he was still Secretary of State, to 1954: throughout, that is, the whole period of the World War.

It is true that the precise scope of my duties did not include foreign affairs ("extraordinary" affairs, as they are called in the language of the Roman Curia); but Pius XII's goodness towards me personally, and the nature itself of my work as *Sostituto* in the Secretariat of State, gave me access to the mind and, I would add, to the heart of this great Pope. The image of Pius XII which Hochhuth presents, or is said to present, is a false one. For example, it is utterly false to tax Pius with cowardice: both his natural temperament and the consciousness that he had of the authority and the mission entrusted to him speak clearly against such an accusation. I could cite a host of particular facts to drive this point home, facts that would prove that the frail and gentle exterior of Pius XII, and the sustained refinement and moderation of his language, concealed—if they did not, rather, reveal—a noble and virile character capable of taking very firm decisions and of adopting, fearlessly, positions that entailed considerable risk.

Nor is it true that he was a heartless solitary. On the contrary, he was a man of exquisite sensibility and the most delicate human sympathies. True, he did love solitude: his richly cultivated mind, his unusual capacity for thought and study led him to avoid all useless distractions, every unnecessary relaxation;

but he was quite the reverse of a man shut away from life and indifferent to people and events around him. Rather, it was his constant desire to be informed of everything. He wished to enter fully into the history of his own afflicted time: with a deep sense that he himself was a part of that history, he wished to participate fully in it, to share its sufferings in his own heart and soul. Let me cite, in this connection, the words of a well-qualified witness, Sir D'Arcy Osborne, the British Minister to the Holy See who, when the Germans occupied Rome, was obliged to live confined in the Vatican City. Writing to the *Times* on May 20th Sir D'Arcy said: "Pius XII was the most warmly humane, kindly, generous, sympathetic (and, incidentally, saintly) character that it has been my privilege to meet in the course of a long life."

Again, it is not true to say that Pope Pius XII's conduct was inspired by a calculating political opportunism. It would be just as true—and as slanderous—to assert that his government of the Church was motivated by considerations of material advantage.

As for his omitting to take up a position of violent opposition to Hitler in order to save the lives of those millions of Jews slaughtered by the Nazis, this will be readily understood by anyone who avoids Hochhuth's mistake of trying to assess what could have been effectively and responsibly done then, in those appalling conditions of war and Nazi oppression, by the standard of what would be feasible in normal conditions—or in some hypothetical conditions arbitrarily invented by a young playwright's imagination. An attitude of protest and condemnation such as this young man blames the Pope for not having adopted would have been not only futile but harmful: that is the long and the short of the matter. The thesis of "The Deputy" betrays an inadequate grasp of psychological, political and historical realities. But then the author was concerned above all to write an interesting play.

Let us suppose that Pius XII had done what Hochhuth blames him for not doing. His action would have led to such reprisals and devastations that Hochhuth himself, the war being over and he now possessed of a better historical, political and moral judgment, would have been able to write another play, far more realistic and far more interesting than the one that he has in fact so cleverly but also so ineptly put together: a play, that is, about the vicar who, through political exhibitionism or psychological myopia, would have been guilty of unleashing on the already tormented world still greater calamities involving innumerable innocent victims, let alone, himself.

It would be as well if the creative imagination of playwrights insufficiently endowed with historical discernment (and possibly, though please God it is not so, with ordinary human integrity) would forebear from trifling with subjects of this kind and with historical personages whom some of us have known. In the present case the real drama, and tragedy, is not what the playwright imagines it to be: it is the tragedy of one who tries to impute to a Pope who was acutely aware both of his own moral obligations and of historical reality—and was moreover a very loyal as well as impartial friend to the people of Germany—the horrible crimes of German Nazism.

Let some men say what they will, Pius XII's reputation as a true Vicar of Christ, as one who tried, so far as he could, fully and courageously to carry out the mission entrusted to him, will not be affected. But what is the gain to art and culture when the theater lends itself to injustice of this sort?

With my sincere respects, devotedly yours,

G. B. CARDINAL MONTINI
Archbishop of Milan /652/

Rolf Hochhuth

REPLY TO POPE PAUL VI

His Holiness Pope Paul VI wrote his opinion of *The Deputy* shortly before his elevation, and it has only recently been published. Though I am reluctant to do so, his statement compels me to quote from portions of my "Historical Sidelights" clarifying the role he played as Undersecretary of State during the deportation of the Roman Jews. The secretary of the German legation, Gerhard Gumpert of the Economic Division, testified as follows at the Nuremberg Trials:

"Later, when I bade goodbye to Weizsäcker because I was being transferred to the Embassy in Northern Italy, he spoke of this incident once more and said in so many words: 'That was another stinking mess.' In reaction to the reports, he said, they had got cold feet in Berlin and stopped the deportations immediately. He added: 'I can also tell you that at the time I spoke very confidentially with Montini and advised him that any protest by the Pope would only result in the deportations being carried out in a thoroughgoing fashion. I know how our people react in these matters. Montini, incidentally, saw the point.'"

What we have here is a morass. Weizsäcker's closest collaborator, von Kessel, tries to force the Vatican to drop its reticence. When at least one German bishop takes him up on his suggestion, Weizsäcker /75/ temporarily makes the bishop's demand his own. He threatens Berlin with an ultimatum by the Pope; this obviously means that he regards such an ultimatum as a deterrent. But simultaneously he tells the Pope's closest associate that a statement by the Holy Father "would only result in the deportations being really carried out in a thoroughgoing fashion." And Montini, or as the case may be, the Pope, are only too glad to hear that, although they know, although every child in Rome knows, that the first Jews were already being loaded into the boxcars; that the round-ups are going on regardless; and that Weizsäcker's words are therefore—to put it mildly—sheer twaddle.

Finally, by the following weekend (October 25–26), when the *Osservatore Romano* reports that "the Pope's universal and fatherly works of mercy . . . know no limits," the first 615 Roman Jews had already arrived in Auschwitz, and 468 of them were already in the crematorium.

Thus when Pope Paul VI declares today that any protest "would have been not only futile but harmful: that is the long and the short of the matter," it merely indicates that his position has not changed since 1943, when he decided in accordance with Hitler's representative. Yet this position is surely questionable in view of the fact that Kappler, the head of the German Gestapo in Rome, hastened to halt a deportation train in order to free two Jews simply on the basis of an *unofficial* request by Pope Pius XII, an incident confirmed by Dr. Wemmer, Weizsäcker's deputy. Can it, therefore, be claimed that an

"Hochhuth antwortet Papst Paul VI," Basel, Switzerland, July 1963, as it appears in *Der Streit um Hochhuths "Stellvertreter"* (Stuttgart: Basilius Press, 1963), pp. 75–77. Trans. by the editors.

official papal protest would have been ineffective? And how does Pope Paul VI justify the fact that only a few days after the deportations, his superior at that time, Cardinal Maglione, the Secretary of State, at the request of Weizsäcker, issued a statement on the front page of *Osservatore Romano* attesting to the exemplary behavior of the German occupation forces towards the Vatican and the Curia? This statement on the good conduct of the Nazis greatly dismayed the Allied press, as it had been reporting the horrible events taking place in Rome regarding the Jewish deportations. Weizsäcker writes: /76/ "The propaganda of our enemies tried to present the German soldiers as despoilers of Rome and as a prison guard to the Pope." A public denial by the Cardinal Secretary of State was a priceless propaganda advantage to the murderers, who were not despoiling Rome but merely slaughtering the Jews. Once again Christianity, through its present highest representative, had given the kiss of Judas to the Jews, only a few days after the poorer Jewish families (the rich ones had found sanctuary more easily) had been herded in the streets outside St. Peter's and loaded into vans bound for "destinations unknown." (Nor did the Vatican wish to know them.) /77/

Associated Press

VATICAN PAPER REPLIES

VATICAN CITY—(AP)—The Vatican weekly, L'Osservator Della Domenica, Friday put out a special 80-page issue defending the World War II role of Pope Pius XII. It said the pontiff was being tried posthumously.

The magazine, weekend edition of L'Osservator Romano, contained articles by prelates, churchmen and others—both Roman Catholic and non-Catholic—who had worked with Pius XII. Photographic copies of previously unpublished documents were also carried.

An introductory editorial said:

"Today a posthumous trial of Pius XII is being conducted. But too many persons have forgotten that Pius XII had fought with all his strength to avoid a world conflict . . . and spare mankind from intolerable suffering."

The special issue came out amidst public discussion of the Pope's war role as a result of Rolf Hochhuth's controversial play, "The Deputy," and a number of recent books and articles. The play suggests that the Pope might have done more to halt the Nazi persecution of the Jews. Vatican officials have maintained that he did all he could.

A second editorial said: "History crushes lies and errors without pity. It leaves only truth, and truth now puts and will put a halo of glory around Pius XII."

The special edition—the most comprehensive defense of Pius by a Vatican publication since the controversy developed—was entitled "The Pope, Yesterday and Today."

Associated Press dispatch, Vatican City, June 27, 1964. Father Martini conducted the historical research on which the issue of *L'Osservator Della Domenica,* discussed in the article, is based; his conclusions first appeared in "La vera storiá e *Il Vicario* di Rolf Hochhuth," a translation of which is on pp. 164–177 of this book.

Brief articles covered the World War I reign of Benedict XV, and the pre-World War II pontificate of Pius XI.

But the bulk of the articles dealt with Pius XII, especially his actions on behalf of Jews during World War II. They told of his help for Italian Jews and the shelter granted Jews by Roman Catholic churches and institutions.

Tom Prideaux

HOMAGE AND HATE FOR THE DEPUTY

In metropolitan New York, the largest Jewish city in the world and one of the biggest Catholic cities, the opening of *The Deputy* was bound to start a grand chorale of controversy. But there were some unexpected discords and odd harmonies. Catholics disagreed with each other about the virtue of the late Pope Pius XII. Jews defended Catholics. Preachers, rabbis, priests, editors and church historians tangled vehemently—but with a new and perhaps prophetic goodwill. . . .

At the New York opening, while five sets of picketers chanted outside, audiences were quiet and attentive. But they were locked inside during intermission lest some picketer start trouble. Since then every performance has sold out, and detectives search the house daily for bombs. Calmly, Cardinal Cushing of Boston said, "I don't think it would do any harm for any intelligent person to see the play." But Cardinal Spellman, whose archdiocese includes Broadway, called the play "a slanderous . . . outrageous desecration of the honor of a great and good man."

Among all the forums and articles on *The Deputy*, a little local TV show, WABC's *New York, New York*, packed in the liveliest range of opinion. Edward Keating, editor of the Catholic magazine *Ramparts*, when he was asked if he thought the play would intensify division between Catholics and Jews, replied, "No . . . exactly the opposite, because it requires Catholics to face a very subtle anti-Semitism in the church that Pope John, incidentally, was trying to get rid of."

Reinhold Niebuhr, the noted Protestant theologian, excoriated "the shocking inadequacy of all Protestants and Catholics in their reaction to the Nazi terror in general." Rabbi Marc Tanenbaum objected to "the caricature of the Pope," but Dr. Niebuhr defended the playwright for using the Pope as a Christian symbol. "I wasn't very struck by Pope Pius XII," he added, speaking of the Pope himself, "although I wouldn't make him a scoundrel. . . ."

At the end Rabbi Tanenbaum summed up: "Even the Eichmann trial has not succeeded in touching Christian consciences as deeply."

To judge *The Deputy* strictly on its dramatic merits, then, seems beside the point. Pieced together, as it has been, from the author's huge stockpile of dramatic material—he first wrote it in five acts to run more than seven hours—the play sometimes seems crude and jerry-built. It is less play than polemic, and more morality play than tragedy. It can hardly figure importantly in the history of modern drama, but it belongs unmistakably to the drama of modern history. /28D/

From "Homage and Hate for 'The Deputy,'" *Life*, March 13, 1964, p. 28D.

NBC Monitor

INTERVIEW WITH HERMAN SHUMLIN

MR. McGEE: Herman Shumlin, the man who brought *The Deputy* to the United States, has been in the American theater for thirty years, but it's doubtful that ever before has he had anything to do with so controversial a drama as German playwright Rolf Hochhuth's indictment of Pope Pius XII. Still, though, Mr. Shumlin does have the reputation of being Broadway's "angry old man," and angry men seem to thrive on controversy. Certainly, they usually have something important to say. So we are happy to welcome you to *Monitor,* Mr. Shumlin.

MR. SHUMLIN: Thank you.

MR. McGEE: Tell us, why did you bring *The Deputy* to the United States?

MR. SHUMLIN: Well, that's a peculiar question. You might as well ask me why I produce any play. Usually people don't ask me that question unless the play fails. Then they ask, "Why did you produce it?" But the question has come up, and I will tell my simple reasons. Number one, I feel it is a very good play; number two, I think it is the first play played in too many years which has something to do with the life in which we live, and I think it is most important that the theater concern itself, as it was intended to do, with the life in which we live and not only with pleasant musical shows or little comedies, which I have nothing against. But the theater, according to George Bernard Shaw, is the main pulpit in the world. I have always believed that with him, and I think it is true. It is most interesting—the play, as you know, was published as a book; the full-length play which was to run for eight hours has many interesting comments by the author, Rolf Hochhuth. The Grove Press has published it, and they never received one word of protest from anybody. But the theater is quite different. There was a tumultuous avalanche of disapproval, of efforts to suppress the play, of antagonistic actions against the play. That is quite remarkable, and I think it proves the importance of the theater, and that's very important to me.

MR. McGEE: Well, what is the central point—personalities aside for the moment—what is the central point that the play has to make?

MR. SHUMLIN, The central point of the play is silence, or rather *against* silence—silence in a sense of people conforming and people refusing to take responsibility of their citizenship, of their morality, of their religion, of their beliefs, who stand by and do nothing when wicked things are done in the world. We have it all the time. We have it here. We need to face it, and we need to stand up as men and accept our responsibility and not always think of our own convenience, of the difficulties that might happen to us if we stood up and spoke, of losing our jobs, and soon and so forth, because that's what's happened—too long. I feel right now it is important, and *this* is what the play is about.

MR. McGEE: Now, I have heard an argument for many, many years about destroying one's effectiveness by speaking out, the argument being that you should consider even your willingness to sacrifice an arm in a good cause. Just how much effectiveness might a one-armed man have in the future in that cause? What about that idea?

Transcription of a taped interview with Herman Shumlin on Monitor, The NBC Weekend Radio Service, produced by Bob Maurer, March 14, 1964.

MR. SHUMLIN: I never heard the argument before, Mr. McGee. It is kind of curious. I think that the priest who went to Molokai with the lepers did not worry about losing his arm or his nose or his ears or his fingers, because he was a Christian who believed that he must help people. And I think that Joan, now *St.* Joan, by courtesy of the Roman Catholic Church, who first arrested her, condemned her, and burned her at the stake, also spoke out and lost her life. And I think you can remember a great many others who have been most effective in the world.

MR. McGEE: Not to press the point too hard, Mr. Shumlin, but what I am getting at is this: this question of destroying one's effectiveness, that it is possible that you have some influence with a group whose course needs to be changed, but that if you do too much too soon in trying to persuade them to change their course, you can destroy any possibility of having any influence on them.

MR. SHUMLIN: It is always *too* soon. It is never the right time, is it, to do anything? Always wait, and then nothing will ever happen to you.

MR. McGEE: Now, Pope Pius may have been silent on the execution of millions of Jews, but there were those in the Roman Catholic Church, in the Vatican, who did act and, it would seem, with the Pontiff's full knowledge. One such was Angelo Cardinal Roncalli. Ira Hirschmann, author of the book *Caution to the Winds,* was President Roosevelt's personal envoy and War Refugee Board representative to the Middle East in 1944, and he knows something of those actions. Well, Mr. Hirschmann was in the Monitor studios this week, and he told us something of Angelo Roncalli's accomplishments. I would like you to listen, if you would, to what Mr. Hirschmann had to say, and then, if you will, Mr. Shumlin, make some comment.

MR. HIRSCHMANN: There was a desperate situation, as Eichmann was killing Jews by the thousands in Hungary, and in an effort to find some possible means of saving some before the world war came to an end, I was sent by a representative of the International Red Cross to meet the Apostolic Delegate in Istanbul. His name was Angelo Roncalli. In spite of the frustrations I had had from governments and other institutions in my efforts at rescuing minorities, Roncalli greeted me warmly and finally suggested a plan for rescue in Hungary in which the long arm of mercy of the Catholic Church was to reach out to be helpful. The plan was based on giving baptismal certificates to Jews, mostly in Budapest, which the Nazis recognized as exit permits at that time. He suggested it. We called it Operation Baptism. Our underground worked together with members of the Church, and some thousands of Hungarian Jews came out to safety. Many of them I have met in this country and in Israel, and they owe their lives to the intercession of this man, Angelo Roncalli. He became Pope John, and I could understand that he was chosen for that post when I observed this humanitarian manifestation of this very great man.

MR. McGEE: So it would seem that the Roman Catholic Church acted to save Jews who might otherwise have been put to death, even though the Pope personally remained silent.

MR. SHUMLIN: Oh, yes. There is no doubt about that, and the play says that. The play speaks of, for example, the action of the Nuncio, who was the Apostolic Delegate in the city of Pressburg in Slovakia, who, by his actions, prevented the deportation of Jews from Slovakia for two years—on his own, entirely on his own. Now, as to Roncalli, who later became Pope John—I am sorry I don't have it with me, I had it in my hand just before I left my home to come here—but I have a news item from the London *Express* which says that the diary of Pope John, or Roncalli, is in the possession of a certain monsignor, whose name I cannot now remember, I am sorry to say—I could have brought it down if I had known this was going to be referred to—which says that he was visited at more or less the same time by Chief Rabbi Herzog of Palestine, as it was then known, who asked Roncalli to help and asked him to get in touch with the Pope and plead with him to do something. And Roncalli's diary says that the Pope answered Roncalli's appeal, but the letter said he could do nothing. Roncalli then went ahead on his own. He was a good man, Roncalli, and a good Pope, I think.

MR. McGEE: Now, some have said that the Pope has been singled out for what they feel to be a disproportionate share of the responsibility of this, and that it would extend to Britain, the United States, Sir Winston Churchill, the late President Roosevelt. And they question why they were not selected as subjects of the drama rather than the Pope.

MR. SHUMLIN: I can agree with that. The whole subject is enormous, and, as I say, Hochhuth, the author, in his play had to take what in time, in space, would take six to seven hours to perform—out of all reason—to cover the subject as far as he has. It would be impossible in one play to put everything in. I hope, really, that this play, *The Deputy*, will be the first of a number of plays which will truly examine, truthfully examine, *all* the leaders of the world: Roosevelt, Churchill, Protestants, Jews—everyone. We need to face the truth in every direction and not hide under ignorance, under a blanket of suffocation of the truth. The Pope happened to be the only person, the only neutral person, whose voice could not be disbelieved as being on one side or the other, and, therefore, he is not only symbolic but *actually* the person at whose feet the whole problem was laid.

MR. McGEE: We have a little time remaining. These two questions, it seems to me, might go to the heart of the matter and their arguments being advanced. Some say that had the Pope spoken, it would not have aided things, and that had he spoken, he might have made things worse. There are two sides to it. Would you turn them over for us?

MR. SHUMLIN: Well, there was a Protestant minister, Provost Gruber, from Berlin, who spoke out against Hitler's action and who was put in a concentration camp, where he remained throughout the war. When that question was put to him, he said, "What *could* have been worse?" Now, it is interesting to me, however, when you take that a little further and say that if he had spoken out, some Catholics might have been killed. Well, I find that a most remarkable statement, a most remarkable picture. Does the soldier have anything to do with his life when he accepts his uniform, his pistol, his gun, and is told to go somewhere and fight and perhaps give up his life as many have done? Why isn't the Pope in the same situation? Why aren't you? Why aren't I? We are! There must come a time when we stand up as men and not as businessmen and not as preservers of an institution, but simply as men. The Pope is called the Vicar of Christ. He is the head of the most important religious body, the most important community in the western world, numbering a half a billion people. Certainly, his chief position is a religious one, one as the Vicar of Christ. He is supposed to represent Him and to do as He did. I think He would have spoken.

MR. McGEE: Yes, I think so, too. We have been talking with Herman Shumlin, director and producer of *The Deputy*, the man who brought the play about Pope Pius XII to Broadway, the play that deals with the wartime pontiff's alleged guilt by silence in the slaughter of six million Jews, but a play that deals in a much broader sense with the rut of complacency in which too many of us have fallen.

NBC Monitor

INTERVIEW WITH FATHER ROBERT A. GRAHAM, S.J.

MR. McGEE: As I said a couple of minutes ago, Monitor received a good many requests that we hear the other side of the story after we had as our guest Herman Shumlin, the producer of *The Deputy,* the highly controversial play that is now showing on Broadway after long runs in Europe. We had Mr. Shumlin because that is what this segment of Monitor is for: to take an in-depth look at the stories of the moment that are in the news. And in that light, and as part of our continuing look at *The Deputy,* we talked with the Reverend Robert Graham, associate editor of *America,* the national Catholic weekly magazine. . . . Father, do you think *The Deputy* places too much blame on the Pope, or should any blame be placed on the Pope?

FATHER GRAHAM: Well, I certainly think that you cannot blame it all on the Pope. The play presents him in a most disgusting, revolting way. He makes a very clear charge in the play—not in the play but in its "Historical Sidelights," which he has at the end to bolster up his alleged historical foundation. He says, "Perhaps never before in history have so many human beings paid with their lives for the passivity of a single statesman." Well, now, that is a very sweeping and very grave charge, and in the course of the play, he also describes that sort of a policy as being a criminal one. Inasmuch as we are here in reaction to the appearance of Mr. Shumlin on Monitor, I think it is right to report that I asked Mr. Shumlin on a previous radio broadcast that I had with him, "Do you think that Pope Pius XII was a criminal?" And he replied, "Yes." And I asked him again, "You mean that he didn't just make a mistake? That he operated and worked out of unworthy and evil motives?" "Yes, sir," he said, very plainly. Now Mr. Shumlin is trying to allege that the play does not portray him as a criminal. Well, the play *does,* and all the protests to that effect don't stand the test of an analysis of the play.

MR. McGEE: Do you think *any* blame should be placed on the Pope?

FATHER GRAHAM: Well, to the extent that he was a human being, certainly. But to single him out, a historical personality, and to make him the scapegoat, to make him the target of an indictment and by a trial by Broadway using historical arguments that are so completely distorted in the light of the concept of the papacy, which the papacy does not itself entertain. He has responsibilities, terrible responsibilities, not to one nation, not to any one time of history, but over a longer and wider scope, and to judge a Pope's moral responsibilities in that falsified perspective—as though he were a simple, individual man whose every word would not have repercussions on the lives and the well-being of millions of people—that is an unfair criterion on which to judge the Holy Father.

MR. McGEE: Am I understanding you to say, sir, that he could possibly have done more harm than good had he spoken?

Transcription of a taped interview with Father Robert A. Graham, S.J., on Monitor, The NBC Weekend Radio Service, produced by Bob Maurer, March 21, 1964.

FATHER GRAHAM: He certainly could have done more harm than good. But who knows? The point is, if the Pope made any mistake in judgment — how to proceed. That is quite possible, but that is not the point of the play, which is a question of character assassination. He attributes motives, most unworthy motives — financial preoccupation with his investments, world fanaticism, anti-Communism that is so fanatical that he would rather have Hitler stay around the scene than to see Communism come to Europe, or vanity, and power politics, which is completely contrary to all we have known of Pius XII. And then, also, there is a little trace of anti-Semitism, which I believe is the worst and meanest sort of an accusation to make against Pope Pius XII. He doesn't say it in so many words, but he implies it.

MR. McGEE: Do you think they have any motives?

FATHER GRAHAM: I do not know what his motives are. I am not going to speculate on what Mr. Hochhuth's or the producer's motives are in relation to the Holy Father. I stick to what I said — that they are mistaken in attributing these base and mean motives to Pope Pius XII.

MR. McGEE: We have talked about the possibility of doing more harm than good had the Pope spoken out. Is there any possibility that he could have altered the course of history by speaking out?

FATHER GRAHAM: That, of course, is a hypothetical question. But it seems to me that those who have any knowledge of the facts of the wartime years would agree that the Pope had a very solid foundation from his own experience, among others, in not pushing the matter further than he actually did. He was in a position of terrific responsibility where you have to weigh between speaking too much or not speaking enough. Who really knows? Who is in a position to decide that? And it is, as I have said, one of the mean and unworthy and outrageous features of this play that it ascribes the worst motives without any historical foundation.

MR. McGEE: Do you think it's done any harm to the Catholic Church?

FATHER GRAHAM: Well, no, no. I think that the reputation of Pope Pius XII is secure in history. It is typical, I think, and revealing that we had to wait for twenty years before any new "revelation" of Pius XII has come forth. If this is a sample of what can be said against Pope Pius XII, then I can be quite confident that nothing will be said in the future that is any worse or any better founded than this play.

MR. McGEE: I am recalling, or trying to recall — I am not sure that I can do it word for word — a statement that Mr. Shumlin made, but it was to this effect: that the Pope is supposed to be the Vicar of Christ on earth and, by his interpretation — perhaps it's right — that he should conduct himself as Christ did or Christ would have under these circumstances. He concluded that Christ would have spoken out against the Nazi atrocities against the Jews, that the Pope did not, and therefore he had failed in his role as vicar.

FATHER GRAHAM: Well, I believe I can answer that, Mr. McGee. After all, Christ did not denounce the evils of His day. He denounced the Pharisees, but He didn't go forth in a general career of denouncing every evil wherever He found it. He drove the moneychangers out of the temple, but what other evils were there in Israel in those days which Christ Himself did not castigate? And yet He was Christ; He was carrying on His mission, His religious mission.

MR. McGEE: One final question, sir. Do you anywhere in the play or in the book that has been written about the play find any manifestation of a sympathetic understanding?

FATHER GRAHAM: Not the slightest. For Mr. Hochhuth, the papacy is

merely a power machine. In this respect, by the way, I find that his image of the papacy is exactly that which I read in the Communist literature against the Vatican. He has no real concept —
MR. McGEE: Are you suggesting, sir, that they have parallel convictions?
FATHER GRAHAM: Yes, oh, yes, the —
MR. McGEE: Are you suggesting that he is in any way a Communist?
FATHER GRAHAM: No, I do not say that.
MR. McGEE: I ask this so we may clear this out.
FATHER GRAHAM: No, no. But the parallel is there. When I read that, I said to myself, "This is the approach which I notice in the Communist publications, namely that the papacy is a power instrument consumed with concern for its money, and fanatically anticommunist, and, of course, 'fascist.'" And that, of course, is the Communist portrait. I do not believe Mr. Hochhuth has any real conception, regardless of all he says, has any real conception of the fundamental and authentic, religious and spiritual self-consciousness which prevails in the Holy See.
MR. McGEE: Thank you very much, sir. I've enjoyed talking with you.

Alfred Kazin

REVIEW OF THE DEPUTY

On Easter Sunday, 1943, when all resistance from the Warsaw Ghetto had been crushed, the holiday crowds on their way from Mass "pushed through the streets to catch sight of Warsaw's newest spectacle . . . Batteries of artillery were set up in Nonwiniarska Street, from which the Germans kept up a steady barrage against the ghetto. And everywhere the flame, and the stench of roasting human flesh. The sight was awesome — and exciting. From time to time a living torch would be seen crouched on a window sill and then leaping through the air. Occasionally one such figure caught in some obstruction and hung there. The spectators would shout to the German riflemen, 'Hey, look over there! . . . no, over there!' As each figure completed its gruesome trajectory, the crowds cheered" (Alexander Donat, "Our Last Days In The Warsaw Ghetto").

The interest that the spectators took in this carnage was "medieval," in the sense that the public massacre of Jews had in the Middle Ages provided the onlookers with a sense of their own righteousness. It must have been frightful to watch Jews burn, but in the Middle Ages they were feared and marked off with so much holy zeal that to *watch* them burn established your own credit with God. The Poles suffered atrociously at the hands of the Nazis, but at Easter time, a favorite time for pogroms, the average Pole could still attend church, walk the streets, sit in a park, work in an office, get legally married, attend to his children — and thus despise and fear the Jews, who were being hunted down with such raging hatred by a great power already at war with half the world, that it was impossible for the average Pole, growing up in an anti-Semitic society, not to feel disgust and loathing for the Jews precisely because they were so much hated. Just as in the Middle Ages the townspeople of Mainz, Toledo, Worms, and York, watching Jews being burned, could not help despising and fearing people who provoked so much odium, so in 1943

From *The New York Review of Books*, March 19, 1964, pp. 1–3.

even many a patriot in the resistance was exasperated by the sufferings of the Jews—who were always the same and whose sufferings were the same, and who were so bewildered yet fatalistic as they were mown down in the hundreds, with their babies, by a single machine gunner smoking a cigarette. How could you identify with people who suffered so much and had no friendly Polish neighbors to escape to? How could you help drawing away from what the S.S. professors, watching an "action," fastidiously (and in Latin) called "the asshole of the world?"

Suffering can make people disgusting. The people whose martyrdom was called an "extermination," even to the destruction of a million of their children, made them not objects of compassion, but a disease to stay away from. The Nazis made it easy for the majority to stay away, to look away, to hold their noses, to shrug their shoulders. All very natural—if you gag at the viscera of a dog some passing car has ripped open on the highway, what would you feel at all those mounds of human hair, gold teeth, children's toys smeared with excrement and blood?

The sufferings of the Jews made them unbearable—and this was the war that the Nazis won. Of course there were many individuals throughout Eu- /1/ rope, and even a whole people, the Danes, who were not sickened by Jewish suffering, who felt the terror of children as an outrage to Christianity, who saw that "Europe," "the West," "the free world," "the Church," could become empty terms if it were permitted to shovel the Jews out like so much dirt. The Polish priest Maximilian Kolbe took another man's place in one of the "starvation cells" at Auschwitz and died after weeks of agony. Provost Lichtenberg, of St. Hedwig's Cathedral in Berlin, prayed openly for the Jews, asked to accompany deportees to camp, and died on his way to Dachau. A Catholic editor in Bologna, Focherini, lost all seven of his children in a camp because he was active in saving Italian Jews. Many of the lower clergy in France and Holland conspired to save Jews, and saved hundreds. But millions were killed, and it is doubtful that whole communities, towns, districts would have been wiped out if the American government, the British government, the Vatican, had not been able to bear with equanimity the destruction of so many civilians who were not Americans, British, or Catholic. Of course the reasons of state given for their inaction by the heads of state were entirely tenable and normal—as normal as Chamberlain's refusal, as Prime Minister, even to look at the reports of Nazi atrocities sent to him by British diplomats in Germany. Roosevelt had smart diplomatic reasons for not performing any extraordinary action. Pius XII saw no reason to confuse the millions of German Catholics fighting for Hitler. In the face of the total terror against all the Jews—every Jew in the world was marked for destruction—*Realpolitik* paid off. And soon the "normal" world came back. By now many a German civil servant, professor, doctor, policeman, judge, must wonder if he was really he who one day in 1944 drove children into a pit to be shot, who watched the naked women screaming for twenty minutes as the gas came on.

Yet obviously this effort to reclaim "normalcy" and "good sense" has not worked for everyone. Although life is rich in West Germany and Chancellor Erhard fits even better into a Texas barbecue than the late President Kennedy would have done, the Germans don't seem to achieve "normal" status. Herr Adenauer was the very quintessence of a good German mayor, but he was always being embarrassed by associates like Dr. Globke, who did nothing but frame the Nuremburg race laws. The other day it developed that Herr Erhard's Refugee Minister, Dr. Hans Kruger, had been a Nazi judge in Poland.

Then the chief of Herr Erhard's own security guard, Herr Peters, who had flown down to the LBJ ranch to guard his boss, was identified as the member of a murder squad in wartime Russia, and took his life to save the government further embarrassment. The Germans would love to get back to "normal" life and to be unequivocally trusted by their allies in NATO, but all sorts of young Germans themselves, like Rolf Hochhuth (born in 1931), are outraged by the claim to bourgeois respectability on the part of so many people who twenty years ago were robbing, torturing and killing all over Europe.

It is rage against the unbearable moral obtuseness of the German philistine, now restored to the complacent gluttony of the good old days plus the self-righteousness of "the free world," that is obviously behind Hochhuth's play. What the author must have said to himself was: How can I attack hypocritical "authority" at its most vulnerable point? How can I shake these symbols of a moral tradition that no longer exists? Who was the one leader during the war whose *Realpolitik* symbolizes more than any other's the moral failure of *Europe* during the war? The Vicar of Jesus Christ on earth, the "deputy" and "representative" of Christ, the Pope . . . Pius XII. Not once did he condemn the massacre of the Jews specifically and by name. He did not speak out even when Italian Jews (many of them baptized Catholics) were being rounded up under the Pope's very windows. He never once ordered priests to pray for the Jews. He never saw to it that spiritual aid was given to the Catholics of Jewish origin (many of them priests and nuns) transported to the camps. He never threatened (as even his predecessor had done before the war) to break the Concordat with Hitler. He never even threatened to excommunicate Hitler, Goebbels, Himmler, and other Nazi leaders who had been baptized as Catholics. /2/

Hochhuth's calculated provocation has worked. Pope Paul VI, when still Cardinal Montini, was moved to special remonstrances against Hochhuth; his defense of Pius XII was included in each programme at the London production of *The Deputy* and was repeated during his brief stay in Israel. The play has aroused violent protests from members of the Bundestag, the German hierarchy, theater audiences in Vienna and Paris—in Paris some members of the audience, crying *A bas les juifs!*, leaped to the stage and tried to keep the actors from going on—and American Jewish organizations, which sought to dissuade Herman Shumlin from putting the play on after Billy Rose had dropped it. In answer to Hochhuth, whose play charges Pius XII with indifference to the Jews, it has been pointed out that many Jews were given refuge in monasteries, that priests and nuns risked their lives to save Jews, that the Pope once offered Vatican funds to meet the Nazi demand for ransom. None of these points answers to Hochhuth's main charge—he is not attacking the Catholic Church and his work is even dedicated to Father Kolbe and to Prior Lichtenberg. And he rejects Cardinal Montini's claim that Pius XII wanted to protest the atrocities suffered by the Jews, but was silent for fear that he would bring worse down on them. What would have been worse?

Hochhuth offers us both a documented play and a documentary of the times. He makes extremely serious charges in the play and in his historical notes, and so invites the counter-charges that inevitably make up discussion of the play. Yet that is the kind of play it is. It is not a work of art, not a transmutation into imaginative symbols. It is a tract in dramatic form that attempts to humanize what C. P. Snow called "the worst episode in human history"; it is a dramatization of "reality," a vast script out of which different productions can be made and have been made. It is probably impossible, and even intolerable, to fit Auschwitz to the common scale and moral satisfactions of a work of art. Hochhuth's script — humane, polemical, "daring" — was captive to the delusion that anything can be put on the stage and explained on the stage long before he sat down to write. But for a young German writer, there is a spiritual necessity in at least trying to cut through the silence that prevails between the Jews and the Germans. Hitler Germany is the nightmare from which we are all trying to awaken. A German writer who was fourteen years old in 1945 must go down into that hell if he wants to write anything meaningful about his country and his people in the future. I salute Hochhuth for not shirking that journey into hell, for seeking to understand himself in the light of modern German history.

Hochhuth's whole effort here, it seems to me, is to make a dramatic kaleidoscope that will involve people now in the fate of the Jews as it couldn't and didn't involve them before. But as a playwright of the whole Nazi terror, as a documentary maker in dramatic form, he's been too appalled, disturbed and even fascinated by the cruelties of the Nazis even to be able to think of events and people as figures in his own imagination. Piscator, who did the Berlin production, claims in his pretentious preface to the German text that the play has links with Schiller's historical dramas, which Piscator sees as a type of "dramatic novel." And it is true that Hochhuth, whose characters speak in vaguely rhythmic lines that are meant to recall dramatic verse, has put Pius XII and other recent historic personages into some kind of costume drama; he wants to create an effect of historical "art" around the terrible facts. But his play is too eclectic, it is too consciously truth and fiction at once, to suggest anything more moving than his own struggle with these materials.

Hochhuth's "book" has left his producers with so many possibilities and freedoms that it is no wonder that the Berlin and London productions emphasized different sides of it, and that the New York production is sharply different from the others. Shumlin has freely adapted the play, virtually cutting Kurt Gerstein out of it, and has added passages of his own, some of which plainly depart from Hochhuth's own voice. The New York production is bare, crude, and shockingly listless in places; much of it is an anti-Nazi movie of the John Garfield period. If it weren't for Emlyn William's venomously stylized performance in Act II as Pius XII, and the sheer unavoidable horror of the truth as it comes through by the end, the New York production would be amazingly dull. (Most of the excitement opening night came from the American Nazis noisily picketing the play. The audience was asked not to leave the theater during intermission, which was more of a shock than it got from the first act.)

As a "book," complete with sixty pages of historical documentary and stage directions that are understandable assurances that a play about murder factories is possible but should not be taken as "the whole truth," Hochhuth's work lends itself to the most tendentious kind of Broadway production. There are just too many characters, scenes, comments, charges, notes. It opens in the house of the Papal Nuncio to Berlin, when an heroic "spy" in the S.S., Kurt Gerstein (another real person), breaks in to beg the Nuncio to get the Vatican to protest against the murder factories. It ends in Auschwitz, with the unnamed Doctor who assigned the victims directly to the gas chambers debating God's silence with the young Jesuit who, anguished by the Vatican's silence, put a yellow star of David on his soutane and accompanied Jews to Auschwitz. Between these two scenes of direct historical reference, we are taken to Berlin for rapid glimpses of Eichmann living it up in the company of a Rhineland industrialist, mapping Krupp's future holdings in Russia, a Nazi "scientist" who collects Jewish-Bolshevist skulls for his anatomical collection, and other such charmers out of a horror film; we are in Rome to hear a Cardinal defend the Pope's silence to a Papal court; we attend as Pius XII heatedly defends his policy while Jews are being rounded up in Rome by Nazi policemen who are now amiable bureaucrats in Bonn.

So all the oppressors and victims and onlookers are represented in the play, and everything is made—how Hochhuth would like to make it—believable, actable, dramatic, moving. If in design Hochhuth's play *is* costume drama (Rome: a palace . . . The Vatican: the Pope's chambers), in language it is very like the "living theater" of the 1930s. The "rhythmic" lines are *not* prose only in the sense that they allow a character to give us information in "spoken" form—

> *One million eight hundred thousand Jews*
> *in Poland alone*
> *have been murdered already—and since this figure*
> *was given officially to the Papal Legate*
> *in Washington this July by the Ambassador*
> *from Warsaw to the White House . . .*

But the tone is not right: *no* tone is right for this kind of thing on the stage. Hochhuth moves up to Auschwitz, in the last act, full of fear and trembling for his own presumption; but he does think he can put it on the stage and make it dramatically swallowable. So we can hate "The Doctor"—based on Joseph Mengele, who made the final selection of the victims, and who is still at large—as this mad scientist boasts about "whistling Freud's sister up the chimney," or shows the brains of a pair of Jewish twins, or tells the Jesuit that he has put endless Jews to death so as to "provoke" God to answer.

Of course Hochhuth doesn't really understand this "Doctor," who in Elie Wiesel's memoir of Auschwitz, *La Nuit*, is remembered as pointing out his victims with a *conductor's baton*. These Auschwitz scenes, with their attempt to give the Doctor a pseudo-theological and very "German" rationale in philosophy for his frightful crimes, are pretentious and false. The bitter truth, the ultimate humiliation for us humanists and anti-Nazis, is that the "Doctor" was not a theologian, not a false theologian, not even an anti-theologian, but a sadistic clown, a frivolous maniac and gangster. That is the horror for us, who for thirty years now have tried to make Hitlerism accountable to our humane culture—the horror is that so many frivolous, hysterical, ignorant, *trivial* people could have captured the hearts of millions of Germans and have killed millions of human beings for reasons no more "significant" and "historical" than their own murderous vanity and rage. One is now supposed to honor Napoleon for the millions of deaths he caused because he was the vehicle of historical progress. In the case of Hitler and his gang, no delusion is possible. Like the boy who stabbed an enemy in a gang war and as he took the knife out, said to the corpse, "Thanks very much!", Hitler operated on the weakness of his victims and the fear he inspired in the outlookers. He had no serious historical ideas, no tenable hopes. All those millions died to the frenzy of murdering gangsters. They died *meaninglessly*. And how do you make art out of what is inherently meaningless, was never a contest? Nowhere has totalitarianism as a climate, or totalitarianism as a subject, been able to produce a work of art. What it does provoke, from the millions ground down in our time by the Moloch of "History" or "Race," is occasional personal testimony. The victims alone can testify to the power of these murderous abstractions. Their own existence is the moral authenticity they have saved from the encompassing conformism and cruelty.

Hochhuth's polemic is irrefutable on one point. If it was all for nothing, if this was a massacre of the helpless and the innocent that in the end became as horrible in its felt insignificance as any industrial process, shouldn't those who believe that God is present in history, that He once came to earth as man — shouldn't they have protested against so much frivolity and meaninglessness — not in love for the Jews, but in defense of Christianity itself? On August 23, 1942, Archbishop Saliège cried out in Toulouse — "Why does the right of asylum no longer exist in our churches? Why are we a vanquished people? Lord, have pity upon us! Our Lady, pray for France! These Jews are men, these Jewesses are women; these aliens are men and women. All is not permissible against them, against these men and women, against these fathers and mothers. They belong to mankind. They are our brothers, as are so many others. No Christian can forget that."

What would have happened in Europe in 1943, 1944, 1945, when Jews were being killed at the rate of a thousand an hour — how many children would have been saved from the fire — if the Vicar of Christ on earth had said that? /3/

Emile Capouya

CRY AGAINST A DECISION OF SILENCE

This interesting play had a stormy reception in Germany and France, and at its opening in New York was picketed by various persons — all of whom had read the play, no doubt, or at least had heard of someone who had read it. We might as well deal at once with the so-called controversial aspects of the drama. I say so-called because I find it hard to believe that they can sustain any genuine controversy, inasmuch as they are either matters of historic record, such as the supineness of the Vatican in its relations with Hitler, or else characterizations of personages in the play (some of them clerical personages) and ascriptions of motive to them — and that, I had always imagined, is the playwright's business.

Since the author deals with historical facts, he has some responsibility to represent them fairly. After all, we don't want him to falsify our sense of reality. Mr. Rolf Hochhuth has exhibited a very German thoroughness in that connection, for the text of the American edition of the play is followed by an appendix, quoting the journals, memoirs, and historical studies upon which he drew in creating his characters and incidents. As it happens, I had occasion to look up some thirty of Mr. Hochhuth's references, and I found that in those instances he quoted very fairly indeed, in no way misleading the reader about the significance of his citations in their original context. The playwright has the further responsibility, in a historical drama, of ascribing motives to his characters that have some relation to the actions chronicled in the historical record. In dealing with his ecclesiastical characters, including the play's hero

"Cry Against a Decision of Silence," *Saturday Review*, March 21, 1964, pp. 41–42.

and martyr, Father Riccardo Fontana, Mr. Hochhuth has fulfilled that responsibility; the persons of his drama are as humanly believable as persons engaged in extraordinary actions can well be.

Audiences, and readers, must certainly wince at the scene in which Pope Pius XII is represented as hesitating between two evils, the sacrifice of the Jews destined to be murdered wholesale by Hitler, and the sacrifice of the Church's worldly interests. In a scene that reminds one irresistibly of Shylock's "My ducats! My daughter!," the Pope is shown dictating a mild and equivocal reproof, addressed to the man who is burning Jews, Poles, Gypsies, Catholic priests, and other undesirables, and then he is shown consulting with his financial adviser about the fate of certain investments threatened by the Nazi reverses in Russia. But the Papal message referred to is, in all its inadequacy, a matter of history. And does anyone suppose that the Church does not have investments? Does it malign the Church to suggest that it pays reasonable attention to its investments? Of course not. Rather, the shock that this scene generates comes from the direct suggestion that the Holy See considered the death of millions of people to be of secondary importance to its own temporal security, which can be symbolized for dramatic purposes by investments, or in plain English, money. But that is just what the Vatican's historic choice amounted to, and if Pius XII did not in fact take up the two matters of the Nazi victims and the safety of the Church's investments in the course of a single morning, that is, historically speaking, neither here nor there. Dramatically speaking, it is of the first importance that the two activities be represented at the same time, so that we can learn something about the nature of sin.

The reason offered by the Church for its failure to intervene directly and unequivocally in the murders done in the concentration camps—say, by a threat to denounce the Concordat with Hitler, or to excommunicate any Catholic who participated in torturing, gassing, and burning men, women, and children in the camps—is that higher spiritual interests of universal scope demanded that the Vatican put its temporal security before every other consideration. Unfortunately, that is an excellent reason. It is so good an excuse that men resort to it before any other when they wish to justify acting badly in the extreme crises of life. The Church's moral position on this issue is even a little ahead of that of the governments of the United States and Great Britain, which made no real protest to Hitler between 1933 and 1940, and thereafter did only such things as suited their presumed military interests, including the demand for unconditional surrender; those governments have scarcely troubled to justify their position, while the Church has. For that matter, why did Americans not instruct their government to act properly? It's a free country, isn't it? Why did no American Jews threaten an organized protest against their government's indifference? In all these cases, the answer is the same: because they put other considerations ahead of the agony of millions of their fellow human beings.

It has been argued that Mr. Hochhuth has distorted history by concentrating so heavily on the Church's culpability. That is true but impertinent. He has indeed failed to indict all the parties to the concentration camp and extermination camp murders, except in passing and by implication, singling out instead the German nation and the Vatican. But that is already a subject of a size to tax a playwright, and I do not see how he could be asked to expand it to include every guilty person or group. Moreover, by talking about the Germans and the Vatican, Mr. Hochhuth focuses our attention on the moral es-

sence of the problem. He opposes the spirit of murder to the spirit of Chris-
/41/ tian love, and discovers—to our horror—that in this century Christian
love knowingly yielded to the spirit of murder. That is the point of the play; it
is an important point; it is true. It is still true. And I refer not to one priest's
decision that you may forcibly resist your neighbor's attempt to claim sanctuary
in your fallout shelter, but to the preparations that the great powers have
made and are making to murder mankind—with no effective protest from
labor unions, clergymen, or missile manufacturers.

It is hard to form an opinion of the purely literary merit of the play from
the English text. The lines read easily enough, but they are in verse, and the
verse is not distinguished. I do not know whether this is true of the German
original, but no shame attaches to the translators, Clara and Richard Winston,
in any case, for it is always an accident if verse can be successfully translated.
Clearly, the scenes are conceived with great theatrical imagination. There is
the hotel cellar where Nazi officials resort for beer and bowling, the audience
chamber of Pius XII, and nightmare scenes in Auschwitz. But at climactic
moments of the play, when the language should carry the tension, it fails to
do so—at least for a reader. How the lines sound in the theater is, of course,
another matter, and to determine that we must see the play.

Aside from any question of transcendent literary value, is the play effective
when read? On the whole, enormously so, but with disappointing lapses in
which the reader's good will and historical imagination are all that hold it
together. Statistics concerning the brutalities practiced by the Germans are
presented by the characters on many occasions; these are hard enough to
assimilate in real life, and on the stage their effect is numbing and, eventually, monotonous. One scene strikes me as extraneous to the organic shape of
the play, though it is moving enough in itself—the one in which a family of
Italian Jews, preparing to flee to a monastery, are prevented from doing so by
the arrival of an SS man and two Italian militiamen, who take them away for
eventual extermination. And one crucial character is, for me, imperfectly
realized.

History records a doctor who was charged with selecting from among the
new arrivals at Auschwitz the people who would be worked to death and
those who would be murdered at once. Apparently, he was a man of parts,
gallant to ladies and kindly with children. Mr. Hochhuth has decided that he
must have been the Devil, which seems reasonable. But his Mephisthophelean
doings on Mr. Hochhuth's stage do not, on the whole, impress me. He se-
duces and humiliates women, he holds theological disputations with the martyred Father Riccardo, and he kills people. But he is disappointing as the Evil
One. It seems to me that I have known mere human beings who could have
done as well as the Doctor in thought and deed, if they had had his opportunities. It may be that this role can reveal itself only when played by an actor of
great force. In any case, it eluded me in the study.

To judge hastily—for the play is still young in our imagination—*The Deputy*
fails as drama to the extent that it succeeds as preaching. Art is usually more
effective when less direct; Mr. Hochhuth's artistic attitude is more like William
Lloyd Garrison's than William Shakespeare's. Possibly, though, this is a case
where moral intensity does as well as art, and moral intensity Mr. Hochhuth
certainly has. The words *"Mit brennender Sorge"* seem more appropriate to him
than to their famous author. In any event, I have no doubt that *The Deputy* is
the most important recent drama now being played on any stage in the Western world. /42/

Susan Sontag

ALL THE WORLD'S A STAGE

The supreme tragic event of modern times is the murder of the six million European Jews. In a time which has not lacked in tragedies, this event most merits the unenviable honor for reasons of magnitude, unity of theme, historical meaningfulness and sheer opaqueness. No one really understands. For the event cannot be wholly accounted for either in terms of passions, private or public, or of error or of madness, or of moral failure or of overwhelming and irresistible social forces. Some 20 years after, there is more controversy about it than ever. What happened? How did it happen? How could it have been allowed to happen? Who are responsible? This great event is a wound that will not heal; even the balm of intelligibility is denied to us.

Yet, if we did know more, that would not suffice. In saying this event was "tragic," we allow other demands than those for factual historical understanding. By tragic, I mean an event—piteous and terrifying in the extreme—whose causation is super-charged and over-determined, and which is of an exemplary or edifying nature that imposes a solemn duty upon the survivors to confront and assimilate it. In calling the murder of the six million a tragedy, we acknowledge a motive beyond the intellectual (knowing what happened and how) or the moral (catching the criminals and bringing them to justice) for comprehending it. We acknowledge that the event is, in some sense, incomprehensible. Ultimately, the only response is to continue to hold the event in mind, to remember it. This capacity to assume the burden of memory is not always practical. Sometimes remembering alleviates grief or guilt; sometimes it makes it worse. Often, it may not do any good to remember. But we may feel that it is *right*, or fitting, or proper. This moral function of remembering is something that cuts across the different worlds of knowledge, action and art.

We live in a time in which tragedy is not an art form but a form of history. Dramatists no longer write tragedies. But we do have works of art (not always recognized as such) which reflect or attempt to resolve the great historical tragedies of our time. Among the unacknowledged art forms which have been devised or perfected in the modern era for this purpose are the psychoanalytic therapy, the parliamentary debate, the political rally, and the political trial. If then the supreme tragic event of modern times is the murder of the six million European Jews, the most interesting and moving work of art of the past ten years is the trial of Adolf Eichmann in Jerusalem in 1961.

As Hannah Arendt and others have pointed out, the juridical basis of the Eichmann trial, the relevance of all the evidence presented and the legitimacy of certain procedures are open to question on strictly legal grounds. But the truth is that the Eichmann trial did not, and could not, have conformed to legal standards only. It was not Eichmann alone who was on trial. He stood trial in a double role: as both the particular and the generic; both the man, laden with hideous specific guilt, and the cipher, standing for the whole history of anti-Semitism, which climaxed in this unimaginable martyrdom.

The trial was thus an occasion for attempting to make comprehensible the incomprehensible. To this end, while the impassive bespectacled Eichmann sat in his bullet-proof glass cage—tight-lipped, but for all that like one of the

"All the World's a Stage," *Book Week*, March 1, 1964, pp. 1, 12–13.

great shrieking but unheard creatures from the paintings of Francis Bacon — a great collective dirge was enacted in the courtroom. Masses of facts about the extermination of the Jews were piled into the record; a great outcry of historical agony was set down. There was, needless to say, no strictly legal way of justifying this. The function of the trial was rather that of the tragic drama: above and beyond judgment and punishment, catharsis.

The very modern feeling for due process which the trial appealed to was also genuine, but the ancient connections between the theater and the courtroom went deeper. The trial is preeminently a theatrical form (in fact, the very first account in history of a trial comes from the drama — it is in the third play, "The Eumenides," of Aeschylus' trilogy, "The Oresteia"). And as the trial is preeminently a theatrical form, the theater is a courtroom. The classical form of the drama is always a contest between protagonist and antagonist; the resolution of the play is the "verdict" on the action. All the great stage tragedies take this form of a trial of the protagonist — the peculiarity of the tragic form of judgment being that it is possible to lose the case (i.e., be condemned, suffer, die) and somehow triumph nonetheless.

The Eichmann trial was such a drama. It was not the tragedy itself, but the attempt, dramatically, to deal with and resolve the tragedy. It was, in the profoundest sense, theater. And, as such, it must be judged by other criteria in addition to those of legality and of morality. Because its purposes were not simply those of a historical inquest into the facts, an attempt to determine guilt and affix punishment, the trial of Eichmann did not always "work." But the problem of the Eichmann trial was not its deficient legality, but the contradiction between its juridical form and its dramatic function. As Harold Rosenberg has pointed out, "The Trial undertook the function of tragic poetry, that of making the pathetic and terrifying past live again in the mind. But it had to carry out this function on a world stage ruled by the utilitarian code." There was a fundamental paradox in the Eichmann trial: it was primarily a great act of commitment through memory and the renewal of grief, yet it clothed itself in the forms of legality and scientific objectivity. The trial is a dramatic form which imparts to events a certain provisional neutrality; the outcome remains to be decided; the very word "defendant" implies that a defense is possible. In this sense, though Eichmann, as everyone expected, was condemned to death, the form of the trial favored Eichmann. Perhaps this is why some feel in retro- /1/ spect, that the trial was a frustrating experience, an anticlimax.

It remains to be seen if art of a more easily recognizable type — art which need not pretend to be neutral — can do better. By far the most celebrated of all the works of art which take up the same functions of historical memory served by the Eichmann trial is "The Deputy" *(Der Stellvertreter)*, the lengthy play by the young German playwright Rolf Hochhuth, performed throughout Europe this past year to the regular accompaniment of riots in the theaters. . . .

Here we have a work of art as we ordinarily understand it — a work for the familiar theater of 8:30 curtains and intermissions, rather than for the austere public stage of the courtroom. Here there are actors, rather than real murderers and real survivors from hell. Yet it is not false to compare it with the Eichmann trial, because "The Deputy" is first of all a documentary work. Eichmann himself and many other real persons of the period are represented in the play; the speeches of the characters are drawn from historical records.

In modern times, this use of the theater as a forum for public, moral judgment has been shunted aside. The theater has largely become a place in which private quarrels and agonies are staged; the verdict which events render upon characters in most modern plays has no relevance beyond the play itself. "The Deputy" completely breaks with the private boundaries of the modern theater. And as it would be obtuse to refuse to evaluate the Eichmann trial as a public work of art, it would be frivolous to judge "The Deputy" simply as a work of art.

Some art—but not all—elects as its central purpose *to tell the truth;* and it must be judged by its fidelity to the truth, and by the relevance of the truth which it tells. By these standards, "The Deputy" is an extremely important play. The case against the Nazi party, the SS, the German business elite, and most of the German people—none of which is slighted by Hochhuth—is too well known to need anyone's assent. But "The Deputy" also stresses—and this is the controversial part of the play—a strong case for responsibility against the German Catholic Church and against Pope Pius XII. This case I am convinced is true, and well taken. (See the ample documentation which Hochhuth has provided at the end of the play, and the excellent article by Guenter Lewy, "Pius XII, the Jews, and the German Catholic Church," in the February issue of Commentary.) And the importance—historical and moral—of this difficult truth at this time cannot be overestimated.

Let me repeat: "The Deputy" is a documentary play. In a preface (unfortunately not translated) to the German edition of the play, the famous director Erwin Piscator, who gave "The Deputy" its first production in Berlin, wrote that he saw Hochhuth's play as a successor to the historical dramas of Shakespeare and Schiller and the epic theater of Brecht. All questions of quality aside, these comparisons—with the classical historical drama and with epic theater when it deals with historical subjects—are misleading. It is the whole point of Hochhuth's play that he has barely transformed his material. Unlike the plays of Shakespeare or Schiller or Brecht, the play of Hochhuth stands or falls by its fidelity to the complete historical truth.

This documentary intention of the play also indicates its limitations. The fact is that as not all works of art aim at educating and directing conscience, not all works of art which do have a moral function entirely satisfy as art. I can think of only one work of art of the type of "The Deputy"—an act of historical memory of the tragedy of the six million—the short film "Night and Fog" *(Nuit et Brouillard)* by Alain Resnais, which satisfies equally as a moral act and as a work of art. "Night and Fog" is short, highly selective, emotionally relentless, historically scrupulous, and—if the word seems not outrageous—beautiful. "The Deputy" is not a beautiful play. Nor does one necessarily ask that it be. Nevertheless, if I can assume the immense interest and moral importance of the play, the aesthetic questions need to be faced. There is the matter of length, for example. I don't find "The Deputy's" length objectionable. Probably it is, indeed, one of those works of art—like the novels of Dreiser, the operas of Wagner, the plays of O'Neill—which positively benefit from their outlandish length. .

Nevertheless, whatever "The Deputy" may be as a moral event, it is not playwriting of the highest order. One reason is the style—a colorless but correct German arranged in blank verse form on the page. The language of this English version is flat, neither formal nor truly idiomatic. ("The Legion is extraterritorial—be off with you / Or I'll send for the police.") Hochhuth may have put his lines in blank verse to emphasize the seriousness of his subject, or to reveal the banality of Nazi rhetoric. But I can't imagine any plausible way.

of *speaking* these lines which convey the effect (either one) that Hochhuth intended. A greater fault is the thick chunks of documentation which Hochhuth has piled into the play. Much of the play as written reads as an elaborate casebook in dramatic form. It is clogged with information.

There are, to be sure, a number of extremely powerful scenes, particularly those involving the demonic SS Doctor. Yet the fact remains that one of the principal and recurrent—and almost, by nature, undramatic—reasons for characters confronting one another in a scene is that of *informing each other of something.* Hundreds of names, facts, statistics, reports of conversations, items of current news are crowded into the speeches. To read "The Deputy"—I have not yet seen it performed—is an exhausting, an overwhelming, and a tremendously moving experience. But this is, I believe, because of the supreme importance of its content—not because of its style or dramaturgy, both of which are extremely conventional.

I imagine that "The Deputy" could, of course, be completely satisfying on the stage. But its effectiveness on the stage places an unusual burden upon the director. A good production of "The Deputy," I would think, must be tense and stylized and modern—not overly realistic or ideological. Hochhuth himself has provided one of the best ideas for stylization. In listing the characters in the play, he has made certain groupings of those who appear in only one scene; all the roles in a single grouping are to be played by the same actor. Thus the same actor is to play both Pope Pius XII and Baron Rutta of the Reich's Armament Cartel. In another grouping the same actor is to play a Father in the Papal Legation; Witzel, an SS sergeant, and a Jewish Kapo. "For recent history," Hochhuth explains, "has taught us that in the age of universal military conscription it is not necessarily to anyone's credit or blame, or even a question of character, which uniform one wears or whether one stands on the side of the victims or the executioners." Apart from the ironic, very modern statement of the interchangeability of historical and personal roles, this seems to be an excellent theatrical idea. Along the same lines, in Peter Brook's production of the play in Paris, the actors all wear identical blue cotton suits, over which, when identification is needed, are slipped the cardinal's scarlet coat, the priest's soutane, the Nazi officer's swastika armband, and so on.

A final point. The play has caused riots in Berlin, Paris, London, almost everywhere it has been performed, because it depicts (not just reports) the late Pope Pius XII refusing to use the influence of the Catholic Church and oppose, either openly or through private diplomatic channels, the Nazi Final Solution.

There is reason to believe such protests by the Church might have had some efficacy. When the German Catholic Church strongly opposed Hitler's euthanasia program for the elderly and incurably ill Aryans /12/ —the trial run for the Final Solution of the Jewish Problem—it was stopped. The Vatican had made strong pronouncements on such public issues as the Russian invasion of Finland. And there are documents which indicate that the Pope, like many conservative European rulers of the time, did approve of Hitler's war against Russia and for that reason did not want to actively oppose the German government. For this scene in particular, Hochhuth's play has been slandered by many Catholics as an anti-Catholic tract. But either what Hochhuth reports is true or it is not. And, assuming that Hochhuth has his facts (and his notion of Christian courage) right, a good Catholic is no more bound to defend all the actions of Pius XII than he is to admire the libertine Popes of the Renaissance. Dante, whom no one would accuse of being anti-Catholic, consigned Celestine V to hell. Why may not a modern Christian—Hochhuth is a Protestant—argue that it is not the Pope but the Berlin provost, Bernard Lichtenberg (who publicly prayed for the Jews from his pulpit and volunteered to accompany the Jews to Dachau), or the Franciscan monk, Father Maximilian Kolbe (who died hideously in Auschwitz), who is the true Deputy, the true Vicar of Christ.

In any case, the attack on the Pope is scarcely the only subject of "The Deputy." A great deal depends on the selection that a director and adaptor will make from a printed text, which would run some eight hours if performed in full. The Pope appears in only one scene of the play. The story is centered on the two heroes—the Jesuit priest Riccardo Fontana (mainly based on Provost Lichtenberg, with something of Father Kolbe) and the remarkable Kurt Gerstein, who joined the SS in order to gather facts to bring to the attention of the Papal Nuncio in Berlin. Hochhuth has not placed Gerstein and Fontana (Lichtenberg) in any "grouping," lumping them with other persons to be played by the same actor. There is nothing interchangeable about these men. Thus, the main point that "The Deputy" wishes to make is not a recriminatory one. It is not an attack on the hierarchy of the German Catholic Church and the Pope and his advisors, but a statement that absolute honor and decency—though it may entail martyrdom—are possible, and mandatory for a Christian. It is precisely because Hochhuth shows us persons who have chosen, that he has a right to accuse the others who refused to choose, to speak out, of an unforgivable cowardice. /13/

Wilfrid Sheed

THE DEPUTY

To discuss "The Deputy" simply as a play would be like being the only person in Philadelphia who doesn't read the _Bulletin._ Aesthetically there is no precise language for dealing with a melodrama which uses live ammunition; historically speaking all the bodies on the stage are still warm; and Mr. Hochhuth himself follows his play around the world in person making sure that nobody fails to hiss the villian.

It is an extraordinary pilgrimage, this odyssey of Hochhuth, and the usual limits of play-criticism seem altogether too small for it. Mr. Hochhuth probably knows this better than anybody. When Walter Kerr gave the play a painstakingly judicious review, Hochhuth said, in effect, why doesn't Mr. Kerr come out and tell us he is a Catholic? Why does he pretend to be impartial? (Incidentally if Hochhuth's marginal comments could be reduced to a system, they would go something like this: "The Deputy" is not anti-Catholic, but no Catholic can possibly judge it fairly; the Pope is a great moral leader to whom we all turn—but since he believes in an after-life, nothing can be expected of him either, and so on.)

I believe Mr. Hochhuth is right about impartiality. But, by one of those small lapses of sensibility that have also enabled him to ask why New York allows storm-troopers in its streets, and to discredit the motives of one of our more distinguished play-reviewers, I believe he has managed to over-simplify the varieties of Catholic prejudice.

"The Deputy," _Jubilee_ April 1964, pp. 25–26.

Many Catholics—especially those likely to be reviewing plays—actually start out with a bias in favor of the play. There are several good and bad reasons for this. To begin with, Pius XII is a type that has gone completely out of style. A few years ago, he was a lot of people's idea of a good man. His asceticism was not held against him, and neither was his rather flowery rhetoric. Hochhuth considers the rhetoric particularly damning; but those of us who were raised on pastoral letters know that it is only old-fashioned ecclesiastical rhetoric, which does not in the least preclude genuine feeling—although, like rancid romanticism in general, it is easily used for faking it.

Nowadays, Pius XII is also called an aristocrat, as if that were the last word in abuse, as if nothing decent could be expected of such a man; and he is called a mystic and a diplomat, other bad words of the moment. He is, in short, a victim of fashion, and no better moment could have been chosen to attack him. (Nineteenth-century piety certainly was a bad fashion in many ways, as ornate and stylized as bad nineteenth-century architecture, but to proceed as though Pius XII invented and monopolized it is to lack any sense of period.)

But beyond personal considerations, many Catholics have long felt uneasy about belonging to such an apparently top-heavy political organism. A freakish pressure is put on one man, instead of being shared by the whole body. The response of the Church to a political situation should be the response of its people, not the response of one representative. If, as Hochhuth seems to believe, a protest from the Pope is the only kind of Catholic protest that means anything anymore, it can only be that the nature of the Church has become seriously distorted: so that people can see and hear only one Catholic. Furthermore, if this lop-sided emphasis on the papacy has led us to the point where Pius XII must stand scapegoat for the whole of Christendom, it may be just as well to have a play that points out the brutal consequences.

Yet one more reason for bias in the play's favor is that many Catholics would genuinely like to share in the guilt of the Jewish massacres. This sounds dilettante—it is very much "in" to feel guilty these days—but it is in fact deadly serious. The complicity of Catholics in anti-Semitism is one of those nagging things that never quite seems to get shaken off; it was part of the climate in which Hitler functioned—and even after Hitler, you still find Catholics who don't take the gas-ovens very seriously, who feel that the Jews have made rather too much fuss about them (in fairness, it might be added that the English, after four hundred years of persecution, commonly have the same feeling about the Irish). The liberal Catholic wants to feel guilty for two; he wants to feel guilty for every anti-Jewish wisecrack he has ever tolerated, for every insipid Catholic response to Hitler and his Final Solution, for every failure to realize that, while the Pope is indeed Christ's vicar, the persecuted are Christ. /25/

So all in all, Mr. Hochhuth had quite a lot going for him. The goon-squads with the placards were only part of the story. There are more shades of Catholic opinion than Mr. Hochhuth may be aware of. If he has alienated potential Catholic supporters, he has done so entirely on his own merits. If he had merely written a vacuous play, he might have kept them. The theme does a great deal of his work for him. The night after I saw it (this is the kind of information that is usually not worth handing on), I dreamed about storm-troopers. The SS has become a mythic archetype of horror. Hochhuth's version of the SS is comparatively mild—yet even so, it penetrates the world of dreams immediately.

The procession of Jewish victims is also extremely moving—although, thanks to Hochhuth's art, more so the first time than the second. With such scenes, the play can afford to be bad; it can afford to have its structure compressed from seven hours into two and a half—and to be turned into a spastic, shapeless melodrama in the process. But it cannot afford to be incredible: and this, for Catholics, however much they may wish to sympathize, the Deputy must finally be.

Unlike Jane Austen, who never wrote a scene in which only men were present, Hochhuth has written a major scene in which only priests are present— and what a scene. In a less solemn setting it would almost pass for comedy. The Pope, who is described in the author's notes as icily intelligent, turns out to be a trembling old fuddy-dud. The hero, in spite of having been through Jesuit boot-camp, is a callow effeminate hysteriac (the author's way of conveying genuine emotion is always to have his characters shriek and quiver, so this may mean less than I suppose.) The Pope's adviser is a sly, self-indulgent old fop, a comic-opera bishop of the old school—but here as elsewhere, it is not so much that these characters are silly as that they are silly in the wrong way. The most rabid anti-cleric would not accept them as priests at all.

The high-point of this scene, comically-speaking, arrives when the Pope, who has just been accused by the young Jesuit of the gravest crime there is, breaks into demented plainsong. Even those of us who have voiced reservations about the curial mentality have never pictured its members chanting away their troubles in quite this way; to find the icily intelligent Pope doing so is to abandon all belief, all sense of involvement. Whatever the Pope did, he didn't do that.

Inevitably the question comes up, what did the Pope do then? Mr. Hochhuth's notes, which by the way are far more interesting than his play, seem to make it clear that he knew what was being done to the Jews. The author makes a persuasive case that papal intervention would have helped the Jews— although one has to wonder how hollow Pius's rhetoric would have sounded if intervention had led in fact to further persecutions (more of this in a moment).

Hochhuth's notes on Pius XII himself are much less convincing. He cites unfavorable personal opinions as if they carried more weight than such opinions normally carry (no public figure would be safe, by this method). Pius XII has the misfortune anyway of being remembered most clearly in decline—the visions, the hiccoughs, a not very impressive exit—and Hochhuth's version of an icy, shrewd pseudo-mystic manages to blend the old man and the young one into a singularly unpleasant composite.

But vices should not be multiplied unnecessarily. It was said fairly often, even in his prime, that Pius experienced great difficulty in making decisions, and this may be close to the truth of the matter. The decision to denounce Hitler when the latter was in full paranoid cry would not have been an easy one for anyone to make; for a man with a tendency to neurotic indecisiveness, it must have been excruciatingly painful.

To suggest that it wasn't painful at all is simply slanderous. To suppose that Pius deliberately abandoned the Jews for the sake of financial profit is to take a funny view of aristocratic pseudo-mystics—although it fits well enough with self-seeking career diplomats, of course. (Turning him into a compendium of failings helps enormously in establishing motive.)

No doubt Pius XII was a complicated man and no doubt Mr. Hochhuth is not, and there are limits to how much the one can usefully say about the other. But the story remains a tragic one in several respects. There is something eery about the way in which the author follows his play everywhere like a bird of prey, making sure that no one forgives Pius, carrying on his vendetta against (pope or no pope) a dead man. But there may be a usefulness, too, in this weird crusade.

The papacy has been asked to perform two divergent roles: to speak for Christ, and to preside over the manifold concerns of the visible Church: to be a saint and to be a politician. These are superhuman demands to make of one man. Even if he has the greatness for both, there will be problems.

Consider it this way: supposing beyond a shadow of doubt that a denunciation by Pius would have led to further slaughter (Hochhuth jumps back and forth between arguments of principle and arguments of expedience, so there is no kind of answer to this hypothesis in the play). As the representative of Christ he must denounce evil come what may. We do not—especially after the event—want the Pope to be a politician first.

But if he had said the words, and brought on the slaughter, what would the survivors be saying of Pius XII today—this other-worldly mystic, sending other men to their deaths, while he sat in safety? What was a vaporing saint doing in a position of political responsibility in the first place? And what kind of play would Hochhuth have written about such an empty posturer?

It is possible to argue that that wasn't the situation. But it is at least as possible to argue that Pius XII thought it was. And that of course would be another tragedy—a tragedy concerning the whole structure and interpretation of the Church. In the period under consideration, Christ was believed, in the widest sense, to have only one representative on earth: and that one was not free to speak, owing to other obligations. /26/

Harold E. Fey

THE DEPUTY CONTROVERSY

Twenty-five years after Pius XII acceded to the papal throne he received a dubious anniversary tribute in the form of a controversy over his reputation. The dispute, as everyone must know by now, was touched off by the appearance in Germany of Rolf Hochhuth's play *The Deputy.**

Though the young German playwright has adduced no essentially new historical material, he has treated his theme so provocatively that Pius XII and his era are being re-examined with an intensity and a passion seldom accorded historical figures and events by the immediately succeeding generation. The mystery of the appeal of nazism, the motives of Hitler and his associates, the debauching of a generation—all these are being debated today in the hope that generations to come may avoid the demonism that blackens western Europe's record through the 1930's and 1940's. It is in the context of our continuing examination of that record that Hochhuth's drama must be viewed.

"The 'Deputy' Controversy," *The Christian Century*, April 22, 1964, pp. 507–508 (editorial).
*In Germany, *Der Stellvertreter;* in England, *The Representative.* For reviews and reports on the German production, see The Christian Century of August 7 and October 16, 1963. /507/

What part did Pius XII play in the moral fault of a civilization when by his relative silence he did little to place Hitlerism and the nazi extermination of central Europe's Jews on the conscience of the world? We could have hoped for a better instrument for our examination of the record than the play which has aroused so much comment in Europe, which opened in New York on February 26 and which in book form has become a best seller (Grove, $5.95).

It is a flawed drama. Most critics agree that the Broadway producers have excised many important motifs from the overlong free-verse play. Still, Hochhuth and his adapters have raised a major moral issue, and in so doing they have stirred the emotions of great numbers of people. In Europe the production has now and again been greeted with riots and sometimes with formal and strident Roman Catholic disapproval.

The New York production has been on the boards long enough for us to read a number of lessons from the controversy centering upon it. For one thing, its reception indicates a growing maturity in interfaith relations in this country. The brotherhood groups which have done so much to help that maturity come about have underestimated the degree of their own success. Some of them overplanned in their efforts to forestall potential interfaith tension which they feared might result from any play which could portray a pope so critically, only to find their fears groundless. The picketing of the theater has not been significant. And though official U.S. Catholicism has naturally been very critical of the play, few Catholics in high office have pleaded for a ban or a boycott. Many other Catholics have not only solicited a fair hearing for the play but have identified themselves with some of its positions and opinions.

The Deputy is not anti-Catholic; Hochhuth dedicated his work to two anti-nazi Catholics, some of his heroes are Catholic, and he pays Catholicism the compliment of looking to it with hope for moral leadership. But it *is* anti-Pius XII, is scornful of the kind of decayed Christendom over whose dying empire that pontiff presided. Non-Roman Catholics have some difficulty understanding why any individual should be set aside from searching criticism; most of them look on popes as they do Presidents or preachers. But even if a Catholic is prepared to subject a pope to top-to-bottom criticism, he may legitimately protest if that criticism is not wholly fair. At this point the two sides in *The Deputy* debate are joined.

Rolf Hochhuth's play would have won no hearing, indeed could not have been staged or regarded as in any degree plausible, had Pius XII looked really good on the nazi-Jewish question. He did not always come out bad, but he was not really good, either. "It is no longer permitted to anyone to be mediocre," his predecessor had said in an earlier critical time. Pius XII was at best mediocre. In Hochhuth's argument, mediocrity, temporizing, compromise and virtual silence were evils of great magnitude even when set against that sin of first magnitude committed in once-Christian Germany. That Pius helped protect some Jews, that he helped some gain safe passage—in Hochhuth's view that does not count; only a consistent or at least a more frequent attempt to throw the moral weight of Roman Catholicism against Hitler and his exterminators would have been an act consonant with Christian moral claims.

The debate has come to center on whether Hochhuth's work is historically accurate and whether it /507/ constitutes character assassination. This is unfortunate, because it inhibits the personal conscience-searching Hochhuth is seeking. If his play can be dismissed on "character assassination" grounds, all its lessons will be lost. The documentation he has appended to the play lends weight to his argument that Pius was guilty of omission, but it is not wholly convincing. The historians are divided. Not all Pius's record has been made public; perhaps it never will. Hochhuth has worked with materials open to all of us, and on that basis he has rendered his moral judgment; on that skeleton he has hung the flesh of his play.

We believe that *The Deputy* can best be understood and turned to profit if the connotations of the title are fully explored. Unfortunately, for Americans "deputy" calls to mind the bumbling helper tagging along at the western sheriff's heels. The true *Stellvertreter*, however, is one set forth in history in the place of another. Hochhuth sees this "vicar" set at the apex of the whole Christian complex. And when he seeks a *Stellvertreter*—one to stand in the place of the official vicar who has failed, one to represent Christianity, morality—he finds him in Riccardo Fontana, the young Jesuit who went forth to stand at the side of the Jews. Here Hochhuth is working with what is for him rather sophisticated symbolism (subtlety is not his art), and it is important that he keep cool if the idea of proxy is to be worked out effectively. Instead, he warms up to his subject, then becomes overheated. His animus against Pius XII is undisguised both in the play and in the historical apparatus appended to it. His failure to decide whether to condemn Christendom and thus lead us to search ourselves as he has searched himself, or, on the other hand, to attack Pius XII as semimoral and thus the "evil man"—in that failure lies the structural flaw of the play.

Apart from this flaw, *The Deputy* can serve us well. We may well ask whether by a stronger stand on the part of Pius XII many Jews would actually have been saved. Was Hitler such a revengeful madman that he would only have treated them worse after an appeal from the Vatican—if such treatment were possible? Hochhuth implies that things could only have been better, but that the answer is not important. He is contending that what is important for the representative of God among men, the vicar of Christ on earth, is not that he should be the shrewder calculator on behalf of the state and of human lives, but that he should act in accord with Christian mandates.

By and large, Protestants have refrained from exploiting *The Deputy*. On the lowest levels of Protestant nativism in America the spirit has been anti-Semitic as well as anti-Roman Catholic, and one cannot be anti-Pius and pro-Hochhuth without standing with the Jew. On the responsible levels there is too much knowledge that throughout the nazi era German Protestantism was in no way superior to German Catholicism, and that the record of Protestantism in relation to the world cannot bear too much scrutiny. As for American Jews, they are divided, though for domestic reasons most of them are understandably reluctant to speak out too noisily against the pope.

Somehow we are all on our own as we try to extract the lessons from Hochhuth's parable. We are led to ask ourselves many questions—about history and morality, about calculation and courage, about Jewish-Christian relations. *The Deputy* may be an unsatisfying parable, but there it is, and it must be faced. As a matter of fact, certain historical studies, more restrained in tone than Hochhuth's piece, have said much the same thing and have gone virtually unnoticed. The German playwright has at least and at last put the matter on the front page and on the public agenda. Hochhuth has the moral passion to awaken us, but not the moral passion to guide us.

And Pius himself? If his record is pure, the Vatican and the historians can begin to establish it. If it is weak, we must conclude that Hochhuth has been fair to him. If the record is mixed—as it seems to us—then all depends on how one looks on moral mediocrity on the highest level of expectations. If Hochhuth has been too severe and Pius has been maligned, perhaps posthumously that pope can begin to serve as the representative among men he was not in life. A vicar of Christ is supposed to be prepared to suffer shame for a good cause. If the Christian record has now been set firmly on the Christian conscience, he has suffered in a good cause. /508/

APPENDIX

STUDY OUTLINE OF THE DEPUTY

General

1. The events and many of the characters of *The Deputy* are either historical or solidly based on historical material. This would seem to suggest that the play is *realistic,* yet Hochhuth describes some of the scenes as *surrealistic.* (a) Define the terms *realistic* and *surrealistic.* (b) To what extent is *The Deputy* realistic? surrealistic?
2. Consider the following casting directions provided by Hochhuth:

> The characters grouped here by twos, threes or fours should be played by the same actor — for recent history has taught us that in the age of universal military conscription it is not necessarily to anyone's credit or blame, or even a question of character, which uniform one wears or whether one stands on the side of the victims or the executioners. (p. 11)

> A German staff sergeant of the Waffen-SS and two Italians of the Fascist Militia swarm into the room. The sergeant's name is WITZEL; in 1943 he resembled the typical thirty-five-year-old German, just as in 1960, when he held the post of Chief Inspector of the Municipal Government in D., he looked like most fifty-year-old Germans. Perhaps it should be mentioned that he is very "correct" — the rude, obscene, blustering tone he uses toward Jews and other defenseless persons, because that is the custom, doesn't really belong to him. Quite instinctively, WITZEL has picked up this brutal loquacity from his superiors; he even parrots their turns of speech. As soon as his superiors change after the war, he will just as quickly unlearn these habits. By 1959 he has become a dependable citizen. His love of order makes him dislike neo-Nazi agitation as much as strikes or a burst water main. He is so typically a person of his time that his clothes define him, not his face. Consequently, he can play the FATHER in the first scene and the Jewish KAPO in the last; when he changes roles, he should not even be disguised by a mustache or a pair of glasses. (p. 132)

> The men . . . are "fictional," but we are acquainted with them not only from the second scene of the first act. We have known them a long time, for we see them daily either on the roller coaster of the German *Wirtschaftswunder* or in our own bathroom mirror. (p. 230)

(a) What is the implication of these descriptions? (b) Do these descriptions affirm or contradict the charge that the play is nothing more than an indictment of Pius XII?
3. At the beginning of the play, Hochhuth states: "It would seem that anyone

who holds a responsible post for any length of time under an autocrat
— whether it be Hitler or Pius XII — surrenders his own personality" (p. 14).
(a) Discuss the various ways in which Hitler and the Pope are compared in
the play. (b) Discuss the similarities between the Nazi officers and the high
church officials portrayed in the play.

4. What is the meaning of the title of the play?

Act One

1. Act One is entitled "The Mission." What is the mission?
2. How does the epigraph "Beware of the man whose God is in the skies"
   apply to what takes place in this act?
3. Throughout the play, Hochhuth makes use of visual and auditory effects
   to carry forth his themes. (a) In Scene One, how do the setting and the
   action — the serving of tea — contrast with the subject under discussion? (b)
   What is revealed by the Nuncio's request for cake?
4. Scene Two affords an even greater contrast between the subject under discussion and the place and occasion of the discussion. (a) What characteristics of the Nazi officers are revealed by the contrast? (b) How does the
   replacement of the rumble of bowling balls with the rumble of bomber
   squadrons contribute to the effectiveness of the scene?
5. Of the Doctor, Hochhuth says, "Seemingly human . . . [he] is in reality
   comparable to no human being" (p. 32). Consequently, he chooses to portray the Doctor as an incarnation of the devil. (a) Considering the subject,
   is Hochhuth justified in evoking a supernatural figure in a play depicting
   historical events? (b) Does the injection of a supernatural figure weaken or
   strengthen the author's attempt to portray humanity's shared guilt for the
   destruction of the Jews?
6. How does the opening of Scene Three contrast with the previous two
   scenes? Is the setting indicative of the mood of this scene, i.e., building
   rather than destroying?
7. One of Hochhuth's themes is that what a man wears — his uniform — does
   not necessarily indicate what is in his heart. Thus, one may wear the uniform of an SS officer and be a saint, or be dressed in papal robes and be a
   criminal. How does the conclusion of Scene Three contribute to this
   theme?
8. Discuss the following speech made by Riccardo (p. 81) as an example of
   dramatic irony:

> . . . At home in Rome
> (*with pride, slightly declamatory*)
> such things would be impossible. From the Holy Father
> down to the chestnut peddler in the piazza,
> the entire nation would rise up
> against such cruelties, if Jewish fellow citizens
> were arrested. Or at any rate, arrested
> by policemen of a foreign government.

9. Hochhuth has been accused of attempting to whitewash the German

people by shifting the blame for the destruction of the Jews to others.
Consider Gerstein's speech (pp. 80–81):

We Germans are no worse
than other Europeans. First of all the
great majority have no specific knowledge
about the killings, though, of course,
a lot of soldiers in the East have watched
the massacres, and the whole nation looks on
while Jews are shipped out of the cities
like cattle. But anyone willing to help—what can he do?
Are we to castigate a man
who does not want to die for others?
Not long ago the Jews employed in Berlin factories
were to be sent to Auschwitz. The police
did not descend at once, but first informed
the factories. And the result was that
four thousand Jews managed to disappear.
They were hidden by Berliners, fed by them—
four thousand—and every Berliner
involved is risking his own life!
The lives of his whole family as well.
You see, not every German has forgotten
the debt he owes to Germany's name.
And there are scoundrels everywhere. In Holland
the Dutch police are working hard
to round up every Jew; in France they don't cooperate
with so much zeal, but still they do their part.
In Hungary too, but worst of all in the Ukraine . . .
The Ukrainians shoot their Jews themselves . . .
Some time ago, when seventeen thousand Jews
were shot in Maidanek, a lot of Poles
got drunk to celebrate this festive day. Only
on rare occasions can a Jew in Poland find a place to hide
outside the towns. His kindly neighbors
turn him over to the German murderers
for a small bounty. *We* have no right to speak,
Father. The Germans
bear the greatest guilt. Their leader
has conceived the program. As for the *people*—
the other peoples hardly are much better.

(a) In your opinion, is this speech an attempt to whitewash the German
people? (b) Do you feel that Hochhuth is historically justified in writing
thus? Why, or why not?
10. The Doctor's visit to Gerstein in this scene serves several important purposes: it adds an element of suspense; it points out the risk involved in
Gerstein's position; and it introduces several philosophic considerations
of importance to the play. In the course of his visit the Doctor character-
izes Gerstein as "the only one worth talking to." (a) What is there about
Gerstein that makes him particularly attractive to the Doctor? (b) In what

ways are the two men alike? In what ways do they differ from the average
SS officer?

Act Two

1. In this act, Hochhuth employs a number of devices to emphasize the
Church's devotion to the past and to ritual, while it overlooks the pressing
moral issues of the day. (a) How does the opening scene establish this prem-
ise? (b) What is the occasion being celebrated, and how does it contribute
to the author's view of the Church?
2. What is the significance of the title of this act, "The Bells of St. Peter's"?
Is it ironic?
3. In Act Two, we find Riccardo totally committed to "the mission," highly
critical of the Pope, and, by his very presence, in defiance of the hierarchy
to which his life has been dedicated. Considering Riccardo's background
and training, the change is an extremely radical one. (a) Would one expect
such a total reversal of values to be accompanied by a great inner conflict?
(b) In answer to Riccardo's question of whether his course of action had been
preceded by "some terrible ordeal," Gerstein says (p. 77):

> I must disillusion you, Father.
> There was no terrible ordeal,
> no pangs of conscience, none at all.
> Hitler himself has written: the rights of men
> invalidate the rights of states. . . .

(c) Does this answer also give sufficient explanation of Riccardo's own
course? Why, or why not?
4. In both Act One and Act Two, the point is made that "Truth is with the
victor." (a) Discuss Fontana's cynical statement (p. 105) that the victor

> . . . controls the historians.
> And . . . the history of the world . . .
> comes to have meaning only when
> historians have assigned it one. . . .

(b) Do you feel that the author himself ascribes to this theory of the meaning
of history? Why, or why not?
5. What aspect of the Church does the Cardinal who interrupts the two
Fontanas represent? How does the orchid he bears contribute to the picture?
6. Some critics consider Fontana the best-drawn character in Hochhuth's play,
the only one demonstrating a man painfully divided in loyalties and, hence,
intensely human. Do you agree or disagree with this view? Why?

Act Three

1. The Visitation in Roman Catholic liturgy refers to Mary's visit to Elisabeth,
the mother of John the Baptist, and symbolizes love of neighbor. How does
this title apply to the events of Act Three?
2. In Scene Two of Act Three, there is a peculiar situation in which conventional values are reversed so that the only way to accomplish good is through
duplicity, treason, and murder. Thus, Gerstein and Riccardo seem to stand

for the principle that "the end justifies the means," the principle that led to the building of Auschwitz in the first place. (a) Is this situation philosophically consistent with the author's attitude towards the Nazis? (b) Is it consistent with Christian philosophy?

3. Throughout the play, the older men advising Riccardo try to no avail to get him to modify his views. (a) Compare Riccardo's and the Abbot's approaches to the problem of individual responsibility and their reactions to the destruction of the Jews. (b) In the light of the plans and statements made by Riccardo in this act, consider the words the Cardinal spoke to him in Act Two (pp. 115–116):

> Riccardo — you idealists are *inhuman*.
> We realists are more humane, because
> we take men as they are.
> We laugh at their faults, for we know we share them.
> An idealist does not laugh — can Herr Hitler
> laugh? Has he personally any faults?
> No, he cannot laugh at this world;
> he wants to improve it.
> Anyone who differs with his ideals is exterminated.
> This rules out compromise, I fear.
> He must first smash a world so that he can
> confer *his* peace upon it. No, thanks.
> We realists are compromisers, conformists —
> very well, we make concessions.
> But why not? It's a case of staying alive
> or being consistent, you know.
> Let us never forget that both the devil
> and the saints were placed in this world by God.
> Between them stands man, whose only choice
> is always between two sins, you know, Riccardo.

(c) Do you agree or disagree with this view of idealists? Why?

4. One critic has said that the theme of Hochhuth's play "does a great deal of the work for him" because "the SS has become a mythic archetype of horror." (a) Do Scenes One and Three of this act have the powerful emotional impact of mythic archetype? (b) To what extent is the effectiveness of these scenes the result of the material itself? To what extent is it the result of Hochhuth's dramatic skill?

5. Consider the characterization of Salzer in the third scene of this act. Does he possess any saving grace? Are there any remnants of humanity in him?

Act Four

1. Act Four takes its title from the passage of Dante's *Inferno* that is used as an epigraph. Although there is considerable controversy, some scholars maintain that the words "him, who made, through cowardice, the great refusal," refer to Celestine V (St. Peter Celestine), who was elected Pope in 1294. Celestine V, much celebrated for his asceticism, was little interested in matters of state and administration. He quickly abdicated his position in order to escape administrative responsibilities and have full time to give to his de-

votions. Does Hochhuth's presentation of Pius XII parallel the situation of Celestine V? Base your answer on specific acts and passages.

2. One critic has pointed out the great irony in the first speech of the Pope, in which he mentions his "burning concern." The words *mit brennender Sorge* (with burning concern) are also the title of Pius XI's 1937 encyclical denouncing "the whole Nazi conception of life as utterly, and necessarily, anti-Christian." How does the use of these words point up the differences between Pius XI and Pius XII? What is Pius XII's "burning concern" according to Hochhuth's portrayal?

3. Hochhuth's characterization of Pius XII has, of course, been the focal point of criticism of the play. Is Hochhuth's Pope credible, or, as more than one critic has suggested, would the play have gained if Hochhuth had allowed him some sort of humanity?

4. Hochhuth has denied the fact that his portrayal of the Pope is meant to indicate that the Pope's silence was based on concern for the Vatican's investments, stating that Pius XII is characterized as a "statesman of some standing" who presents serious arguments and apprehensions to support his position. In your opinion, does the Pope emerge as the author, according to the above statement, intended him to, or do his financial interests and temperamental indecisiveness dominate the portrayal?

5. In Act Three, Riccardo decries the fact that all the rescue work authorized by Pius XII does not impose "the slightest sacrifice upon the Pope . . . not even the merest shadow of a risk." Had the Pope spoken out as Riccardo wished in Act Four, would the action have involved any risk to his person? To his reputation? To the Church?

6. Is Riccardo's statement denouncing the Church's "use" of Hitler to accomplish its ends consistent with his own position in Act Three?

7. Consider Riccardo's decision to go to Auschwitz as the deputy of God. (a) Is it the decision of an idealist or a fanatic? (b) Is Riccardo, as Gerstein charges (p. 157), assuming greater guilt by doing so?

> Forsaking us will only make you guilty.
> Forget the salvation of the Church.
> You would no longer have
> it in your power
> to aid a single human being. Riccardo,
> you'd only take on greater guilt yourself!

8. At the end of Act Four, the Pope is shown washing his hands in a scene that calls Pontius Pilate to mind. What is the meaning of this conclusion?

Act Five

1. Discuss the title of this act, "Where Are You, God?" in reference to: (a) the opening monologues of the victims. (b) the Doctor's statement of his motives (p. 247):

> Because I wanted an answer!
> And so I've ventured what no man
> has ever ventured since the beginning of the world.
> I took the vow to challenge the Old Gent,
> to provoke him so limitlessly

that He would have to give an answer.
Even if only the negative answer
which can be His sole excuse, as
Stendhal put it: that He doesn't exist.

(c) Riccardo's statement (p. 270):

For the past week
I have been burning the dead ten hours a day.
And with every human body that I burn
a portion of my faith burns also.
God burns.
Corpses — a conveyor belt of corpses.
History is a highway paved with carrion . . .
If I knew that He looks on —
(*With revulsion.*) I would have to — hate Him.

(d) the announcement about the Vatican at the end of the act.
2. Compare the following statements:

The truth is, Auschwitz refutes
creator, creation, and the creature. (p. 248)

No sacrifice is wasted, although history
may fail to register the sacrifices. God does. (p. 104)

Do you agree with either of these statements? Why, or why not?
3. Does Riccardo lose his faith in God? Before answering, consider (a) the three temptations offered him — opportunities to leave Auschwitz — and his responses to them. (b) his dying words.
4. Is Riccardo's death a futile sacrifice or a fulfillment of his duty as a priest?
5. Consider the change that takes place in Riccardo in the course of this play. (a) Discuss the contrast between the untried Riccardo of Act One and the Riccardo of the last scene of the play. (b) What events account for this growth of character? (c) Is Riccardo a tragic figure in the classic sense? Explain.

TOPICS FOR LIBRARY RESEARCH PAPERS

1. The Sins of Their Fathers: A New Generation of German Writers
2. Stirring the Public's Conscience: Ibsen, Shaw, and Hochhuth
3. *The Deputy* and the Tradition of the Morality Play
4. Eichmann: Conscienceless Beast or Obedient Bureaucrat?
5. Pius XI and Pius XII: A Comparison
6. White Ministers in the South: 1860 and 1960
7. Anti-Semitism in the United States
8. Hochhuth's Debt to Sartre and Brecht
9. Literature as a Call to Action: Harriet Beecher Stowe's *Uncle Tom's Cabin*
10. German Protestants and the Final Solution
11. Hochhuth's Doctor and the Mephistophelean Tradition in Literature
12. Nero and Hitler: Some Parallels
13. The Jewish People: Race or Religion?

14. Modern Drama Views the Man of Conscience: *Murder in the Cathedral, A Man for All Seasons,* and *The Deputy*
15. The Pope as Symbol in Contemporary Literature: Claudel's *The Hostage,* Anouilh's *Becket,* and Hochhuth's *The Deputy*
16. What Is History? An Attempt at Definition
17. Father Fontana and the Jesuit Ideal
18. Kurt Gerstein and the Christianity of Kierkegaarde
19. The Burden of the Past: Hochhuth and Faulkner
20. Can It Happen Here? The Sociology of Dictatorship
21. Germany Today: A Lesson Learned or Forgotten?
22. Jewish World Leaders in World War II
23. The Auschwitz Trial, Frankfurt, 1964 – 1965
24. Thomas Mann in World War II
25. Rolf Hochhuth and the Theater of Ideas

SUGGESTIONS FOR FURTHER READING

Historical

The best primary source for the facts on Nazi policy in World War II is *Nazi Conspiracy and Aggression,* 12 vols. (Washington: Government Printing Office for the Office of the Chief Counsel for the Prosecution of Axis Criminality, 1946 – 1948). These books, the "red series," consist of eight volumes of documents, a two-volume index, and a two-volume supplement. Vol. I, pp. 949 – 1023; Supplement 1, pp. 1209 – 1290, and Supplement 2, pp. 1580 – 1605, are particularly pertinent. For the most complete coverage of the Nuremberg Trials, see *Trials of the Major War Criminals before the International Military Tribunal,* 42 vols. (Nuremberg: International Military Tribunal, 1947 – 1949). Thirty volumes in this series, the "blue series," contain court proceedings; the remaining twelve consist of documents in evidence. The volumes most directly concerned with the events and background used by Hochhuth are 6, 8, 20, and 22. Also of interest, though difficult to obtain in this country, is *International Military Tribunal,* 18 vols. (London: Her Majesty's Stationary Office, 1946 – 1951). The trials of lesser war criminals, including those of the Nazi "doctors" and the Auschwitz commandant Rudolf Hoess, will be found in *Trials of War Criminals Before the Nurnberg Tribunal under Control Council Law No. 10,* 15 vols. (Washington: Government Printing Office, 1948 – 1954), known as the "green series." The trials of war criminals being held in Germany by the West German government are being covered in detail by the international press. Though the proceedings are not likely to be available in English, day-by-day reports will be found in The *New York Times;* consult the *New York Times Index* for date and page references.

Numerous memoirs by those directly involved in, or eye witnesses to, the events discussed by Hochhuth have been published and constitute another important source of primary material. Two books that have been widely quoted by commentators on both sides of the controversy over *The Deputy* are Ernst von Weizsacker's *Memoirs* (Chicago: Henry Regnery Co., 1951) and Ulrich von Hassell's *The Von Hassell Diaries: 1938 – 1944* (Garden City, N.Y.: Doubleday & Co., Inc., 1947). In the United States alone, over a dozen separate accounts of concentration camp life by survivors have been published. Two of the more popular ones currently available in paperback editions are Dr. Miklos Nyiszli's *Auschwitz: A Doctor's Eyewitness Account* (New York: Crest Books, 1963) and Primo Levi's *Survival in Auschwitz* (New York: Collier Books, 1963). A memoir presenting a characterization of Pius XII quite different from that given by Hochhuth is Domenico Cardinal Tardini's *Memories of Pius XII* (Westminster, Md.: The Newman Press, 1961); Cardinal Tardini was an intimate of Pius XII for several decades and was in residence at the Vatican during World War II. For a first-hand account of the Nazi demand of a ransom of gold from the Jews of Rome, see Eugenio Maria Zolli's *Before the Dawn: Autobiographical Reflections* (New York: Sheed and Ward, 1954), pp. 159–161; Zolli was Chief Rabbi of Rome at the time the demand was made. A 425-page bibliographical work, *Guide to Jewish History under Nazi Impact,* was prepared by Jacob Robinson and Philip Friedman and published in 1960 by the Yivo Institute in New York; it is the definitive bibliography on the subject.

Secondary sources on the Nazi era are many. One of the best and most widely available general histories of the period is William L. Shirer's *The Rise and Fall of the Third Reich* (New York: Simon and Schuster, Inc., 1960; in paperback, Crest Books, 1962). In addition to Raul Hilberg's excellent study of the "final solution," *Destruction of the European Jews,* excerpts of which appear in this book, two others deserve mention: Léon Poliakov's *Harvest of Hate* (Syracuse, N.Y.: Syracuse University Press, 1954) and Gerald Reitlinger's *The Final Solution* (New York: The Beechhurst Press, 1953). Poliakov, archivist at the Paris Center of Contemporary Jewish Documents, has written widely on the subject for the French and German press and is generally considered one of the foremost authorities on it. It was Poliakov who wrote the first scholarly article on the Vatican's attitude towards the Jewish problem during World War II, "Le Vatican et la question juive," which appeared in France in *Le Monde Juif,* December 1950 and February 1951. The accusation that the Pope's silence caused much needless suffering was raised at the time of the death of Pius XII by W. Rabi in "Les silences de Pie XII," *L'Arche,* November 1958. The Catholic press in the United States was quick to challenge the charge, and two articles, "Did Pius XII Fail the Jews?" *America,* November 29, 1958, p. 261, and "Pope Pius XII and the Jews," *Commonweal,* November 7, 1958, pp. 153–154, are of interest largely because they indicate the scope of the discussion before *The Deputy* reached the scene. A book on the subject of the Pope's wartime responsibilities and actions is *The Vatican and the War* by Camille M. Cianfarra (New York: E. P. Dutton & Co., Inc., 1958). A more recent study of the Vatican's relationship with Hitler's Germany is George O. Kent, "Pope Pius XII and Germany: Some Aspects of German-Vatican Relations, 1933–1943," *The American Historical Review,* LXX:1 (October 1964), 59–78. Kent's article is based largely on the reports of German diplomats involved in the negotiations and is particularly detailed in comparing Pius XI and Pius XII in their policies and attitudes toward National Socialism. A study of the Catholic Church in Germany during World War II is *German Catholics and Hitler's War* (New York: Sheed and Ward, 1962) by Gordon Zahn, professor of sociology at Loyola University, Chicago. Though Zahn's book documents the general acceptance of and accommodation to National Socialism, it is true that there was internal resistance to Hitler, too. For the facts of the resistance movement and its composition and actions see Hans Rothfels' *The German Opposition to Hitler* (Chicago: Henry Regnery Co., 1948) and Terrence Prittie's *Germans Against Hitler* (New York: Little, Brown & Co., 1964).

Literary

The only other work of Hochhuth's that has appeared in English is a short story, "The Berlin Antigone," in *Evergreen Review*, No. 32 (April-May 1964), pp. 70–73.

For a detailed picture of the German literary scene out of which *The Deputy* emerged, see the following articles: H. Schwab-Telisch, "Theater in West Germany Today," *Theatre Arts*, No. 47 (June 1963), pp. 16–21, and Hans Egon Holthusen, "Crossing the Zero-Point: German Literature Since World War II," *French and German Letters Today* (Washington, D.C.: Government Printing Office for the Library of Congress Reference Department, 1960), pp. 39–53. For additional discussion of the concepts of epic theater, see Heinz Politzer, "How Epic Is Bertold Brecht's Epic Theater?" *Modern Language Quarterly*, XXIII (June 1962), pp. 99–114.

Schiller and Brecht are the two German playwrights with whom Hochhuth has been most frequently compared. Excellent translations of the works of both are available in paperback and other economically priced editions. Recommended are Friedrich von Schiller's *Don Carlos: Infante of Spain* (New York: Frederick Ungar Publishing Co., 1962) and Bertold Brecht's *Mother Courage* (New York: Evergreen Books, 1964).

Reviews and Commentaries

In addition to the two anthologies covering the reactions of the German-speaking world to *The Deputy* from which we have quoted in the text, three other full-length books have been published on the subject of Hochhuth's play: Jacques Nobécourt, *"Le Vicaire" et l'histoire* (Paris: Éditions du Seuil, 1964), *Processo al Vicario* (Italy: Edizioni Paoline, 1964), and Eric Bentley, *The Storm Over The Deputy* (New York: Grove Press, Inc., 1964). In addition to his extended study of the play and its background, Nobécourt provides a 38-page appendix summarizing the various arguments about the play and quoting passages from German, French, English, and American reviews and a 35-page supplement of documents relevant to the issues discussed. The Italian work is more one-sided, being a refutation, based on historical sources, of Hochhuth's charges against the Pope and a repetition of the oft-made accusation that the playwright is intent on easing his own conscience and that of the other members of his generation.

Two major reviews omitted from this book because of space considerations but necessary to an understanding of the American response to *The Deputy* are those which appeared in the *New York Times Book Review* of March 1, 1964. The *Times* took the unusual precaution of having both a Catholic, George N. Schuster, and a non-Catholic, Robert Gorham Davis, review the book. Nonetheless, numerous letters from readers protesting one interpretation or the other were sent and published in "Letters to the Editor," *New York Times Book Review*, March 15, 1964. Another review, of interest because of the author's qualifications to speak on the subject and the fact that he represents the minority Catholic view, is by Gordon Zahn, "'The Vicar': A Controversy and a Lesson," *The Critic*, October-November 1963, pp. 42–46.

A number of newspapers and periodicals both here and abroad issued special editions devoted to discussion of *The Deputy*. Of these, undoubtedly the most important both for its source and its content was *L'Osservator Della Domenica*, June 26, 1964. This was a special issue entitled "The Pope, Yesterday and Today." The most accessible of the printed forums in this country is *Commonweal,* February 28, 1964.

Of the reviews of the Broadway production, Walter Kerr's received a certain notoriety as being the one singled out for criticism by Hochhuth on the grounds that the reviewer's Catholicism disqualified him for the task of evaluating the play (*New York Herald Tribune,* February 27, 1964); see also the *Herald Tribune's New York Magazine* for Sunday, February 23, 1964, for an article by Hannah Arendt on the subject of culpability for the destruction of the Jews.

Students desiring additional references are urged to consult the *Readers' Guide to Periodical Literature,* the *International Index,* and *The Catholic Periodical Index.* The Catholic press has, naturally, been in the foreground in discussing the play, and *America* alone has published eighteen separate items on the subject. In all, over a hundred articles have appeared in English so far. For news items pertaining to various reactions to *The Deputy* and Hochhuth, in New York and elsewhere, consult the *New York Times Index.*